01 14 ل

BLANK
SPACE

BLANK SPACE

SPACE

A Cultural History of
the Twenty-First Century

W. DAVID MARX

VIKING

VIKING
An imprint of Penguin Random House LLC
1745 Broadway, New York, NY 10019
penguinrandomhouse.com

Designed by Nerylsa Dijol

LIBRARY OF CONGRESS CONTROL NUMBER: 2025018816

ISBN 9780593833995 (hardcover)
ISBN 9780593834008 (ebook)

Printed in the United States of America
2nd Printing

The authorized representative in the EU for product safety and
compliance is Penguin Random House Ireland, Morrison Chambers,
32 Nassau Street, Dublin D02 YH68, Ireland, https://eu-contact.penguin.ie.

In memory of
Sean and Caleb

CONTENTS

Part Four
2020–2025

INTRODUCTION

At more than three million copies sold, the Seattle band Pearl Jam's debut, *Ten*, was the top-selling rock album of 1992—a complete disaster. "With any more popularity," fretted lead singer Eddie Vedder, "we were going to be crushed, or our heads were going to pop like grapes." He started wearing a helmet everywhere.

The trouble began earlier in the year, when MTV put the band's videos into heavy rotation. An invitation soon followed to join the second-ever Lollapalooza tour, a traveling carnival of alternative music and freak shows that evangelized suburban teens on the joys of mosh pits, body piercing, psychedelic drugs, and left-leaning politics. Pearl Jam eagerly took an early slot on the bill. "I plan to bring my Polaroid camera and hang out just talking to the crowd," Vedder told *Spin*. "It's like putting a finger on the pulse of what young America's doing."

Then came the video for their third single, "Jeremy," a song about an alienated teen who commits suicide at school. This "scathing critique of conformist mainstream American culture" became an unlikely pop sensation, and after MTV aired it nearly hourly, *Ten* shot to number two on the *Billboard* charts. At each stop on the tour, throngs of enthusiastic fans stormed Lollapalooza's gates to secure spots for Pearl Jam's daytime set.

Most bands would have celebrated the moment. But Pearl Jam were rooted in a punk ethos that valued artistry and community over revenue and renown. Like many other musicians at the time, they feared being labeled sellouts—artists who watered down their creative vision for mainstream appeal. As critic Chuck Klosterman explained in *The Nineties*, "The concept of 'selling out'—and the degree to which that notion altered the meaning and perception of almost everything—is the single most nineties aspect of the nineties." Earlier in 1992, Kurt Cobain of Nirvana derided Pearl Jam as "corporate puppets . . . trying to jump on the alternative bandwagon," and with every additional copy of *Ten* sold, the criticism stung harder.

Tormented by success, Pearl Jam made a firm decision: They would no longer produce music videos. And they turned down interviews and photo shoots. Pearl Jam stood athwart popularity, yelling "Stop." During recording sessions for Pearl Jam's follow-up album, producer Brendan O'Brien told Vedder that his new composition "Better Man" would be a surefire hit. "I immediately knew I'd just said the wrong thing," recalled O'Brien; Vedder promptly cut the song from consideration.

Yet their second album, *Vs.*, released on October 19, 1993, without radio-friendly singles or promotional videos, broke records for first-week album sales. Kids flocked to midnight release parties, smashing record store windows in their excitement. Pearl Jam's principled stand resonated with their fans: If rock bands were so desperate for money, they might as well be bankers.

Lollapalooza remained an important cultural institution in the twenty-first century, though reimagined as an annual multiday festival at Chicago's Grant Park. At the 2022 event—exactly thirty years after Pearl Jam joined the tour—rapper Lil Baby headlined the Bud Light Seltzer stage on day one, and pop star Dua Lipa wrapped up day two on the T-Mobile stage. The closer on the Tito's Handmade Vodka stage was the sixty-year-old electronic dance music producer David Solomon, also known as DJ D-Sol.

Though only three years older than Eddie Vedder, Solomon had little allegiance to the punk ethos. He spent his college days as a rugby-playing frat bro and only discovered electronic dance music in his early fifties. Solomon's professional résumé was more impressive than his discography: He had worked in Bear Stearns' junk bond division, helped secure Lululemon's IPO, and was now CEO of Goldman Sachs. He arrived in Chicago on Goldman's Gulfstream G650, met clients in the morning, and later that night "spun remixes of ABBA, Walk the Moon, and Queen for a sea of sports jerseys craving mindless clubbing."

Electronic dance music originated in a small Detroit circle of Black futurist teens in the 1980s; by the 2010s, it was the soundtrack for bachelor parties at Las Vegas megaclubs. So there was nothing shocking about a suit like David Solomon learning to DJ. But his invitation to Lollapalooza alongside the world's top pop stars was astonishing. He wasn't even a sellout; he was the living embodiment of financial capital itself.

———

This book is a cultural history of the early twenty-first century, tracing the people, products, artworks, and events that have reshaped how we live. By tying these specific cultural moments into a unified narrative, it reveals a single profound shift that defines the era: Where society once encouraged and provided an abundance of cultural invention, there is now a *blank space*. Over the past twenty-five years, culture has prospered as a vehicle for entertainment, politics, and profiteering—but at the expense of pure artistic innovation. The shift in Lollapalooza's lineups, from Pearl Jam to the CEO of Goldman Sachs, is a symptom of a larger illness. David Solomon could only share a stage with real musicians in a world that assigns similar value to commerce and creativity.

The profundity of cultural invention in the twentieth century gave us a false faith in its permanence. For the legions of consumers content with the output of the "culture industry," there was always an important minority who channeled their dissatisfaction into becoming *cultural inventors*. They forged new ideas, beliefs, norms, styles, behaviors, and aesthetics that challenged convention. This included subcultures, often born from marginalized groups, who built solidarity through distinct looks and sounds that subverted mainstream norms. Countercultures advocated new value systems. Artists reshaped established culture at its symbolic core, tweaking human consciousness to reveal new ways to perceive the world. And finally, the creative class synthesized these innovations to craft their own sophisticated tastes. These groups didn't just change the content of cultural expression but changed its very form: new styles, new goods, new behaviors. And when the creative industry imitated these innovations, it spurred cultural change at a macro level.

In the twenty-first century, there have been fewer cultural inventors, and where they exist, they seldom wield as much influence on the broader culture. This is not the "death" of culture in toto; the culture industry, luxury sector, and online creators are producing more content than ever. But the most radical forms of cultural invention have become scarce.

We already feel the effects of living in this blank space. Over a decade ago, music historian Alex Ross lamented that the internet's promise of a "long tail" of infinite cultural diversity never materialized: "Culture appears more monolithic than ever." In 2023, *New York Times* critic Jason Farago declared that culture "has come to a standstill": "We are now almost a quarter of the way through what looks likely to go down in history as the least innovative, least transformative, least pioneering century for culture since the invention of the printing press."

Compare this to the explosion of cultural invention during the first twenty-five years of the twentieth century: Avant-garde movements such as fauvism, cubism, futurism, expressionism, Dada, de Stijl, and surrealism expanded the definition of art. Later in the century, stylistic change remained a core part of pop music: Punk supplanted prog rock, rap buried funk, and alternative conquered hair metal and synth pop. And all these radical forms possessed enough depth to still inspire us today.

Since the turn of the century, this rapid progression has slowed. Box office hits are almost exclusively reboots or sequels, from endless *Star Wars* retreads to countless incarnations of Spider-Man and Batman. The most notable music acts of 2006—and 2024—included Taylor Swift and Beyoncé. Unlike previous decades, the 2000s produced few distinct styles. The decade even failed to take on a canonical name: It's sometimes called the "aughts," sometimes the "noughties." The 2010s fared no better. In the words of philosopher Franco Berardi, there has been a "slow cancellation of the future."

Why has cultural invention decelerated in an era of endless cultural production? Some critics argue that trends now move too quickly to cohere into lasting movements, what music critic Simon Reynolds described as a "paradoxical combination of speed and standstill." This was already evident at the end of modernism. In 1967, music scholar Leonard B. Meyer predicted that cultural stasis would not be "an absence of novelty and change—a total quiescence—but rather the absence of ordered sequential change." He likened it to molecules in Brownian motion: constant activity but no forward progress. Today our experience of "everything everywhere all at once" reduces even the most rapid shifts to static noise.

Others have pointed to structural shifts in how culture is created and disseminated. Critic Scott Timberg attributed much of the "culture crash" to the decline of middle-class media jobs, which traditionally supported cultural production. Yet there are now more than three hundred million people worldwide who consider themselves "content creators." Meanwhile, Kyle Chayka, in 2024's *Filterworld*, blamed algorithmic platforms like TikTok and Instagram for "flattening" culture. But the blank space emerged well before the advent of these apps.

At a broader level, these changes in culture are inexorably linked to neoliberalism, the hypercapitalist economic system that organizes society to expedite the free flow of capital across global markets. Neoliberalism has quietly shaped the incentive structures that guide individual human behavior. By elevating extreme profit seeking as the highest human goal, neoliberalism alters what gets made, how it gets distributed, who benefits—and how we feel about that process.

But culture ultimately emerges from our mutual expectations of each other, which means that resistance is always possible. Even when capital-ism's tidal wave is crashing over society, individuals can choose to build dams and levees to keep the water at bay. The market wanted Pearl Jam to assume the role of superstars; they said no.

So why have so many cultural pioneers of the twenty-first century said "Yes, please"? Why have the most successful artists and creators lost interest in cultural invention, leaving behind this blank space? The history in the fol-lowing pages focuses on how the events of the past twenty-five years shifted our cultural *values* toward neglecting, if not rejecting, creative invention. Greed is not the sole issue. So many people sought to make culture into mere entertainment, commerce, and politics because they believed it was the right thing to do. They made their choices under guidance from five dominant ideologies that have transformed cultural production and consumption over this century:

1. **Omnivorism:** The rejection of cultural hierarchies, which promoted equal interest in all genres, tastes, and historical styles

2. **Poptimism:** An extension of omnivorism, celebrating commercial culture and treating popularity as the ultimate democratic arbiter of quality

3. **Entrepreneurial Heroism:** The glorification of business savvy as equivalent to artistic genius, especially when profit is positioned as a tool for social justice

4. **The Counter-Counterculture:** The backlash against liberal ideals that weaponizes "cool" against inclusivity and progressivism

5. **Digital Norm Evasion:** The championing of technology for its power to bypass traditional social mores

Together, these ideologies fostered an explosion of content creation and encouraged a new kind of pluralistic monoculture in which anything goes. This increased activity, however, came at the expense of genuine cultural in-vention. Meanwhile, the century's most impactful subcultural resistance to the mainstream has arguably emerged from radical conservatives, a group with no meaningful concern for artistic innovation.

With eerie precision, the aforementioned ideological shifts align with the theoretical predictions in the eighties about postmodernism. In 1987, literary critic Terry Eagleton described postmodernism as "impudently embracing the language of commerce and the commodity," turning tradition into "irreverent pastiche" and creating "contrived depthlessness." Philosopher Fredric Jameson argued that these weren't intentional aesthetic choices but reflected the "cultural logic of late capitalism."

Certainly, the century's ideologies emerged from the unconscious embrace of neoliberal assumptions about society. But their urgency is best understood as an inevitable reaction to the triumph of liberalism at the end of the twentieth century. By 2001, upstarts looking to fight the establishment felt the need to turn against standard liberal values. On the left, omnivorism and poptimism hyperextended the liberal veneration of inclusivity to further lift marginalized voices. And in the process, they became more accommodating to explicitly commercial culture. Digital norm evasion, initially a progressive effort to disrupt stifling conservative morality, eventually empowered conservative forces to fight civility and avoid accountability for "cancelable" offenses.

Not everyone embraced these ideologies, but they guided many of the century's most influential figures. Even in a so-called populist era, a small cadre of celebrities continues to define what is possible, desirable, and righteous. Yet the blank space also opened the door for so many charlatans and reprobates. With creators no longer required to pursue artistic excellence, culture became a lowest-common-denominator battle for attention. Where there is no value other than money, honor is meaningless; and where there is no honor, there cannot be shame. And without shame, infamy and esteem become indistinguishable. This state of affairs rewarded sociopaths who were willing to weaponize their own disinhibition and amorality to dominate the public discourse. The most controversial people swung the era's narratives so far toward themselves that the twenty-first century's artistic masterpieces often feel like outliers rather than exemplars of our times.

This bred a pervasive nihilism among creators, fans, and critics—one that insists there's nothing wrong with the blank space as long as we are entertained and our cultural heroes earn a decent living. By that standard, the past twenty-five years have delivered: We've had plenty of excitement, and celebrities have been compensated like never before. Billions of people now make and share content every day, and many creators are literal billionaires.

Yet this reductionist thinking misses the most important dynamic of culture: Its health requires the regular emergence of fresh formats and aesthetics. Radical art forms expand the ways we can see the world, broaden our values, and prepare us for the future.

And we have come to rely on these shifts to mark time: The fifties brought flannel-suit suburban conformity and poodle-skirt sock hops; the sixties saw Beatlemania and psychedelia; the seventies, New Age and punk; the eighties, New Wave and yuppie culture; and the nineties, grunge and hip-hop. The lack of stylistic innovation in the twenty-first century has certainly contributed to the widespread feeling of cultural malaise.

Only inventive culture supplies long-term benefits to humanity. Kitsch never asks us to change; empty entertainment provides fleeting thrills. Propaganda discourages symbolic complexity to achieve immediate legibility. And without constant invention, all these other functions wither and die. Passive consumers may tolerate the blank space for a while, but eventually they, too, will grow restless. And we see how this cultural stagnation has political consequences. The rejection of liberal values that empowered the MAGA movement did not begin in government; it first took on contemporary relevance in the deep cynicism of downtown fashion scenes and nihilistic online forums. And this long-term project to rebrand conservatism as cool and transgressive succeeded precisely because we removed cultural invention as a potential countervailing force.

As much as this book attempts to offer a global cultural history of the twenty-first century, the focus on the most influential individuals admittedly overrepresents the United States. Despite decades of globalization, American cultural dominance persists through Hollywood films, Silicon Valley platforms, streaming TV shows, and pop idols. There was also a notable decline in influence from previous cultural powerhouses: The UK's dominance in pop music faded, as did the centrality of French, German, and Italian auteurs in cinema. That said, international cross-pollination has accelerated, with American culture now facing competition from Latin and Caribbean pop, European luxury brands, Korean music and beauty products, Japanese streetwear, and Scandinavian fast fashion and hygge.

Capturing a twenty-five-year history presents inevitable challenges of scope and scale. No single book can chronicle every significant event or artifact. Cultural histories demand curation, and this one, by necessity, omits much remarkable music, art, fashion, media, games, and slang. My own unconscious biases further shape these exclusions. This period aligns with my early adulthood: I graduated from university in June 2001, moved to a Queens apartment on September 7, 2001, with a clear view of the Twin Towers, wrote for New York publications about the music and fashion of the early 2000s, encountered Paris Hilton and her paparazzi on Melrose Avenue, lived in Asia as Japanese and Korean culture went global, and worked in tech during the rise of the mobile internet. But I couldn't be everywhere nor take an interest in everything. To paraphrase the fictional memoirist Hannah Horvath, this book may not be *the* cultural history of the twenty-first century, but it is *a* cultural history. Other authors will surely identify omissions worthy of deeper exploration, such as gaming, and I eagerly anticipate their contributions.

While this history centers on the misadventures of certain wealthy and famous individuals, we must remember that culture ultimately belongs to all of us. If we dislike what has transpired, it's within our power to reverse these trends. The pages that follow chart a clear timeline to diagnose the causes of stagnation and map out potential paths toward cultural renewal. Even if a radical transformation of the global economic structure remains unlikely, we still possess the most powerful tool for cultural change: the ability to choose our own norms and values. Above all, we must begin with reviving a collective belief in the necessity of cultural invention.

This mission feels even more urgent when reliving the past twenty-five years as a single narrative. We gain not just a clearer understanding of what went wrong but also a renewed sense of purpose: to reclaim culture's role as a force for aesthetic innovation and transformative change.

Part One

2001–2008

DOWNTOWN NEW YORK AFTER 9/11
Cool Takes a Rightward Turn

I n spring 2001, the rapper Boots Riley wanted a sensational cover for his group the Coup's fourth album, *Party Music*, planned for an autumn release. Riley, who joined the Progressive Labor Party as a teenager, asked his photographer to help create a visual "metaphor for destroying capitalism." They decided on an image showing Riley pressing a large button on a guitar tuner resembling a bomb detonator, while his DJ, Pam the Funkstress, raised two conductor's batons in triumph. Behind them is the implied outcome of their music's revolutionary power: the Twin Towers of the World Trade Center erupting in red fire and gray smoke.

The Coup's record label, 75 Ark, prepared to print this album cover on the morning of September 11, 2001, just as al-Qaeda terrorists hijacked American Airlines Flight 11 and flew the jet into the World Trade Center's North Tower. Seventeen minutes later, United Airlines Flight 175 hit the South Tower. As news reached 75 Ark about the real-life carnage eerily echoing the cover art, label staff made urgent calls to immediately halt printing.

"The 21st century began on September 11, 2001," novelist Douglas Coupland later wrote—a sentiment that has since become conventional wisdom. The attacks left nearly three thousand dead, shook the world, and shattered the relative peace the West experienced in the nineties. The horror of 9/11 demonstrated that governments no longer monopolized mass destruction, nor could they fully protect their citizens. The hijackers never fired a shot; they simply weaponized the infrastructure of modern life by turning airplanes into missiles. The most chilling aspect of the attack was the sense that it marked only the beginning of a long global conflict. Hunter S. Thompson captured this foreboding in his immediate response: "We are At War now—with somebody—and we will stay At War with that mysterious Enemy for the rest of our lives."

As financial markets reeled and geopolitics shifted, pop culture underwent rapid and profound changes. Gallup recorded a 90 percent approval rating for President George W. Bush—a sharp turnaround among liberals who, just months earlier, had seethed over the Supreme Court's decision to stop the Florida recount and award him the presidency over Al Gore. Bush's administration, stocked with hard-line conservatives and steered by the shadowy influence of Vice President Dick Cheney, had inspired immediate opposition. In the summer of 2001, New York street culture magazine *Tokion* sold T-shirts emblazoned with Bush's face crossed out alongside the slogan "Not My President."

But the post-9/11 climate brought swift censorship of such antiestablishment expression. Media conglomerate Clear Channel advised stations to avoid playing certain songs, including Tom Petty's "Free Fallin,'" Queen's "Another One Bites the Dust," and the entire Rage Against the Machine catalog. *Tokion* pulled its anti-Bush T-shirts. Boots Riley expressed his "deepest sympathy" for the victims but resisted altering his album artwork, arguing it could "interrupt the stream of lies" surrounding US culpability. The label overruled him. *Party Music* debuted in November with a subdued cover of a flaming martini glass.

Explicit leftist critique was silenced almost overnight. Susan Sontag received scathing criticism for questioning the Bush administration's characterization of the hijackers as "cowards." Bill Maher's *Politically Incorrect* was canceled after he made a similar point. German composer Karlheinz Stockhausen's description of 9/11 as the "greatest work of art for the whole cosmos" prompted upstate New York's Ossia ensemble to cancel a planned performance of his music. White House press secretary Ari Fleischer told the nation, "People have to watch what they say and watch what they do."

Unlike during previous moments of war, there would be no call for collective sacrifice. Instead, Bush urged Americans to embrace consumption as an act of defiance against terror: "Fly and enjoy America's great destination spots. Get down to Disney World in Florida."

With leftist dissent squashed and shopping reframed as a patriotic duty, the next move was to roll back the cynical detachment that had defined much of the nineties. Just a week after the attacks, *Vanity Fair* editor in chief Graydon Carter proclaimed "the end of the age of irony." *Time* memoirist Roger Rosenblatt agreed: "For some 30 years—roughly as long as the Twin Towers were upright—the good folks in charge of America's intellectual life have insisted that nothing was to be believed in or taken seriously." There was no place for cool in the hot war on terror.

But the death of irony proved premature. Comedians quickly adapted to the post-9/11 landscape. The left-leaning satirical newspaper *The Onion*, which had moved earlier in the year to the city from Madison, Wisconsin, had to cancel their first New York issue. The editors eventually found a path forward for the newspaper: recognizing the grief of everyday Americans and tapping into their sense of "righteous anger" toward the hijackers. On September 27, *The Onion* reappeared with a 9/11-themed issue; the headlines blared, "American Life Turns into Bad Jerry Bruckheimer Movie" and "Not Knowing What Else to Do, Woman Bakes American-Flag Cake." Faxes piled up at *The Onion* offices "thick as a phone book," filled with praise from military, police, and affected families. Less than three weeks after the attacks, *The Onion* gave New York City a new hope that comic irreverence could survive even the worst national tragedy.

Irony, in fact, would be essential for the next twenty-five years of culture—not only as a coping mechanism, but as a blanket pass that allowed artists and critics to celebrate kitsch and toy with regressive ideas. And this all began in New York City's burgeoning downtown scene.

———————

"Rest of Country Temporarily Feels Deep Affection for New York," declared *The Onion* in its 9/11 issue—a satirical jab that would prove prescient.

Throughout the nineties, New York City's cultural dominance had waned. Grunge emerged from Seattle, gangsta rap thrived in Los Angeles, and Orlando emerged as a cultural hub for teenpop icons like Britney Spears and *NSYNC, aided by Swedish producers. Across the Atlantic, the rise of Britpop made London the world's new style capital under the banner of "Cool Britannia."

One of New York's few cultural successes during this period was Larry Clark's controversial 1995 film, *Kids*. This grim, amoral portrait of teenage boys inflicting violence, doing drugs, and spreading HIV cemented the careers of screenwriter Harmony Korine and indie "it" girl Chloë Sevigny. Yet it reinforced the stereotype of New York as an urban wasteland, a mythos increasingly detached from reality. New York underwent an economic boom in the 1990s. Crime rates plummeted, graffiti was removed from subway cars, and gentrification yuppified Lower Manhattan and Brooklyn. Three years after *Kids*, HBO's *Sex and the City* would showcase the same city as a playground of aspiration and wealth. As writer Jennifer Keishin Armstrong later observed, "To this day, it's why women still move to New York."

Even so, downtown artists clung to an edgier identity that found glamour in danger: the spirit of Andy Warhol's Factory, punk dive bars, and gold-chained rappers posing in front of burned-out Bronx buildings. By 2001, the Lower East Side had emerged as the creative hub for this carefully curated cool, borrowing heavily from *Kids'* portrayal of sex, drugs, and rock and roll. Yet, as comedian Marc Maron lamented, this aesthetic was "built on the carcass of seventies New York." Without the economic desperation that had birthed the original punk counterculture, downtown's grit often felt like posturing.

What New York artists lacked in authenticity they made up for in timing. By the end of the nineties, mainstream American pop culture had lost its edge. Grunge died with Kurt Cobain in 1994, leaving behind alterna-lite acts like Alanis Morissette and Hootie & the Blowfish. MTV, once a haven for countercultural experimentation, shifted focus in 1998 to mainstream programming like *Total Request Live*, which fueled the rise of factory-made teenpop stars and flyover-country favorites Limp Bizkit and Korn.

Downtown New York hungered for something rawer and more authentic. Salvation arrived in the form of a rock band called the Strokes. This five-piece rejected grunge's dirges and teenpop's polish, opting instead for a stripped-down rock sound with no synthesizers, samplers, or turntables. The band eschewed mosh-pit angst for bouncy bops where the instruments all worked in service of the beat. And the lyrics never dove deeper than the ennui of cryptic girlfriends and Friday morning hangovers.

Fittingly, the Strokes embodied the contradictions of downtown New York. Their greasy hair and dirty clothes obscured their privilege. Lead singer Julian Casablancas, offspring of model agency founder John Casablancas and Miss Denmark 1965, Jeanette Christiansen, met guitarist Nick Valensi and drummer Fabrizio Moretti at the private Dwight School in Manhattan. Casablancas first encountered guitarist Albert Hammond Jr., the son of hit LA songwriter Albert Hammond, at the legendary Swiss finishing school Institut Le Rosey. They reconnected in New York after high school and formed the band. Hammond's father bought them equipment for professional gigs, and models from Père Casablancas's agency in the audience created buzz for their early concerts. The Strokes landed a profile in fashion mag *V* before getting a record deal, and they appeared on the cover of the UK's *NME* before putting out an album. They eventually signed with major label RCA, run by veteran mogul Clive Davis. As music critic Ryan Schreiber wrote at the time, the Strokes were "a band that's seen enough publicity in 2001 to make bin Laden jealous."

Their 2001 debut, *Is This It*, became an instant classic, winning critical acclaim and reintroducing downtown New York's aesthetic to a global audience. The band's triumphant emergence convinced the industry that the new century would play out like the previous one: find hip bands and then package them up for mass global consumption. Interscope signed the female-fronted Yeah Yeah Yeahs. British record label Ministry of Sound advanced a rumored $2 million to the obscure performance art project Fischerspooner based on a demo tape and gigs at galleries and the Starbucks on Astor Place. Across town, James Murphy and Tim Goldsworthy of label DFA Records created a new sound merging disco beats with rock instrumentation that challenged Europe's techno dominance on the dance floor. This cohort of New York bands, along with Detroit's the White Stripes, wrote the new rules for global independent music over the next four years. They inspired and brought new attention to like-minded acts around the world: Kings of Leon in Nashville, the Killers in Las Vegas, the Hives in Sweden, the Vines in Australia, as well as British bands the Libertines, Franz Ferdinand, and Arctic Monkeys.

Despite the hype, the rock revival struggled to dominate the airwaves as grunge had in the nineties. The Strokes earned the label of "last real rock stars" but could never match the popularity of their critically loathed post-alternative contemporaries like Creed, Nickelback, and System of a Down. Electroclash fizzled as its artists rejected the categorization, and downtown's influence on the music market waned. Overall, the pop music of the subsequent decades owes very little to downtown New York. The rock revival's most enduring legacies may be the White Stripes' "Seven Nation Army" and the Killers' "Mr. Brightside" being repurposed as jock jams.

Even as its musical impact diminished, downtown New York succeeded in giving the twenty-first century its first major zeitgeist, reestablishing "cool" as raw, decadent, and a little dumb. This aesthetic found fertile ground in post-9/11 America, where consumerism became patriotism and leftist ideas were verboten. Downtown was no longer a haven for starving artists—it became a playground for the privileged, bankrolled by multinational corporations and wealthy investors. Drug-fueled parties, clandestine trysts, and backroom deals became the norm in the "cocaine era of New York." Andrew W.K., whose 2001 album cover depicted him with greasy hair and a bloodied nose, captured the city's post-tragedy ethos in a simple mantra: "Party Hard."

The nihilistic bacchanal of downtown New York in the early 2000s came across as nonideological—or, depending on the potency of the drugs, even anti-consciousness. But beneath the grime and chaos, subtle anti-liberal undercurrents were brewing.

Historically, "hip" countercultural figures positioned themselves as social progressives opposing the conservative establishment. Scholar Joel Dinerstein observes that coolness was traditionally defined by rebellion against the status quo guarded by conservative "squares." By 2001, however, this dynamic had inverted. The liberal coalition of the Clinton years, combined with the mainstreaming of alternative music and sympathetic media, had eroded conservative taboos around marijuana, nonmarital sex, gender norms, and homosexuality. Progressive ideals, once transgressive, were now repositioned as middle-class virtues. As philosopher Jean Baudrillard wrote about France in 1997, "Why has everything moral, orthodox, and conformist, which was traditionally associated with the right, passed to the left?" This shift created a crisis among the rebels, as cool, by definition, must always be oppositional.

Kids offered a template for rebellion: Sex, drugs, and rock and roll could still scandalize polite society when given a predatory edge. While the 1990s embraced psychedelics as tools for therapeutic self-discovery, New Yorkers turned to heroin and PCP for blunt self-destruction. Artists Dash Snow and Dan Colen epitomized this ethos with their "hamster nests," performance pieces where they got high on a cocktail of pharmaceuticals and shredded newspapers in a hotel room until the space resembled a rodent's habitat. Women in the scene shed the pastoral feminism of Lilith Fair, opting to party as hard as the boys. Karen O of the Yeah Yeah Yeahs became an icon with her wild, drunken stage antics, while electroclash rapper Peaches turned unfiltered id into an anthem with "Fuck the Pain Away."

If the Strokes gave the early aughts their sound, photographer Terry Richardson gave them their look. The son of sixties fashion photographer Bob Richardson, Terry grew up amid countercultural degeneracy. His father left the family to date a seventeen-year-old Anjelica Huston, eventually spiraling into homelessness. Terry attempted suicide as a teen and began using heroin at eighteen. By the mid-1990s, he had pulled his father off the streets to collaborate on photography projects, only to strike out on his own when Bob proved too erratic.

Richardson's breakthrough came quickly. His first shoot at *Vibe* was included in a major museum exhibit, and his provocative campaigns—like an ad for Katharine Hamnett exposing the models' pubic hair—made him a star. "I like sex and I like women," Richardson explained in 2000. "Any photographer wants to take pictures of the things they like." He soon became famous for his pseudo-porn chic, placing models against blank walls with blown-out lighting, arranging bodies in louche sexuality, and making obvious references to the exchange of bodily fluids. This calculated outrageousness earned him campaigns for Nike, Gucci, Levi's, and Miu Miu. By 2001, his work for French cosmetics brand Sisley included a model licking a snake's phallic head and another squeezing milk from a cow's udder onto her face.

Richardson often made himself the star of his own work. When not stark naked, he appeared in a signature look of red plaid flannel shirts, tight faded jeans, thick-rimmed glasses, and mutton chops with a handlebar mustache—like an adult film actor unfrozen from the seventies.

Richardson's photography dovetailed with a new set of gender norms that critic Ariel Levy labeled "raunch culture." In this latest stage of feminism, women celebrated sexual objectification as empowerment, thumbing their noses at the seriousness of second-wave feminists. "Female chauvinist pigs" embraced "the sleazy energy and aesthetic of a topless club or a *Penthouse* shoot." Lad magazines like *Maxim* and *FHM* capitalized on this shift, coaxing top female actors into appearing in "greased" poses, wearing "scraps of fabric," and mimicking pornographic imagery. "Things got very repressed in the 90's," noted downtown gallerist Jeffrey Deitch. Richardson's photos, his supporters claimed, similarly liberated the viewer from the straitjacket puritanism of nineties political correctness. His work was "honest" about sexual desire, and defenders claimed that this extended to the female models who engaged in sexual acts with him for the photos. When art critic Jerry Saltz took college students to see a Richardson exhibit, he noted, "At first, the girls sat back. Then they all started carrying on about how it looked fun. . . . They were all delighted."

Raunch culture's grip extended into low culture, as epitomized by the Girls Gone Wild video series. These videotapes and DVDs, sold through late-night infomercials, captured young women at spring break or Mardi Gras flashing the camera or engaging in casual lesbian scenes. Creator Joe Francis, a USC graduate, made a fortune in packaging up this amateur voyeurism. He pocketed at least $10 million from his first project, Banned from Television, which bundled violent and graphic footage deemed too extreme for TV. With Girls Gone Wild, Francis visited the American South to capture fresh material, luring women to "go wild" in exchange for cotton tank tops. By 2001, the franchise had sold 4.5 million units, and Francis lived lavishly, owning private planes, luxury cars, and Andy Warhol lithographs. MGM announced a Girls Gone Wild feature film, and the chart-topping rapper Eminem was brought in to shoot his own video. (Neither came to fruition: Francis claimed Eminem abandoned the project after feeling intimidated by their major differential in height.) Peter Guber at Mandalay Entertainment gushed that Francis "has a smell for the whole young market. He has entrepreneurial ability." The secret, Francis often told journalists, is that "feminists love us, because girls are doing what they want to do."

Despite their different markets, Joe Francis and Terry Richardson were two sides of the same raunch culture coin. Both enjoyed equal impunity: No one could criticize Francis's raunch positioned as entertainment, and no one could criticize Richardson's raunch positioned as art. Yet, as author Rachel Shukert quipped, "Only one of those sets of pictures is going to wind up in some chic gallery on Rivington Street or in the pages of French *Vogue*."

Even as complaints about harassment surfaced from Richardson's models, downtown New York media and celebrities continued to champion him. After gallerist Jeffrey Deitch began to represent Richardson, he faced a rebellion from his staff. He placated dissenters with extra paid holidays. What mattered was that Richardson stayed.

"Terry was in deep shit with all of those first-year feminist types," explained *Vice* magazine cofounder Gavin McInnes about the near walkout at Deitch's gallery. Richardson's style helped define *Vice*'s visual aesthetic as it positioned itself as the unofficial in-flight magazine for New York's descent into self-destructive juvenilia. "We were in a community of musicians, drug abusers, and prostitutes," boasted fellow *Vice* cofounder Suroosh Alvi, "and we all needed something to read." *Vice* soon became the defining media outlet of the early 2000s, and by slowly anchoring its vision of cool to right-wing ideology, it presaged cultural shifts that would unfold over the next two decades.

Conservative politics was not *Vice*'s original aim. Alvi, the son of Pakistani Canadian professors, studied philosophy at McGill University before spending his twenties addicted to heroin. During a rehab session, he resolved to become a magazine editor. His convoluted start involved welfare-funded work on a nonprofit Haitian community publication, which became *Voice of Montreal*, then *Voice*, and finally *Vice*. Alvi added illustrator Gavin McInnes, who brought along his childhood friend Shane Smith. At the time, McInnes and Smith were in a punk band called Leatherassbuttfuk; Smith had just returned from Hungary, where he earned a living through illegally arbitraging currency. Smith was so high on LSD when they first met that Alvi could barely understand him; Alvi assigned him the magazine's business operations.

With McInnes and Smith on board, *Vice* pivoted from a community publication to a "blend of outright fabrication and almost confessional sincerity." One fabrication proved particularly fruitful: The founders falsely claimed Canadian software mogul Richard Szalwinski wanted to buy the magazine. When Szalwinski read the lie, he invested $1 million of his real money for 25 percent ownership. The windfall funded *Vice*'s move to New York in 1999, where it quickly became central to downtown culture, attracting photographers like Terry Richardson and Ryan McGinley, as well as indie comedians David Cross and Sarah Silverman. Excess and outrage weren't just editorial strategies—they were a way of life. "That's why we're here in New York,"

McInnes wrote in 2002. "It's our job to party our asses off, find out what's going on, and convey it to people."

The magazine gained notoriety for its provocative columns and sensational stunts. McInnes's "Do's and Don'ts" column skewered or celebrated New Yorkers' street style, while advice columns pushed readers toward maximum nihilistic indulgence in drugs, sex, and rock and roll. *Vice*'s October 2002 "1980s" issue epitomized its approach: The editors persuaded surf-wear brand Ocean Pacific to place a back-cover ad that resembled a mirror dusted with cocaine residue.

While Terry Richardson provided *Vice* with the feel of amateur porn, the editors also leaned into "white trash" aesthetics. Blue-collar chic offered another way to shock wholesome liberals. Rapper Eminem had defended himself well as a white rapper by elucidating his working-class origin story in the hit film *8 Mile*. In parallel, *Vice* embraced Pabst Blue Ribbon beer, trucker caps, and other symbols of the lower-middle-class lifestyle as tools to reinforce its anti-intellectual "mindless fun" ethos. At the same time, McInnes also dismissed the nineties ideals against selling out as "juvenile and naïve," explaining that capitalism was inseparable from their content. "When you see [a guide to anal sex] in a glossy magazine with ads, it changes the joke," he told the *New York Press* in 2002. For McInnes and his team, corporate funding wasn't just a business goal—it was integral to the humor.

At first, *Vice*'s attack on political correctness and the upper-middle classes made sense within standard notions of transgressive cool. But McInnes quickly used his platform to launch direct political attacks on liberalism. He had once aligned with the left, performing in bands with crossed-out swastikas painted on his chest. But by the 2000s, his beliefs were best summarized by the tattoo on his back: "DESTRUCTION 创造 [creates]." Inspired by Jim Goad's *The Redneck Manifesto*, McInnes embraced atavistic views on gender, sex, and race, which he funneled into *Vice*. After 9/11, he became a self-proclaimed "Western chauvinist," positioning himself against liberal inclusivity and sensitivity. A former staffer described *Vice*'s early 2000s content as "largely an extension of McInnes's psyche."

McInnes thrived on provocation. He told the *New York Press* that women "want to be dominated" and dismissed anti-rape slogans like "No means no" as "puritanism." He described Williamsburg, Brooklyn, as a "big dorm," adding, "at least [the kids are] not fucking n*****s or Puerto Ricans. At least they're white." When confronted about this open racism, McInnes played the irony card. Anyone offended, he argued, didn't get the joke. Comedian Sarah Silverman defended the magazine to *The New York Times* in 2003, claiming, "If you think *Vice* is misogynistic, then you are a self-centered white woman."

McInnes's right-wing realignment soon extended beyond shock tactics into the political arena. In 2003, he interviewed the editor of Pat Buchanan's *The American Conservative* for *Vice*, and then contributed an article to the former, declaring that "it's getting cooler to be conservative." He bragged that *Vice* was shifting young people away from liberalism, replacing the "dumb community's days" with a "new breed of kid that isn't afraid to embrace conservatism."

In the past, abrasive countercultural aesthetics served as barriers to mainstream absorption. But this new right-leaning counter-counterculture that McInnes cultivated—rock machismo, raunchy photography, admiration for "white trash," and political incorrectness—proved easily marketable to provincial audiences. A spiritual sibling to *Vice* was the popular MTV reality show *Jackass*, with its bro-ey actors performing dangerous stunts.

The Strokes, Terry Richardson, and *Vice* were still niche players in global culture during the post-9/11 era, but they laid the groundwork for a larger youth movement: hipsters. As essayist Mark Greif observed, hipsters blended "rebel subculture" with "dominant class" tastes, creating "a poisonous conduit between the two." Hipster fashion—skinny jeans, Chuck Taylor sneakers, vintage 1980s clothing, tattoos, and trucker caps—spread through Urban Outfitters and American Apparel, the latter borrowing Terry Richardson's aesthetic for its provocative ad campaigns. Hipster enclaves like Williamsburg, Brooklyn, became cultural hubs, while the style infiltrated urban centers worldwide. The 2005 UK Channel 4 six-episode TV series *Nathan Barley* parodied the hipster archetype in London, including a *Vice*-esque publication called *SugarApe* (stylized with the *Suga* in tiny letters), a Terry Richardson–like auteur who photographs urinating celebrities, and a multimedia website called trashbat.co.ck, which its creator described as "two people leaping from the Twin Towers and they're fucking on the way down."

While there were always doubts about whether sixties hippies and nineties alternateens truly believed in their movements' tenets, hipsters abandoned even the pretense of ideological substance. Greif described hipsterism as "bohemia without the revolutionary core," in which alternative consumerism replaced any genuine countercultural ethos. But this void arguably took shape in downtown New York, where transgression thrived on commerce, multinational companies, and reactionary politics—all justified through ironic detachment. Few noticed at the time, but the end result was conservatism beginning its rebrand as edgy and countercultural.

Looking back, downtown New York was a false start for twenty-first-century culture—the last gasp of nineties-style rock and roll and the peak of idolizing white male hedonism. Yet its breakout stars gave the century its first major aesthetic: a mix of decadence, irony, and anti-liberal sentiment. By making transgression compatible with consumerism and right-wing ideology, downtown New York helped erase the stigma of selling out. In this new world, being transgressive wasn't about radical cultural innovation—you just had to party hard and find the right corporate sponsor.

HIP-HOP HYBRIDIZATION
Cultural Omnivores Fuse Genres to Create a New Pop

One of the defining songs of post-9/11 New York was LCD Soundsystem's "Losing My Edge," released in July 2002. Over a driving house beat, producer James Murphy delivers a deadpan, aging-hipster lament: "I'm losing my edge / to better-looking people with better ideas and more talent / And they're actually really, really nice." Inspiration struck Murphy after he returned from a concert at the Tribeca Grand, where he met a younger, good-looking, talented—and really, really nice—music producer: Pharrell Williams of the production unit the Neptunes.

By the time Murphy's track was released, Pharrell and his production partner Chad Hugo had already reshaped the sound of American Top 40 radio. In the 1990s, hip-hop had grown from an urban subculture into a global force, but clear genre boundaries persisted between rap, R&B, pop, rock, and electronica. Beginning in 1998, the Neptunes racked up a long stream of hits by blurring these lines, creating a signature sound that united disparate audiences. By 2003, their productions accounted for a staggering 43 percent of US radio singles. "The music industry's mandate," wrote critic Hua Hsu in 2004, "is to minimize risk, and for roughly four years, hiring the Neptunes has been as close to a sure bet as the machine allows." Even as they dominated radio playlists and packed dance floors, the Neptunes won over critics for their "hybrid-minded compositions and outsider sentiments," which Hsu noted made them seem "smarter than they are famous."

Such acclaim was an extraordinary feat for two earnest middle-class kids from Virginia Beach. Hugo, the son of Filipino immigrants, was a navy brat, while Pharrell's father worked as a handyman and his mother held a PhD in education. Both attended church regularly; Pharrell split his Sundays between Baptist and Pentecostal services. The racial integration of Virginia Beach exposed them to a melting pot of musical influences: Michael Jackson, Prince, and Stevie Wonder mingled with the rock of Queen, Yes, Steely Dan, Bon Jovi, and Guns N' Roses. From an early age, Pharrell crossed racial and cultural lines. As a Black teenager immersed in the predominantly white skateboarding scene, he wore checkerboard Vans and rocked hairstyles with "a billion parts cut in my head," signaling his dual allegiance to hip-hop and skating.

Pharrell and Hugo's partnership began in middle school band camp, where they bonded over their shared love of music. By high school, both were integral members of their award-winning drum lines and spent weekends recording songs in Hugo's attic on a four-track recorder. Their eclectic tastes gravitated toward artists who pushed boundaries, such as A Tribe Called Quest, whose socially conscious hip-hop and loopy beats left a lasting impression on Pharrell.

Hip-hop's roots in the South Bronx long gave New York rappers a sense of cultural ownership, but their dominance faced a major challenge from a host of regional styles in the 1990s. The rise of West Coast gangsta rap, led by Dr. Dre and Snoop Dogg, legitimized other cities, including Atlanta (OutKast), Detroit (Eminem), and Philadelphia (the Roots). Virginia Beach later joined this list thanks to Missy Elliott and her producer Timbaland, who was so close to Pharrell that he considered him a "cousin." Across the street from Pharrell's high school stood the studio of legendary producer Teddy Riley. In 1991, while working on Michael Jackson's album *Dangerous*, Riley hosted a talent show where he discovered Williams and Hugo and hired them on the spot. He thought their original compositions were too "ahead of their time" and not "ready for the marketplace." But Riley asked Hugo to play saxophone on multiple records, and in 1992, Pharrell wrote Riley's guest verse for Wreckx-n-Effect's track "Rump Shaker." The song hit number one on the rap charts.

Dropping out of Northwestern University, Pharrell regrouped with Hugo in Virginia Beach to make music full time. The Neptunes crafted a sound that redefined hip-hop and R&B production: snare-heavy funk breakbeats, vaguely ethnic riffs, disco guitar licks, and the occasional punk rock snarls. Their goal was strategic, as Hugo admitted: "We were trying to reach all the demographics" with music that worked in both "clubs and suburbs." Their breakthrough came with N.O.R.E.'s 1998 hit "Superthug," featuring a pseudo–Middle Eastern clavichord line and a Blondie-inspired vocal hook. For Kelis's "Caught Out There," they veered further left field, pairing grunge-style catharsis with her unforgettable scream: "I hate you so much right now / Ahhhhhhh."

Just as the Neptunes and Timbaland pushed boundaries, legendary New York rapper Jay-Z chose the opposite approach. On "Moment of Clarity," from his 2003 release, *The Black Album*, he confessed, "I dumbed down for my audience to double my dollars." For Jay, commercial success justified artistic compromise: "I can't help the poor if I'm one of them." The Neptunes contributed to his financial goals with the club-ready "I Just Wanna Love U (Give It 2 Me)," an infectious anthem powered by Pharrell's falsetto. Britney Spears, eager to shed her teenpop image, then turned to the Neptunes for "I'm a Slave 4 U," a sultry track originally written for Janet Jackson. Meanwhile, Pharrell also took notes from the downtown rock revival, telling *Rolling Stone* in 2002, "Everybody else is doing one-dimensional stuff, except the Strokes and the White Stripes."

The Neptunes' success only fueled their ambition. They penned "Rock Your Body" for Michael Jackson, and when he declined, the song launched Justin Timberlake's solo career instead. Their first *Billboard* number one came with Nelly's 2002 hit "Hot in Herre," a funk-laden anthem inspired by Chuck Brown's 1979 go-go track "Bustin' Loose." As critic Katie Moulton noted, the song bridged "late-'90s throwback tunefulness and the suburban hip-pop that would define mainstream music for the rest of the 2000s."

Artists always face a crossroads when they top their field. They can, like Jay-Z, "dumb down" and repeat themselves to ensure financial stability. Or, like the Neptunes, they can use the privileges of their high status to go even wilder. Under the name N.E.R.D, they released an experimental rap-rock album. For Virginia Beach hip-hop duo Clipse, they produced "Grindin,'" a minimalist track built on car-door-slam-like sounds that even the rappers initially struggled to comprehend. Its success emboldened them to craft another unconventional hit: Snoop Dogg's "Drop It Like It's Hot." *Billboard* later named it the "most popular rap song of the decade," praising its pink noise hisses, tongue clicks, and sparse 808 beats. For the first time, Pharrell stepped out from behind the mixing desk, delivering the song's opening verse and cementing his status as a star in his own right.

The music business is an exercise in chaos management: Hit artists are here today, gone tomorrow. To offset this volatility, savvy managers seek stable revenue streams, and apparel emerged in the 1990s as an obvious choice. Early rappers flaunted aspirational global brands like Kangol, Adidas, and Polo Ralph Lauren, often mirroring the style of local drug dealers. By the 1990s, Afrocentricity in the rap community inspired Black entrepreneurs to launch their own labels, including Cross Colours, FUBU, and Karl Kani.

Those successes paved the way for managers and record executives to expand their influence into fashion. Russell Simmons, cofounder of Def Jam Recordings, launched Phat Farm in 1992. The Wu-Tang Clan introduced Wu Wear in 1995. Sean "Puff Daddy" Combs elevated the game with Sean John in 1998, debuting his line at Bloomingdale's. Jay-Z followed with Rocawear in 1999. As hip-hop journalist Sowmya Krishnamurthy writes, clothing lines soon became an essential element of the "artist starter pack": "Drop an album and then release a clothing line."

Yet even as racial boundaries blurred in music, they persisted in fashion. White suburban teens embraced rap, blasting it from their run-down Honda Civics, but many hesitated to adopt the style fully. Racism surely played a role, but savvy teens also respected the community-mindedness of brands like FUBU ("For Us, By Us"). This led to parallel markets for Black and white styles, with crossover attempts often fraught with controversy. When Timberland boots became a hip-hop staple, the company's CEO publicly implied that Black customers weren't its "target customer," prompting calls for boycotts. Embracing Black audiences proved equally controversial for Tommy Hilfiger, prompting detractors to start false rumors that Hilfiger had made racist remarks on *The Oprah Winfrey Show*.

The eventual bridge across this Black-white divide emerged from an unexpected corner of the fashion industry. In 1984, Laguna Beach surfboard maker Shawn Stussy launched Stüssy, a line of casual clothing featuring graffiti-inspired graphics. Its popularity with skaters, artists, and DJs led to the creation of the International Stüssy Tribe, a collective of young creatives from New York, London, Los Angeles, and Tokyo. As demand surged, Stüssy made an epoch-making decision: to limit production and distribution to specific retailers, focusing on exclusivity rather than mass appeal. "We have no desire to get bigger," Stussy told the *Los Angeles Times* in 1992. "We feel we could continue doing business for many more years, sleep at night, enjoy kids growing up and not be a victim of our business." Together with complementary brands such as LA's FUCT and XLARGE, Stüssy forged a new urban casual clothing style known as "streetwear."

Unlike previous clothing trends, streetwear wasn't about avant-garde fashion design or unusual silhouettes. The core garments were just casual basics: T-shirts, sweatshirts, jeans, shorts, and sneakers. The selling point was the graphics and the logos, and the artificial exclusivity lent an aura of high fashion.

Streetwear became the uniform of urban subcultures: stylists, DJs, musicians, and their hangers-on. Members of the International Stüssy Tribe were involved with the creation of Phat Farm as well as iconic London shop Hit and Run. Japanese Tribe member Hiroshi Fujiwara pioneered Japan's first streetwear brand, Goodenough, in 1990 and helped his disciples open their own lines, Undercover and NEIGHBORHOOD. In New York, James Jebbia opened Stüssy's SoHo flagship store in 1991, where its success inspired him to launch Supreme, a skateboarding shop with a now-iconic red-box logo modeled after the work of artist Barbara Kruger.

This street culture scene, however, remained quite confined to a niche of cool kids in the big cities. Even with roots in skating, Pharrell Williams knew little about streetwear; he anchored his personal style to Polo Ralph Lauren, the ultimate crossover brand equally welcome at country clubs and block parties. Pharrell got his first lessons in European luxury labels from Kelis, and with the expanding zeros on his royalty checks, became a self-described "brand label whore." Pharrell then followed the lead of Jay-Z and Puff Daddy in ordering large bespoke jewelry necklaces and rings from Uzbek Jewish American Jacob Arabo, a.k.a. "Jacob the Jeweler."

During Pharrell's visits to Arabo's shop, he kept hearing about another prominent client: Nigo of the Japanese streetwear brand A Bathing Ape (a.k.a. BAPE). Nigo, born Tomoaki Nagao, was a former protégé of Hiroshi Fujiwara (Nigo means "number two" in Japanese, from "Hiroshi Fujiwara Number Two," due to their facial similarities). Throughout the 1990s, Nigo grew BAPE from a streetwear micro-brand making *Planet of the Apes*–inspired T-shirts into a mammoth retail empire. As a devotee of Andy Warhol, Nigo found his canvas for cultural expression not just in street art but in commerce. He hyperextended the original Stüssy business model: Fans could only buy BAPE's limited-edition clothing, often sold as "double-name" collabs with other brands, at its official stores. Young Japanese streetwear fans lined up outside each morning to strip the BAPE shops bare in a few hours. By the turn of the century, A Bathing Ape had sleek retail spaces across the regional cities, a shoe line (BAPE STA), a women's line (Bapy), a kids' line (Baby Milo), a record label ((B)APE SOUNDS), a restaurant (BAPE CAFE!?), and a hair salon (BAPE CUTS). In the US, streetwear was a tiny community; in Japan, it was a money-printing machine. Yet almost no one could buy BAPE outside of Japan, a scarcity that prompted the British magazine *The Face* to call A Bathing Ape "truly underground" in 1999.

Visiting Nigo's showroom, Pharrell was captivated by the scale and vision of BAPE. "It was the most amazing thing I had ever seen," Pharrell recalled.

The two quickly bonded, and Nigo offered to design Pharrell's planned clothing line, Billionaire Boys Club (BBC).

Weeks later, Nigo rushed to the US with the first samples of Billionaire Boys Club shirts for use in the video for Pharrell's debut solo track, "Frontin'" (a song initially composed for Prince). Nigo made a cameo appearance in the video alongside Jay-Z. In the video, Pharrell styled BBC more Japanese than nineties hip-hop, a slimmed-down skater silhouette topped with the kind of trucker hat beloved among downtown hipsters. In 2021 *GQ* named "Frontin'" "the most influential music video in menswear history."

Pharrell's partnership with Nigo helped introduce BAPE to the US, turning a once-obscure Japanese streetwear brand into a status symbol. Within a few years, BAPE's bright camouflage hoodies—especially the shark-head designs that zipped over the face—were everywhere, from hip-hop videos to paparazzi shots. The brand didn't just redefine aspiration and desire in America; it also created beef. A long-running feud between rappers Lil Wayne and Clipse erupted over who first wore A Bathing Ape. But as a Japanese brand, BAPE had a unique advantage—it could bypass America's racial fashion divides. Streetwear was no longer confined to a single identity; it could be for everyone.

The rise of streetwear also introduced a new mindset to global consumers. Teens began treating clothes like collectibles, buying limited releases to keep "on ice" for future resale. Brands from Nike to Louis Vuitton took note, hiring streetwear legends to learn how to do "drops." Pharrell and Nigo designed sunglasses for Louis Vuitton, and by 2005, Chanel's Karl Lagerfeld photographed Nigo for the cover of *Interview*.

The fusion of hip-hop and streetwear wasn't just about style—something had changed in the culture. Pharrell and Nigo built their friendship on broad omnivore tastes, and their partnership razed boundaries between music, fashion, and art. They had spurred a new global aesthetic that would reshape aspiration and consumer behavior. As Nigo observed, "In America nobody ever used to line up to buy sneakers, but now it's starting to happen."

Standing alongside Pharrell Williams and Nigo at A Bathing Ape's New York launch party in January 2005 was another rising star: a Chicago-born producer-rapper named Kanye West. At the time, Kanye's debut album, *The College Dropout*, had just been nominated for ten Grammy Awards and was widely celebrated for its innovative blend of hip-hop, soul, R&B, and gospel. Much like the Neptunes, Kanye achieved the rare trifecta of approval in music, writer Rob Mitchum noted, "from pop radio, hip-hop purists, and reactionary rock critics."

Kanye was raised in an intellectual and politically engaged household. His mother, Donda, was a civil rights activist turned professor with a doctorate in education. His father, Ray, a former Black Panther, worked as a photojournalist and Christian marriage counselor. They divorced when Kanye was three, and he spent his childhood navigating diverse environments, from gang-heavy Chicago neighborhoods to suburban enclaves. He also did a stint in Nanjing, China, where his mother taught on a Fulbright fellowship. "Living in Chicago and all my friends are gangbangers, and then I'd go to the suburbs in the summertime and I'd be known as 'the Black kid,'" he later recalled.

As a young teen, West told his mother he wanted to make hip-hop, so she set him up in unofficial apprenticeships with producers in Chicago's fledgling rap scene. By fifteen, he'd learned enough to provide beats for local groups. After a few semesters at the American Academy of Art and Chicago State University, he dropped out and moved to New York to pursue music full time. His signature production style, which sped up and pitched soul samples into "chipmunk" hooks, quickly caught the attention of industry insiders. Like Pharrell and the Neptunes, Kanye first went big alongside Jay-Z, producing key tracks for the rapper's *The Blueprint*, released on September 11, 2001.

But Kanye's ambitions extended beyond the mixing desk. He spent the years after 9/11 cruising around studios and record label offices, removing

his orthodontic retainers before showing off his rap skills. "Every motherfucker told me that I couldn't rhyme," he later griped. The top MCs at the
time—DMX, 50 Cent, and Nas—were macho and battle-hardened. Kanye's
lyrics were a mix of socially conscious cynicism, too-clever puns, and insider
critique of the Black middle-class experience.

Roc-A-Fella Records reluctantly signed Kanye in 2002, hoping he'd make
an album that showcased other rappers over his acclaimed beats. When the
label refused to prioritize his solo debut, Kayne self-financed a video for
"Through the Wire," a song he recorded while recovering from a near-fatal
automobile accident. The video helped Roc-A-Fella finally see what Kanye
was aiming for: He wasn't a conventional rapper but a hip-hop auteur who
could "bridge the gap" between the street-oriented beats of mainstream rap
and the artistic edge of backpack rap. West embodied this mission in his personal style, wearing diamond-encrusted pieces from Jacob the Jeweler on his
front and a Louis Vuitton backpack. Like Pharrell, he loved Ralph Lauren
and created a mascot called Dropout Bear, modeled on the Polo Bear.

The production on his debut album *The College Dropout* reflected an
omnivorous approach to music that expanded upon the Neptunes' template.
He pulled from the entire history of Black music as well as the latest international sounds, such as auto-tuned vocals and the house music of French act
Daft Punk. *The College Dropout* ends with nine minutes of spoken word
about Kanye's long struggles to be respected as a rapper. But the haters were
wrong, and he was right: *The College Dropout* sold over two million copies in
2004 and received best album of the year accolades in *The Village Voice's*
annual Pazz & Jop poll of music critics.

Kanye also made fashion a cornerstone of his identity. His early ambition
was to become "the best-dressed rapper in the game." He took early cues
from Pharrell, whom *Esquire* crowned "the best-dressed man in the world" in
2005. Pharrell's brightly colored Polo shirts became Kanye's uniform, often
layered for effect. Pharrell's affinity for A Bathing Ape inspired Kanye to
adopt the brand, making himself an unofficial ambassador.

The two men first met backstage at a Jay-Z concert in 2002, and their work, which often felt in dialogue, would define the next two decades. Both Pharrell and Kanye were voracious omnivores, exploring global culture and bringing unexpected influences into hip-hop. Jimmy Iovine, the veteran music mogul behind Interscope Records, signed the Neptunes in 2004 and gave them their own label, Star Trak. This partnership extended their genre-blurring sound to a broader roster of artists, including Gwen Stefani on her minimal, cheerleader-chant hit "Hollaback Girl" (backed by four Japanese "Harajuku Girls") and Swedish garage rockers the Hives on *The Black and White Album.*

Kanye, too, expanded his reach with unexpected collaborations with the likes of Adam Levine of Maroon 5. He brought aboard producer Jon Brion in an attempt to become "the rap version" of Fiona Apple, and his third album *Graduation* in 2007 incorporated elements of German krautrock and French electronic music. Its hit single "Stronger," built around Daft Punk's masterpiece "Harder, Better, Faster, Stronger," dominated charts, solidifying his reputation as the leading genre blender.

As Pharrell and Kanye reshaped hip-hop, they inspired a new generation. Kanye launched the careers of protégés like R&B singer John Legend and rapper Kid Cudi (who worked at A Bathing Ape in New York). In late 2007, "Stronger" competed for the top slot on the *Billboard* Hot 100 with "Crank That" by seventeen-year-old rapper-producer Soulja Boy, who embraced the rising prominence of streetwear: "Haters gettin' mad 'cause / I got me some Bathin' Ape." Pharrell's and Kanye's abilities to draw from disparate cultural sources and synthesize them into mainstream hits ensured their influence on global culture for the next several decades. And in doing so, they established that the fusion of genres was a reliable and dynamic source of cultural power for the new century.

POP, IDOLS, AND CELEBRITY

Poptimism Paves the Way
for Gossip and Sleaze

3

On October 23, 2004, twenty-year-old teenpop idol Ashlee Simpson—the younger sister of pop star and reality TV sensation Jessica Simpson—appeared on *Saturday Night Live* as the musical guest. When her backing band launched into the second song, "Autobiography," a technical malfunction triggered the vocal track from her first performance, "Pieces of Me." Millions of viewers realized that Simpson had lip-synched. As the band fumbled, Simpson danced an awkward jig before fleeing the stage in tears.

Scandal erupted. Fans flooded her website with angry comments, calling her a fraud. Media outlets eagerly framed her as a modern Milli Vanilli. The incident seemed like a career-ending debacle: a manufactured pop star caught pretending to perform.

Eight days later, Harvard-educated music critic Kelefa Sanneh wrote a defense of Simpson in *The New York Times*. Her critics had succumbed to "rockism": the virulent ideology "idolizing the authentic old legend (or underground hero) while mocking the latest pop star; lionizing punk while barely tolerating disco; loving the live show and hating the music video; extolling the growling performer while hating the lip-syncher." Rockists upheld straight, white guitar bands as the only worthy subjects of critical attention; when they bothered to pay attention to hip-hop, they overindexed rock-influenced groups like OutKast and the Roots.

For Sanneh, the solution was to reject rockism's elitist hierarchies and celebrate pop music on its own terms. Why, he asked, should Nirvana's "neo-punk" be considered "more respectable than Ms. [Mariah] Carey's neo-disco?"

The anti-rockist ethos later became known as "poptimism." Its emergence marked a seismic shift in cultural criticism. For most of the twentieth century, the spiritual leader for critics was neo-Marxist theorist Theodor Adorno, who maligned popular culture as manipulative propaganda. Writers in this lineage advocated for true artists and fought against the cynical excesses of the culture industry. They saw their job as separating art from kitsch, and in the early aughts, that meant elevating the Strokes and the White Stripes as good and impugning Creed and Hoobastank as bad.

Sanneh countered that pop music—and by obvious extension, the entirety of pop culture—shouldn't be dismissed as kitsch nor as bad art but appreciated as a complex manufactured product. In this, poptimism not only acknowledged postmodernist trends in culture but also paid them full fealty. Echoing Fredric Jameson's idea that "postmodernism is the consumption of sheer commodification as a process," Sanneh implored us to enjoy pop music as a "glorious, incoherent, corporate-financed, audience-tested mess."

This reorientation arrived at a pivotal moment for pop. By the early 2000s, the dominance of rock was waning. The bestselling artists weren't guitar bands but hip-hop (Eminem, 50 Cent), R&B (Alicia Keys, Beyoncé), and country (Alan Jackson, Shania Twain). Meanwhile, the rock bands that thrived commercially, like Staind and Evanescence, faced critical derision. And the indie rock darlings of the era, like the Strokes and the White Stripes, captured the imaginations of critics but never came close to the cultural ubiquity of pop titans like Usher or Avril Lavigne.

This cultural shift made poptimism not only timely but also politically resonant. For its advocates, celebrating pop music became a way to champion the voices of marginalized communities. Hip-hop and R&B, genres rooted in Black culture, were already dominating the charts, while Latin artists like Ricky Martin and Shakira gained global followings. By working to elevate these genres and artists, poptimism justified itself in the progressive ideals of diversity and inclusivity.

Yet, just as poptimism ascended, resistance emerged in the form of a website: Pitchfork Media. Launched in 1996 by Ryan Schreiber as a zine-like venture, *Pitchfork* championed indie rock, avant-garde experimentation, and left-field artists. Its reviews, scored to decimal-point precision, became beloved for their meticulous discussions of underground releases and infamous for brutal takedowns of indie stalwarts Sonic Youth and Liz Phair. In what became known as the Pitchfork Effect, high scores on the site launched the careers of many indie bands, such as Arcade Fire, Broken Social Scene, and Clap Your Hands Say Yeah. Dan Hougland at legendary NYC independent record shop Other Music noted in 2004, "The writer for *Spin* makes more money, but the Pitchfork dude has way more power."

Where poptimists celebrated chart-topping artists and glossy production, *Pitchfork* upheld the idea that true art was inherently oppositional. Music that appealed to the masses was, by definition, compromised. Looking back two decades later, Schreiber argued that the "responsibility of the music press" was to "champion artists who are otherwise not gonna be heard by listeners or maybe not heard as quickly . . . things that were a little bit left field, outside of the mainstream, more adventurous, experimental."

In the poptimist logic, however, *Pitchfork*'s favorite musical acts were simply *lesser* artists for refusing to pursue mass appeal. At *Pitchfork*'s first Chicago festival in 2005, Kelefa Sanneh dismissed the lineup for that very reason: "The two stages at Union Park weren't filled with bands that seemed destined to blast into the stratosphere, or even the troposphere. Instead, the stages were filled with bands that are already about as popular as they will ever be." Previous generations of avant-garde artists saw alienating mass audiences as either a requirement or an unavoidable consequence of pushing art forward. But in the poptimist value system, experimental artists were nobodies until they found large audiences. Not selling a lot of records—or worse, not even trying to—became grounds for critical dismissal.

The "rockism versus poptimism" debate was never a mainstream concern; it was a battle waged on internet forums and in the pages of alt weeklies. But its downstream effects upended culture. Over time, poptimism became the dominant mode of twenty-first-century criticism and informed how the creative classes approached art. Mass-marketed success became an important signifier of ambition and innovation rather than a betrayal of artistic principles. The idea of selling out—once a potent cultural critique—further faded into irrelevance.

Despite *Pitchfork*'s distaste for manufactured pop, the site was hardly rockist. Its reviewers explored an eclectic range of music from around the world, reflecting a profound shift in how fans discovered and consumed music at the turn of the century. Technology had begun to radically reshape listening habits, pushing fans to embrace greater diversity in their musical tastes.

In the nineties, CDs and cassette tapes made music portable, allowing high school and college students to create soundtracks for their daily lives. But these formats came with limitations: CDs were expensive, were often hard to find, and offered finite options. The internet changed all that. College students with campus broadband could now swap music files with friends or scour primitive file-sharing platforms, using software like Winamp to play their growing digital collections.

The next breakthrough came in June 1999, with the launch of Napster, a peer-to-peer file-sharing network that connected music-obsessed youth across the globe. Napster didn't just make music free—it made it limitless. Fans no longer had to gamble on an expensive album or stay within the confines of a favorite genre. Instead, they could download tracks from any artist, style, or era, from Brazilian bossa nova to death metal.

In January 2001, Apple released iTunes, a sleek desktop app that organized MP3 libraries and allowed users to rip digital files from their own

CDs. By that fall, Apple took the next step in revolutionizing music consumption with the release of the iPod. For a generation leaving college with
cherished music collections trapped on desktop hard drives, the iPod provided a gateway to mobility. This pocket-size device could hold an entire
music library—up to a thousand songs—that could be taken anywhere. Physical media, with its cumbersome cases and linear listening, began to feel
obsolete. CDs quickly fell out of favor, and kids pivoted to digital files, even
if much of the music in their collections was questionably sourced.

The iPod didn't just change where music was stored; it redefined how
it was consumed. Its shuffle feature allowed users to jump across artists,
albums, and genres in unpredictable ways, turning personal libraries into
infinite playlists of surprising juxtapositions. This randomness became an
aesthetic in its own right, encouraging fans to embrace eclecticism as a virtue. Around the same time, advances in digital music production software
unlocked new creative possibilities. DJs and producers began repurposing existing sounds to create mash-ups—tracks that combined vocal and instrumental elements from different songs into surprising hybrids. Early pioneer
the Freelance Hellraiser set the tone with "A Stroke of Genius," blending
Christina Aguilera's "Genie in a Bottle" with the Strokes' "Hard to Explain."
In 2002, a duo of Belgian brothers, Soulwax, released the seminal *As Heard
on Radio Soulwax Pt. 2*, where Salt-N-Pepa's "Push It" met the Stooges' "No
Fun," and Skee-Lo's "I Wish" collided with the Breeders' "Cannonball."

The mash-up phenomenon culminated in 2004 with *The Grey Album*,
a groundbreaking demo tape by producer Danger Mouse. The album combined Jay-Z's *The Black Album* vocals with instrumental fragments from the
Beatles' White Album, earning critical acclaim, sparking debates over copyright, and annihilating the line between rap and rock. Two years later, American producer Girl Talk pushed the form further, creating songs stitched
together from dozens of recognizable pop hits. What once seemed like a
niche experiment in DJ culture had become a mainstream phenomenon,
with artists using digital tools to craft new pop directly from the remnants of
old pop.

———

Record labels had long grappled with a central dilemma: Their biggest profits came from teenpop and crowd-pleasing hits that critics dismissed as derivative and uncool. Under the ideology of poptimism, however, this was no longer a problem. Poptimism championed the cultural industry's manufacturing processes—ghostwriting, pitch correction, and cosmetic enhancements—reframing them as part of the artistry. The most cynical gambits of the industry were recast as virtues. Market success wasn't just tolerated; it became the supreme marker of importance. Revenue was the ultimate validation of popularity and cultural significance. *Business* was no longer the necessary evil in the music business; it was a source of excitement.

Perhaps this shift reflected a broader cultural reality: Music was losing its place as the central pillar of pop culture. For all the ingenuity of OutKast's "Hey Ya!," the most defining musical moment of 2003 arguably wasn't a song. It was Madonna open-mouth kissing Britney Spears and Christina Aguilera at the MTV Video Music Awards—a moment of pure spectacle that repurposed music as the mere backdrop to television drama.

MTV, once the arbiter of music culture, began shifting its focus upon discovering that young audiences preferred its reality TV programming. The breakthrough came with *The Real World*, a low-budget cinema verité experiment that followed the unscripted lives of young adults sharing a New York apartment. The show's success birthed spin-offs like *Road Rules*, with each iteration shedding even the slightest artistic pretensions. By the early 2000s, as MTV's financial and operations teams gained influence over programming, reality TV dominated the network. Music was sidelined as reality TV became the bait to keep teen viewers tuned in after *Total Request Live*.

The first wave of MTV reality shows still maintained some connection to music: *Cribs* explored celebrity homes; *The Osbournes* brought cameras into the chaotic household of heavy metal singer Ozzy Osbourne; and *Pimp My Ride* brought a hip-hop sensibility to a car show. Teenpop sensation Jessica Simpson starred alongside her then-husband Nick Lachey of boy band 98

Degrees in *Newlyweds: Nick and Jessica*, a show that, as TV critic Emily Nussbaum noted, "turned stars into ordinary people" rather than the other way around.

This fusion of music and reality TV came to a head with *Making the Band*. The show chronicled the assembly of boy band O-Town by mogul Lou Pearlman (who was later convicted of fraud and died in custody). The drama of manufacturing the band proved more compelling than their actual music, and viewers embraced the behind-the-scenes spectacle. And it worked as a business model: The show generated free promotion for O-Town, whose first album debuted at number five on the *Billboard* charts.

The symbiosis between music and reality TV culminated with *American Idol*, which debuted on June 11, 2002. Adapted from the British *Pop Idol*, the US version introduced amateur singers to a panel of judges: the supportive Randy Jackson and Paula Abdul, and the villainous Simon Cowell. The show's first finale, in September 2002, became the highest-rated program of the summer. But music industry executives were initially skeptical of a broader cultural impact; for RCA boss Clive Davis, the idea that a reality show could produce genuine musical stars seemed "essentially unthinkable." But Kelly Clarkson, the inaugural winner, proved them wrong. Her debut album topped the charts, selling 2.8 million copies in the US.

Once *American Idol* became successful enough, the music became secondary to the drama. This perhaps explains why the show was a long-running hit, yet Clarkson and fourth-season winner Carrie Underwood were the only two champions to achieve major success in the music market.

The deprioritization of music on *American Idol* reflected broader trends in the music industry. With the rise of iPods and file-sharing services, music sales plummeted throughout the 2000s, bottoming out in 2014. Teens were still listening to music, but fewer were paying for it. As the Neptunes and Kanye West expanded musical boundaries, Top 40 radio's core audience became increasingly apathetic. In this shrinking market, niche artists could dominate specific segments without achieving widespread fame. The country singer Gretchen Wilson claimed a bestselling album with little footprint beyond her devoted fans. Poptimism oddly arrived at a moment right as pop music was losing its dominance over youth culture.

————

In his 1962 book, *The Image*, historian Daniel Boorstin lamented the rise of celebrity culture, arguing that modern fame had supplanted an era in which "a man's name was not apt to become a household word unless he exemplified greatness in some way or other." For Boorstin, the twentieth century marked the fall of a golden age of heroes to the hollow triumph of the celebrity—"a person who is known for his well-knownness." Despite his critique, celebrity culture only accelerated throughout the century, fueled by the growth of mass media. Yet his argument still stung: To be famous for being famous carried shame. Icons with talent and achievements still received higher esteem than stars who lacked substance.

This distinction couldn't last in the poptimist era, where the processes of fame—marketing, spectacle, and self-promotion—were lauded as valid forms of cultural production. Poptimism blessed musicians for using ghostwriters, vocal correction, and lip-synching as part of their performances. It was a short leap from this logic to exalting celebrities with no artistic output at all.

Enter Paris Hilton, the aughts' quintessential celebrity. Hilton wasn't just famous for being famous; she was famous for openly wanting to be famous for being famous. She was first understood as an aristocratic heiress, but this label wasn't quite accurate. Her great-grandfather Conrad Hilton made his fortune as a hotel magnate, yet he never elevated his clan into the pantheon of Old Money. Instead, the Hiltons gravitated toward Hollywood glamour, with Conrad taking actress Zsa Zsa Gabor as his second wife. Paris's grandfather, Barron, sued to reclaim a share of the family estate to expand the hotel business and found the Los Angeles Chargers. By the time Paris was born, her father, Richard, had made his own fortune in luxury real estate, and her mother, Kathy, had transitioned from childhood acting and modeling into Beverly Hills society life.

Paris Hilton's early years were both privileged and tumultuous. As a teenager living at the Waldorf Astoria in New York, she became a regular on the party circuit, earning frequent mentions in Page Six for her wild nights out. After a string of expulsions from prestigious schools, Hilton was sent by her parents to a boarding school for troubled teens founded by members of the Synanon cult. The experience was brutal; Hilton later recounted enduring humiliation and abuse, and despite multiple escape attempts, she was repeatedly returned to the institution.

Back in New York as a young adult, Hilton turned her party-going lifestyle into a budding career. She strategically cultivated media attention, tipped off paparazzi as to her whereabouts, and demanded payment from event organizers for attending their parties. The *New York Post* noted that "the most outrageous New York City–based heiress is hotel-darling Paris Hilton, 19, a part-time model with a tendency to flash her thong." In 2000, famed photographer David LaChapelle shot her for *Vanity Fair* in her grandmother's house with a mesh top and no bra, flipping off the camera. Hilton had grand aspirations: "I want to be famous," she once told a friend. "I want people to know who I am to be aware of me and I want them to like me so I can sell them things. . . . I want people to appreciate my opinion as a tastemaker. As an icon. And I want to monetize that, like a *lot*."

For all of her aspirations of becoming a tastemaker, she didn't care much about taste. She appeared in a low-budget film called *Sweetie Pie* that was shelved. She joined real estate magnate Donald Trump's modeling agency T Management: "I wanted to model and Donald was like: 'I want you at my agency.' So now I'm with them and I'm loving it." In November 2001, just two months after the 9/11 attacks, Hilton arrived at the opening of the Palms Casino Resort in Las Vegas wearing a dress with $1 million in gambling chips sewn on.

A decade earlier, Hilton's lack of talent in the performing arts would have capped her ascent. But by 2003, reality TV opened a new career path. Bunim Murray Productions decided to build a reality show around Hilton and her friend, Lionel Richie's daughter, Nicole. Modeled after the 1960s sitcom

Green Acres, The Simple Life cast Hilton as a ditzy Manhattan socialite in rural Arkansas, leaning heavily on her catchphrase, "That's hot." Hilton embraced the character as both a shield and a "ticket to financial freedom." "Paris Hilton," she later admitted, was "the character I played—part Lucy, part Marilyn." (The split personality became even clearer when Hilton revealed that she switches between a deep register of voice in more comfortable settings to a high register when acting as "Paris Hilton.")

Weeks before *The Simple Life*'s premiere, however, Hilton faced a major crisis when a mysterious website teased clips of her performing in a homemade pornographic video. She assumed the video was fake; there was "no way for a regular person to upload something like that onto the internet. The technology for humiliating someone on that level hadn't been invented yet." But the video was indeed real, made in 2001 by Hilton's much older divorcé boyfriend Rick Salomon when Hilton was just nineteen. When Salomon released it as *1 Night in Paris*, charging fifty dollars per view, Hilton believed her "life was over."

But Hilton, guided by crisis communications expert Dan Klores, weathered the storm. She reframed herself as a victim of exploitation, declined most interviews, and made a self-deprecating appearance on *Saturday Night Live*. The tape, rather than ruining her, further cemented her status as a cultural phenomenon. By the end of 2004, she was one of Barbara Walters's "10 Most Fascinating People," alongside the founders of Google and conservative political mastermind Karl Rove. Ariel Levy summed up Hilton's paradoxical appeal: "Paris Hilton isn't some disgraced exile of our society. On the contrary, she is our mascot."

Hilton's rise marked a shift in the cultural understanding of fame. In previous decades, notoriety still carried social penalties. Hilton proved that controversy—and even widespread hatred—could be a career asset. *Guinness World Records 2007* named her the most "overrated" celebrity, but she accepted such derision as part of her winning formula. Poptimism made this new kind of fame possible. Perhaps only a small minority of fans loved her with utter sincerity, but the new moral demand to respect their tastes resulted in a collective acceptance of Hilton's stardom.

Hilton's mode of fame presaged the rise of the influencer economy. She monetized her image across a host of less-than-respected industries, from private-label fashion goods to fast-food chains. Her Carl's Jr. commercial, where she provocatively washed a Bentley in a bikini, set new benchmarks for salacious marketing campaigns. Paparazzi followed her every move, fueling a growing celebrity gossip industry that expanded beyond print tabloids to online blogs and forums.

While celebrities' most prurient moments began to dominate entertainment news, there were still strong restrictions against such raunch on prime time. The 2004 Super Bowl halftime show, in which Justin Timberlake exposed Janet Jackson's breast, ignited a national debate about decency in entertainment. The FCC imposed hefty fines on CBS, while MTV, which produced the show, scrambled to contain the fallout.

But the Super Bowl fiasco also marked one of the last times central authorities could enforce limits on content. In February 2004, when Rick Salomon showed up on Howard Stern's radio show, the two men discussed lurid sexual preferences and Salomon boasted of bedding an underaged Drew Barrymore. Then a listener called in and used racial epithets. Clear Channel suspended Stern and later fired him. Sirius Satellite Radio stepped in to steal the shock jock with a $500 million deal. The saga proved that new forms of technology would always be there to let creators get away with evading norms— and this was just the beginning.

———

Three years after 9/11, the waning scene in downtown New York looked to the glossy, celebrity-driven culture of Los Angeles for a new source of energy. This was evident at the Misshapes, New York City's next iconic party. Like *American Idol*, Misshapes downplayed music in favor of spectacle, with amateur DJs offering chaotic sets that sounded like an iPod on shuffle mode. The real attraction was its photo wall, inspired by Japanese street photo magazine *FRUiTS*, where attendees posed for portraits that later appeared online. Participation offered a pathway to minor internet notoriety. As writer Tricia Romano observed, "We were all watching reality TV and we were all starring in our own nightlife type of reality TV online."

Madonna, ever the cultural barometer, made a surprise visit to Misshapes in October 2005, drawing such massive crowds that the party needed larger venues moving forward. The arrival of digital cameras and web pages democratized party photography, turning private nightlife antics into public performance. Photographer Mark Hunter, a.k.a. the Cobrasnake, emerged as the medium's first breakout star. Hunter, an assistant to street artist Shepard Fairey, shot blown-out candids of wild party scenes, launching his teenage girlfriend Cory Kennedy as "the internet's first 'it' girl." Reflecting on her rise, Kennedy recalled, "People sweating, running around, jumping over and on each other. . . . It was action packed and it was a very positive vibe."

The Cobrasnake's photos captured the further collapse of subcultural boundaries in real time. His lens gave equal attention to downtown scenesters like *Kids* actor Chloë Sevigny and artist Dash Snow as to Los Angeles celebrity elite such as Paris Hilton, the Olsen twins, and DJ Steve Aoki. A decade later, this aesthetic would be dubbed "indie sleaze," a merger of creative-class sensibilities and raunch culture. Fashion trends followed suit, with LA's garish glamour overtaking New York's gritty sophistication: velour tracksuits from Juicy Couture, rhinestone-emblazoned Ed Hardy shirts, and trucker hats from Von Dutch. (Von Dutch was the nickname of American mechanic Kenny Howard, an open admirer of the Third Reich who used "Sieg Heil" as a sign-off for personal letters.)

By the mid-2000s, gossip and celebrity rivaled music and film as the dominant pillars of pop culture. Paris Hilton epitomized this shift, often outpacing Britney Spears in Google searches. Spears herself leaned into reality TV to maintain relevance, starring in *Britney and Kevin: Chaotic*, a critically panned series chronicling her volatile marriage to Kevin Federline. (Jimmy Kimmel labeled him "the world's first-ever no-hit wonder.") After her marriage to Federline dissolved, Spears made a new friend: "One of the people who was kindest to me when I really needed kindness was Paris Hilton."

Spears celebrated her new freedom by hitting the town with Hilton and blunting her depression with Adderall. On November 26, 2006, paparazzi culture reached its apex when an army of photographers spotted Hilton, Spears, and fellow tabloid superstar Lindsay Lohan huddled in the front seat of Hilton's car—a $20,000 photo that became known as the "Holy Trinity."

But Spears's struggles also underscored the darker side of this media frenzy. Her public breakdowns in 2007—shaving her head, attacking a photographer's SUV with an umbrella—signaled the collapse of the teenpop era. In that moment, Paris Hilton stood out as the clearest model for achieving cultural relevance. She released her own album, *Paris*, showing that gossip opened the path to a music career and not always the other way around.

Then Hilton decided to become an entrepreneur: "I'm glad I got the partying out of my system when I was young, because now I'm so over it and I can focus on my career." She had two particular business heroes: Sean "P.Diddy" Combs and her old family friend Donald Trump. "He's built this whole empire—hotels, casinos, resorts, a television show." At that moment, Trump was enjoying a career resurgence thanks to his reality game show, *The Apprentice*. In the Trump model, Hilton flooded the market with cash-grab handbags and body sprays. She slapped her name on an inferior club in Orlando, Florida, in partnership with the Iranian American businessman Fred Khalilian (who was arrested in 2023 for attempting to employ a hitman to kill a documentary filmmaker).

In 2006, Hilton hired her longtime friend Kourtney Kardashian's younger sister Kim to organize her closet. Kourtney and Kim were the daughters of Robert Kardashian, a lesser-known lawyer on O. J. Simpson's triumphant legal team, and Kris Jenner, who remarried with Olympian Caitlyn Jenner (prior to her transition). Like Hilton, Kim Kardashian also had big dreams of being famous. While trying to make money running her closet-organizing business, Kim Kardashian often met with an editor at *In Touch Weekly* to pitch gossip stories about herself. The problem, the editor kept having to reiterate, was that readers had no interest in reading about complete unknowns like Kim Kardashian. She at least needed to be on TV. Hilton allowed Kardashian to appear in a few episodes of *The Simple Life*, and the two began attending events together.

In January 2007, rumors appeared in the press that the adult company Vivid planned to release a homemade video of a gum-smacking Kim Kardashian having sex with her boyfriend Ray J, the brother of R&B singer Brandy. How did Vivid acquire this video? This question has been one of the great mysteries of the twenty-first century, with recriminations on both sides. Girls Gone Wild founder Joe Francis, who had been linked romantically with both Paris Hilton and Kourtney Kardashian in the early aughts, revealed in 2023 that Kim and Ray J asked him to broker the deal. Whatever the truth, the pornographic video *Kim Kardashian, Superstar* appeared on March 21, 2007, and sold massive numbers.

A few months later, Paris Hilton spent a few weeks in jail for violating her probation for an earlier alcohol-related reckless driving charge. *The Simple Life* aired its last episode on August 5, 2007. Lindsay Lohan planned to release her own reality show on E!, but she pulled out of the project after being arrested for cocaine possession and driving under the influence. Needing to plug the hole in programming for fall, E! announced a new reality show from Bunim Murray Productions and *American Idol* host Ryan Seacrest: *Keeping Up with the Kardashians*. Poptimism opened the door for Paris Hilton, and now Hilton opened it further to accommodate the entire Kardashian family.

THE NERD INTERNET

Circumventing Norms to Create Niches,
Make Money, and Find Hope

4

Early internet culture boasted an immaculate countercultural pedigree. Its lineage began with Stewart Brand—a disciple of Ken Kesey and his Merry Pranksters—who founded the techno-utopian magazine *Whole Earth Catalog*. Brand believed that tools and technology were critical for expanding human consciousness. (Kesey agreed; personal computing would be "the next thing after acid.") The *Whole Earth Catalog*, later described by Steve Jobs as "a sort of Google in paperback form," offered a vision of interconnected knowledge and creativity. Brand then became the First Man of Tech: He attended Burning Man, gave a talk at the first TED conference, coined the phrase "Information wants to be free," built early online communities like the WELL (Whole Earth 'Lectronic Link), and influenced thinkers who would shape early online media, including institutions like *Salon*, Craigslist, the Electronic Frontier Foundation, and *Wired*.

The next link in the Brandian chain was an alternative zine called *Boing Boing*, launched in 1988 by Mark Frauenfelder and his wife, Carla Sinclair, about "comic books, cyberpunk science fiction, consciousness technology, curious phenomena." After reaching an impressive 17,500 print run, the *Boing Boing* zine hit a wall in the late 1990s when its distributors went bankrupt. Frauenfelder later heard about a fledgling company called Blogger pushing a new technology called "web logging." On January 21, 2000, he gave the Boing Boing website its own "blog" and posted a few links each week.

Almost immediately, the aspiring science fiction author Cory Doctorow began to pester Frauenfelder with ideas for additional posts. Frauenfelder appointed Doctorow to serve as a guest editor, and he promptly increased *Boing Boing*'s content schedule from a few blog posts a week to six or seven posts a *day*. Traffic exploded. By the early 2000s, *Boing Boing* was the "Web's most popular blog," serving as a hub for nerd culture, anarcho-left politics, and the gleeful celebration of niche creativity. The editors lived by the old Brandian tenet that "information wants to be free." Doctorow released an e-book of his first novel at no cost under a Creative Commons license. And they first ran *Boing Boing* as a passion project, paying the enormous hosting costs themselves. When they finally decided to procure advertisers to cover costs, they only agreed to promote brands they liked: Google, *Wired*, and O'Reilly Media.

But the site's dominance was possible only in a primordial era of online culture. Slow dial-up modem connections constrained early internet activities to emailing, chatting with friends on apps like AOL Instant Messenger, reading text-heavy news sites such as the Drudge Report, and trading digital music files. E-commerce felt uncertain and risky; Amazon only sold books, CDs, and DVDs. While the internet seemed to hold vast potential for profitability, the dot-com crash of 2000 showed that no one had yet figured out a sustainable business model, even with 361 million people worldwide online.

But few bemoaned the internet's distance from the mainstream—that was the point. From the days of the WELL, the internet gave people with unusual tastes a place to congregate, share information, and create content with limited appeal to outsiders. Millions of people with strange hobbies and interests could participate anonymously, with few personal sacrifices. Web forums allowed S&M aficionados to discuss the best whips and ball gags without revealing their faces or names.

This flourishing oasis for connoisseurs, nerds, deviants, and militants stood in stark contrast to the early aughts entertainment industry, where a wave of corporate consolidations, mergers, and acquisitions pressured executives to prioritize big returns and quick profits. Patience for auteurs and slow-burn successes all but vanished. At the box office, only franchises and sequels seemed to stand a chance: *The Lord of the Rings*, Harry Potter, *Star Wars*, *Terminator 3*, *Bad Boys II*, *Shrek 2*. Even before the launch of the Marvel Cinematic Universe, superhero movies like *Spider-Man* and *Fantastic Four* had already flooded the market.

Rather than pursuing lowest-common-denominator content for steady profits, the internet nurtured culture that mainstream media had ignored, from unfilmed scripts to MP3s from unsigned bands. Aspiring pundits at think tanks, such as Ezra Klein and Matthew Yglesias, pumped out daily analysis on health care policy too in-the-weeds for most news outlets.

Meanwhile, online gaming communities began to reimagine collective play. Massively multiplayer online games (MMOs) such as *World of Warcraft* introduced players to immersive worlds where they could collaborate, compete, and create identities untethered from real-world limitations. *Second Life*, inspired by the utopian visions of Brand and Burning Man, allowed users to build virtual societies, transcending geographic and physical boundaries. "Many residents of Second Life," wrote Leslie Jamison in *The Atlantic*, "understand it as a utopia connecting people from all over the world—across income levels, across disparate vocations and geographies and disabilities, a place where the ill can live in healthy bodies and the immobilized can move freely." While *Second Life* faltered under its steep learning curve, *World of Warcraft* emerged as a cultural juggernaut, shaping internet slang ("n00b," "ZOMG," "pwned"). It also popularized the subscription revenue model, raking in $1 billion a year by 2013.

These subcultural experiments exemplified what *Wired* editor in chief Chris Anderson later called "The Long Tail." In his influential 2004 article, Anderson argued that the internet's true power lay in catering to niche audiences. "Our culture and economy," he wrote, "are increasingly shifting away from a focus on a relatively small number of 'hits' (mainstream products and markets) at the head of the demand curve, and moving towards a huge number of niches in the tail." Anderson's vision suggested that the future belonged to digital platforms capable of aggregating diversity and obscurity into profitability. The internet could forever be weird—and even make money.

———

Nerds may have been the original settlers of the digital frontier, but by the mid-aughts, online tools had become simple enough to welcome the techno-illiterate as well. Most of these newcomers had neither heard of Stewart Brand nor were familiar with the techno-utopian ideals that shaped early internet culture. Yet they understood the medium's unique power to circumvent traditional social norms—a technique that would quickly attract large audiences to be monetized.

Hardcore pornography was an obvious example. For decades, society relegated explicit content to shadowy theaters, seedy video stores, and discreet mail-order catalogs. The internet revolutionized access: Viewing was anonymous, instantaneous, and as simple as checking the weather.

Meanwhile, internet news sites began exploiting the medium's openness to publish stories that traditional outlets deemed too risky. Where mainstream media hesitated to cover rumors of President Bill Clinton's relationship with intern Monica Lewinsky, the Drudge Report eagerly broke the story. Similarly, the Smoking Gun drew massive audiences by posting celebrity mug shots and court filings—public records that traditional outlets rarely touched. And while no TV entertainment programs could air photographs of Paris Hilton stepping out of a car without underwear, those very images became catnip for gossip blogs. Nick Denton's Gawker Media empire capitalized on this dynamic: "Giving people the things they wouldn't admit they wanted," journalist Ben Smith observed. Initially focused on insider media gossip, *Gawker* became infamous for exposing salacious secrets, broadcasting sex tapes, and outing closeted executives.

Similarly, Perez Hilton—the flamboyant alter ego of Cuban American Mario Armando Lavandeira Jr.—built his blog *PageSixSixSix* on speculative celebrity gossip, unverified claims about drug use, and crude paparazzi photos.

His disclaimers were as shameless as his content: "Postings may contain erroneous or inaccurate information. The owner of this site does not insure [sic] the accurateness [sic] of any content presented on perezhilton.com." Operating out of an LA Coffee Bean & Tea Leaf, Lavandeira epitomized the new breed of internet entrepreneur, entirely disconnected from techno-utopianism or the DIY ethos of the nineties. He didn't hide his motivations: "I want to sell out as fast and as hard as I can."

The paparazzi-gossip ecosystem hit its professional stride in November 2005 with AOL's launch of TMZ (later acquired by Fox). Harvey Levin, the site's founder, combined the sensationalism of Perez Hilton with corporate backing and a formidable legal team. TMZ's first major scoop—video of a car crash involving Paris Hilton and her then-boyfriend, Greek shipping heir Stavros Niarchos—set the tone for its relentless pursuit of celebrity scandal. Cultural critic Anne Helen Petersen later called TMZ "the most influential and important media organization of the last decade," precisely because, as she put it, "it's not in good taste. It's brazen, proud of its gaudiness."

TMZ broadened the appeal of celebrity gossip, expanding into a white middle-aged male audience and providing the oft-disparaged industry with mainstream acceptance. For Paris Hilton, this evolution was simply inevitable: "Celebrity gossip was the Chicken McNugget of the new information age: not especially good for you but delicious. And irresistible." The internet, with its ability to sidestep the gatekeepers of traditional media, was the best place to feast.

In 1999, user experience expert Darcy DiNucci predicted a dramatic evolution in the internet's potential. Writing for *Print* magazine, she coined the term *Web 2.0* to describe a future in which the web moved beyond static, "brochure-like" pages confined to PCs. Faster broadband speeds, she argued, would "transform" the internet, allowing it to integrate with TVs, car dashboards, phones, appliances, and other devices, creating a dynamic, participatory experience. This article might have remained a footnote in computer history if not for the 2004 Web 2.0 conference, where tech luminaries Tim O'Reilly and John Battelle made her term a rallying cry for a new internet. The "web as platform" would empower users to become creators, not just consumers, heralding a more democratized, participatory digital culture.

While the term *Web 2.0* quickly became a cliché, its underlying transformation was real. User-generated content reshaped the internet in profound ways. Services like Friendster (2002), Myspace (2003), and Facebook (2004) made online spaces intuitive, encouraging users to create profiles, share photos, and connect with real-life friends. YouTube, launched in 2005, allowed anyone with a camera to upload videos and share them with the world. A year later, the "microblogging" service Twitter went live, allowing anonymous users to connect with one another over 140-character posts. Digital commerce also became easier for small-scale transactions thanks to the growth of PayPal, run by the likes of Peter Thiel, Elon Musk, and Reid Hoffman. With the immediate success of these services, *Time* chose "you"—that is, the entire public—as its 2006 Person of the Year.

Yet the early cultural products of Web 2.0 were, by most standards, amateurish. Slow connections made watching and uploading videos difficult. In 2006, TMZ posted video footage of oil empire scion Brandon Davis ranting against actress Lindsay Lohan's "firecrotch" as Paris Hilton laughed in the background; almost no one had a fast enough connection to watch it. The first YouTube hits were quite primitive. Two Chinese art students called themselves Back Dorm Boys and lip-synched the Backstreet Boys' "I Want It That Way" inside a cramped dorm room. "Star Wars Kid" was an unintentionally comedic video of a Canadian teenager wielding a golf ball retriever like a lightsaber. These low-quality productions could hardly compete with the prestige TV of the era, like *The Sopranos* and *The Wire*. The initial wave of Web 2.0 content often felt like a digital riff on *America's Funniest Home Videos*: bloopers, fails, and moments of accidental hilarity.

Web 2.0's defining feature—its accessibility—was both its greatest strength and most dangerous flaw. In particular, the ease of anonymity and pseudonymity encouraged equal amounts of creativity and cruelty. (When Stewart Brand once held an experimental anonymous online conference, things became so chaotic he forever forbade unsigned posting on WELL.) The unwitting stars of internet humor, such as Mark Allen Hicks (dubbed "Afro Ninja" after a failed audition tape) and Ghyslain Raza (the "Star Wars Kid"), faced relentless public ridicule. Hicks tried to reclaim his narrative by leaning into his accidental fame but admitted, "If I had a choice to do it all over again . . . I would pass." Raza endured so much bullying that he was forced to leave school.

There is no question, however, that anonymous web forums soon emerged as the central engine of internet culture. Rich "Lowtax" Kyanka opened Something Awful to host humor pieces attacking *Boing Boing*–style techno-idealists. "Everybody was talking about how the internet was going to revolutionize everything and everything was going to be great," recalled Kyanka, "but nobody ever talked about how shitty the internet could also be." Something Awful became a proving ground for early online humor, producing beloved Twitter comedian @dril and kick-starting the internet's obsession with funny cat photos.

In 2003, a fifteen-year-old Something Awful user named Christopher Poole, posting under the handle "moot," opened his own site, 4chan, in imitation of the low-tech Japanese bulletin board 2channel. 4chan's policy of complete anonymity made it a free-for-all—and an even more powerful laboratory for the internet's in-jokes. Rickrolling, a bait-and-switch meme linking users to Rick Astley's cheesy 1987 hit "Never Gonna Give You Up," was born there, along with countless other internet tropes.

Yet 4chan's lack of accountability also unleashed darker forces: "Trolling" for "lulz" (a slang term for laughs) often crossed into harassment and cruelty. Even without direct influence from Gavin McInnes's *Vice*, 4chan found a similar energy in its uneasy blend of anti-liberal humor and antisocial malice.

The internet's promise of access to unfiltered information also tilled fertile soil for conspiracy theorists. In 2005, the crudely made documentary *Loose Change* exploded onto the web, offering an alternative narrative for the

9/11 attacks. The film argued that the Twin Towers were brought down by pre-planted explosives rather than hijacked planes. This popularized the phrase "Jet fuel can't melt steel beams," which became a banner phrase to describe all internet conspiracy theories. Initially dismissed by mainstream media, *Loose Change* attracted a large audience online, spreading across forums and social networks to millions, including filmmakers David Lynch and Kevin Smith, and celebrities Rosie O'Donnell and Charlie Sheen. In the past, mainstream media could fully marginalize such fringe theories, but digital platforms allowed their advocates to create compelling content that sat alongside more orthodox material. Digital technology also made it easy to update the content. The makers of *Loose Change* frequently re-edited the film with new information and improved special effects.

An executive producer for a later version of *Loose Change* was Alex Jones, a Texas-based radio DJ who first gained notoriety for defending the Branch Davidians after the Waco siege and who believed that the US government was behind the Oklahoma City bombing. Jones once pushed his theories on a public-access channel in Austin; on the internet, he could now vie for the attention of the entire globe.

As webcam videos from the Guangzhou Academy of Fine Arts reached international audiences, media pundits required new vocabulary to describe the internet's rapidly evolving cultural dynamics. The most immediate metaphor was borrowed from infectious disease: "going viral." Malcolm Gladwell's 2000 bestseller, *The Tipping Point*, argued that ideas could behave like "social epidemics," spreading exponentially as individuals shared them with their peers. This framing felt intuitive—cultural contagion was just like the flu.

But what to call the individual unit of viral culture? In 1990, law school student Mike Godwin adapted a term from evolutionary biologist Richard Dawkins's 1976 book, *The Selfish Gene*: *meme*. Dawkins had coined the word to describe "a unit of cultural transmission" that propagates itself through imitation, much like genes do biologically. His examples ranged from catch-phrases to clothing styles to architectural techniques. Though his compar-ison to genetics was often criticized as simplistic, the term *meme* gained traction, especially online, where it became useful for tracking the spread of cultural phenomena.

As internet users traded inside jokes—like the mistranslated gaming phrase "All your base are belong to us"—and cataloged their diffusion across forums and blogs, *internet meme* entered the vernacular. Scholar Limor Shif-man later defined the term as "(a) a group of digital items sharing common characteristics of content, form, and/or stance, which (b) were created with awareness of each other, and (c) were circulated, imitated, and/or trans-formed via the Internet by many users." Rickrolling was a meme. So was the Star Wars Kid. Memes quickly became a way to link disparate ideas through metaphor, transforming shared images into shorthand for broader cultural commentary.

Despite their utility, *virality* and *meme* mischaracterized the mechanics of online information flows. Dawkins imagined memes as self-propagating entities like viruses, but internet culture depended upon active participation. Gladwell's model of exponential spread fared no better. In practice, most vi-ral content didn't slowly spread from person to person but relied on "dark broadcasters"—key nodes in the network like 4chan or *Boing Boing*—that amplified its reach before mainstream media picked it up. The most popular viral music videos, for example, achieved steady growth over time rather than in an explosive curve.

Virality, with its sharp spikes and rapid declines, was less an internet in-vention than a digital hyperextension of old-timey fads, like phone booth stuffing or Pet Rocks. The difference lay in accessibility: The web made it easier to participate, and the sheer volume provided an endless stream of low-stakes amusement. Yet viral content often lacked the lasting impact of even the most ephemeral novelty song.

Memes, however, radically transformed communication itself. Web 2.0 platforms encouraged users to express themselves through images as much as text, sparking a competition to put the cleverest comments on the funniest photos. Despite their limitless potential, memes coalesced around a shared visual language. One defining example emerged from an anonymously uploaded image on Something Awful: a fluffy gray British shorthair cat with its mouth agape, captured in the Impact font with the grammatically incorrect plea, "I Can Has Cheezburger?" The image became a template for countless "LOLcat" memes, inspiring an eponymous website dedicated to collecting and monetizing these jokes. Its companion site, Know Your Meme, became the definitive encyclopedia for tracking the internet's evolving humor. From this point forward, no subcultural innovation would go unnoticed; every inside joke, slang term, and urban myth could be cataloged and explained in real time.

Marketers took notice of the viral content's similarity to the concept of buzz. So when news leaked in 2005 of a B-movie called *Snakes on a Plane*, starring Samuel L. Jackson, internet posters began joking that the actor should deliver the line: "I have had it with these motherfucking snakes on this motherfucking plane!" The line wasn't in the script, but the studio, eager to harness the buzz, reshot scenes in spring 2006 to include it. This back-and-forth between fans and filmmakers seemed to herald a new Hollywood, one where studios could pre-guarantee success by catering directly to online audiences. An entire book, *Snakes on a Plane: The Guide to the Internet Sssssensation*, hit shelves before the film's release. Yet the movie was a box office disappointment. The addition of Jackson's foul-mouthed line, along with other salacious elements, bumped the film's rating to an R, which limited its audience. As one industry analyst noted, "Internet interest in a movie doesn't necessarily translate to good box office." The extremely online had yet to prove themselves as tastemakers.

Despite all the cultural energy, the internet was far from a reliable profit engine. Even Google, which was minting money with its digital advertising tool

AdWords, experienced a rocky lead-up to its initial public offering. The big money remained in enterprise software companies like Microsoft, chip manufacturers like Intel, and infrastructure builders like Cisco. Yet as online media began aggregating audiences of educated, high-income users, many believed websites could eventually become profitable businesses.

The problem was that no one had figured out how. Google's AdSense offered bloggers an early monetization tool: automated low-quality banner ads that provided modest revenue streams. Sites like *Boing Boing* took a boutique approach, securing sponsorships from companies like Verizon and American Express. While this model made the site millions in revenue, the founders kept a zine mindset and never attempted a major expansion.

Nick Denton had a more ambitious vision. Extending his gossip blog, *Gawker*, into a media empire, he launched a tranche of niche sites like *Deadspin* (sports), *Valleywag* (Silicon Valley), *Jezebel* (feminism), *io9* (sci-fi), and *Jalopnik* (automobiles). His theory was that bloggers, being cheaper and faster than traditional journalists, could target specific interests and collectively sustain a profitable network. But perhaps there was an even more lucrative idea on the horizon: recruiting actual celebrities and established experts to write blog posts, which would better attract mainstream audiences to the internet.

Arianna Huffington, partnering with AOL veteran Kenneth Lerer and internet provocateur Jonah Peretti, tested this idea in May 2005 with *The Huffington Post*, a site she conceived as a liberal counterweight to the Drudge Report. Huffington's site aggregated news articles and hosted blogs from celebrities like John Cusack. Yet the public wasn't clamoring for political essays from Hollywood stars. Early struggles led Peretti to build out a separate site called *BuzzFeed*, where he tested his theories about virality. The site pioneered low-stakes content that appealed to younger audiences.

The morass of lo-fi nerd culture, however, prevented websites from replicating the business models of legacy institutions like Condé Nast. Glossy titles such as *Vogue* and *Vanity Fair* sold cultural cachet to anxious upper-middle-class readers, which attracted luxury advertisers despite unverifiable circulation data. In theory, online publishers offered advertisers a much fairer deal: Every web page came with measurable metrics like "unique visitors" and "page views." But with top-tier luxury brands staying away, web publishers relied on aggregating low-quality advertisers. More traffic meant more money, incentivizing online publications to prioritize traffic over prestige. Clickbait and lascivious content were the best bets to boost numbers. *Gawker* posted celebrity sex tapes, while *BuzzFeed* churned out nostalgia-soaked "listicles."

As a new media mogul, Jonah Peretti was idiosyncratic. He mostly obsessed over cracking the secrets of virality. As former colleague Ben Smith noted, "He wasn't concerned with taste or quality or brand or consistency. He just wanted to know what would get traffic." Peretti used this data-driven approach to revitalize *The Huffington Post*, creating a sophisticated system of search engine optimization (SEO) that catered to Google's algorithms. They engineered articles with keyword-rich headlines, strategically named URLs, and hidden HTML elements to ensure high visibility in search results. This formula drastically increased the site's traffic, solidifying its place as a leading digital media outlet. And here began the practice of prioritizing content to satisfy Google's "machines" more than to cater to the long-term needs of human readers.

Despite these innovations, online culture remained constrained by its distribution. Reading websites still required sitting at a desktop computer, limiting the audience to mostly white-collar professionals and tech-savvy youth. Mobile phones like the BlackBerry gained popularity among business users, while T-Mobile's Sidekick became a modest hit thanks to celebrity endorsements from Snoop Dogg and Paris Hilton. But these devices offered a very limited online experience.

The entire internet changed on January 9, 2007, when Apple CEO Steve Jobs unveiled the iPhone. Combining a phone, camera, and web browser into a single device with a sleek touch screen, the iPhone promised to make the internet much more accessible. Tech industry skeptics dismissed it as a toy; for Microsoft CEO Steve Ballmer, the iPhone was doomed because it was "not a very good email machine." They were wildly mistaken. Within a decade, the iPhone and its Android competitors gave billions of people pocket-size computers capable of constant connectivity, transforming how the world accessed information and shared experiences.

With the iPhone's arrival, the internet began to break free from both its countercultural and professional-class origins. Anyone could now be online, anywhere, at any time. The era of the nerd internet would soon be over—but it had one final act.

———

"Online politics" of the mid-aughts, journalist Ben Smith observed, "was basically synonymous first with opposition to President George W. Bush and then with the name of a young senator from Illinois, Barack Obama." At just forty-six years old, Senator Obama was known for a rousing 2004 speech at the Democratic National Convention and his unambiguous opposition to the Iraq War. Unlike most politicians of his era, Obama combined youthful charisma with powerful oratory, making him a hero to the burgeoning online liberal movement known as the netroots. *The Huffington Post* endorsed Obama early, reflecting the digital groundswell of support. He became the first "hip" candidate in decades; Terry Richardson photographed him for the cover of *Vibe* magazine.

Obama's candidacy rode on a growing backlash to President Bush, who lost support each year as a destabilized Iraq erupted into violent chaos. Michael Moore's 2004 anti-Bush film, *Fahrenheit 9/11*, earned $222 million at the box office, becoming the highest-grossing documentary of its time. Pop culture rallied too: Green Day's *American Idiot* offered an album of anti-Bush anthems, while Kanye West gained national prominence after declaring during a 2005 Hurricane Katrina telethon, "George Bush doesn't care about Black people." By 2006, as violent civil war overtook Iraq, Bush's approval rating cratered. In a 2006 Associated Press poll, he was named both "top hero" and, by twice the vote, "top villain."

Obama's campaign tapped into this shifting cultural zeitgeist. Street artist Shepard Fairey's "Hope" poster became the defining image of 2008, reimagining political iconography through the lens of pop art. Viral videos like "Barack Obama-sistible" and "McCain Girls: Raining McCain" demonstrated the internet's potential to fuse absurdist humor with advocacy. The playful energy of the campaign, however, gave way to sobering realities in September 2008, when the global financial crisis hit. Lehman Brothers went bankrupt; other banks teetered on the edge of collapse. This all culminated in an electoral sweep for Barack Hussein Obama, who was elected the forty-fourth president of the United States.

By the time of his victory, the new century's key ideological trends had already taken hold. Downtown New York scenesters and anonymous forum posters found thrills in a new transgressive, nihilistic form of conservatism. Hip-hop found its formula for enduring domination in an omnivorous approach. Poptimism gave full blessing to manufactured pop idols and gossip culture, while Jay-Z and Paris Hilton made entrepreneurialism cool. The internet found its momentum in offering a seamless way to evade social norms. This helped liberals organize around resistance to the Bush regime, culminating in the election of the first Black president. As much as Obama's victory promised a new focus on expertise and thoughtful politics, however, there would be no return to the nineties. His election may have marked a new era, but he was powerless to reverse the cultural shifts already in motion.

Part Two

2009–2015

THANKS, OBAMA

As Capitalism Survives, Poptimism Thrives

5

O n the morning of October 9, 2009, Barack Obama awoke to unexpected news: He had won the Nobel Peace Prize less than nine
months into his presidency. Even Obama's own team was baffled
by the honor, given that the deadline for nominations had been just twelve
days after his inauguration. The Nobel Committee explained that the award
was meant to "promote what he stands for," hoping it might bolster his standing amid fierce Republican opposition. Instead, the announcement only intensified criticism. Conservative radio host Rush Limbaugh said the Peace
Prize was now worth what they're "putting in Cracker Jacks these days."
Obama himself reportedly sought to skip the ceremony.

Today his prize at least serves as a historical marker—a symbol of the last
collective moment of liberal optimism, when Obama's presidency seemed
like the dawn of a new political era. He was young, charismatic, and progressive, promising to rebuild the economy and wind down the War on Terror.
Yet his presidency unfolded alongside a full-blown crisis of capitalism. The
global financial crash wiped out $19 trillion in household wealth, leaving
millions without jobs or homes. Before he could tackle systemic change, he
had to first keep the country from unraveling.

At the level of culture, the legacy of Obama's presidency was more symbolic than transformative. In 2024, *Vulture* critic Nate Jones retroactively
labeled the era's defining aesthetic as "Obamacore"—a time marked by an
"earnest, optimistic, energized, celeb-obsessed, self-conscious, cringeworthy"

spirit. Meanwhile, CNBC coined *recession pop* to describe the buoyant anthems of Katy Perry and the Black Eyed Peas, which offered escapism during hard times. Both terms capture the bright, hopeful cultural mood of the era, but they overstate the direct influence of political and economic trends on the moment.

Obama's eight years in office are best understood as the further entrenchment of existing trends from the early aughts: most notably, the poptimist embrace of mass culture and the veneration of entrepreneurs. If anything, the powerful symbolism of Obama's presidency fostered great complacency among liberals. Many believed that the election of a Black president had forever repudiated racism and that their charismatic hero would fix everything. But then, as Republican obstructionism stalled Obama's agenda, hope curdled into cynicism. Both optimism and despair resulted in a similar disinterest in political intervention, in many ways mirroring the collective embrace of the culture industry's most brazenly commercial output.

Today we understand the profundity of how the economic crisis affected people around the globe. Economic policy journalist Annie Lowrey argued that the downturn left America "more unequal, less vibrant, less productive, poorer, and sicker." In the short term, however, cultural life showed surprising resilience. There was no Weimar Republic hyperinflation or *Grapes of Wrath* Dust Bowl devastation. Music, TV, film, and books continued to arrive on schedule, as if the crisis were a mere flesh wound.

At least temporarily, the crash did close out a period of money-forward tastes. "People were dripping in gold," recalled Christina Binkley of *The Wall Street Journal*. "Fashion had been really loud and it was a huge party, and then that shifted literally overnight." After the crash, the wealthy still shopped but with greater discretion. French luxury brand Hermès was rumored to have replaced its signature orange shopping bags with generic brown ones to avoid attracting attention. The middle classes didn't lose their new lust for luxury goods, but they hunted for bargains on Gilt Groupe and embraced direct-to-consumer substitutes, like Warby Parker's ninety-five-dollar glasses. Meanwhile, people stayed home more often, boosting TV ratings, particularly for sports.

Economist Tyler Cowen predicted in 2009 that "popular culture's catering to the wealthy may also decline in this downturn. We can expect a shift
away from the lionizing of fancy restaurants, for example, and toward more
use of public libraries." This shift never materialized, because within a year,
the fortunes of the ultrawealthy bounced back. Wall Street profits hit $19
billion in 2010, approaching pre-crash levels. "On Wall Street," wrote journalist George Packer, "the financial crisis felt like a speed bump." As the rich
resumed spending, the culture industry faced less pressure to reorient itself
toward lower-priced goods.

The mechanics of the crash itself remained opaque to most Americans,
mired in the impenetrable jargon of "subprime mortgages," "credit default
swaps," and "synthetic exposure." The media felt a need to explain what
happened, elevating prescient voices like Dr. Doom—economist Nouriel
Roubini—who had long warned about mortgage defaults, and Nassim Nicholas Taleb, whose "black swan" theory gained new relevance. Michael Lewis's
The Big Short, in celebrating the few maverick investors who profited by betting on the housing crash, became a touchstone for understanding the crisis.

Hollywood also weighed in, but few recession-themed films resonated
with audiences. Director Baz Luhrmann fast-tracked his adaptation of *The
Great Gatsby*, believing the story could illuminate the moment's excesses. (It
didn't debut until 2013.) Michael Moore's documentary *Capitalism: A Love
Story* (2009) failed to recoup its $20 million budget, while films like *Inside
Job* (2010), *Margin Call* (2011), and *Too Big to Fail* (2011) garnered only modest attention. *The Big Short*, with Margot Robbie explaining subprime mortgage bonds in a bubble bath, arrived in 2015, only after the crisis had faded
from the national conversation.

Behind the scenes, however, the recession was reshaping Hollywood. In
the mid-2000s, major banks began to pour money into film production,
which studios deployed on second-rate projects. After the crash, financiers
demanded that their money fund marquee films at the least possible risk.
This required a new strategy in an industry where predicting hits is inherently uncertain. Their "best bet," explained journalist Daniel Bessner, was

basing films on preexisting intellectual property—familiar stories, characters, and brands that came with built-in audience recognition.

The shift toward IP intensified as studios increasingly relied on international markets to offset declining American movie theater attendance. Sequels and franchises dominated because of their universal appeal. The Marvel Cinematic Universe launched with *Iron Man* in 2008. The *Twilight* saga began the same year, spawning five box office hits. Animated films like *Despicable Me* (2010), with its toy-friendly Minions and Pharrell Williams score, were engineered for global success. By 2011, nine out of the ten top-grossing films were sequels. The lone exception, *The Smurfs*, was based on the popular 1980s Saturday morning cartoon.

Christopher Nolan emerged as one of the few directors succeeding with original material, most notably with *Inception* (2010), a cerebral action film about dreams within dreams. Yet such outliers were rare. "Low-revenue arthouse films," observed journalist Gareth Rubin in the depths of the recession, "have all but disappeared from distribution lists."

James Cameron's *Avatar*, released in late 2009, epitomized the era's priorities. Its cutting-edge 3D visuals made it the highest-grossing film of all time, yet it left little cultural impact. Unlike *Star Wars*, which inspired fan tributes and added new words and phrases to the vernacular, *Avatar* failed to achieve much lasting relevance. Critics blamed its prioritization of technological spectacle over basic storytelling. One of its few legacies was a *Saturday Night Live* sketch in which Ryan Gosling mocked its use of the generic Papyrus font for the film's logo. The joke stuck, with even a 20th Century Fox executive admitting the lazy font choice was the only "part that went viral."

The sorry state of cinema was one example of how the crisis gave financial institutions greater control over culture. This was not an obvious outcome at the time. At least on paper, the Great Recession seemed ripe for the emergence of a sixties-style counterculture. Grassroots leftist action, however, struggled to coalesce into a unified movement until Occupy Wall Street (OWS) in late 2011. Earlier that year, Canadian anti-commerce magazine *Adbusters* called for a protest on Wall Street to begin on September 17. Hundreds heeded the call, occupying nearby Zuccotti Park for two months, their cramped quarters echoing with the constant beats of drum circles. The movement inspired allied protests across the United States and around the world.

OWS thrust the issue of income inequality into the national conversation with a memorable slogan: "We are the 99%." The phrase, attributed variously to economist Joseph Stiglitz or anarchist anthropologist David Graeber, drew attention to the fact that the top 1 percent of Americans controlled 40 percent of the country's wealth. French economist Thomas Piketty would later articulate the structural forces behind this inequality. He argued that returns on wealth consistently outpaced wage growth, further enriching the very top of society and undermining "the meritocratic values on which democratic societies are based." OWS framed this disparity as a battle between the people and a small, entrenched oligarchy. This message had potential to bridge ideological divides, but political factions soon weaponized competing definitions of "elites." Liberals targeted their ire at billionaires and Wall Street executives, while conservatives pointed fingers at coastal professionals and the academy.

While the "99%" slogan resonated, OWS's aesthetics alienated many Americans. Gallup polls showed tepid public sentiment toward the movement, which also struggled from internal discord. Graeber encouraged anarchistic governance structures, which hampered decision-making. The incessant drum circles irritated both city officials and fellow protesters. Despite a compromise limiting drumming to two two-hour sessions, rogue musicians continued late into the night. "Two hours is too little," drummer Elijah Moses told *The Wall Street Journal*. "There's too much time in a day for us to only have two hours in a damn revolution, you know?"

Police cleared Zuccotti Park on November 15, 2011, effectively ending the protests. In their aftermath, sympathetic commentators praised OWS for revitalizing the American left, elevating income inequality into a major issue, and reinvigorating protest culture. Bernie Sanders and Alexandria Ocasio-Cortez later harnessed this momentum. Critics like Andrew Ross Sorkin argued, however, that OWS would be "an asterisk in the history books, if it gets a mention at all." The movement's failure to achieve tangible victories reinforced theorist Mark Fisher's idea of "capitalist realism," in which we could no longer even imagine a "coherent alternative" to the current economic system.

Surprisingly, OWS struggled to find a foothold in mainstream pop culture. Celebrity endorsements came from predictable leftists like Michael Moore, Cornel West, Boots Riley, and Rage Against the Machine. (Radiohead failed to appear at Zuccotti despite rumors of a free concert, which Marxist critic Malcolm Harris later admitted he made up.) Many African Americans withheld their support. As journalist Stacey Patton observed, Black Americans asked why they should "ally with whites who are just now experiencing the hardships that Blacks have known for generations."

Hip-hop mogul Russell Simmons stood out as an exception, attending the protests "almost every day for months" and offering to fund Zuccotti Park's cleanup. Yet he failed to galvanize the broader hip-hop community. Kanye West made a brief appearance wearing gold chains but was careful not to make any statements. Two months earlier, he and Jay-Z had released *Watch the Throne*, an album described as a "marvel of affluenza" and a tribute to "wealth-happy maximalism," accompanied by $300 limited-edition Givenchy T-shirts. Critic Hua Hsu noted, "Rarely has an album seemed so simultaneously in and out of touch with the exigencies of American life."

On the album, Jay-Z, who was already worth $450 million at the time and had appeared on the cover of *Forbes* with Warren Buffett, dedicated his verses on *Watch the Throne* to bragging about his blue-chip art collection. During OWS, his Rocawear brand sold twenty-two-dollar T-shirts emblazoned with OCCUPY ALL STREETS, admitting it had no intention of sharing profits with protesters. Speaking with novelist Zadie Smith, Jay-Z defended his position: "The 1 percent that's robbing people, and deceiving people . . . that's criminal. . . . Not being an entrepreneur. This is free enterprise. This is what America is built on."

Critics saw Jay-Z as emblematic of hip-hop's shift from social consciousness to unfettered capitalism. Even libertarian journalist Conor Friedersdorf castigated Jay-Z as "the most aggressively unapologetic member of the 1 percent in America." Jay-Z was not just a businessman but a self-professed "business, man"—personhood as a corporation. Hsu noted that he embodied "the luxury goods, the art collection, private compounds, the Oprah-level American Dream." Music critic Greg Tate lamented that by 2004, hip-hop had ceased to be "an agent of social change" and instead celebrated "the money-shakers and moneymakers."

The year 2011 offered two pathways through the economic crisis: the collective intervention of OWS and the self-enrichment of Jay-Z. Culture went along with the latter. Two days before Zuccotti Park was cleared, *GQ* honored Jay-Z as "King" in its Men of the Year issue. In the accompanying interview he discussed preparing for the birth of his first child with Beyoncé—and needing to outfit his Maybach with a baby seat.

On the July 31, 2011, episode of *Keeping Up with the Kardashians* (season 6, episode 7: "The Haves and the Have Nots"), Kim, Khloé, and Kourtney Kardashian, along with Kendall and Kylie Jenner, pressured matriarch Kris Jenner to address her light bladder leakage. "You can't be at a black-tie event and peeing on yourself," Khloé scolded. After receiving a diagnosis of stress incontinence, Jenner didn't just seek medical treatment. She contacted the Kimberly-Clark Corporation, pitching herself as an influencer for Poise, the leading brand in absorbent protection products. Her philosophy was consistent: "Let's not make it a problem, let's make money."

Keeping Up with the Kardashians premiered on October 14, 2007, riding a wave of interest in Kim Kardashian's leaked sex tape. Critics long dismissed the show's bad taste and shameless commercialism. *The Washington Post* decried its content as ranging from "the simply self-absorbed to the downright despicable," while *The New York Times* described the Kardashians as "a family that seems to understand itself only in terms of its collective opportunism."

Yet, for millions, the series became a cultural touchstone—a live-action TMZ blending gossip and raunch. Early episodes followed Kim posing for *Playboy*, Khloé being pulled over for a DUI, and family friend Joe Francis of Girls Gone Wild calling in from jail. Critics may have sneered, but audiences tuned in, enthralled by the family's indefatigable hustle.

The Kardashians' rise was part of a broader shift in television during the Great Recession. While movies leaned into bombastic blockbusters, television shifted to cheaper, unscripted programming. By 2010, scripted shows like *Friends*, *CSI*, and *Everybody Loves Raymond* had waned, and reality TV dominated prime time, with *American Idol* and *Dancing with the Stars* consistently topping the charts. The format's international appeal turned it into a juggernaut of global low-cost entertainment.

Reality TV's explosion in the US began with *Survivor* in 2000. Executive producer Mark Burnett, inspired by the 1997 Swedish program *Expedition: Robinson*, pitched the idea of a wilderness survival competition to every major network. The project was initially dismissed as too lowbrow, but CBS gave Burnett the green light after he promised to produce it cheaply.

Survivor was an immediate success, drawing an audience of fifty-one million Americans. The show was so central to the pre-9/11 zeitgeist that Destiny's Child scored a 2001 hit with "Survivor," as the group's internal shake-ups resembled the show's dynamics of being "voted off the island." Its success unleashed a flood of imitators: *Fear Factor*, *The Bachelor*, and *Joe Millionaire*. Even scripted shows like *The Office* adopted reality TV's aesthetic, with the US version hiring *Survivor* cinematographer Randall Einhorn to emulate its documentary-like style.

Burnett's idiosyncratic and often cynical views on unscripted television set the new standards for the entire industry. First, product placement became integral to the format. Burnett personally pocketed a percentage of revenue from all the overt logo displays in *Survivor*. As journalist Bill Carter noted, "The appearance of products was anything but subliminal. Logos of running shoes, towels, even the occasional beer repeatedly popped up on the screen." Even in a show about primitive living in nature, there was no line between content and advertising. Second, Burnett rejected traditional documentary ethics. Instead of relying solely on raw footage, he embraced "dramality," reshooting scenes as "do-overs" and using stand-ins for aerial shots. Audio snippets, dubbed "sweet-and-lows," were layered into scenes to bend reality to better fit the storylines.

Burnett's next major hit, *The Apprentice*, took reality TV's embrace of capitalism to new heights. After befriending real estate developer Donald Trump at a screening of *Survivor*, Burnett developed a show casting Trump as the archetypical business magnate. Premiering in 2004, *The Apprentice* presented Trump as a "tough-but-fair executive who doles out savvy business advice and decisively fires underperforming employees." For Trump, the series was a rebranding opportunity after years of financial troubles. Collaborating closely on the show, Burnett came to consider Trump a "soul mate."

As *The Apprentice* waned in popularity around 2008, Burnett found renewed success in *Shark Tank*. The series, in which entrepreneurs pitched ideas to venture capitalists, dramatized the process of financing, and turned entrepreneurs and investors alike into cultural icons.

Networks loved the genre for its cost-effectiveness: The producers didn't have to hire unionized writers. Most reality TV stars were amateurs who needed only minimal payouts. They also signed contracts that granted producers the right to manipulate their words and actions for drama. Viewers, critic Emily Nussbaum observed, were "offered something authentic, buried inside something fake." Audiences saw themselves among the "real" people in "real" situations. From amateur singers on *American Idol* to ordinary people facing extraordinary circumstances on *Survivor*, reality TV reflected the viewers' aspirations and anxieties. "More than any other cultural product," Nussbaum wrote, reality TV "functioned as a mirror of the people who watched [it]."

Reality TV thereby created the easiest pathway yet to national fame. Participants on reality shows moved fast to turn their fleeting stardom into cash, from *Survivor* cast members making paid appearances to *American Idol* reject William Hung booking gigs as a motivational speaker. Nussbaum described the new career of reality TV as something of "an extreme sport, one whose risks they embraced." The entire genre's mantra, immortalized by a contestant on *The Bachelor*, was "I'm not here to make friends."

In line with Jay-Z's aristocratic rap, reality TV's "egalitarian" nature worked well with a renewed interest in entrepreneurial hustle. By the time the Kardashian-Jenner clan launched *Keeping Up with the Kardashians* in 2007, they had learned a lot from reality TV pioneers like Burnett. They understood that their on-camera performances could drive sales to their business ventures. Episodes promoted their clothing chain Dash, QVC fashion line K-Dash, cosmetics labels, and endless brand collaborations. The Kardashians also mastered the art of monetizing scandal. As Amy Chozick wrote for *The New York Times*, "Family turmoil feeds the celebrity news cycle, which drives interest in the TV show, which then helps to publicize an ever-increasing number of sponsorships and branded products." The show's most lucrative product, however, was Kim Kardashian herself. "I really do believe," Kim told *The New York Times* in 2010, "I am a brand for my fans."

Reality TV also appealed to cynical viewers who enjoyed laughing at the participants' vulgarity and excess. *Keeping Up with the Kardashians* was a gaudy pageant of new-money flamboyance, while MTV's *Jersey Shore* offered a caricature of a working-class Italian American hedonism. Its stars—Snooki, DJ Pauly D, and the Situation—achieved instant notoriety, with their antics fueling public fascination. The Bravo franchise Real Housewives invited viewers to loathe its wealthy, combative protagonists. As critic Safy-Hallan Farah noted, the title itself signaled the irony: "A housewife . . . appears to 'have it all'—every desirable feature under capitalism, such as riches, beauty, and feminine accoutrements—yet none of it makes her a paragon in the eyes of other women." Real Housewives superfan Abby Steffens told *The Observer*, "I do not want them as my friends. I don't want to sit down and have a drink with them. I'm terrified of them! But that's what makes them great TV." Villainy became a pathway to financial success, as crazier antics led to higher appearance fees. After *Jersey Shore* aired footage of Snooki getting punched in the face at a bar, her event fees quintupled from $2,000 to $10,000.

At its peak, reality TV's format proved so versatile that mid-tier celebrities wanted in. Shows like *Dancing with the Stars* and *The Celebrity Apprentice* offered washed-up actors, athletes, and socialites a second chance at fame. Even the Kardashians dipped their toes into crossover territory: Kim guest-starred on the show in 2010, while Khloé competed as a formal contestant.

The genre's defining tension—a showcase for both undiscovered talent and grotesque degeneracy—was epitomized by *Britain's Got Talent* in 2009. The show wheeled out Susan Boyle, a frumpy forty-seven-year-old Scottish woman with autism, and primed the audience to expect a William Hung–type travesty. Instead, she stunned judges and audiences alike with her virtuosic rendition of "I Dreamed a Dream" from *Les Misérables*. The clip went viral online, making Boyle an overnight sensation, and her debut, *I Dreamed a Dream*, was a top-selling album that year.

Beneath its hyperlocal trappings, reality TV ushered in a quiet globalization of culture. Successful formats were exported and adapted worldwide, creating a shared narrative language that crossed borders. Japan's *The Tigers of Money* inspired the UK's *Dragons' Den*, which in turn became Mark Burnett's *Shark Tank*. Real Housewives expanded from Orange County, New York, Atlanta, and New Jersey to twenty-one international territories, while *Jersey Shore* landed in Poland as *Warsaw Shore* (on the famed "shores" of the Vistula River).

Keeping Up with the Kardashians continued for twenty seasons, cementing Kim Kardashian's place as Paris Hilton's obvious successor. Both women shared a lack of ethical qualms about monetizing their infamy. As this ethos spread, it was no surprise that gossip site TMZ became one of the most important sources of journalism. The tabloid website broke stories that defined the era, from Michael Jackson's death to Tiger Woods's infidelity scandal and harrowing police photos of Rihanna after Chris Brown assaulted her. In such a media environment, entertainers engaged in self-debasement as an obvious career step. In these years, Kanye West moved beyond his initial reputation as a mere musical prodigy and political gadfly into a gossip superstar. At the 2006 MTV Europe Music Awards, he stormed the stage to protest his video "Touch the Sky" losing to Justice vs. Simian. This was merely a prelude to the 2009 MTV Video Music Awards, where Kanye interrupted Taylor Swift's acceptance speech for Best Female Video to proclaim, "I'mma let you finish, but Beyoncé had one of the best videos of all time!" The incident was widely condemned (Obama called West a "jackass"), but Kanye had never been more famous—and neither had Taylor Swift.

By the late aughts, downtown New York's post-9/11 creative surge had dissipated. The Strokes, once heralded as the saviors of rock, went on hiatus after the lukewarm reception of their third album, 2005's *First Impressions of Earth*. Their reputation, critics noted, plunged to "Mariana Trench–like depths." Veteran art critic Calvin Tomkins, surveying the downtown scene in 2007, observed that despite plenty of "high-decibel energy," no one seemed poised "for stardom on a larger stage." The scene's darker undercurrents also took a toll: Skater and *Kids* star Harold Hunter succumbed to a cocaine-induced heart attack in 2006, artist Dash Snow overdosed on heroin in 2009, and the scene's most promising fashion designer, Benjamin Cho, disappeared from runways in 2008 and died in 2017.

The spirit of downtown New York, however, continue to supply high-end consumer brands with their edgy aesthetics; Belvedere vodka famously hired Terry Richardson for its "Luxury Reborn" ads. But by the Obama years, New York snobbery had little to offer a poptimist age dominated by mass-market tastes. The spiritual gap between the Jersey Shore and Williamsburg, Brooklyn, was far larger than the geographical distance. Top 40 radio largely bypassed the early 2000s rock revival, while reality TV stars like Kim Kardashian embodied a total rejection of urbane sophistication.

Into this cultural moment emerged Stefani Germanotta, better known as

Lady Gaga. Her rise demonstrated how twenty-first-century performers hoping to engage with "cutting-edge" culture rarely achieved more than recycling a palette of zany antics. Gaga borrowed liberally from the century's subcultural aesthetics without ever becoming a true conduit for radical ideas.

Growing up in an upper-middle-class household in Uptown Manhattan, Germanotta was a Catholic school girl with a passion for musical theater. At seventeen, she attended the Collaborative Arts Project 21, a conservatory affiliated with New York University's Tisch School of the Arts, before dropping out to pursue a career as a nineties-style singer-songwriter. Her early performances with a scrappy rock band at open-mic nights yielded little success, though she landed minor acting roles on *The Sopranos* and the MTV reality show *Boiling Points*. Her break came when a fellow musician introduced her to producer Rob Fusari, who envisioned her fronting a Strokes-inspired band. Germanotta came across as very "Jersey Shore," but Fusari took her on as a producer and a lover. Inspired by the Queen song "Radio Ga Ga," Fusari christened her Lady Gaga, and they began crafting rock ballads together.

As rock music's commercial influence waned, Fusari pivoted Gaga toward dance music. After a brief stint with Island Def Jam, which dropped her in 2006, Gaga spent a year immersing herself in the Lower East Side. Late to the party but eager to catch up, she absorbed its aesthetics: cocaine, Andy Warhol's philosophy of art, and burlesque performances with indie singer Lady Starlight, which attracted the attention of Interscope Records' Jimmy Iovine.

In Iovine's account of their meeting, "an Italian girl with brown hair" walked in, and she "started telling me about Andy Warhol, and dance music, but yet industrial, and paintings. . . . She confused me so much that I signed her." Partnering with up-and-coming Moroccan Swedish producer RedOne, Gaga transformed her love of eighties heavy metal into a market-friendly electropop sound, trading guitar riffs for synth lines. As she refined her stage persona, Gaga embraced the aesthetic of drag culture, platinum blond hair, and over-the-top fashion inspired by Warholian iconography and gay icons like Liza Minnelli.

Music critic Simon Reynolds noted, "Everything about Gaga came from electroclash." Her debut single, "Just Dance," epitomized this synthesis, blending David Bowie–inspired makeup, Karen O's fashion, and the party visuals of the Cobrasnake's indie sleaze photography. The track's rap breakdown nodded to electroclash icon Peaches. Reynolds observed that beneath the avant-garde veneer, her songs were "ruthlessly catchy noughties pop glazed with Auto-Tune and undergirded with R&B-ish beats," giving the impression of innovation while remaining rooted in familiar conventions. And the constant product placement for Beats by Dre headphones in Gaga's videos secured multiple revenue streams for Iovine.

Unsurprisingly, Gaga also found her visual language in downtown New York. Terry Richardson shot her 2011 photo book, including a now-iconic image of her in a wet, see-through Supreme T-shirt and dark sunglasses. The partnership served Richardson well: Gaga's identity as a strong feminist and LGBTQ+ ally gave him further progressive validation. Gaga's foray into the art world extended to collaborations with pop artist Jeff Koons, who designed the cover of her 2013 album, *Artpop*, and Serbian artist Marina Abramović, whose conceptual training bolstered Gaga's high-art credentials. Together with Kanye and Pharrell, these alliances made her a key player in centering neo–pop art as part of mainstream culture.

Gaga did offer a crucial departure from downtown New York: Where the New York scene relied on age-old notions of snobbish exclusivity, she built her persona around radical inclusivity. She told fans they, too, could free themselves by donning edgy looks and inhabiting ever-shifting avatars of selfhood. Critic Liz Jones dismissed Gaga as "not remotely new or innovative," calling her success a triumph of self-promotion. But this relatability was precisely the point. For a generation searching for identity, Gaga's "chimerical sprite" persona, as Rachel Syme put it, offered permission to redefine oneself endlessly. Her young fans didn't want artistic innovation; they wanted an accessible model for role-playing a more glamorous, boundaryless life. Gaga became the embodiment of the era's contradictions: Becoming a "fame monster" was positioned as the ultimate path to self-liberation.

For some, Gaga represented a bright spot of calculated weirdness in a pop landscape dominated by reality TV mediocrity. Lollapalooza founder Perry Farrell likened her to a "Plastic Ono Band meets Madonna meets Elton John." Rachel Syme believed that Lady Gaga "opened the doors for more female hitmakers to be cheekily bizarre." In 2013, Miley Cyrus asked Terry Richardson to direct the sensational video for Gaga-clone track "Wrecking Ball," in which she appears nude.

Yet, in hindsight, Gaga's provocations feel shallow. Her 2010 MTV Video Music Awards meat dress provoked mild outrage from animal rights activists but left little cultural impact. As Simon Reynolds wrote, "Collapsing past into future, and edgy hipsterism into mainstream showbiz, Gaga voided the meaning of either." Her defining anthem, "Born This Way," framed as a rallying cry for individuality and queer rights, was widely derided as a blatant rip-off of Madonna's 1989 hit "Express Yourself." This misstep invited unflattering comparisons with the former Queen of Pop, whose boundary-pushing career had unfolded at higher stakes and with greater finesse. Where Madonna sparked national scandals with her book *Sex*, Gaga partnered with Oreo on a limited-edition flavor.

But perhaps Lady Gaga was the most radical pop possible in the poptimist era. Jimmy Iovine didn't need her to challenge the conventions of art— he just needed new beats to sell Beats. Scholar Natasha Degen defined her overall aesthetic as "art pop," which "claims high-art cachet while never challenging the commodification of culture." Gaga's success—as one of the loudest voices proclaiming allegiances to both radical creativity and marginalized communities—augured how much commerce would go on to fully triumph over art.

Such commodification wasn't confined to pop music. The art world itself mirrored the era's poptimist tendencies. Street art, which initially seemed poised to reinvigorate the gallery scene, devolved into kitsch. Banksy's 2010 documentary, *Exit Through the Gift Shop*, attempted to make a cautionary tale out of Mr. Brainwash, a sub-Warholian prankster who excited the market with cliché pieces, such as Michael Jackson with Marilyn Monroe's blond locks, and Einstein holding a sign that reads "Love is the answer." Banksy's critique hardly stuck; Madonna asked Mr. Brainwash to design an album cover for her third greatest hits collection, *Celebration*.

But how would one know the difference between art and kitsch in a pop-timist world? For all the possibilities around reimagining society in the wake of the Great Recession, the culture went deeper into capitalist logic: the collective celebration of entertainers' personal enrichment and the entrepreneurial chutzpah of reality TV stars. There was certainly no artistic explosion or moral revolution. In all the era's cultural pursuits, commerce was the answer.

TECHNO-OPTIMISM

Evading Norms to Fight the Bad Guys and Make Billions

6

On December 17, 2010, an impoverished fruit and vegetable vendor named Mohamed Bouazizi pushed his cart onto the streets of Sidi Bouzid, Tunisia, when police confronted him over his lack of permits. They confiscated his cart and scales. Bouazizi claimed that a female officer slapped him in the face. Humiliated and desperate, he threatened to burn himself alive if the authorities didn't return his belongings. When no one listened, he doused himself in paint thinner and set himself on fire.

Bouazizi's act of defiance ignited a wave of protests across Tunisia, eventually toppling its president-for-life, Zine El Abidine Ben Ali. The success of Tunisia's revolution emboldened similar movements across the Middle East. By February 2011, Egyptian protesters forced the resignation of their own autocratic leader, Hosni Mubarak. Together, these uprisings became known as the Arab Spring.

Western media not only celebrated the courage of the young protesters but also hailed an unexpected hero: social media. The events in Tunisia and Egypt were dubbed "Facebook revolutions." Where Americans used the internet to share photos of their meals or follow the daily musings of Kim Kardashian, protesters in the Middle East were harnessing these same platforms to dismantle dictatorships. With Obama's rise and now the Arab Spring, the internet promised hope for a better world. The democratization of information was ushering in a democratization of politics. Technology was people power.

Silicon Valley platforms were indeed indispensable to these uprisings. Egyptian protesters described how they used "Facebook to schedule the protests, Twitter to coordinate, and YouTube to tell the world." Wael Ghonim, Google's marketing executive in the Middle East, became a key figure after creating a Facebook page protesting the death of a fellow activist. As the protests escalated, the Egyptian government blocked Twitter and Facebook and ultimately shut down the internet altogether—a decision Ghonim later called their fatal mistake: "They forced everyone . . . to go to the street to be part of this."

For Silicon Valley, the Arab Spring was a major public relations victory. A 2012 YouTube blog boasted, "Video plays a particularly important role in illuminating what occurs when governments and individuals in power abuse their positions," noting that Egypt saw a 70 percent increase in videos uploaded during the protests. Ghonim himself proclaimed on *60 Minutes* that the internet was more powerful than the US presidency: "It was good that [Obama] supports the revolution. . . . But we don't really need him."

These events appeared to not only validate the core belief of the Stewart Brand techno-utopians—"Information wants to be free"—but go even further: Information would make us free.

As political gridlock thwarted Obama's domestic agenda, such technocratic market solutions became an attractive alternative. Books like *New Yorker* staff writer James Surowiecki's *The Wisdom of Crowds* argued that large groups made better decisions than elites, mirroring the internet's participatory nature. His colleague Malcolm Gladwell's *The Tipping Point* and *Blink* promised social transformation through small changes and quick decisions. Steven Levitt and Stephen J. Dubner's *Freakonomics* dissected the oddities of human behavior to reveal rational economic patterns, while in the book *Nudge*, "libertarian paternalists" Richard H. Thaler and Cass R. Sunstein introduced "choice architecture" as a way to shape behavior without restricting freedom. All these books shared a fundamental belief that data-driven solutions could improve society without direct governmental interference or having to change voters' minds.

Surowiecki's "wisdom of the crowd" thesis found its most immediate validation in Wikipedia, a crowdsourced website that became the largest and most accessible repository of knowledge in human history. By offering free, multilingual information to anyone with an internet connection, Wikipedia embodied the democratizing promise of the internet. "What can we put into the hands of people under oppressive regimes to help them?" asked its founder, Jimmy Wales. "For me, a big part of it is information, knowledge—the ability to defeat propaganda by understanding it."

Wales himself became a celebrity, beloved across the political spectrum. His friend, U2 front man Bono, hailed Wikipedia as "the democratization of information in a world where knowledge is power." Yet the same participatory ethos inspired more radical projects. WikiLeaks, founded by Australian ex-hacker Julian Assange, aimed to host "restricted or censored material of political, ethical, diplomatic or historical significance." Assange believed the internet's anonymity and global reach could empower whistleblowers to expose corruption and injustice, supporting democratic movements worldwide.

WikiLeaks gained its first support from the anti-war left for releasing classified documents about US actions in Afghanistan and Iraq. In 2010, it made global headlines by publishing top-secret war documents provided by intelligence analyst Chelsea Manning. This leak, and Manning's subsequent imprisonment, cemented Assange's status as the face of "hacktivism"—a controversial new frontier in the fight for transparency.

Where WikiLeaks weaponized the release of classified information, the decentralized hacktivist group Anonymous demonstrated the strength of a diversified digital arsenal. Emerging from the anarchic forums of 4chan's /b/ board, Anonymous pioneered tactics such as distributed denial-of-service (DDoS) attacks, doxing, and even juvenile pranks such as ordering hundreds of pizzas to an enemy's home. Initially, these "raids" were done for the "lulz," with no explicit political ideology. But as the group targeted figures like racist right-wing radio host Hal Turner, it began to appear as a chaotic but principled force.

Anonymous's 2008 campaign against Scientology, Project Chanology, marked its transformation into a recognizable activist group. Protesters in Guy Fawkes masks—leftover merchandise from the 2005 film *V for Vendetta*—rallied in front of Scientology churches worldwide. The masks became a symbol of resistance, and Anonymous, once seen as an online mob, appeared like a heroic counterforce against once-untouchable antisocial forces.

These early successes emboldened Anonymous to take on bigger targets. Hackers supported the protesters during Iran's 2009 elections, hampered MasterCard's, Visa's, and PayPal's websites for refusing to serve WikiLeaks, and pledged to go after a murderous Mexican drug cartel. They provided technical support to Tunisian protesters during the Arab Spring, defaced the Tunisian president's website with a pirate ship, and launched DDoS attacks against the government. Under the banner of "Freedom Ops," Anonymous helped shape the internet's role as a tool for revolution.

Despite their shared belief in the internet's power, the figures driving these movements came from wildly different ideological backgrounds. Wikipedia's Wales was an Ayn Rand–loving libertarian from Alabama; Anonymous's Christopher Doyon (a.k.a. Commander X) idolized Yippie Abbie Hoffman and Black Panther Eldridge Cleaver. Julian Assange, as scholar Peter Ludlow observed, couldn't be neatly "characterized in terms of left versus right so much as individual versus institution." The internet united these disparate actors under a common goal: to disrupt entrenched power structures.

Yet Anonymous's contradictions were impossible to ignore. While supporting Occupy Wall Street, members freely used homophobic slurs. They protested racism in the online game *Habbo* by arranging a group of Black avatars into a swastika. Their nihilistic pranks often veered into outright cruelty, from harassing grieving families of dead teenagers to targeting epileptics with flashing lights. But in the techno-optimist spirit, these flirtations with fascist imagery were again excused as ironic. At Baltimore's Otakon anime conference in 2007, teens attending a 4chan panel marched around with Sieg Heil salutes—performative fascism for the lulz.

Online activism in the early 2010s may have felt like a Wild West, but it appeared to net out as a positive force. Backed by the power of crowds, the internet's invisible hand could seemingly channel even the most destructive energies toward meaningful collective action.

———

The rumors about *The Social Network* sounded ludicrous: David Fincher, the director of cult hits *Seven* and *Fight Club*, was teaming up with screenwriter Aaron Sorkin of *The West Wing* to make a film about the early days of Facebook, a website founded five years prior. Facebook executives were less amused. The company was progressing toward its initial public offering, and the leadership team was nervous about scrutiny over the site's messy origins. Top Facebook executives Sheryl Sandberg and Elliot Schrage asked to view an early cut of the film. They hated it. When their suggested edits were rejected, they convinced themselves it would flop, another "failed attempt to bottle a generation." To their credit, no one had made a particularly accurate movie about computers or the internet, as evidenced by 1995's *The Net* and *Hackers*.

They were wrong. *The Social Network* premiered on September 24, 2010, to rave reviews and packed theaters. Propelled by a pulsing electronic score from Nine Inch Nails' Trent Reznor and Atticus Ross, the film transformed Facebook's story into a tale of ambition, betrayal, and excess. Jesse Eisenberg portrayed founder Mark Zuckerberg as a sarcastic dweeb with the wit of Dorothy Parker, while Justin Timberlake played the company's first president, Sean Parker, as a pop idol. *The Social Network*, thanks to a forty-eight-year-old director, a forty-nine-year-old screenwriter, and forty-five- and forty-two-year-old musical composers, managed to finally "bottle" the internet generation.

The real Zuckerberg complained about his portrayal being so jaded and girl-crazy: "They just can't wrap their head around [the idea] that someone might build something because they like building things." And the film did overdramatize the mundane truth of Facebook's backstory. But Facebook ultimately benefited from the cinematic glow. *Time* named Zuckerberg Person of the Year for 2010. Tech company founders were becoming folk heroes. Zuckerberg's Harvard dropout predecessor, Bill Gates, had made his fortune with utilitarian tools like DOS and Office—the ball bearings of the digital age with little cultural cachet. As Steve Jobs once quipped, "The only problem with Microsoft is that they just have no taste." Zuckerberg himself wasn't particularly cool, but Facebook was: The platform brought social dynamics online—party photos, dating prospects, stalking high school crushes—and introduced millions to the internet for the first time.

Riding the momentum of social media, the internet had transformed in a few short years from a hobbyist haven for nerds to the epicenter of global culture. Tech companies became the new media powerhouses, shaping tastes and trends. Steve Jobs had revitalized Apple with colorful iMacs and the iPod before revolutionizing the world with the iPhone. Unlike the BlackBerry, the iPhone wasn't just functional—it was aspirational, seamlessly blending design and culture. The iPhone crushed every device that had come before. Japanese manufacturers spent two decades developing the world's most advanced mobile phones; by early 2010, the iPhone captured 72 percent of the Japanese phone market.

Google, meanwhile, redefined corporate culture with its T-shirt-clad workforce, free meals, and whimsical campuses. "Google is not a conventional company," founders Larry Page and Sergey Brin wrote. "We do not intend to become one." They chose Eric Schmidt as their first grown-up CEO because he was the only candidate who had been to Burning Man. Zuckerberg borrowed heavily from Google's unofficial playbook for how to run Facebook, commissioning artist David Choe to spruce up its office walls with a graffiti-inspired mural. (The stock Choe took as payment later ballooned to $200 million.) This vision of work as fun was so compelling that dying companies hired Google executives to spearhead revivals. Marissa Mayer failed to save Yahoo!, but she became a media darling in the process.

Consumers, meanwhile, supported tech companies' "disruption" when it meant fighting entrenched industries. In 2006, former PayPal executive Elon

Musk unveiled the Tesla Roadster, reframing electric vehicles from tree-hugger oddities to Silicon Valley status symbols. Dubbed "sex on wheels" by *Wired*, the Roadster drew celebrity fans like Arnold Schwarzenegger, George Clooney, and Leonardo DiCaprio. Tesla followed with the Model S in 2009, promising a future of affordable electric cars for every price range.

The rise of the smartphone then unlocked a sprawling app economy. Companies like Netflix pivoted from DVDs to streaming, while Spotify provided immediate access to nearly all the world's music. Ride-sharing app Uber disrupted the taxi industry in 2009, and Airbnb upended hospitality two years earlier, letting anyone turn a spare room into a hotel. Instagram, launched in 2010, brought casual photography into the mainstream with its nostalgic filters and square formatting. Snapchat introduced disappearing messages in 2011, creating new avenues for intimacy and privacy. Dating apps like Grindr (2009) and Tinder (2012) redefined relationships for the digital age.

On October 6, 2011, a double rainbow appeared over Silicon Valley just as news broke that Steve Jobs had passed away the previous day from pancreatic cancer. Only nineteen days later, Walter Isaacson's biography hit bookshelves, solidifying Jobs as a historical and cultural legend on par with Thomas Edison. His unconventional uniform of black Issey Miyake turtlenecks, stonewashed Levi's 501s, and New Balance sneakers took on an iconic air. Jobs didn't just sell products; he sold an optimistic and tasteful vision of the future. The year of his death, Apple overtook ExxonMobil as the world's most valuable company—proving that entrepreneurs, not just artists, could reshape the entire culture by channeling the spirit of radical innovation.

On July 28, 2010, Huntsville, Alabama's WAFF 48 news channel visited the Lincoln Park public housing complex to interview Kelly Dodson about an attempted rape in her bedroom. "I was attacked by some idiot from out here in the projects," Dodson recounted. Her brother Antoine rushed in to defend her, forcing the assailant to flee through the window. On camera, Antoine, with his long hair under a red bandanna, delivered an impassioned, poetic plea: "He's climbing in your windows, he's snatching your people up, tryin' to rape 'em, so y'all need to hide your kids, hide your wife, and hide your husband, 'cause they're raping everybody out here." Dodson later explained that his outburst stemmed from his own experiences as a rape survivor: "I didn't want what I said to be swept under the rug."

The clip quickly went viral, propelled by Reddit and *BuzzFeed*, with millions reveling in Dodson's freestyle delivery. Before it even hit YouTube, the footage reached the Gregory Brothers—a musical group known for remixing news clips into comedic songs. Within two days of the incident, they turned Dodson's rant into "Bed Intruder," a seventy-five-second rap that became 2010's most-watched YouTube video. Without radio play or industry backing, the song charted on *Billboard*, fueled by iTunes downloads. Half the proceeds went to the Dodson family, enabling them to move to a safer neighborhood. Dodson performed "Bed Intruder" at the 2010 BET Hip Hop Awards; he noted about the entire ordeal, "Blessings come in disguise."

"Bed Intruder" wasn't without controversy. Critics argued it trivialized a serious crime, and others questioned the ethics of the musicians—four white Brooklynites—profiting from the difficulty of living in public housing. New York University professor Jason King told NPR, "The aesthetics of Black poverty—the way they talk and they speak and they look—sort of becomes this fodder for humor without any interest in the context of the conditions in which people actually live." Compounding the backlash, the whole story may have been made up. Huntsville resident Rashaad Cooper claimed in 2014 that he was simply having a "fling" with Kelly Dodson, and when he rejected her advances, she "got mad and bipolar and started throwing stuff, trying to fight me." Antoine Dodson denied this account yet went along with its underlying premise by fighting Cooper in a pay-per-view celebrity boxing match hosted by O. J. Simpson trial star Kato Kaelin. (Dodson won in the first round, a moment that viewers missed because the video froze.)

Despite these gray areas, "Bed Intruder" exemplified how the internet was rewiring the mechanics of fame and cultural production. The Gregory Brothers had monetized their video through the YouTube Partner Program, earning ad revenue from millions of views, while iTunes allowed them to bypass record labels entirely. As Andrew Gregory noted, "In one fell swoop, there could be a piece of work that all these people would see, more than the entire amount of people that saw us on a three-month tour."

This new democracy of self-monetization went hand in hand with an amplification of voices long underrepresented in traditional media. Mommy bloggers tackled taboo topics such as postpartum depression, breastfeeding, and post-childbirth sex. YouTube brought more visibility to a diverse set of creators. In particular, Asian Americans, only 7 percent of the US population, were very well represented among early YouTube stars. Makeup artist Michelle Phan established the popular genre of beauty tutorial videos, and in winning corporate sponsorships and starting her own makeup company, she arguably pioneered the influencer profession. Black Twitter emerged as a cultural powerhouse, propelling shows like *Scandal* to major success. Viral campaigns such as the Ice Bucket Challenge showcased how nonprofits could harness social media for good, raising millions for ALS research.

Even those mocked online found ways to reclaim their narratives. In 2007, autistic graduate student Adam Nyerere Bahner, a.k.a. Tay Zonday, uploaded an earnest anti-racist song called "Chocolate Rain." With its repetitive piano hook and idiosyncratic vocal delivery, the video became a meme, initially drawing ridicule on forums like 4chan. But the buzz catapulted Zonday into national fame, proving that even the internet's targets could turn mockery into opportunity. Soft drink brand Dr Pepper paid him to make an over-the-top rap video parody called "Cherry Chocolate Rain," in celebration of its Diet Cherry Chocolate soda.

By 2010, even fringe subcultures like the Juggalos were gaining unexpected validation online. The movement's core act, Insane Clown Posse (ICP)—often labeled as "the worst band of all time"—received a new pop culture prominence after the group's viral video for "Miracles" went viral for its widely disparaged lyric "Fucking magnets / how do they work?" As *Pitchfork*'s Sean Fennessey noted, there was now "an honest affection for the subculture Violent J and Shaggy 2 Dope built from the ground up. Over time they became oft-underestimated owners of a tiny piece of unwanted subculture—the ignored and humiliated. But put enough unwashed together, and the masses rise."

The internet didn't just give former outcasts a chance for redemption; it also forged new paths to creative success. In earlier eras, building an online audience was a mere stepping stone toward a career in traditional media. Policy wonk bloggers like Ezra Klein and Matthew Yglesias parlayed their followings into high-profile jobs at *The Washington Post* and *Slate*, respectively, while mommy bloggers moved from AdSense-reliant websites to lucrative endorsement deals with major brands.

But the biggest cultural shift came from Web 2.0's revenue-sharing models. Platforms like YouTube allowed creators to monetize directly, making a career in content creation an end goal rather than a means to traditional industry acceptance. Posting regularly could yield a middle-class income—without needing to win over a single gatekeeper. This radically changed the logic of amateur creativity. Before the internet, the stereotype of an aspiring filmmaker was someone with artistic pretensions—represented in the scrappy, outsider ethos of nineties indie auteurs such as Richard Linklater, Spike Lee, and Quentin Tarantino. Once tech platforms began paying for views, this incentivized a new type of creator who simply talked into their camera and constantly honed their content to attract the broadest possible audience. This also shifted the median internet poster from the anonymous or pseudonymous forum lurker to performative creators who revealed their faces online—a change that was crucial for making internet culture more accessible to regular teens.

As YouTube became central to pop culture, it also became a clear pathway for unknown talent to ascend into global fame. In 2007, twelve-year-old Justin Bieber uploaded a video of himself singing Ne-Yo's R&B ballad "So Sick" from his home in Stratford, Ontario. Encouraged by positive feedback, he posted more performances, eventually catching the attention of Scooter Braun, an ambitious young talent scout in Atlanta. Bieber's devout Christian mother, Pattie, was initially hesitant about Braun ("God, you don't want this Jewish kid to be Justin's man, do you?"). But after church elders blessed the arrangement, Bieber flew to Atlanta, where R&B star Usher eventually signed him over interest from rival Justin Timberlake.

Bieber's meteoric rise was a modern Cinderella story, a celebration of the internet's ability to circumvent traditional gatekeepers at dizzying speeds. His debut EP in 2009 made him an instant teen idol, performing for President Obama and dominating pop culture with his 2010 hit "Baby." At its peak, the song's video was the most watched in YouTube history, and Bieber accounted for 3 percent of all Twitter traffic. His ascent also demonstrated the efficiency of the internet in identifying marketable talent. For record labels, YouTube became a farm league, in which view counts served as a reliable metric for an artist's viability. Bieber wasn't just a fluke; grassroots popularity in cyberspace now served as a critical step toward global stardom.

Less scrupulous companies exploited the internet's promise of democratization, crafting backstories that gave the illusion of authenticity—the so-called industry plants. A notable early example was lonelygirl15, a YouTube channel launched in 2006 that rapidly gained popularity for the vlogs of charismatic teenager Bree Avery, who turned out to be a fictional character played by a paid actress.

This tactic persisted into the next decade. While in Canada, Bieber and his then-girlfriend Selena Gomez heard a catchy pop song, "Call Me Maybe," on the radio by the relatively unknown Canadian pop singer Carly Rae Jepsen. Recognizing its potential, Bieber asked Braun to sign Jepsen, and together they orchestrated a viral marketing campaign. Bieber and Gomez filmed a lip-synch video in the homemade YouTube aesthetic, sparking a wave of fan engagement that propelled the song into one of the year's biggest hits. The song's meteoric rise had less to do with democratic mechanisms than with carefully managed celebrity endorsement.

The internet's chaotic nature, however, ensured that virality wasn't always a product of calculated campaigns. Hate clicks remained just as powerful as genuine admiration. On February 10, 2011, thirteen-year-old Rebecca Black uploaded the music video for "Friday," a song her parents commissioned for $4,000 as a birthday present. The track, with its shrill vocals and banal lyrics—"Yesterday was Thursday / Today is Friday"—became an object of instant ridicule. Comedy Central's *Tosh.O* turned it into a meme, and music blogger Lyndsey Parker observed that its popularity stemmed not from any redeeming qualities but because it was "so unbelievably BAD." For a brief moment, Black's "Friday" eclipsed even Bieber's view counts, showing the internet's power to elevate even the most reviled content into cultural phenomena.

The internet's inherent volatility opened new possibilities for trends to emerge from anywhere, breaking up the Anglo-American dominance on global pop culture. In the 1990s the South Korean entertainment industry realized early that the domestic market was too small to sustain their ambitions and set their sights on exporting K-pop. To create a globally appealing sound, Korean agencies taught their stars multiple languages, collaborated with foreign producers, and leaned on the expertise of the Korean diaspora. Initially, they targeted Japan, but their true breakthrough came online. In the YouTube era, K-pop quickly outpaced J-pop, thanks in part to contrasting industry strategies. While Japanese record labels clung to physical media and withheld full-length videos from YouTube to preserve domestic DVD sales, Korean companies like SM, YG, and JYP embraced the platform as a global stage. They uploaded high-production videos with subtitles in multiple languages, betting on the internet's potential to create their own Cinderella stories.

The unofficial scheme to achieve global K-pop domination paid off much faster than anyone expected—just not in the way anyone expected. On July 15, 2012, the middling thirty-four-year-old rapper Psy (Jae-sang Park) uploaded his new video, "Gangnam Style," to YouTube. Within weeks, it shattered view-count records. Psy had a colorful backstory: The son of a Korean semiconductor manufacturer, he was sent to Boston in 1996 to study English and then business management but instead gravitated toward the Berklee College of Music. Upon returning to Seoul, Psy released a series of albums that Korean authorities labeled obscene. Further scandal erupted when he skipped mandatory military service by claiming special software expertise. By twenty-five, Psy had served a month in jail for marijuana possession, cementing his reputation as the bad boy of Korean pop.

In 2012, Psy recorded "Gangnam Style" as a satirical dance-rap track mocking the ostentatious new-money culture of Seoul's affluent Gangnam district. The video was a chaotic mix of mild hip-hop parody, Korean pop culture in-jokes, celebrity cameos, and absurdist humor—complete with a silly horse-riding dance and a slow-motion rage scream at a woman's raised buttocks in a yoga pose. Aside from the phrase "Hey, sexy lady," the lyrics were entirely in Korean, and even in translation, they required a deep familiarity with Seoul's socioeconomic dynamics to pick up on the nuanced class commentary. All in all, it was not a song designed for global domination.

But to Western audiences, "Gangnam Style" felt utterly novel. Few were familiar with K-pop's slick production, neon aesthetics, and synchronized choreography. That July, rapper T-Pain tweeted, "Words cannot even describe how amazing this video is . . ." which helped launch the song into a sprawling pop culture phenomenon. At a Dodgers game in Los Angeles that August, Psy was spotted by the stadium Dance Cam, and after briefly hesitating, he performed his now-iconic horse-riding dance to thunderous applause. By September, Scooter Braun had signed Psy to his label, exclaiming, "There is one reason . . . to be a part of history, to do something no one has ever done before." The internet had not only introduced K-pop to a global audience but also transformed a controversial, mid-career rapper into an unlikely international sensation. By the year's end, Korea's Ministry of Culture, Sports and Tourism gave Google a special achievement award for its role in spreading K-pop globally, and "Gangnam Style" became the first YouTube video to surpass two billion views. Technology was no longer just a vehicle for globalization; it was becoming a means of cultural equalization.

Yet by 2012, there were already signs that the internet couldn't solve every global challenge. That year Jason Russell of the nonprofit Invisible Children uploaded a thirty-minute documentary, *Kony 2012*, to raise awareness of murderous Ugandan warlord Joseph Kony's Lord's Resistance Army and its use of child soldiers. Despite its grim subject matter, *Kony 2012* went viral, thanks to endorsements from Oprah Winfrey, Justin Bieber, and Kim Kardashian. Within a week, it had set a record with a hundred million views.

But the phenomenon quickly unraveled. Just a week later, Russell suffered a public mental breakdown in which he was reportedly "masturbating in public and vandalizing cars." Although the reality was less salacious than initial reports, with his team blaming "exhaustion, dehydration and malnutrition," the damage was done. On Twitter, the hashtag #Horny2012 replaced #Kony2012, and the movement's credibility collapsed. Invisible Children burned through $32 million in donations, while public concern for Uganda vanished as quickly as it had appeared. By year's end, the Kony 2012 campaign was little more than an internet in-joke, occupying a cultural shelf just above "Chocolate Rain." Joseph Kony remains at large.

MILLENNIALS

A Poptimist Generation Aspires to Entrepreneurial Glory

On May 18, 2012, Mark Zuckerberg, clad in a dark gray hoodie and mall-store jeans, rang the bell at Facebook's Menlo Park headquarters to commence the company's initial public offering. Just days after his twenty-eighth birthday, Zuckerberg was worth $19 billion. The IPO spread wealth across his Harvard crew: Chris Hughes made $935 million; Dustin Moskovitz, $5.1 billion; and even Eduardo Saverin, the supposed victim of Zuckerberg's betrayal in *The Social Network*, walked away with $2.9 billion.

This IPO, coming less than three years after the global financial crisis, formally minted the first self-made billionaires born between 1981 and 1996—the so-called millennials. This single act of market capitalization set a new aspirational standard for an entire generation. Just as the millennials ascended into adulthood, one of their own redefined success by becoming a billionaire—without putting on a suit.

Yet while Zuckerberg ascended, most millennials felt deeply underwater. Coming of age in the aftermath of the global financial crisis, many faced chronic economic insecurity for the next decade. "Very few of us," wrote millennial journalist Anne Helen Petersen, "felt anything close to *secure.*" Even college graduates feared sliding into the "precariat," fated to eke out unstable livelihoods in the gig economy. In the wake of 9/11, journalist Hunter S. Thompson warned that children of the era were "doomed to be the first generation of Americans who will grow up with a lower standard of living than their parents enjoyed." That prediction became a generational identity. Only 33 percent of Americans believed their children would surpass their parents' quality of life.

While the scientific validity of dividing generations into boomers, Gen X, and millennials remains debatable, it's clear that the pessimistic millennial self-narrative profoundly shaped how young people understood themselves. *The Washington Post* declared them "the unluckiest generation in U.S. history," because, as *The Atlantic*'s Annie Lowrey lamented, they were "saddled with debt, unable to accumulate wealth, and stuck in low-benefit, dead-end jobs." Around the world, millennials felt the deck was stacked against them: More than half of European millennials believed that "success in life is pretty much determined by outside forces."

Neil Howe and William Strauss coined *millennial* in their 1991 book, *Generations*, based on the idea that the cohort's oldest members would graduate high school in 2000. Despite early competition from rival *Gen Y*, the term became common parlance by *Time*'s 2013 cover story "The Me Me Me Generation." By the Obama years, millennials were hard to ignore: At 1.8 billion strong, they were the largest generation of adults on the planet, primed to shape global culture through sheer numbers.

Millennials grew up in the depths of poptimism. As teens, they idolized Britney Spears, Justin Timberlake, and Beyoncé; as young adults, they helped elect Barack Obama and were the first users of Facebook and core readers of *BuzzFeed*. Yet they shocked pundits with their disdain for the traditional markers of adulthood: golf, cars, casual sex. By the mid-2010s, the media better clarified their particular tastes: the "millennial whoop" (a recurring melodic pattern in pop songs) and "millennial pink" (a "grapefruit shade of apricotty salmon" ubiquitous in fashion and design).

Rather than unique aesthetics, however, millennials' defining trait was their collective response to economic uncertainty. Living in a world of tech IPOs, Kardashian hustle, and celebrity entrepreneurs, millennials suffered from "relative deprivation"—the nagging sense that everyone *else* was getting rich. For many, the solution was more capitalism—but their kind of capitalism. Zuckerberg once used business cards that read "I'm CEO, bitch," and now he was the twenty-ninth richest person in the world.

Perhaps some millennials embraced leftist critiques of capitalism, but even they admitted that their generation was mostly swept up in capitalist realism. Marxist writer Malcolm Harris argued that young people conceived of themselves as "human capital" to be optimized, driving an obsession with credentials, efficiency, and career advancement. Yet this ambition created narrative contradictions: Millennials were both hard-charging strivers and "lazy, entitled narcissists," stereotyped as demanding promotions and large salaries without paying their dues. What older adults didn't understand, however, is that they were in a rush.

The antidote to precarity is stability, and in the wake of the Great Recession, no one wanted to be an unambitious, itinerant hipster. There was no millennial respect for bartenders in porkpie hats making craft cocktails. They wanted careers. In 2015, David Infante of *Mashable* proposed a replacement term for hipster: *yuccie*, short for "young urban creatives." Yuccies, he wrote, were "infected by the conviction that not only do we deserve to pursue our dreams; we should profit from them." Their dream was "getting rich quick and preserving creative autonomy."

Yuccies gravitated toward internet-enabled careers like "social consultants coordinating #sponsored Instagram campaigns for lifestyle brands" or "brogrammers hawking Uber for weed and Tinder for dogs." While the term *yuccie* was dead on arrival, its attempted coinage reformulated the idea of the creative class: Millennials now equally weighted "creative" and "class." As Anne Helen Petersen observed, millennials "internalized the need to find employment that reflects well on their parents (steady, decently paying, recogniz-

able as a 'good job') that's also impressive to their peers (at a 'cool' company)."
Neither being a corporate drone nor being a starving bohemian solved their
dilemma; millennials wanted lucrative careers that aligned with their personal brands.

But building a personal brand required more than professional achievements. It also demanded a curated aesthetic across social media feeds—
foreign travel, rare goods, and perfectly plated meals—while quietly omitting
menial aspects of life like flying in economy. Older generations often mis-
took this conspicuous consumption as pure avarice, but millennials often
justified it as a coping mechanism for being priced out of cars, homes, and
children. Others saw their lifestyle spending as advertisements for themselves: Establishing a vision of present success would lead to even greater
success in the future.

This dogged pursuit of consumerist sophistication tended to alienate millennials from traditional domesticity. Basic household chores required a rebranding of their own. In 2013, Kelly Williams Brown coined the term
adulting in a book about the bewildering responsibilities of adulthood, such
as folding towels and cleaning toilets. Brown's playful framing resonated
deeply, transforming mundane tasks into heroic feats of self-reliance. Writer
Kathryn Jezer-Morton believed that "*adulting* sums up the anxiously self-
reliant ethos of early-aughts millennials as accurately as the *Whole Earth
Catalog* summed up the back-to-the-land fantasies of early 1970s boomers."
It was also quite pathetic: *Jezebel*'s Madeleine Davies wrote, "An award for
fulfilling your basic responsibilities as a human is pretty much the most
childish thing imaginable."

While Occupy Wall Street types attributed their generation's materialism
to the structural inequality of late capitalism, young right-wingers embraced
the rat race with gusto. Like the 1990s stockbrokers who memorized the
"greed is good" speech from *Wall Street*, millennial finance bros and entrepreneurs found their mantra in a scene from Martin Scorsese's 2013 film,
The Wolf of Wall Street, in which junk bond salesman Jordan Belfort exalts,
"There is no nobility in poverty. I've been a rich man and I've been a poor

man—and I choose rich every fucking time." If millennials were doomed as a generation, then it was every person for themselves. Only those with what psychologist Angela Duckworth called "grit"—the "passion and perseverance" to succeed in long-term goals—deserved to win.

This ideology became a meme when Australian property magnate Tim Gurner blamed millennials' inability to afford homes on their love of avocado toast and lattes. His own success, Gurner claimed, came from his work ethic: "When I had my first business, when I was nineteen, I was in the gym at six a.m. in the morning and I finished at ten thirty at night and I did it seven days a week, and I did it till I could afford my first home. And there was no discussions around, could I go out for breakfast or could I go out for dinner or whatever it was. I just worked." This ethos reflected the pervasiveness of "hustle culture" or the "grind mindset"—the belief that relentless effort and discipline could overcome any obstacle.

The parallels to athletics were explicit. The "grind" language appeared in a 2012 motivational video created for the Texas Christian University baseball team. Its narrator intoned, "A legion of voices are shouting their unanimous permission for you to hit the snooze button and go back to dreamland—but you didn't ask their opinion. The voice you've chosen to listen to is one of defiance. . . . Welcome to the grind." Social media served as a virtual clubhouse for bragging about disciplined lifestyle routines. During a week in June 2014, Twitter users were posting 9.3 "rise and grind" tweets per minute during peak hours.

Nowhere was the grind mindset more celebrated than in the tech world. Yahoo! CEO Marissa Mayer famously attributed Google's success to its early employees' grueling 130-hour workweeks. There were no weekends or holidays in the grind; tireless execution trumped clever ideas. Upon visiting a coworking space run by her husband, Mayer said, "If you go in on a Saturday afternoon, I can tell you which startups will succeed, without even knowing what they do." Silicon Valley became a cult of self-improvement, with engineers trading their schlubby 1980s archetype for slim physiques, North Face vests, and a constant search for "hacks" to improve their lives. The stakes were enormous: Where Wall Street promised six-figure bonuses for twenty-hour workdays, Silicon Valley dangled the prospect of billions through IPOs or acquihires.

The grind became even more efficient with technology. BlackBerrys, email, chat, and Skype allowed workers to maximize every waking moment across time zones. Yet the all-encompassing work culture often led to burnout, a fate Tim Ferriss narrowly avoided. A Princeton graduate, Ferriss started a business selling unregulated cognitive supplements under the brand BrainQuicken but found himself consumed by the work, even during vacations. Desperate to reclaim his time, he outsourced tasks to overseas assistants in lower-wage countries. From this experience, he found his true calling: packaging up his wisdom to sell to others.

With mentorship from *Chicken Soup for the Soul* cocreator Jack Canfield, Ferriss distilled his methods into *The 4-Hour Workweek: Escape 9–5, Live Anywhere, and Join the New Rich*. Released in 2007, the book became an instant bestseller, promising a path to wealth, freedom, and mobility. Hustling, Ferriss argued, wasn't about grinding endlessly but about achieving "passive income" that let you escape the grind entirely. His advice— outsource menial tasks, check email sparingly, and focus on high-value activities—resonated with millennials desperate for control over their lives.

But Ferriss himself embodied the contradictions of hustle culture. A friend told *The New Yorker*, "Tim is a total fraud, you know. 'Four-hour workweek'? He is *constantly* busting ass." Ultimately, Ferriss's philosophy was less about escaping work and more about fully optimizing every aspect of life. As Rebecca Mead of *The New Yorker* wrote, his book promoted "a kind of hyperkinetic entrepreneurialism of the body and soul, with every man his own life coach, angel investor, Web master, personal trainer, and pharmaceutical test subject."

Whether readers embraced *The 4-Hour Workweek* to accelerate their hustle or decelerate their ambitions, its popularity heralded a new communal attitude toward work. The ideal twenty-first-century career was a sprint, not a marathon. Ferriss's "New Rich" accepted the grind, but only to accumulate enough wealth to never work again. It was a seductive resolution to millennials' financial anxieties and their disdain for corporate serfdom.

There was also a palpable lack of alternative models for the "good life." Socialism and bohemianism lost their allure, and Old Money nonchalance held little appeal even for those raised in privilege. Zuckerberg, who fenced at Phillips Exeter before founding Facebook in Harvard's Kirkland House, epitomized the new entrepreneurial elite. Similarly, Ferriss, whose family owned a seventeen-acre estate in the Hamptons, attended St. Paul's School and Princeton, and began scheming about opening a chain of Taiwanese gyms long before graduation.

Seventy-three percent of American millennials believed that hard work was crucial to "getting ahead in life"—and yet they also resented that fact. Many sought refuge in the FIRE movement: "financial independence, retire early." Early adopters were "stoic ultraminimalists" who embraced delayed gratification, subsisting on beans today to fund globetrotting tomorrow. Over time, the most popular strain became "FatFIRE," in which hacks and shortcuts promised to yield fortunes large enough for early, luxurious retirement. If Zuckerberg could make billions by cloning Friendster and Myspace, certainly others could find their own stash of gold in the app economy. Software was an enticingly low-overhead business: Write some code, join a display ad network, and pick a name that dropped vowels, like Tumblr, Scribd, or Grindr.

This entrepreneurial heroism also shaped millennials' take on feminism, encapsulated in the idea that liberation comes, as described by Jia Tolentino, "when an individual woman gets enough money to do whatever she wants." In 2013, Facebook COO Sheryl Sandberg published *Lean In*, advising women on how to further break through the glass ceiling. But the digital economy offered a shortcut: platforms where women could sell products made by women for women. Enter the "girlboss" era, defined by journalist Marisa Meltzer as a "cohort of young, mediagenic female founders" who fused empowerment messaging with entrepreneurial ventures. The movement surfaced in the culture when Sophia Amoruso, CEO of apparel company Nasty Gal, titled her memoir *#Girlboss*.

The phenomenon soon extended beyond Amoruso. Emily Weiss spun a *Teen Vogue* internship into appearances on the reality show *The Hills*. She then built a popular blog, working on it early in the morning before heading to her day job. That blog became a launching pad for Glossier, a direct-to-consumer beauty brand that eventually achieved a $1 billion valuation. Audrey Gelman founded the Wing, a women's social club marketed as a chic hub of empowerment. (She also made the gossip pages for her romantic relationship with Terry Richardson.) Even if the entire *girlboss* label carried patronizing undertones, Meltzer noted that it "captured the imagination of a younger generation" by putting "women in business front and center in culture." The modern Cinderella didn't wait for a prince; she hustled her way toward fortune. Amoruso, a "hipster dynamo dream girl," went from "anarchist shoplifter to multimillionaire."

In contrast to the tech bros dreaming up scalable digital services, girlbosses typically sold physical products or managed physical spaces—but the internet was still integral to their rise. Amoruso launched Nasty Gal on eBay, selling vintage pieces found at Goodwill. After buying the URL nastygal.com from pornographers, she migrated to her own website, eventually securing venture capital to expand. Social media amplified her reach: First Myspace, then Facebook, and finally Instagram helped her surpass $300 million in annual sales.

Despite their initial success, the girlboss icons flamed out quickly. Nasty Gal went bankrupt, the Wing shut its doors, and Weiss stepped down as Glossier's CEO. (Even more injurious, the TV adaptation of Amoruso's *#Girlboss* was dubbed "Netflix's first truly terrible show.") Perhaps, as Meltzer suggested, the girlboss was always a media mirage. While the most visible female entrepreneurs floundered, many successful women were running unglamorous but thriving businesses in America's heartland, invisible without the support of publicists.

Still, in the mid-2010s, the girlboss movement offered an aspirational narrative: Hardworking women could become billionaires by simply following their passions. These women fused entrepreneurial hustle with polished

Instagram lifestyles, providing a road map for young women to imagine their own success stories. Sophia Amoruso, at just nineteen, tattooed the Virgin Records logo on her arm, which may have been in tribute to the label's musical output, but as Richard Branson noted, it "brought her spectacular entrepreneurial good luck." By this point, youth culture and capitalism were no longer in opposition. The world may have set up millennials for failure, but the best revenge was their paper.

One of the first millennials known to Americans was LeBron James. Born in Akron, Ohio, to a sixteen-year-old mother and absent father, James spent his early years in nonmetaphorical precarity. His mother's boyfriend, whom James called Dad, served three years in prison for cocaine trafficking. James missed nearly a hundred days of fourth grade. Everything changed when he and his mother moved in with a youth sports coach, where he picked up basketball. By his teenage years, James was leading a team of local middle school legends who became high school legends at St. Vincent–St. Mary.

Much like other millennials, James focused on professional success from a young age. By sixteen, he was already six feet seven and anointed King James. Before he graduated high school, James graced the cover of *Sports Illustrated* and mingled with his heroes Michael Jordan and Jay-Z. The media framed his identity almost entirely in commercial terms: Would he skip college to go pro? How much would his salary be? Which sneaker brand would secure his endorsement?

In 2003, James was the number-one pick in the NBA draft, joining his hometown Cleveland Cavaliers. His Nike contract dwarfed his rookie salary, and he quickly became one of the league's top players, earning accolades and the adoration of fans. That goodwill evaporated in 2010 when James, as a free agent, produced a reality TV show, *The Decision*, to announce his next team. With celebrities lingering off-camera (including a napping Kanye), James declared, "I'm going to take my talents to South Beach"—that is, join the Miami Heat. He was as good as dead to Cleveland fans; the Cavaliers' owner called him a "coward." The broader public found the spectacle self-indulgent. As journalist Ian Crouch noted, James was seen "if not as an out-right villain, then at least a dogged and self-serious mercenary."

Critics blamed this misstep on his generational identity. Millennial writer David Cho defended James in *The Awl*, arguing that "LeBron is no more egomaniacal than the rest of us his age." To Cho, James's move to Miami re-flected "a generation that's been told that we can do anything that we want." After winning two championships in Miami, James returned to Cleveland in 2014, a decision *Ebony* framed in generational terms: "Just like what many Millennials have experienced in their 20s, it takes making a tough decision to realize what we really want in life." John Gorman of *The Cauldron* added, like any good millennial, James is "looking for *meaningful work*, to truly make a difference and expand his skill-set in novel ways beyond merely working on his post-up game. He's more than a court general, he's a court entrepreneur."

Such generational profiling can feel like a horoscope—a map of stock traits to apply as needed. Yet James did embody the millennial belief in en-trepreneurial heroism. Athletic dominance was not enough; he sought to be understood as a businessman and celebrity. He read Malcolm Gladwell, founded a marketing company, took counsel from Warren Buffett, hosted *Saturday Night Live*, and stole scenes in the 2015 comedy *Trainwreck*. His ultimate goal was to become a billionaire—not because he had a specific purpose for that amount of money, but because that number of digits repre-sented the pinnacle of achievement.

Globally, Cristiano Ronaldo served as LeBron's millennial counterpart in the world's most popular sport. Named after Ronald Reagan, Ronaldo rose from humble origins on the Portuguese island of Madeira to be one of the most celebrated and highest-paid footballers of all time. But his ambitions extended far beyond the field. In addition to his lifetime Nike contract, Ron-aldo invested in a Portuguese media company, launched hair transplant clin-ics in Spain, and built his own CR7 brand of hotels, restaurants, and consumer goods. He dismissed critics with characteristic bravado: "Because I am rich, handsome and a great player people are envious of me."

In this posture toward the world, both LeBron and Ronaldo faced the same label often applied to the entire millennial generation: narcissist. The 2013 *Time* cover story on millennials had declared, "The incidence of narcissistic personality disorder is nearly three times as high for people in their 20s as for the generation that's now 65 or older." Critics like Jeffrey Kluger lamented that millennials were displaying narcissism "on a pandemic level," with the selfie becoming the definitive emblem of their self-obsession.

Scientific studies have debunked the idea that millennials are more narcissistic than Gen Xers or boomers, but the frequency of the accusation revealed how deeply this narrative was etched into millennial lore. This was an unfair aspersion: In an age where personhood was reduced to résumés or bank balances, millennials simply adapted to the demands of the era faster than their elders.

Vice made the most of its millennial workforce with what it jokingly called the "22 Rule": "Hire 22-year-olds, pay them $22,000, and work them 22 hours a day." By the 2010s, *Vice* had shed its roots as a debaucherous downtown NYC gossip rag in a bid to become millennials' most trusted source of global news. With Gavin McInnes exiled and the explicit right-wing politics sidelined, cofounder Shane Smith took center stage. Under his leadership, *Vice* reimagined itself as a multimedia platform. Under guidance from filmmaker Spike Jonze, Smith believed that millennials craved a mix of hard news and entertainment. *Vice* crews traveled to global hot spots like Afghanistan, Liberia, and North Korea, producing gonzo-style documentaries that captured attention online and attracted major advertisers like Intel, which invested $25 million in a branded content series.

Yet *Vice* remained a Gen X operation attempting to speak for a millennial audience. By the 2010s, millennials were old enough to tell their own stories—and they no longer gravitated toward the cynical detachment that long defined earlier notions of "cool." As scholar Joel Dinerstein writes in *The Origins of Cool in Postwar America*, the aesthetic disposition "cool" was at first "synonymous with authenticity, independence, integrity, and nonconformity; to be cool meant you carried personal authority through a stylish mask of stoicism." This required wearing a "mask of cool" to project "toughness and self-mastery." Sixties suburban teenagers dulled down coolness into a mere signifier of style or novelty purchased in the marketplace. Yet even in the 1990s, vestiges of the original definition remained: a standoffishness, an oppositional attitude toward conformity, and an aversion to indulging in schmaltzy emotions. Early 2000s downtown artists like Dash Snow and the Strokes felt a need to mask their privilege under layers of performative grime and disaffection.

Millennials, however, forged their own version of cool that was earnest, aspirational, and inclusive. In alignment with poptimism, authenticity no longer required detachment from mainstream norms; it thrived in openness about personal ambition. Odd Future, the rap collective led by Tyler, the Creator, exemplified this shift. From one angle, they were the rightful inheritors of Pharrell and Kanye's omnivore hip-hop, blending rap with skater thrash, smooth soul, and far-out electronic sounds. Growing up near Inglewood, California, Tyler navigated his own liminal racial identity from a young age: He was "too white for the Black kids, too Black for the white kids." He found a clear direction for his musical aspirations in Pharrell's 2006 debut solo album, *In My Mind*—a polarizing record dismissed by Jimmy Iovine as "a complete fucking failure."

Odd Future had avant-garde instincts but also felt the millennial need to go big and had the digital savvy to make it happen. Tyler discovered fellow rapper Earl Sweatshirt, then sixteen, on Myspace, and the group released nine free mixtapes and albums in a single year via Tumblr. While Odd Future quickly won over young music nerds (mostly "skinny white kids"), older critics wrung their hands over their *Vice*-like lyrics: gay slurs, misogyny, fantasies about sexual violence, and shout-outs to Hitler and Terry Richardson. Simultaneously, however, the group embodied the generational pivot toward inclusivity, with members whose identities spanned sexualities and genders. *Pitchfork*'s Briana Younger observed that Odd Future "challenged shallow societal representations of Blackness" while embracing disparate musical styles and identity politics within the same dialogue. Odd Future's most successful alumnus, Frank Ocean, captured this sensibility in his groundbreaking solo career. Ocean's 2016 album, *Blonde*, became one of the decade's most celebrated works, his success underscoring the collective's enduring impact on pop culture.

Yet despite millennials being "the most racially diverse generation in American history," the broader cultural narrative initially positioned white creators as its vanguard. An early architect of millennial cool was Ezra Koenig, who founded Vampire Weekend in 2006 with three fellow Columbia University students. The band rode the poptimist wave to find a sound grounded in genre-blending, polished aesthetics, and impeccable commercial instincts—perhaps the very sound of neoliberalism. "We were all massive Strokes fans," he admitted, but as the rock revival grew stale, Koenig and his friends searched for a "new kind of guitar identity and rhythmic drum identity." Koenig belonged to a post-Neptunes culture, where kids of all backgrounds danced to the same Top 40 hits.

Vampire Weekend eventually settled on an Upper West Side songbook that broke with downtown New York's gritty, detached aesthetic. Lyrically, Vampire Weekend explored class anxiety without touching traditional class politics. Unlike the anti-wealth fury of Pulp's anthem "Common People," Vampire Weekend protagonists seemed to fantasize about rich girlfriends whisking them away to family estates. They reveled in the thrill of privilege: Louis Vuitton, Benetton, Oxford commas, Washington Heights, bleeding madras, and Cape Cod. Rostam Batmanglij's Wes Anderson–esque keyboards created an imagined utopia where "world music" reflected the customs of a singular, fictional nation-state. While artists like Paul McCartney, Paul Simon, and Talking Heads had all faced backlash for previously dabbling in

African music tropes, Vampire Weekend dove in headfirst. Critic Simon Reynolds found "the lack of hesitation with which they go about their borrowing" to be their most fevered transgression.

As a vanguard for millennials, Vampire Weekend pioneered the "mask of no mask." They never pretended to be anything other than Columbia kids. Kris Chen, their A&R rep at XL Recordings, described this transparency as key to their appeal: "They didn't give a shit about being cool. We all know that's the ultimate in *being* cool." The strategy paid off. Their buzz on MP3 blogs secured them a *Spin* cover story before they even released an album. Vampire Weekend's self-titled debut sold half a million copies and received widespread acclaim. Their 2010 follow-up, *Contra*, debuted at number one on the Billboard charts. Honda chose their song "Holiday" for its Christmas campaign, perhaps because it sounded like it had been composed for that very purpose.

Across town, writer-director Lena Dunham emerged as another quintessential millennial creative. The daughter of artists Carroll Dunham and Laurie Simmons, she grew steeped in the privileges of an ultraliberal, affluent milieu. At Saint Ann's, a Brooklyn private school with a creative pedigree, she took an interest in playwriting, which evolved into filmmaking during her years at Oberlin College. There, she began honing her signature oversharing style through short YouTube videos like "The Fountain," where she brushes her teeth and bathes in a campus fountain while wearing a bikini.

At twenty-three, with funding from New York's art-world elite, Dunham made a full-length feature, *Tiny Furniture*. The film, a semi-autobiographical portrait of postgrad drift, won Best Narrative Feature at SXSW, catching the attention of director Judd Apatow, who became her mentor. This led to her breakthrough: *Girls*, which premiered on HBO in April 2012, just a month before the Facebook IPO.

Girls was very much Dunham's creation. She wrote, directed, and starred in the show as Hannah Horvath, an aspiring memoirist who famously declared in the pilot episode that she may not be the voice of her generation, but she was "a voice of . . . a generation." Hannah's circle of friends embodied familiar millennial archetypes: Marnie, the uptight gallery assistant; Jessa, the jet-setting bohemian; and Shoshanna, the bubbly, gossip-obsessed NYU student. Set in Brooklyn's gentrified Greenpoint, the show explored the lives of twentysomethings navigating awkward relationships, vague career paths, and the lingering dependence on parental largesse.

Girls was the first TV show about millennials made by a millennial, yet it leaned heavily on self-deprecation. The humor often stemmed from the characters' insecurities and narcissism. Hannah quickly pivots her conversations into diatribes about her own victimization, while everyone struggles through awkward and porn-influenced sex. The show was one of the first to capture how smartphones were degrading social interactions, satirizing the modern hierarchy of communication: "The lowest, that would be Facebook, followed by GChat, then texting, then email, then phone. Face to face is of course ideal, but it's not of this time."

While *Girls* parodied its subjects, it still faced backlash for its narrow representation of millennial life as overwhelmingly white, privileged, and urban. Besides Dunham, whose family was well connected in the art world, the three main costars were the daughters of playwright David Mamet, news anchor Brian Williams, and Bad Company drummer Simon Kirke. Progressive critics lambasted the show's lack of racial diversity, while conservative pundits viewed Dunham's Oberlin-style identity politics as emblematic of millennial degeneracy.

Despite these critiques, *Girls* crystallized a key element of millennial cool: the shift from Gen X detachment to radical vulnerability. In an article on post-hipster youth, *Vice* identified a subset of millennials it labeled "Earnests," who abandoned irony to pursue "real beauty and experience." Nearly every episode featured Dunham stripping naked—not as titillation, but as the highest expression of confessional honesty.

This aesthetic trickled down to less sophisticated millennials as an unabashed embrace of overwhelming corniness. Good taste, after all, is a mask—and the mask of no mask gave young people permission to jettison traditional constrictions of sophistication. This shift was particularly easy in a poptimist world where their elders rejected any elevations of art over kitsch. Nowhere was this clearer than in *Glee*, Ryan Murphy's wildly popular 2009 comedy-drama about a diverse group of socially awkward teens finding solace and identity in their high school glee club.

Each episode featured auto-tuned, karaoke-style renditions of *Now That's What I Call Music* deep cuts, nostalgic oldies like Journey's "Don't Stop Believin'," and viral hits such as "Gangnam Style." Borrowing its initial energy from millennials' beloved *High School Musical* (2006), *Glee* weaponized its campiness as a political statement. Glee clubs, in Murphy's framing, became a metaphor for all marginalized identities. Teacher Will Schuester earnestly tells his students that they are "all minorities," just by virtue of being in the glee club.

This line didn't age well, particularly in an era of heightened awareness around racial and social equality, but *Glee* undeniably expanded representation on network TV. The show featured romantic subplots for actors with Down syndrome and, as *Slate*'s June Thomas noted, "did more to normalize homosexuality than any other show in TV history, perhaps more than any other mainstream work of art." Where queerness in earlier decades felt transgressive—for example, when Nirvana bandmembers French-kissed each other on *Saturday Night Live*—*Glee* made queerness look ordinary, even square. By 2015, 73 percent of millennials, many of whom had been raised on *Glee*, supported same-sex marriage.

Yet for all its focus on immutable identities like race, gender, and sexual orientation, *Glee* and its millennial viewers showed little interest in class solidarity. As millennials became strivers and hustlers, open aspirations to wealth replaced collective resistance. Wes Anderson's films of this era exemplified the sumptuous allure of privilege, while shows like *Gossip Girl* updated the teen soap opera for the internet age, centering its drama on the lives of Upper East Side prep school elites. Framed around a TMZ-like anonymous blog chronicling their misdeeds, *Gossip Girl* indulged both schadenfreude and aspiration. The show's glamorous portrayal of Manhattan wealth translated globally, inspiring adaptations in China, Mexico, Thailand, and Turkey.

Gossip Girl's politics, wrote *Slate*'s Willa Paskin, were "borderline aristocratic." Lana Cooper in *PopMatters* observed that the show transformed its "Poor Little Rich Kids" into sympathetic figures, "regardless of how many rules they break." In fact, critic David Klion wrote, "Everyone on *Gossip Girl* remains filthy rich and free to do whatever they want. They're all morally exonerated for their most reprehensible actions." Even this, however, felt in keeping with millennial candor. *Gossip Girl*'s tagline—"You know you love me"—was, as Paskin put it, "a neat summation of the series's feelings about the preposterously wealthy."

Millennials' unapologetic fascination with wealth reflected a broader cultural shift. Flaunting money was once seen as gauche, but gaucheness itself was no longer socially disqualifying. In a high-pressure, winner-takes-all economy, the most successful millennials displayed their status by living and dressing like children and by outsourcing adult responsibility to focus entirely on self-optimization. The path to the top of the status ladder required neither rebellion nor tasteful detachment but a relentless and open commitment to refining one's personal brand.

Anna Wintour, *Vogue*'s editor in chief, kept the cover of the April 2014 issue under wraps, lest there be leaks. A decoy image of model Kate Upton hung on the layout board with a cryptic note reading "KW and KK." It was no great mystery: The initials stood for Kanye West and Kim Kardashian, the world's "most talked about" couple. Shot by Annie Leibovitz, the cover featured Kim in a white Lanvin wedding gown and Kanye embracing her from behind in a black Saint Laurent blazer. When the issue dropped, it marked a watershed moment: Kanye became the first rapper and Kim the first reality TV star to appear on the cover of *Vogue*.

Kanye and Kim began dating in April 2012, six months after her widely mocked seventy-two-day marriage to basketball player Kris Humphries. The brevity of that union spawned conspiracy theories that the pairing was a publicity stunt, but no one doubted Kanye's true lust. His interest in Kim had long surfaced in his lyrics, and tabloid rumors swirled that he watched her sex tape before sleeping with other women. Kim was soon pregnant, and the couple welcomed their first child, North West, on June 15, 2013.

Then the relationship got quite serious. In October 2013, he rented San Francisco's AT&T Park, projecting "PLEEEASE MARRY MEEE!!!" on the Jumbotron while an orchestra played Lana Del Rey's "Young and Beautiful." Kim said yes. Naturally, E! cameras captured the proposal for *Keeping Up with the Kardashians*, marking it the second engagement of Kim's to be featured on her reality TV show.

Gossip sites loved to brand celebrity couples with hybrid monikers—"Bennifer" for Ben Affleck and Jennifer Lopez, "Brangelina" for Brad Pitt and Angelina Jolie—and "Kimye" at first seemed like the latest addition. But the union of Kim and Kanye represented something far more significant: a further progression in cultural omnivorism. Over the previous decade, Pharrell Williams and Kanye had worked to collapse boundaries between backpack rap, bling, rock, R&B, pop, hipster folk, electronic, Japanese streetwear, and street art. Kanye, in particular, used his fame to elevate sophisticated tastes, from Takashi Murakami's neo–pop art to LA label Band of Outsiders' neo-preppy aesthetic. By the late Obama era, he had helped forge a new kind of monoculture that erased racial and genre divisions.

Yet two particular domains remained stubbornly distinct: high fashion and reality TV. Despite reality TV's popularity, cultural gatekeepers shunned its stars. Paris Hilton never graced *Vogue*'s cover and often had to crash the front row of fashion shows. Even as *Keeping Up with the Kardashians* became a ratings juggernaut, Kim wasn't considered a credible candidate as a cover model. Her nude appearance on the front of *W* magazine in 2011 was understood as an ironic statement by its artist, Barbara Kruger. Designers dismissed her curves as unflattering to their creations, and her family's ventures into cheap clothing lines further tarnished her reputation among tastemakers. While the commercial logic of merging reality TV and high fashion was undeniable, gatekeepers like Anna Wintour staunchly resisted the idea. Dana Brown at *Vanity Fair* later admitted, "We had an unofficial ban on any Kardashians appearing in the magazine. We took a stand."

With such high barriers, Kanye assumed the role of Trojan horse. His insatiable quest for sophistication became a campaign to win over the cognoscenti. This accelerated after his mother's tragic death in 2007. Channeling his grief, he recorded *808s & Heartbreak*, a minimalist electronic pop album drenched in auto-tuned despair. The album redefined hip-hop as emo, paving the way for a new generation of introspective, singsong rappers like Drake. Kanye's visual transformation accompanied the sonic shift: The jacket photo featured him in a sharp, light gray glen-check suit and crisp white shirt, having shed his signature hoodies and jeans.

Kanye's ambition extended beyond music. He teased his own fashion label, Pastelle, though it never came to fruition, and scored a hit sneaker collaboration with Louis Vuitton. His goal, however, was to gain entry into the world of high fashion. In January 2009, Kanye and his Chicago entourage attended Paris Fashion Week only to be turned away from many collections. Seeking attention, he enlisted street photographer Tommy Ton to shoot his crew outside Comme des Garçons' show. In this now-iconic photo, Kanye is flanked by his entourage, including a young Ghanaian American designer named Virgil Abloh.

Just as Kanye fought for fashion legitimacy, his music career hit an infamous snag. His interruption of Taylor Swift's acceptance speech at the VMAs made him a national pariah. "They say I was the abomination of Obama's nation," he later rapped. A planned joint tour with Lady Gaga was scrapped amid the fallout. Swift, on the other hand, made the most of her victimization, releasing the song "Innocent" on her next album—a pointed yet ostensibly tender response that veteran music journalist Alison Stewart called "a small masterpiece of passive-aggressiveness." The incident gave Swift further fuel for her meteoric rise into pop superstardom.

Following the VMA debacle, Kanye withdrew from the spotlight and started from the bottom in luxury fashion. Alongside Virgil Abloh, he moved to Italy to intern at Fendi, earning just $500 a month performing menial tasks like fetching coffee and making copies. He balanced this humbling stint with crafting a musical comeback. Holed up in a Hawaii studio, Kanye assembled a star-studded roster for his new project, including Jay-Z, Rihanna, Pusha T, and Nicki Minaj, alongside 1990s legends like Q-Tip of A Tribe Called Quest and RZA of the Wu-Tang Clan, and emerging talent like Rick Ross and Justin Vernon of Bon Iver. In August 2010, he began teasing the album by releasing tracks as free downloads each Friday.

The resulting comeback album, *My Beautiful Dark Twisted Fantasy*, was an incontrovertible triumph. Released on November 22, 2010, it debuted at number one on the *Billboard* charts and received universal acclaim, including a perfect 10.0 from *Pitchfork*. Critics hailed it not only as his best work, but as one of the decade's defining albums. *Complex* lauded Nicki Minaj's guest verse on "Monster" as the best rap of 2008–2013. Far from issuing remorseful apologies, Kanye leaned into his villainous image, toasting the world's "douchebags" and "scumbags" with glee. To promote the album, he directed *Runaway*, a thirty-four-minute art film shot in the Czech Republic, replete with ballet dancers and references to Greek mythology.

Once again celebrated as one of the world's great musical geniuses, Kanye shifted his attention back to French high culture, forging connections with influential figures like Sarah Andelman from the iconic boutique Colette. He collaborated with French casual brand A.P.C. on a capsule collection. When Kanye began dating Kim, he took on her public image as a personal project. Working closely with his stylist, he revamped Kim's wardrobe, aligning it with Parisian fashion trends from Givenchy, Balmain, Balenciaga, and Margiela. She was an eager participant. Reflecting on her pre-Kanye style, Kim confessed to CNN, "Back in the day, I thought I had the best style. I look back at outfits and I'm, like, mortified." By 2013, Kanye brought Kim to the Met Gala for the first time. Pregnant with their first child, Kim attended but felt deeply out of place. Later, she confessed to breaking down in tears: "I didn't know anyone & I'm sure no one wanted me there lol."

In June 2013, Kanye released *Yeezus*, a harsh, avant-garde album that pushed his experimental inclinations even further. The album earned critical acclaim, with Velvet Underground icon Lou Reed praising it shortly before his death: "The guy really, really, *really* is talented. He's really trying to raise the bar. No one's near doing what he's doing, it's not even on the same planet." The record's closing track, "Bound 2," stood out for its stripped-down use of a 1971 soul sample with no additional beats. The song's music video, in which a bleached-blond and nude Kim straddles Kanye on a stationary motorcycle, reached instant infamy. Actors James Franco and Seth Rogen parodied it shot for shot, with a topless Rogen taking on Kim's role.

By this point, Kanye had done the most to integrate high fashion and contemporary art into hip-hop. Perhaps feeling pressure to keep up, Jay-Z made his own attempt to go avant-garde. He performed a new track, "Picasso Baby," for six straight hours in a New York gallery as part of a Marina Abramović–inspired piece. Despite notable attendees like Rosie Perez, Adam Driver, Judd Apatow, and Glenn O'Brien, the effort fell flat. Critics derided it as "cultural cringe," a transparent bid for highbrow legitimacy. Even Abramović was displeased, alleging that Jay-Z failed to deliver promised support for her institute. (She later retracted her comments, apologizing for the misunderstanding.)

With Kanye's cultural dominance, Kim's newfound status as a high-fashion icon, and an upcoming wedding, Anna Wintour decided the time was right for a *Vogue* profile. Yet the resulting Kimye cover still unleashed a wave of backlash. Within minutes of its release, #BoycottVogue trended on Twitter. *Deadline*'s Nikki Finke suggested the issue should include an airsickness bag, and *Buffy the Vampire Slayer* actress Sarah Michelle Gellar announced she was canceling her subscription.

In the aftermath, Wintour quipped, "I think if we just remain deeply tasteful and just put deeply tasteful people on the cover, it would be a rather boring magazine!" Her comment implicitly labeled Kim and Kanye as distasteful, but it also conceded that taste had become an impediment to profit. This statement alone marked a turning point for the Condé Nast empire and signaled the twilight of cultural capital as an exclusionary concept.

In the twentieth century, magazines such as *Vogue*, *GQ*, and *The New Yorker* set the standards of sophistication for elite society, and that meant that editors dictated what the public wanted rather than responding to its existing desires. *Vanity Fair*'s Dana Brown described these celebrity editors of the 1990s as "the arbiters of taste, the translators of culture and style to the culture-and-style-hungry masses. They decided what was cool, what was important, what was necessary, what made it onto their pages, what people would be talking about, watching, reading, wearing, *thinking.*" While *Vanity Fair* focused on the "New Establishment" of Hollywood stars and media moguls, journalist Amy Larocca noted that *Vogue* historically centered more on "social class than [on] celebrity."

But now the magazine needed to embrace elements of "distasteful" pop culture to maintain its influence. Even *Vogue* could no longer deny the internet logic that hate clicks were as valuable as love clicks. As with Wintour's endorsement of reality TV, there was no longer a meaningful line between good and bad taste. The palace walls had crumbled: High fashion, hip-hop, and reality TV now occupied the same cultural milieu. Wintour's capitulation signaled yet another victory for poptimism. Journalist Amy Larocca dismissed criticisms of the Kimye cover as "puritanical self-righteousness" and "hypocrisy on a colossal scale," and few bothered to mount a defense for the opposite view.

Critic Allison P. Davis suggested that Kanye wasn't solely responsible for Kim's elevation to *Vogue*'s cover: "Culture was shifting in a way that likely made Kim's celebrity status inevitable." Still, Kanye's recognition in elite circles as a creative visionary and alignment with traditional gatekeepers provided more credibility to elevate Kim into those spaces. Later in 2014, *Paper* magazine further escalated Kim's cultural dominance with its infamous cover of her greased bare buttocks that "broke the internet." In the aftermath of the *Vogue* cover, critics began reevaluating the entire Kardashian phenomenon. Kim was no longer merely a bottom-feeding reality TV star or a tabloid fixture but increasingly seen as "self-created, self-aware, and sincere," as Jerry Saltz observed.

This reappraisal reached its zenith in April 2015 with the publication of *Selfish*, a 448-page Rizzoli collection of Kim's selfies. This made her, critics argued, akin to an artist. *Slate*'s Laura Bennett called the book "riveting," describing Kim as "someone who has spent her life devising elaborate ways to get herself seen." *The Atlantic*'s Megan Garber took it further, proclaiming that Kim had invented, "in her way, a new strain of capitalism. Its currency is the selfie. . . . There is, say what else you will about it, something admirable, and refreshing, in that."

Après Kimye, le déluge. Kim's mother, Kris Jenner, attended the Met Gala in 2015 as a guest in her own right. Kim's half sister Kendall Jenner became the highest-paid model in the world, walking for the top French brands. Kanye launched his Yeezy fashion line with Adidas, eventually creating a multibillion-dollar sneaker empire. The debut of his clothing collection may have received tepid reviews, but his second show at Madison Square Garden drew significant attention. Anna Wintour sat in the front row, flanked by Kim and Kimye's daughter, North. Wintour snuck out after forty-five minutes and broke down in tears after getting lost in the stadium basement.

BLURRED TIMELINES

Mining the Past for Grooves, Styles, and Marketing Hooks

Before Alan Thicke played the father on the 1980s sitcom *Growing Pains*, he composed the theme songs for beloved NBC comedies *Diff'rent Strokes* and *The Facts of Life* with his wife Gloria Loring. Their son Robin Thicke was born in 1977, and while he dabbled as a child actor, his true dream was to become a musician. By sixteen, Robin had impressed Jimmy Iovine, who had him write for other artists. When he finally released his own solo album, it flopped. So Iovine introduced him to Pharrell Williams, who signed him to Star Trak Entertainment and set him up with better material. Thicke found success with his 2006 single "Lost Without U," which topped the R&B charts for many weeks and landed him an opening spot on Beyoncé's tour.

In July 2012, Thicke and Pharrell met up again to brainstorm new songs. Thicke mentioned his admiration for Marvin Gaye's "Got to Give It Up," and Pharrell riffed on a cowbell-heavy groove inspired by the track. The result was a song called "Blurred Lines." At least, that was the official story. Later, Thicke admitted he'd been bingeing on Vicodin and alcohol at the time, and Pharrell had effectively written everything.

Whatever the actual creative process, "Blurred Lines" sold over ten million copies and became 2013's song of the summer. Its music video, an homage to Terry Richardson, launched twenty-two-year-old model Emily Ratajkowski to superstardom. The team capitalized on the track's risqué lyrical content, first releasing a video featuring the models in skimpy outfits, followed by an "unrated" version with the same models topless and in nude-tone thongs. (In her memoir, *My Body*, Ratajkowski later alleged that Thicke groped her on set.) Meanwhile, Jimmy Iovine added his signature touch: a third version of the video marketing his Beats Pill wireless speaker.

"Blurred Lines" attracted an initial wave of controversy for its "rapey" no-means-yes lyrics. Thicke's early attempts to deflect blame—pinning the video on its female director—only made things worse. Then came the legal battles. Marvin Gaye's estate accused the song of copying "a constellation of distinctive and significant compositional elements" from "Got to Give It Up." Pharrell, Thicke, and guest rapper T.I. denied wrongdoing, filing a preemptive lawsuit to protect their right to draw upon past influences. But the Gaye family countersued, and the case went to trial. The jury unanimously ruled against Thicke and Pharrell. Going forward, 50 percent of the song's royalties would go to Gaye's family.

Homage, pastiche, inspiration, and borrowing have always been at the core of creativity. The future of culture always builds upon the past: Fashion trends cycle through revived looks, films glamorize bygone eras, and cover songs launch new careers. As music critic Agnès Gayraud writes, "Recorded popular music borrows from all musics: it is a tissue of hybridisations and appropriations." Hip-hop itself was born from rapping over looped samples of older records. Yet borrowing exists on a spectrum—from inspiration to outright plagiarism. Whether or not "Blurred Lines" violated copyright law, the song unequivocally captured the essence of Gaye's "Got to Give It Up." And in its massive popularity, "Blurred Lines" heralded a shift in pop music in which the direct quotation of past genres felt distinctly contemporary. The song was not beloved as kitschy retro or as tongue-in-cheek parody. For listeners in 2013, it *was* 2013—in mirroring a song from thirty-six years earlier.

"Blurred Lines" wasn't an anomaly. Similar 1970s musical conventions appeared in Bruno Mars's colossal 2014 hit, "Uptown Funk," which faced its own accusations of plagiarism. The Gap Band's "Oops Upside Your Head" from 1979 later claimed 17 percent of royalties, while Collage's 1983 track "Young Girls" prompted a lawsuit that was quietly settled.

This surge in retro sounds fueled the earliest complaints that the twenty-first century lacked the creative momentum of the previous one. Artists seemed more energized by mining the past than inventing the future. In 2010, music critic Simon Reynolds labeled this phenomenon *retromania*: "The sensation of moving forward grew fainter as the [aughts] unfurled. Time itself seemed to become sluggish, like a river that starts to meander and form oxbow lakes. If the pulse of NOW felt weaker with each passing year, that's because in the 2000s the pop present became ever more crowded out by the past, whether in the form of archived memories of yesteryear or retro-rock leeching off ancient styles." As the 2010s progressed, this stagnation deepened. Nothing sounded especially groundbreaking or urgent. Genre blending gave hip-hop a burst of innovation in the early 2000s, but a decade later, many mainstream songs continued to pull from an industry template: Swedish pop production, alt-rock melodies, and seventies grooves.

Whether or not there had been innovation out there somewhere, Reynolds was correct that culture no longer progressed through clear successions of styles. A key issue was that there hadn't been a true paradigm shift since the sixties. The term *paradigm*, despite rampant overuse in marketing copy and mocked as meaningless jargon by *The Simpsons*, describes a specific phenomenon in social science: the macro-values that set the logic of our choices and aesthetics. When a new paradigm emerges, the previous established styles lose all their value. Before World War II, America was in a jazz paradigm. The rise of Elvis and the Beatles in the 1950s and 1960s didn't just introduce new tastes; it rendered decades of jazz passé among teens. In "When I'm Sixty-Four," Paul McCartney only nodded to music hall traditions as a nostalgic joke.

In the twenty-first century, cultural tastes stayed remarkably close to the post-Elvis paradigm, in which decades-old music still felt vibrant and contemporary. When Pharrell and Thicke played in the artistic conventions of Marvin Gaye's song, it wasn't ironic—it was the defining groove of the year.

In perhaps the primary example of the stagnancy, the Beatles never faded at all: Their 2000 greatest hits album *1* sold over eleven million copies, making it the bestselling album of the decade. In 2006, Cirque du Soleil launched *Love*, a mash-up extravaganza of Beatles songs that ran for eighteen years. This endurance suggested a winning formula in the 1960s cultural paradigm—transgression, hedonism, and light experimentation—that could be endlessly adapted. Only the drugs and beats changed. But the new part was that, over time, the canon simply expanded, with very little falling out of favor.

By the Obama years, the internet was ubiquitous enough to be a prime suspect in causing cultural stagnation. Simon Reynolds noted, "There has never before been a society that is *able* to access the immediate past so easily and so copiously." Yet the impulse to archive predated the internet. Cable television in the 1980s relied on reruns and documentaries to fill programming gaps; Nickelodeon, short on new kids' content, aired decades-old shows like *The Monkees* and *The Donna Reed Show*. VCRs and DVDs allowed movie buffs to build personal film libraries. The internet only amplified this archivist mentality. Photo books were scanned to become indexed JPEGs in Google Images. YouTube became a trove of obscure music videos, interviews, and commercials. Spotify didn't just make old music available—it treated every era equally, organizing albums from the 1960s alongside the latest releases. By the mid-2010s, old music began to outsell new music.

But ease of access alone doesn't explain the deeper reverence for the past. Retromania depends on older works feeling more valuable than contemporary ones. Baby boomer nostalgia played some role, flooding the market in the late 1980s and early 1990s with revivalist content like the *Freedom Rock* compilation and shows like *The Wonder Years*. Yet the longing for twentieth-century authenticity seemed especially acute in a plastic, poptimist era. Where cool detachment remained aspirational, younger generations gazed back at the archetypes of rebellion: James Dean's brooding defiance, the sixties counterculture, punk's anarchic chaos, and the swagger of eighties hip-hop.

Postmodernist theory had long predicted a heightened interest in retro. The past, flattened into yet another aesthetic ingredient, became an accessory for the present. Omnivore tastes, in embracing everything—mainstream, niche, exotic, and familiar—extended this inclusivity to long-dismissed genres of yore. Seventies rock fans had once derided disco; by the twenty-first century, those critiques were reexamined as racist and homophobic, prompting a collective reassessment of thousands of songs. But there were opportunity costs for these revaluations. As Reynolds observed, "Nothing seems to wither and die. This hampers the emergence of new things."

Meanwhile, risk aversion in the cultural industries further entrenched the past. Nostalgia had always been a useful marketing tool, but in the twenty-first century, it became a cornerstone of the industry's low-risk financial strategy. Film studios leaned on sequels and reboots, while consumer brands mined our childhood memories for anything that could break through the noise. Volkswagen won accolades in 2011 for a TV commercial in which a child dressed in a Darth Vader costume fails to "Force push" objects around the home until getting a response from the family Passat. In preparing to sell Lucasfilm to Disney in 2012, George Lucas wanted to create maximal value for his IP, so he licensed the *Star Wars* franchise to everything possible, from themed merchandise across every category to Brisk iced tea ads. After Disney's $4.05 billion purchase of Lucasfilm, the company announced a new trilogy, plus spin-off films and TV series, ensuring *Star Wars* remained omnipresent throughout the decade. Billions of dollars poured into sustaining the *Star Wars* universe, reducing Disney's reliance on the creation of new IP.

As the 2010s continued, artists kept proving Simon Reynolds correct in their fixation on the past. In 2001, the French house group Daft Punk released their landmark album, *Discovery*, layering vocoders, arpeggiating analog synthesizers, and digitally degraded seventies samples into a unique and futuristic sound. But by 2013, the duo could only look backward. Their final album, *Random Access Memories*, meticulously re-created the lush, live-instrument disco of their childhoods. *Pitchfork* initially awarded the album an 8.8, only to later revise the score to 6.8, arguing that it failed to "push pop music forward."

Yet the album propelled Pharrell forward at a time when his cultural influence had waned. His collaboration on Daft Punk's breakout hit, "Get Lucky," became a global sensation, reigniting his relevance and landing him a new solo deal. Soon after, he contributed a neo-soul track to the *Despicable Me 2* soundtrack. The result, "Happy," became the bestselling song of 2014. Built on gospel-inflected choruses and retro grooves, it was engineered for universal appeal. Music scholar Andrew Fisher observed: "Classic soul and R&B instruments like an electric piano, guitar and riffs [combine with] modern and slick production values to give it a timeless classic feel that has a contemporary edge." The song's twenty-four-hour music video sparked a worldwide phenomenon, inspiring fans everywhere to film themselves dancing and singing along.

While retromania infected mainstream music, the clearest source of artistic innovation yet again emerged from the Black underground. In Atlanta, a nascent hip-hop subgenre called trap rejected seventies' grooves of the past for a minimalist sound. Defined by the *tik-tik-tik* of drum machine hi-hats, crunching snares, and chest-thumping 808 kick drums, trap music was the sound of the city: the streets, the drug-production factories, and the strip clubs. The genre's leading voices—including Gucci Mane and T.I.—had come up in Atlanta's drug trade. Some saw rap as the next step in their financial strategies rather than as an artistic calling. Producers helped a lot: When a rapper like Lil Baby had trouble finding his voice in the recording booth, they would coax him to mumble short phrases, which they chopped and looped into hypnotic vocal hooks.

The Atlanta trio Migos became synonymous with trap's ascent, popularizing the triplet flow, a rapid-fire delivery that quickly made older "boom bap" styles of hip-hop sound outdated. In rap, the paradigm most certainly shifted. Trap was hardly obsessed with compositional experimentation (the labels culled backtracks from an endless number of anonymous grunts who pumped out commodity beats), but its immediacy made it feel more authentic than rival sounds. Sharing a spirit with punk rock, songs were often created in twenty minutes. "If they really take their time on it," Migos's DJ Durel said, "they'll take forty or forty-five minutes" on a track.

Trap's dominance in hip-hop provided a sharp counterpoint to retromania. By rejecting the grooves of the sixties and seventies, trap reasserted a futurist aesthetic, suggesting that audiences could not subsist on nostalgia alone.

———

In the second episode of AMC's *Mad Men*, set in the advertising industry during the early 1960s, the young Sally Draper rushes into the living room with a plastic dry-cleaning bag over her head. Her friend explains, "We're playing spaceman!" Her mother, Betty, scolds her daughter: "If the clothes from that dry cleaning bag are on the floor of my closet, you're going to be a very sorry young lady." Early episodes of *Mad Men* leaned heavily on such historical irony, offering viewers the warm satisfaction of social progress. Civilization now rejected misogyny, racism, and child asphyxiation. Our twenty-first-century economy hummed along toward maximum efficiency by abandoning the three-martini lunch and rescuing women from the prison of secretarial roles.

On the surface, *Mad Men* served as a cautionary tale about badly behaving men, but its allure lay in its aesthetic glamour—particularly in the wardrobes. The men's slim suits, pocket squares, and pomade-slicked hair stood in stark contrast to the schlubbiness of modern men's styles. The counterculture's war on formal dressing had triumphed by the 1990s, leaving men in the sartorial wasteland of Dockers and golf shirts. As Silicon Valley and the creative industries rose in prominence, companies abandoned dress codes to attract freewheeling innovators whose ideation needed the full comfort of hoodies and sneakers. For most Americans outside of investment banking, the era of business casual reigned: soft button-down shirts tucked into khakis with sneakers or loafers.

While European men maintained their reputation for sartorial dignity, dressing well in the US became coded as gay. Designer fashion, in particular, was viewed as a female and queer domain. In the pilot of *Glee*, when football players threaten to toss gay countertenor Kurt Hummel into a dumpster, he pleads, "This is Marc Jacobs' new collection!" The 2003 hit reality show *Queer Eye for the Straight Guy* leaned into the idea that improving a heterosexual man's style was a Herculean task requiring divine intervention. This aversion to fashion was reinforced by the realities of the American physique: Hedi Slimane ultra-skinny Dior Homme suits of the early aughts were hardly designed for men raised on a diet of corn syrup.

Then *Mad Men* arrived, making body-conscious formalwear accessible and, crucially, straight. A well-tailored charcoal suit became a symbol of masculine power—armor for negotiating, drinking, and seduction. As *British GQ* wrote in 2022, "No TV show has had as much impact on men's style as *Mad Men*." The show introduced everyday men to "too-tailored suits, pocket squares, monk-strap shoes, whisky rocks, tie bars and high and tight haircuts." Simultaneously, menswear blogs emerged, reviving long-forgotten knowledge of these items. The *Mad Men* aesthetic dovetailed with the rise of American Thom Browne, whose boxy gray wool suits with cropped jackets and high-cuffed trousers—paired with chunky wing tips and no socks—modernized the classic American look. Over the next decade, he would outfit stars from Hollywood and K-pop to LeBron James.

While retailers had long anchored their businesses around women's seemingly insatiable interest in fashion, the early 2010s saw a surprising surge in menswear sales, even without a formal return to uniforms or dress codes. Dressing up remained voluntary, which gave clothing new significance as a marker of sophistication. In the aughts, European fast-fashion brands like H&M, Zara, and Topshop had served as gateways for middle-class youth to experiment with style. Now many of those same shoppers aspired to the real deal, seeking out higher-end options.

This shift came after the collapse of spending on physical media. In the nineties, men often built their identities around collections of albums, CDs,

DVDs, and film or TV preferences, with logo T-shirts serving as shorthand for cultural affiliations. But as streaming rendered those markers invisible, fashion filled the void, as you can't download a blazer. In a digital era, tangible goods like clothing became even more valuable, crossing gender lines to occupy a bigger role in the zeitgeist.

Fashion has traditionally drawn its social power from exclusion, which might seem at odds with the twenty-first century's poptimist, omnivorous ethos. Yet the internet gave fashion a democratic rebrand, leveraging its vast accessibility to liberate style knowledge from elite circles. Photographer Scott Schuman became a star for his blog and book series *The Sartorialist*, capturing images of stylish "real people" that felt egalitarian (though many subjects were industry insiders). His blog later became a series of bestselling coffee-table books. Similarly, Bryan Grey Yambao rose to global fame for his blog, *Bryanboy*, where his unfiltered takes on fashion resonated with readers. From his bedroom in the Philippines, Bryanboy became the country's most famous export after boxer Manny Pacquiao.

Luxury brands quickly noticed how bloggers could translate niche designer goods into the vernacular of everyday consumers. Marc Jacobs was among the earliest advocates of this new class of influencers. After Bryanboy praised a green ostrich bag from Jacobs's collection, the designer renamed it "BB" and invited Bryanboy to sit in the front row at his shows. In 2009, Bryanboy's seat at Dolce & Gabbana—between representatives from *Vanity Fair* and *Vogue*—symbolized the shifting power dynamics within fashion media.

Even more emblematic of this change was thirteen-year-old Tavi Gevinson, whose blog, *Style Rookie*, turned a middle schooler from suburban Illinois into a bona fide star of the fashion world. Publicist Kelly Cutrone summed up this shift to *The New York Times*: "Do I . . . now have to have my eye on some kid who's writing a blog in Oklahoma as much as I do on an editor from *Vogue*? Absolutely." Within a year, professional fashion editors were complaining about Gevinson's giant bow blocking a clear view of the runway.

While blogging sprinkled techno-optimist magic on fashion—Dolce & Gabbana famously provided loaner laptops to bloggers at their shows—the rising interest in style also seemed to reflect a yearning for formality and flair in a hyper-rationalized world. Designer fashion offered an accessible way to inject individuality into regimented lifestyles and a means to flaunt newfound status in an era of growing wealth.

The new obsession with high fashion found its fullest expression in hip-hop. Migos's 2013 track "Versace" name-dropped the brand over 160 times and signaled the genre's full embrace of Euro-luxe. The group's *Culture II* album featured a collaboration with Bloomingdale's. In the early 2000s, younger rappers followed the trail blazed by Kanye and Pharrell into international streetwear. Odd Future's first mixtape referenced Supreme, Stüssy, A Bathing Ape, and G-Shock watches, reflecting Tyler, the Creator's time spent lurking in online streetwear forums.

Kanye's forays into Parisian fashion cemented his role as hip-hop's style innovator. He attended *The Sartorialist*'s 2012 menswear lunch in Florence, Italy, rubbing shoulders with industry insiders and declaring his intention to "invent a camera where the flash comes at the subject from the side, somehow." His relentless passion gave younger rappers permission to push boundaries. Atlanta's Young Thug became an icon for his avant-garde wardrobe, revealing, "Ninety percent of my clothes are women's," because "women's clothes are [slimmer] than men's clothes." Meanwhile, A$AP Rocky partnered with designer Jeremy Scott in the early 2010s, a realization of his teenage dreams: "We used to save up money to buy his collections."

While hip-hop style thrived on eclectic mash-ups of luxury and streetwear, a different philosophy was brewing in post-hipster circles. In 2013, millennial trend consultancy K-Hole published a pdf called *Youth Mode: A Report on Freedom*, proposing "normcore" as a rejection of omnivore tastes and fashion status wars. The concept was initially abstract, advocating a principled refusal to reveal personal preferences through apparel. But an article in *The Cut* soon associated normcore with a specific aesthetic: "Mall clothes. Blank clothes. The kind of dad-brand non-style you might have once associated with Jerry Seinfeld." The look included gray sweatshirts, Patagonia fleeces, and the full "Steve Jobs": mock turtlenecks, stonewashed jeans, and New Balance sneakers.

Normcore embodied the logical progression of fashion democratization. As blogs and e-commerce made designer goods widely accessible, the ultimate countersignal was to dress as if clothing didn't matter. However, this approach had its limits: As fashion journalist Lauren Sherman noted, normcore made women look less "hip or chic" and more like "a mom." And despite its aspirations toward futurism, normcore was another iteration of retromania. As writer Fiona Duncan pointed out, "The contemporary normcore styles I've seen have their clear aesthetic precedent in the nineties." Unlike other decades, however, 1990s athletic fashion never devolved into kitschy nostalgia. Its drabness ensured that even its revival felt deliberately understated.

By the mid-2010s, fashion had returned to the center of culture. Bloggers had democratized access to sartorial knowledge, rappers delved deep into the worlds of luxury and streetwear, and high-end brands reaped the renewed rewards of this renewed interest. By early 2015, the stock price of luxury conglomerate LVMH more than tripled from its Great Recession low.

―――――――

"There's no way, I don't think," Long Island Republican representative Peter King groused, "any of us can excuse what the president did yesterday." King was outraged because Obama had delivered a speech on the rise of ISIS in Syria—while wearing a tan suit. For liberals, the Obama era began with high hopes of sweeping change and ended with eight years of conservative obstruction and faux scandals about sartorial choices.

Yet, outside the gridlock of formal politics, the overall culture seemed to shift decisively toward cosmopolitan values. Obama's presidency repaired America's global image: In 2016, confidence in the US president "to do the right thing" surged to 86 percent in Germany and 84 percent in France.

Domestically, the Obama years saw dramatic progress in racial and sexual inclusion. In 2011, a majority of Americans supported legal same-sex unions, culminating in the Supreme Court's landmark 2015 ruling in *Obergefell v. Hodges* that enshrined marriage equality. Transgender visibility also increased, with Caitlyn Jenner's public transition receiving widespread support. In 2015, Jenner followed Kimye's *Vogue* cover by appearing on the cover of *Vanity Fair*. By 2016, one third of Americans identified as "socially liberal," the highest percentage ever recorded, while the political power of the religious right waned alongside rising secularization.

The defining cultural moment of Obama's presidency arrived in its final years. On August 6, 2015, *Hamilton* officially premiered on Broadway: Lin-Manuel Miranda's hip-hop-infused retelling of Alexander Hamilton's life with actors of color. "In order to dislike it," wrote *New York* magazine about the preview, "you'd pretty much have to dislike the American experiment." The show's runaway success—with tickets commanding astronomical sums—suggested a nation fully embracing a multicultural, inclusive narrative of its history. Hillary Clinton, securing the Democratic nomination in 2016, mentioned *Hamilton* twice in her acceptance speech.

Obama frequently referenced Martin Luther King Jr.'s quote (of nineteenth-century clergyman Theodore Parker's phrase), "The arc of the moral universe is long, but it bends toward justice." While much cultural progress of the Obama years seemed to affirm that sentiment, the murders of unarmed Black men underscored the limits to progress. George Zimmerman shot seventeen-year-old Trayvon Martin and was acquitted. Two years later, a Ferguson, Missouri, policeman shot Michael Brown six times, igniting protests and a national reckoning on systemic racism. "In America," wrote Ta-Nehisi Coates in his 2015 bestseller, *Between the World and Me*, "it is traditional to destroy the black body—*it is heritage*." Faith in a post-racial America was cracking.

Despite such rising tensions, liberals in 2016 remained confident that the country was trending toward a "permanent Democratic majority"—especially as the ascendant upper-middle class embraced the optimistic, pro-business outlook that had once fueled Republican victories. The booming tech industry also seemed firmly in their corner. Throughout 2016, Clinton held steady leads in the polls, and there appeared to be no widely accepted ideological challenge to a multicultural America. Conservatives were uncool, backward, and strange. With pop culture grounded in ideas of maximal inclusivity, how could a provincial-minded political coalition ever expect to win again?

Part Three

2016–2019

REVANCHISM AND RESISTANCE
Counter-Countercultural Weirdos Take Power but Not Culture

"Donald Trump is here tonight," President Barack Obama announced at the 2011 White House Correspondents' Dinner, as part of his annual comedic monologue. "Now, I know that he's taken some flak lately, but no one is happier, no one is prouder, to put this birth certificate matter to rest than the Donald." Riding high on ten seasons of *The Apprentice* and *The Celebrity Apprentice*, Trump had recently become a fixture on the talk-show circuit, pushing the baseless conspiracy theory that Obama's long-form birth certificate would reveal his true origins in Kenya, not Hawaii. For months, Obama had refused to dignify the accusations with an official response. But three days before the dinner, his staff finally released the full document, and Obama arrived at the event ready to strike back.

Trump, he quipped, could "finally get back to focusing on the issues that matter, like, did we fake the moon landing? What really happened in Roswell? And where are Biggie and Tupac?" The audience erupted in laughter.

Obama was not done. "All kidding aside, obviously we all know about your credentials and breadth of experience." More laughter. "Seriously, just recently, in an episode of *Celebrity Apprentice*, at the steakhouse, the men's cooking team did not impress the judges from Omaha Steaks. And there was a lot of blame to go around. But you, Mr. Trump, recognized that the real problem was a lack of leadership, and so ultimately you didn't blame Lil Jon or Meat Loaf. . . . You fired Gary Busey. And these are the kind of decisions that would keep me up at night."

The room roared with applause. *The New Yorker's* Adam Gopnik, who was in the audience, noted that Trump's "humiliation was as absolute, and as visible, as any I have ever seen: his head set in place, like a man in a pillory, he barely moved or altered his expression as wave after wave of laughter struck him."

Many pundits have pinpointed this moment as the spark that ignited Trump's 2016 presidential run—a campaign fueled by the narcissistic need for revenge. The theory doesn't quite align with the timeline; Trump had floated presidential ambitions as early as 1987 and even formed an exploratory committee for a Reform Party bid in 2000. But the laughter of Washington insiders that night likely added fuel to Trump's long-standing desire to assert his dominance.

This was far from Trump's first skirmish in his long struggle for elite esteem. For decades, New Yorkers had dismissed him as a gaudy arriviste from Queens with over-the-top real estate projects, failed casinos, and a tabloid-optimized love life. No matter how much money he made or how many Manhattan properties he developed, he never earned the respect of high society. As *Spy* magazine famously dubbed him, he was the "short-fingered vulgarian."

Like Paris Hilton's great-grandfather Conrad Hilton, Trump found refuge from elitist derision in mass-market entertainment. He became a pop culture fixture through his bestselling book, *Trump: The Art of the Deal*, a Trump-branded board game that languished in attics across the country, and cameos in *Home Alone 2*, *Zoolander*, and *The Fresh Prince of Bel-Air*. His last name, conveniently a homonym for a winning move in card games, became a shorthand for the excesses of capitalism's hollow promises. Hip-hop lyrics frequently referenced him as a rich guy stock character. (In 2010's "So Appalled," Kanye West rapped, "Balding Donald Trump taking dollars from y'all.")

Less visible to the public was the extent to which Trump's wealth was mostly illusory. He had perfected a version of "fake it till you make it" that conveniently skipped the "making it" part. Despite six bankruptcies, Trump maintained the facade of an affluent mogul living a life of extreme luxury. He demonstrated that debt could be a tool, not a trap, as long as another spate of financial institutions could be persuaded that they wouldn't be fleeced like the last ones. This precarious approach to wealth building made him a national punch line. In a 2000 episode of *The Simpsons* that fantasized about the future, a single offhand mention of a "President Trump" was enough to signal America's descent into dystopian absurdity.

But *The Apprentice* gave Trump an image makeover, introducing him to middle Americans as a bona fide business genius. Creator Mark Burnett meticulously crafted this narrative, driven both by the show's storylines and his personal belief that Trump was "a real American maverick tycoon" in the mold of the industrial titans who built the West. This fabricated persona gave Trump the platform he needed to step directly into politics. His choice of birtherism as his central issue was revealing. While most mainstream Republicans focused their criticisms of Obama on policy, Trump dove straight into racial politics, questioning Obama's legitimacy as an American and, by extension, as president. The message resonated: Soon, half of Republicans believed this baseless conspiracy. Trump's brazen attacks made him a star on Twitter and a folk hero to the right-wing base. By 2012, his influence was so significant that Republican nominee Mitt Romney felt the need to meet him at Trump Tower, though his team draped the setting in solid blue curtains to avoid photos showing the gaudy gold décor resembling "a burlesque house or one of Saddam's palaces."

For many liberals, the 2011 White House Correspondents' Dinner marked the exact moment of Trump's definitive comeuppance. Obama, embodying poise after years of enduring vile personal attacks, reduced Trump to a reality TV caricature, dismissing him as more Meat Loaf than Madison. Few in attendance knew that a day before, Obama had greenlit Operation Neptune Spear, the raid on Osama bin Laden's compound in Pakistan. That week, the president had seemingly vanquished both a global enemy and his most obnoxious domestic detractor. Obama's reelection in 2012 only reinforced the sense that decency and progress would prevail. He left office in 2016 with an approval rating over 50 percent; Hillary Clinton, his handpicked successor, appeared poised to carry the torch.

Nevertheless, Trump persisted. On June 16, 2015, he 'descended the gilded elevator at Trump Tower to announce his candidacy for the Republican nomination. His speech carried the incendiary line: "When Mexico sends its people, they're not sending their best. . . . They're bringing drugs. They're bringing crime. They're rapists." From that moment onward, Trump became the central figure in American politics, which dragged global culture into his chaotic orbit.

At first, Trump's campaign seemed like a surreal postmodernist prank, and cable news indulged him for ratings. His candidacy appeared doomed after he criticized the Iraq War, belittled John McCain's military service, and openly insulted establishment Republicans. When he somehow won the Republican primary, many assumed he'd falter once his scandals caught up with him. The leaked *Access Hollywood* tape, in which he bragged about groping women because "when you're a star, they let you do it," seemed like the final nail in his coffin. This already came upon hideously cruel moments, such as mocking a disabled reporter, attacks on Gold Star parents of a fallen soldier, and his open embrace of fringe conspiracy theories. Steamrolling over ethics and morals worked well for Girls Gone Wild and Kim Kardashian, but national politics surely required upholding the fundamental norms of American society. Clinton's consistent lead in the polls throughout 2016 suggested as such.

Trump won the election. Not even Lena Dunham's pro-Hillary rap video as "MC Pantsuit" for Funny or Die could convince America to elect its first female president.

Trump's victory was a "political 9/11"—an unforeseen event that challenged the collective understanding of American society and culture. Millions of Americans, including large swaths of "moral majority" fundamentalist Christians, voted for a candidate who openly defied traditional moral codes. American pop culture had grown increasingly indecent and vulgar in recent years, and it was perhaps a strategic miscalculation for Clinton to campaign against Trump on grounds of decorum. While there were loud fringe elements in the Tea Party wing of the Republican party—the kind of people who "called [Obama] a socialist, a radical, and a Muslim, but the word that got to the main point started with n"—there was an assumption that bigots alone couldn't elect a president. The expectation was that Trump would lose, start a TV network, and then the "fever" within the Republican Party would break. Even Trump seemed convinced of his inevitable defeat; he refused to dismantle the *Apprentice* set at Trump Tower.

Instead, millions of Americans said yes, *that* reality TV star should be our leader, commander in chief, and national symbol.

As in the aftermath of the 2008 financial crisis, the mass media turned inward to ask why they had so profoundly misunderstood the situation. Accusations that Russia had interfered in the election immediately took center stage, casting a shadow over Trump's presidency. But the more mundane reasons for his victory soon emerged: Moderate voters despised Clinton, viewing her as emblematic of a detached political elite, while Trump, the face of *The Apprentice*, appeared to them as a "jobs guy." White animosity toward demographic change played a significant role, though commentators hesitated to directly attribute the outcome to racism. Instead, journalists leaned on the euphemism of "economic anxiety." This birthed a new media cliché in which coastal reporters journeyed deep into flyover country to interview diner patrons.

The election exposed how pop culture and politics had cleaved into two separate spheres. Liberals viewed their cultural dominance as meritocratic, a natural result of education and sophistication. Conservatives saw this liberal monopoly as exclusionary and victimizing. Even before the election, historian Thomas Frank had pointed to the left's culpability in fostering populist resentment: "We liberals bear some of the blame for [the populist backlash's] emergence, for the frustration of the working-class millions, for their blighted cities and their downward spiraling lives."

For much of the twentieth century, conservatives romanticized rural

America as an idyllic heartland of small towns and good people, contrasting it with the supposed moral decay of big cities. By the 2010s, this narrative had flipped: Cosmopolitan urban centers had become consumer paradises stocked with exotic cheeses and imported hams, while rural Americans languished under the weight of drug addiction and industrial decline. "Kids were dying in the Rust Belt of Ohio and the Bible Belt of Tennessee," writes journalist Sam Quinones in *Dreamland: The True Tale of America's Opiate Epidemic.* "Some of the worst of it was in Charlotte's best country club enclaves. It was in Mission Viejo and Simi Valley in suburban Southern California, and in Indianapolis, Salt Lake, and Albuquerque, in Oregon and Minnesota and Oklahoma and Alabama." The urban professional classes had little sense of just how desperate life had become in much of the country.

Trump's movement succeeded because it tapped into a giant swath of angry people who felt a loss of status. While much was made about his victory as an uprising of the white working class, his most devoted support came from the ranks of wealthy heartland business owners—the self-made petite bourgeoisie who built small empires through car dealerships, fast-food franchises, and pool-cleaning businesses. Like Trump, they were discontented that their economic success had not translated into higher cultural standing. The 2016 election was less a straightforward class war between rich and poor and more a culture war over the distribution of esteem. It played out through the lens of taste: Multicultural, meritocratic coastal liberals, with their slender physiques, Priuses, IPAs, and pan-seared Wagyu steaks, were pitted against heartland small business owners and white working-class voters driving Ford F-150s, drinking bland pilsners, and ordering well-done steaks. Adam Gopnik captured this dynamic: Trump appealed to "a social class [that] sees its perceived displacement as the result of a double conspiracy of outsiders and élitists. . . . *They look down on us and they have no right to look down on us.*"

In the mid-twentieth century, titans like General Electric and General Motors built factories offering stable jobs to white- and blue-collar workers in regional cities. By the twenty-first century, Apple, Microsoft, and Alphabet dominated the economy, mostly hiring a small number of desk workers from elite universities on the coasts. These shifts not only left swaths of the country behind economically but also upended traditional gender dynamics. As elucidated in journalist Hanna Rosin's provocative essay "The End of Men," the nature of postindustrial work increasingly favored women. Meanwhile, pop culture and mainstream media leaned decisively liberal, portraying empathetic, gym-toned liberals as heroes and their opponents as irredeemable, overweight bigots. By the Obama years, wealthy coastal liberals controlled the status quadfecta—economic, social, cultural, and political capital. For Trump and his supporters, the campaign promised a rebalancing, a revenge on the elites who dominated modern American life.

The growing cultural differences moved American politics away from policy disagreements such as social security privatization, military spending, and civil liberties. After the Obama years, the binary was recentered between forces of inclusive liberalism and vengeful illiberalism. The Trumpist movement, with its media savviness and disdain for traditional morality, represented the political culmination of the counter-counterculture that began with Gavin McInnes at *Vice* in 2001. But unlike McInnes's predictions, this new right had yet to become cool. The Trump victory felt like a hostile takeover.

Just as Bush turned his narrow victory over Gore into a sweeping neoconservative agenda, Trump and his team of outsider "alt-right" provocateurs launched a "Make America Great Again" (MAGA) platform aimed at undoing Obama's legacy—politically, socially, culturally, and spiritually. Where Obama sought to unite a "purple" America, Trump took a page from Paris Hilton's playbook: Doing loathsome things had no downside as long as the ensuing outrage won the news cycle. This also echoed the gambit of heels in professional wrestling. Whether in "his rallies, his debates, his interviews, [or] his social-media posts," wrote *Atlantic* staff writer John Hendrickson, "Trump relied on WWE tactics."

Trump's uninhibited stream of un-PC statements was often celebrated on the right as long-overdue resistance to the so-called tyranny of liberal thought-policing. But such statements also intended to inflict maximum psychological damage on educated elites. Twentieth-century philosopher Judith Shklar defined liberals as those who see cruelty as the ultimate evil. Therefore, Trumpism embraced cruelty as a virtue—delighting in the humiliation and despair of its perceived enemies. In *The Atlantic*, Adam Serwer captured this ethos in his essay "The Cruelty Is the Point," noting how Trump supporters found unity and euphoria in their leader's ability to mete out verbal and symbolic punishment: "It makes them feel good, it makes them feel proud, it makes them feel happy, it makes them feel united."

Trump's base believed that his ascendency to the presidency would force the media to treat him with the same respect and admiration they had shown Obama. Early in 2017, there was indeed a brief adjustment, with some media outlets adopting a more empathetic tone toward heartland Americans. Conservative venture capitalist J. D. Vance's Appalachian autobiography, *Hillbilly Elegy*, soared to bestseller status, offering an ostensibly nuanced explanation of white working-class struggles.

Yet the consumer market had only limited potential for political realignment. The biggest global brands—Apple, Nike, Starbucks—depended on the purchasing power of wealthy upper-middle-class consumers, who grew more disdainful of Trump with each passing day. These companies couldn't afford to alienate their best customers. In fact, Trump's victory only heightened pressure on major corporations to align with liberal causes. When conservative football fans and franchise owners decried San Francisco 49ers quarterback Colin Kaepernick for kneeling during the national anthem to protest police brutality, Nike countered by making Kaepernick the face of an ad campaign. With politics in chaos, the educated yet again looked to the marketplace for salvation.

Despite wielding maximal political power, Trumpism struggled to make a cultural dent in the late 2010s. Trump couldn't mobilize significant support among A-list celebrities outside of a few reliably conservative figures, such as Clint Eastwood, Ted Nugent, and Kid Rock. His most visible celebrity fans were fringe figures from reality TV and internet culture. Willie Robertson of *Duck Dynasty* fame lent his support, as did Paris Hilton, an old family friend, who claimed to have voted for Trump before later stating she didn't vote at all. Antoine Dodson of "Bed Intruder" fame celebrated Trump's victory in a video, while avant-rapper Azealia Banks declared: "HE IS MY FUCKING HERO RIGHT NOW. I AM ELATED." Trump also received an endorsement from Tila Tequila, the star of the bisexual dating show *A Shot at Love with Tila Tequila*, who later faced backlash for a blog post titled "Why I Sympathize with Hitler Part I: True History Revealed."

The most shocking celebrity defection to Trumpism came from Kanye West, whose pivot to MAGA came in the middle of a mental breakdown. During a May 2016 guest slot on *The Ellen DeGeneres Show*, Kanye delivered an eight-minute disjointed monologue about trying to work for Payless shoes and having "ideas that can make the human race's existence, within our 100 years, better." That same year, he donated money to both Hillary Clinton and the Democratic National Committee. Yet just days after Trump's victory, Kanye stunned fans at a concert by declaring, "If I would have voted, I would have voted on Trump." At his next show, he launched into a tirade against Jay-Z and Beyoncé before being hospitalized for a "psychiatric emergency" and diagnosed with bipolar disorder.

Two weeks after his breakdown, Kanye emerged at Trump Tower for a private meeting and photo op with the president-elect. Trump told reporters, "We discussed life." Over the next two years, Kanye cemented his loyalty to Trump, frequently sporting a red MAGA cap personally signed by the president. On his 2018 track "Ye vs. the People," he rapped, "Make America Great Again had a negative reception / I took it, wore it, rocked it, gave it a new direction."

———

During the campaign, Hillary Clinton faced sharp criticism for referring to Trump supporters as a "basket of deplorables"—weirdos flouting the basic norms of polite society. Yet Trump's victory undeniably brought some of the most provocative and transgressive figures from the counter-counterculture into mainstream visibility. These men—and they were overwhelmingly men—represented a new breed of far-right actors distinct from the millenarian Christian sects, militia groups, and male-centric organizations like the Promise Keepers that had once occupied the fringes of conservative politics. They were hyper-online provocateurs who sought to reframe the right as culturally savvy and cool by weaponizing media literacy and internet culture.

The Deplorables included Roger Stone, a self-styled political trickster and veteran of the Nixon White House who paired dandyish suits with a swinger lifestyle and acted as a back channel to Russian hackers. Another prominent figure was Richard Spencer, a wealthy heir to a Texas cotton-farming fortune and PhD dropout fired from *The American Conservative* for his extreme views. Spencer openly championed a "blood-and-soil" ideology and advocated for a white ethno-state. Claiming credit for inventing the term *alt-right*, Spencer became the movement's face—his close-cropped "fashy" haircut a potent symbol of his politics. (This nudged celebrities with hairdos similar to Spencer's, such as rapper Macklemore, to make tonsorial adjustments.) Spencer's notoriety peaked during Trump's inauguration, when a masked protester sucker punched him on live television during an interview, which anti-Trumpists watched over and over as a looping GIF.

King Deplorable was slovenly Steve Bannon. He layered multiple button-down dress shirts as if he were a villainous prep-school teen in an early eighties science fiction movie who had accidentally chugged a magical rapid-aging potion. Bannon was a former Goldman Sachs banker, Hollywood film producer, and the CEO for Biosphere 2. In 2004, he met media entrepreneur Andrew Breitbart, and the two bonded over a shared belief that "politics is downstream of culture." After Breitbart's death in 2012, Bannon took over his namesake website and aggressively steered it toward a nativist-right platform, complete with a dedicated section on "Black crime." *Breitbart* popularized the term *globalist* as a slur for liberals and elites. As Trump's chief strategist in the White House, Bannon unveiled an ambitious and chaotic agenda, highlighted by the controversial "Muslim ban," which rescinded visas mid-flight for people returning to the country.

Two years before the election, Breitbart hired Milo Yiannopoulos, a flamboyant British commentator who had previously run a tech gossip site called *The Kernel*. Yiannopoulos rose to prominence covering "Gamergate," an online harassment campaign that targeted nonbinary developer Zoë Quinn, developer Brianna Wu, and media critic Anita Sarkeesian under the guise of concerns about "ethics in game journalism." He cast himself as a champion for male gamers, who, Yiannopoulos believed, had "very little social capital" to resist "feminist bullies." In hindsight, Gamergate provided a blueprint for the right's use of internet-driven harassment, memes, and disinformation as tools for inflicting psychological and social damage on their perceived enemies.

Inspired by his idol Paris Hilton, Yiannopoulos mastered the art of leveraging controversy and gossip to stay in the spotlight. Right-wing leaders at the Conservative Political Action Conference (CPAC) recognized his ability to energize youth around conservative politics and invited him to speak in late 2016. But his ascension came to an abrupt halt when a recording surfaced of Yiannopoulos voicing support for sexual relationships with thirteen-year-old boys. He resigned from *Breitbart*, was banned from most major tech platforms, and faded into obscurity over the following years.

Yiannopoulos once stated, "If you want to be punk these days, you have to be a conservative," a sentiment that echoed *Vice* cofounder Gavin McInnes's vision of counter-countercultural conservatism. Unsurprisingly, McInnes himself reemerged as a prominent alt-right figure in the Trump era. While *Vice* has never officially explained his 2008 departure, McInnes had alienated his colleagues in 2006 after attending a white nationalist conference and boasting about meeting former Ku Klux Klan Grand Wizard David Duke. Post-*Vice*, McInnes maintained his close connections to downtown media circles, continuing to cloak his extremist politics in irony. He later worked with Richard Spencer at the paleoconservative publication *Taki's Magazine* and, in 2016, founded the far-right paramilitary group the Proud Boys, ostensibly named after a song from the Broadway version of Disney's *Aladdin*, though more plausibly derived from notions of white pride.

McInnes envisioned the Proud Boys as a fusion of right-wing ideology and youth culture. The group's manifesto championed "minimal government, maximum freedom, anti–political correctness, anti–racial guilt, pro–gun rights, anti–Drug War, closed borders, anti-masturbation, venerating entrepreneurs, venerating housewives." Members gathered to read aloud from Pat Buchanan's 2001 book, *The Death of the West*, and their uniform—a Fred Perry polo shirt—nodded to the 1970s British skinhead subculture, long romanticized in *Vice's* early aesthetic. Upon Trump's victory, McInnes declared, "I'm in a state of exuberance that we now have a President who rates women on a 1–10 scale in the same way that we do." He promised his followers that "we'll just walk into the White House." Four years later, at the 2020 presidential debate, Trump directly addressed the group, telling them to "stand back and stand by." By then, McInnes had distanced himself from the organization, resigning days after the FBI classified the Proud Boys as "an extremist group with ties to white nationalism." Yet McInnes's influence endured—his ideas had taken root, even if he himself became dispensable.

Trump's presidency also brought conspiracy theorists into the mainstream. In December 2015, as part of his campaign, Trump appeared on Alex Jones's *Infowars* radio show. Jones was already infamous for claiming the victims of the 2012 Sandy Hook Elementary School shooting were "crisis actors." Despite the despicable nature of Jones's rhetoric, Trump praised him on air, saying, "Your reputation is amazing." Trump would go on to repeat *Infowars* staples on the campaign trail, including the baseless claim that Obama secretly supported the Islamic State.

In the aftermath of Trump's victory, conspiracy theories gained alarming traction. One of the most infamous was Pizzagate, promoted by Alex Jones and other right-wing provocateurs. The theory alleged that high-ranking Democrats were running a child sex-trafficking ring out of the basement of Washington, DC's Comet Ping Pong pizzeria. In December 2016, Edgar M. Welch, a twenty-eight-year-old North Carolina volunteer firefighter, stormed the restaurant armed with an AR-15 rifle, determined to rescue the fictional victims. After firing shots and finding no children—or even a basement—Welch peacefully surrendered, admitting, "The intel on this wasn't 100 percent."

The rise of such conspiracy theories illustrated the counter-counter-culture's weaponization of sixties-style defiance, but with its progressive ethos inverted. Where liberals had once championed antiestablishment rebellion, the alt-right recast progressive institutions as oppressive forces. The Black liberal president became "the Man," feminists were labeled "bullies," and affirmative action was derided as "reverse racism." Many white men began to frame themselves as an oppressed group, with 55 percent of white Americans in 2017 claiming "discrimination against white people" was a problem—even though fewer than 20 percent reported direct experiences of it. Misogyny also found fertile ground in online forums like the Red Pill subreddit, where disaffected men reimagined society through a lens of radical gender resentment.

Even as mainstream pop culture largely excluded these ideas, the internet provided a safe space for the counter-counterculture to flourish. Platforms like 4chan became hubs for alt-right ideology, coalescing around a trope that "the left can't meme." One of the movement's most visible symbols was Pepe the Frog, a cartoon character originally created by illustrator Matt Furie in 2005 as a harmless, laid-back amphibian. In 2008, Pepe was co-opted by 4chan trolls, transforming into a mascot for bigotry, irony, and transgression. "Rare Pepe" memes blurred the line between humor and hate, with versions depicting Pepe in Nazi uniforms and KKK robes. By 2016, Pepe appeared in Trump-themed memes, and soon, the Anti-Defamation League designated the character a "general hate symbol." In a nod to Clinton's infamous "basket of deplorables" comment, Donald Trump Jr. tweeted a parody *Expendables* movie poster titled *The Deplorables*, featuring Pepe as part of the ensemble. An entire faction of alt-right extremists under leadership of neo-Nazi Nick Fuentes called themselves Groypers, after an overweight variant of Pepe.

Emboldened by Trump's victory, alt-right figures moved from online spaces to real-world gatherings. Their first major celebration was the DeploraBall, a party for those who claimed to have "memed Donald Trump into the White House." Attendees included Gavin McInnes and Cassandra Fairbanks of the

Russian-funded media outlet *Sputnik,* who wore Pepe the Frog and Comet Ping Pong pins as accessories. But the movement's darker side came into full view on August 11, 2017, at the Unite the Right rally in Charlottesville, Virginia. Protesters—carrying tiki torches and dressed in cut-rate polo shirts and khakis—marched through the city, chanting slogans like "Jews will not replace us." Among them was former *BuzzFeed* employee and live streamer Anthime Joseph Gionet, known as Baked Alaska, who led chants of "White lives matter." The rally turned deadly when a neo-Nazi drove his car into a crowd of counterprotesters, killing Heather Heyer and injuring dozens more. Trump faced bipartisan backlash for stating that there were "very fine people" on both sides of the protest.

As Trumpism normalized fringe beliefs, an even more bizarre conspiracy theory emerged: QAnon. Beginning in November 2017, an anonymous 4chan user named "Q Clearance Patriot" claimed Trump was secretly working to dismantle a global cabal of "Satan-worshiping pedophiles." These cryptic posts, later traced to South African blogger Paul Furber and the owners of 8kun, Jim Watkins and his son Ron, gained a cult following. By 2020, despite widespread deplatforming by major social media platforms, QAnon had attracted a significant base, with 17 percent of Americans believing its core tenets. Supporters emblazoned their slogans—such as WWG1WGA ("Where we go one, we go all")—on hats, T-shirts, and bumper stickers. Entrepreneurs turned QAnon into a cottage industry, selling merchandise and hosting events. The movement reached the halls of power when Marjorie Taylor Greene, an outspoken QAnon believer, was elected to Congress in 2020.

———

In February 2016, during Trump's candidacy, Beyoncé released "Formation," a musically adventurous track with a politically charged video addressing police shootings of Black teenagers and the mishandled Hurricane Katrina response in New Orleans. Critics hailed it as the year's best song, and *Rolling Stone* later declared it "the greatest music video of all time." Her subsequent album, *Lemonade*, inspired by Jay-Z's infidelity, further cemented her status as a cultural icon. The Associated Press named it album of the decade. Both she and Jay-Z publicly endorsed Hillary Clinton's campaign.

On January 21, 2017, the day after Trump's inauguration, signs emblazoned with the lyric "OK ladies, now let's get in formation" appeared at the Women's March, which drew four million people from across the United States—the nation's largest-ever single-day protest at the time. Alongside the poptimist soundtrack, the event introduced a new cultural symbol: the pink, hand-crocheted "pussyhat," with triangular corners resembling cat ears. Trump's presidency galvanized liberals, many of whom had grown complacent during the Obama years. They transformed into a movement collectively known as the Resistance.

The left framed Trump's victory as evidence that widespread bigotry continued to thrive beneath the surface of American society. This conclusion spurred an intensified focus on minority rights, particularly in the domain where they held the most influence: pop culture. "For both Yiannopoulos and his online liberal enemies in the culture wars," wrote critic Angela Nagle, "to be said to have purely cultural politics would not be considered particularly pejorative." A prominent wing of the Resistance hoped to reshape all symbolic elements of life—norms, values, language, behaviors, and products. Philosopher Gilles Lipovetsky anticipated this cultural shift in 2004, predicting a growing demand for "hyper-recognition," a rejection of "every form of the contempt, depreciation or sense of inferiority under which one might suffer." The twenty-first-century civil rights struggle moved beyond the liberal ideals of equal recognition under the law to focus on dismantling the unconscious biases embedded in cultural norms. Virtually every facet of society could be subject to scrutiny and revision.

This expansive push for all-encompassing inclusivity became known as *wokeness*. Originally a term within the Black community to describe political consciousness, *woke* entered broader usage in 2008 as a lyric from Erykah Badu's recording of "Master Teacher." It gained further prominence during the Black Lives Matter movement, evolving by the Trump years into a broader call for the normalization of all marginalized identities within language and culture. *The Guardian* journalist Julia Carrie Wong, echoing philosopher Judith Butler, described wokeness as operating on the premise that "there is no grand distinction between attacking a group's material status and legal rights and attacking its members' dignity by refusing to use forms of address they find tolerable. Both are on a spectrum of disrespect."

Woke principles resonated widely, not only with marginalized groups but also with white liberals. Robin DiAngelo's controversial book, *White Fragility*, became a bestseller, symbolizing the era's emphasis on improving racial relations through self-examination. Film studios and TV networks made a conscious effort to increase opportunities for people of color, while publishers hired sensitivity readers to flag potentially problematic content.

In the rush to protect and uplift marginalized groups, overall value judgments of culture became increasingly tied to identity politics. Content creators began including trigger warnings to prevent potential psychological harm, and institutions established safe spaces where marginalized communities could feel shielded from hostility. These efforts gained traction among college students and teenagers on platforms like Tumblr, creating a vibrant, youth-driven movement. Meanwhile, the right mocked these harm-reduction efforts: They derided the woke left as fragile "snowflakes" while simultaneously getting bent out of shape when their own illiberal views weren't given proper respect.

Beyond reducing psychological harm, hyper-recognition also emphasized heightened awareness of status disadvantages. This meant constantly accounting for signs of disrespect and comparing biases across demographic groups. The principle of "checking your privilege" encouraged people in socially advantaged categories—white, male, straight, able-bodied—to acknowledge and reject the unearned benefits born from inequality. Right-wing columnist Heather Wilhelm intended to mock the Women's March when she described its ideology as "victimhood . . . sorted by category, tallied, and ultimately ranked," but the left openly embraced the notion that not all minorities experienced the same level of disadvantage.

Critical race theory (CRT), particularly scholar Kimberlé Williams Crenshaw's concept of intersectionality, provided a framework for understanding how overlapping minority identities compound oppression. This theory also influenced the left's evolving language. Advocates introduced the term *BIPOC* (Black, Indigenous, and people of color) to reflect the perceived acuity of racial oppression. Similarly, *LGBTQ+* expanded its scope to ensure equal visibility for lesbians, bisexuals, transgender individuals, queer people, and other sexualities and gender identities.

The accounting model of discrimination, however, often spurred infighting among groups. After the resounding success of the Women's March in 2017, the organization fractured due to internal conflicts. Accusations of antisemitism surfaced when organizer Tamika Mallory attended a speech by the Nation of Islam leader Louis Farrakhan. Women's March organizers told marchers not to wear the pink pussyhat, as it would be unfair to transgender women and women of color. "We did not choose the color pink as a representation of some people's anatomy," responded the Pussyhat Project. The hat, they explained, was just supposed to look like a cat.

With same-sex marriage legalized and gay and lesbian representation normalized in media, the cultural spotlight turned to transgender rights. Caitlyn Jenner's 2015 transition gave the movement early momentum, and terms like *cisgender, sex assigned at birth, gender expression,* and *deadnaming* reached the mainstream discourse. A corporate convention emerged in which people were encouraged to introduce themselves with their pronouns—for example, she/her, they/them. Meanwhile, conservatives vilified transgender people, stoking fears about "biological males" competing in women's sports and using public restrooms.

Identity politics also permeated the popular dialogue around film. In 2015, the hashtag #OscarsSoWhite highlighted the lack of diversity in Hollywood awards. The right responded with vitriol, notably targeting the all-female cast of the 2016 *Ghostbusters* reboot, which flopped at the box office. Misogynist *Star Wars* fans launched a harassment campaign against Asian actor Kelly Marie Tran following her appearance in 2017's *The Last Jedi*.

Despite such backlash, Ryan Coogler's 2018 film *Black Panther* demonstrated the commercial and critical potential of progressive filmmaking. With its all-Black cast and director, the Marvel film earned over $1 billion and was hailed as "the most political movie ever produced by Marvel Studios."

Perhaps the most consequential social movement of the Trump era was the #MeToo campaign, which targeted predatory men in media and entertainment. The movement encouraged women to share their experiences of harassment and assault, breaking the silence that had protected powerful men from facing consequences for criminal behavior.

In October 2017, investigative reporting in *The New York Times* revealed multiple allegations of sexual misconduct against Miramax producer Harvey Weinstein. Over the following months, high-profile actresses—including Ashley Judd, Rose McGowan, Mira Sorvino, Asia Argento, Gwyneth Paltrow, Annabella Sciorra, Daryl Hannah, Uma Thurman, and Angelina Jolie—came forward with stories of Weinstein's abuses. The revelations toppled Weinstein's career, leading to his expulsion from his own company and subsequent imprisonment on sexual misconduct charges. Other serial predators also faced reckoning: Bill Cosby was imprisoned in 2018 after decades of accusations finally came to light.

Weinstein's downfall triggered a cascade of allegations and cancellations across industries. Footballer Cristiano Ronaldo faced rape allegations from a nearly decade-old incident in Las Vegas. Kevin Spacey disappeared from Hollywood as multiple men accused him of sexual abuse and assault. Director Ridley Scott reshot Spacey's role in *All the Money in the World* to erase his performance as J. Paul Getty. James Franco vanished from public view following misconduct allegations and lawsuits, while comedian Louis C.K., a defining figure of independent comedy, admitted to sexual misconduct and lost his mainstream career. Longtime TV hosts Charlie Rose and Chris Matthews were also ousted after allegations of harassment. WWE chief Vince McMahon also stepped down in 2022 amid serious sexual scandals. (Joe Francis of Girls Gone Wild's self-imposed exile to Mexico allowed him to evade serious legal accountability.)

In 2017, a reckoning finally came for photographer Terry Richardson. Three years earlier, two models had alleged that Richardson had bullied them into sexual acts during shoots while assistants documented the incidents. For Richardson, such episodes were "people collaborating and exploring sexuality and taking pictures." Gavin McInnes and many insiders continued to defend him; Australian model Abbey Lee insisted, "Terry doesn't force girls to do anything they don't want to." By the time of #MeToo, major clients like Condé Nast, Hearst, and Bulgari finally decided to sever ties. A year later, the New York Police Department launched an investigation, and in 2023, Richardson faced lawsuits under New York's Adult Survivors Act.

The music industry also started to confront its predators. In 2017, *BuzzFeed* reported that R&B singer R. Kelly operated a sex cult, preying on young women. Despite avoiding significant legal repercussions for years—most notably, being acquitted for child pornography charges in 2008—Kelly's career ground to a halt. This reckoning cast a shadow over Lady Gaga's 2013 duet with him called, regrettably, "Do What U Want." At first, she claimed the partnership was an act of solidarity: "R. Kelly and I have sometimes very untrue things written about us, so in a way this was a bond between us." Later she apologized and claimed, "As a victim of sexual assault myself, I made both the song and video at a dark time in my life, my intention was to create something extremely defiant and provocative because I was angry and still hadn't processed the trauma that had occurred in my own life." She shelved the song's music video—directed by Terry Richardson—in which a group of people sexually abuse her while she lies unconscious on an operating table.

As the right condemned #MeToo as a Cultural Revolution–type overreach, the movement's core achievements—holding figures like Weinstein, Cosby, and Kelly accountable—were unambivalent moral victories. Still, the public debate often obsessed over the edge cases: whether misreading social cues on a first date or displaying anger should justify full cancellation. At a basic level, wokeness created a new lens for cultural analysis. Pharrell

Williams revisited "Blurred Lines," conceding, "I realized that we live in a chauvinist culture in our country. Hadn't realized that. Didn't realize that some of my songs catered to that. So that blew my mind."

At its core, the debate questioned whether left-wing activists had the moral right to disrupt the careers of public figures as a form of punishment. In a poptimist culture, where revenue streams are paramount, being removed from public life was tantamount to death. Yet few remembered that pop culture had long required the removal of once-popular celebrities. The mechanism had simply been different—cancellation by taste.

For decades, the avant-garde mindset pushed young artists to forge new styles explicitly designed to outmode and devalue the previous generation. Andy Warhol's pop art made abstract expressionism obsolete. But in the retromaniacal, omnivore culture of the twenty-first century, new aesthetics no longer displaced older artists—nor did young artists even attempt to. The only force powerful enough to remove someone from the cultural spotlight was now moral condemnation: not just for unambiguous crimes and bigotry, but for affiliations with illiberal ideologies. Culture always needs a refresh, and in an era where omnivorism ruled, political denunciation became an effective means to clear out the old.

––––––––––

The cultural battles of the Trump era culminated in the 2020 protests against police brutality following the death of George Floyd, who was suffocated by law enforcement during his arrest over a suspected counterfeit twenty-dollar bill. During the following month, approximately twenty million Americans joined Black Lives Matter–organized marches across the country, with parallel protests erupting worldwide. The Pharrell-produced Kendrick Lamar song "Alright" became its unofficial anthem. Despite deep political polarization, 67 percent of Americans expressed support for Black Lives Matter. The left rallied around slogans like "Defund the police" and "ACAB" ("All cops are bastards"). The right countered with its own iconography, including "Blue Lives Matter" and thin blue line flags, symbolizing law enforcement as the barrier between order and chaos. Conservatives lionized figures like seventeen-year-old Kyle Rittenhouse, whose entire life accomplishment was crossing state lines into Wisconsin with an AR-15–style rifle, killing two protesters, and being acquitted.

That summer of racial strife saw politics further saturate global culture. Multinational corporations issued public statements supporting Black Lives Matter. Anna Wintour apologized to her staff: "I know *Vogue* has not found enough ways to elevate and give space to black editors, writers, photographers, designers and other creators. We have made mistakes too, publishing images or stories that have been hurtful or intolerant. I take full responsibility for those mistakes." Kanye West donated $2 million to the families of George Floyd, Ahmaud Arbery, and Breonna Taylor, including support for Floyd's daughter's education. With passions inflamed, there were only two sides to the conflict, and brands were punished for attempting to find a middle path. Pepsi became a punch line after releasing a jejune commercial in which Kendall Jenner attends a nonspecific demonstration (with protesters brandishing "Join the conversation" signs) and defuses tensions by handing a soda to the riot guards. (Bernice King, Martin Luther King Jr.'s daughter, tweeted, "If only Daddy would have known about the power of #Pepsi.")

As cultural leaders turned introspective, politics complicated the basic mechanics of cultural exchange. In the woke framework, not all cultural borrowing was legitimate. Cultural appropriation, as writer Ligaya Mishan defined it, involved a "member of the dominant culture—an insider—taking from a culture that has historically been and is still treated as subordinate and profiting from it at that culture's expense." The canonical example was mid-twentieth-century white record labels reaping fortunes from Black musical innovations like rock and roll and funk, allowing white copycats from Elvis to Average White Band to become global stars. By contrast, Afrocentric movements in reggae and hip-hop allowed Black artists to retain some creative control, enabling figures like Russell Simmons, Jay-Z, Dr. Dre, and Kanye West to amass vast wealth.

After 2016, policing for cultural appropriation intensified, often extending beyond traditionally marginalized groups. White celebrities like Miley Cyrus and Justin Bieber faced backlash for wearing dreadlocks (which also sparked new debate over whether the term *dreadlocks* itself was pejorative). Kim Kardashian was widely condemned for attempting to trademark the Japanese word *kimono* for her shapewear line, a move denounced as "horrible cultural disrespect." Just as culture came to rely on genre blending and collapsing subcultural divisions, new rules suggested that only the cultural fusions spearheaded by marginalized groups should be permitted.

By the end of Trump's first term, pop culture was no longer a refuge from political and economic anxieties but a direct battleground for ideological conflict. Activists in the poptimist era steered audiences toward virtuous creators and away from maligned ones, weaponizing the consumer market as a political tool. Political factors dominated the overall judgment of art. Terry Richardson was no longer an artist, but "merely a perpetuator of celebrity sleaze with a penetrating flash." And in the hunt to eradicate all biases, critics began to reexamine the entire cultural canon.

Political pundits once dismissed the term *culture war* as a misleading narrative of American polarization, which distracted the public from coming together to find pragmatic policy solutions. But by the Trump era, both political sides agreed that pop culture was the key battlefield. As a result, purely artistic-minded culture receded in favor of social activism. Even in the US, culture echoed Mao Tse-tung's assertion that there was "no such thing as art for art's sake, art that stands above classes, art that is detached from or independent of politics."

TECHNO-PESSIMISM

The Internet Begins Its Villain Era

Veles, a city in Macedonia with around forty thousand people, was once known for its delicate porcelain ceramics. By the 2010s, the economy was in ruins, with youth unemployment just under 50 percent. But in 2016, the champagne began to flow at local dance clubs, fueled by an unexpected new industry: fabricating and plagiarizing news articles about the US presidential election.

These digital entrepreneurs went beyond the usual content farm scam of churning out low-quality articles on trending topics. They created fraudulent clickbait about the Trump–Clinton matchup, promoted it to older Americans on Facebook, and could make in three days what their neighbors earned in a year—all without much knowledge of American politics or even fluency in English.

The trailblazers of this lucrative industry were the Arsov brothers, Trajche and Panche, who launched usapoliticstoday.com in September 2015. As rumors of their wealth spread, dozens of Veles youth flocked to "Facebook Marketing University," an online course run by consultant Mirko Ceselkoski, whose previous clients included Swedish country-techno band Rednex of "Cotton Eye Joe" fame. Ceselkoski's playbook was simple: Open a generic website like usaelectionnews.com, slap on a "Breaking News" banner, find trending stories, and embellish. Pro-Trump fabricated stories, such as the pope endorsing him or Hillary Clinton selling arms to ISIS, proved especially profitable, as conservatives clicked Facebook links more frequently than liberals.

Four days before the election, *BuzzFeed News* exposed the Veles operations. After Trump's victory, the site exemplified how disinformation was shaping global politics. Outgoing president Obama talked "almost obsessively" about Veles as a warning sign for American democracy. Hilary Clinton blamed the "guys over in Macedonia" as one of the reasons for her defeat. Consultant Ceselkoski leaned into his notoriety: His business card read in all caps, THE MAN WHO HELPED DONALD TRUMP WIN US ELECTIONS.

At first, the story's most shocking revelation was the political agnosticism of the Veles content farmers. They backed Trump simply because it paid better. But as *BuzzFeed News* later uncovered, the operation wasn't purely local. The Arsov brothers partnered with two right-wing American propagandists, Ben Goldman and Paris Wade, both from *Liberty Writers News*, who in turn recruited Alicia Powe, a staffer who claimed to have worked for Rudy Giuliani's presidential campaign.

This collaboration revealed a more dystopian form of globalization: Powerful political forces outsourced disinformation campaigns to low-cost labor in developing countries. For the teens, it was all business. "We can't afford anything," one content farmer explained, "and if the Americans can't tell the difference [between real and fake news], it's their fault."

Between the shock of Brexit in June and Donald Trump's election that fall, elites shed their techno-optimism almost overnight. The internet once promised a golden age of global democratization; now, as the cliché went, reality felt like an episode of *Black Mirror*. The utopian features of Web 2.0—lifting marginalized voices and extending monetization tools to everyone—ended up powering disinformation operations that catapulted right-wing politicians into office. Digital marketer Rick Webb, who once "worshipped at the altar of Stewart Brand and Kevin Kelly," captured the disillusionment in his 2017 "internet mea culpa," calling the internet a "terrordome." The new face of tech was no longer an archetypal West Coast nerd but a Macedonian millennial working with right-wing operatives to enrage voters for cash. The internet was lifting youth out of poverty—one clickbait article at a time.

Like so much else in the Trump era, the internet itself became a battleground for political ideology. The left blamed Trump's victory on social media platforms' failure to police bad actors, with growing suspicion that these platforms benefited financially from causing chaos. Academic Ian Bogost reflected, "Social-media operators discovered that the more emotionally charged the content, the better it spread across its users' networks. Polarizing, offensive, or just plain fraudulent information was optimized for distribution." Meanwhile, the right accused Big Tech of censoring conservative voices. Silicon Valley, long seen as a bastion of liberalism, amplified the divide. In 2016, most tech workers donated to Democrats, and industry leaders like Facebook's Sheryl Sandberg, Google's Eric Schmidt, and Netflix's Reed Hastings endorsed Clinton. Many platforms introduced features aligned with woke ideals, further fueling conservative claims of bias.

While some pro-Trump tech figures emerged, they faced public ostracization. Facebook investor Peter Thiel survived as a rare Trump supporter in Silicon Valley, with Zuckerberg defending his presence on Facebook's board of directors as "ideological diversity." Palmer Luckey, who sold his virtual reality hardware company Oculus to Facebook in 2014 for $2 billion, wasn't as fortunate. Teaming up with deplorable Milo Yiannopoulos, he funded a political group, Nimble America, that aimed to "shitpost" dank anti-Clinton memes. When exposed, he apologized for "negatively impacting the perception of Oculus and its partners" before being fired by Facebook in March 2017. He immediately flew off to Japan for a vacation, where he cosplayed in a leather bikini top as the female assassin Quiet from the *Metal Gear Solid* video game series.

Purging right-wing executives and banning a few websites, however, could not prevent all bad actors from using digital tools to sow political chaos and division. Academic Evgeny Morozov had long predicted these developments. Morozov grew up in Belarus and began his career at an NGO working to promote democracy through independent journalism. His experiences made him into a skeptic, and he soon became outspoken in his belief that dictatorships would benefit most from the digital world. "The internet does not and cannot replace politics," Morozov argued. "It augments and amplifies it."

The tech industry dismissed Morozov as a crank. In 2013 he complained that Silicon Valley was a "Teflon industry": "No matter how much dirt one throws at it, nothing seems to stick." But by 2016, his words seemed prescient. The Arab Spring had largely ended with authoritarian retrenchment. The Iranian Green Movement, ubiquitous on YouTube, had fizzled. Social media platforms, far from empowering dissidents, cracked down on activists' accounts while regimes like Saudi Arabia deployed "troll armies" to suppress dissent.

Even grassroots online activism faced setbacks. Crowdsourcing, once heralded as a democratic tool, became a cautionary tale. Reddit users wrongly identified a missing Brown student as the Boston Marathon bomber in 2013. Anonymous, initially seen as a force for justice, named the wrong police officers in the shooting of Michael Brown in Ferguson, Missouri. Meanwhile, the WikiLeaks technique of publishing secret tranches of documents descended into lechery. In 2014, hackers stole celebrities' nude photos from iCloud accounts and published them in an event dubbed "The Fappening."

Morozov also predicted that the internet would destroy common knowledge—the shared understanding that citizens not only have the same information but know that others have it too. This dissolution went beyond lifestyle fragmentation to create entirely oppositional realities. Pundits warned that social media, particularly Facebook, placed users in ideological bubbles. As Morozov put it, "The logical end of this ever-increasing personalisation is of each user having his or her own online experience. . . . Instead of the internet, we may as well start talking of a billion 'internets'—one for each user." This splintering left the liberal professional classes unaware of shifts in public opinion that enabled Brexit and Trump's election.

Morozov was also an early critic of Big Tech's invasive use of personal data for targeted advertising. In 2013, whistleblower Edward Snowden revealed the extent to which American intelligence agencies accessed private user data through sprawling surveillance programs that relied on secret partnerships with Big Tech. What once sounded paranoid—the idea that every online action could be tracked and weaponized—suddenly became undeniable. By 2018, Shoshana Zuboff coined the term *surveillance capitalism* to describe these practices, framing targeted advertising as an "assault on human autonomy" and a "coup from above."

In light of these new developments, the initial excitement about tech had descended into a debate over whether major companies actively hindered democracies or were simply negligent in policing bad actors. Scandals like Cambridge Analytica exemplified this tension. The firm, funded by billionaire Trump donor Robert Mercer, harvested the private data of fifty million Facebook users through personality surveys. Though Cambridge Analytica oversold their data's efficacy, it became a symbol of how sharing personal details could be weaponized. As tech analyst Benedict Evans put it, Cambridge Analytica was a "hoax" but "catalysed awareness of issues that were real." The revelations helped boost a #DeleteFacebook campaign, which coincided with a generational exodus from the platform to Snapchat and Instagram.

Critics of Big Tech often repeated the motto "If you're not paying for the product, you *are* the product." For years, most users accepted this trade-off. The internet offered instant access to global information, free navigation tools, endless entertainment, and seamless communication—at no monetary cost. Depending on your view, it was a deal with the devil or the greatest consumer proposition of all time. The political upheavals of 2016, however, changed the equation. The negative externalities of a digital world had shifted geopolitics. Internet usage continued to increase, but the period of unbridled enthusiasm was over.

———

As Western elites debated deleting Facebook, Zuckerberg's platform became synonymous with the internet in much of the developing world. By the early

2010s, Indonesians would claim they didn't "use the internet," even as they spent hours each day on Facebook. Recognizing this dynamic, Facebook acquired the global messaging app WhatsApp for $19 billion in 2014 and launched internet.org, a grand initiative to bring the internet to the world's impoverished populations. Zuckerberg presented himself as a tech messiah, appearing in an issue of *Time* in front of a rural Indian schoolhouse, surrounded by children he promised to connect through Free Basics, internet .org's flagship program.

By partnering with local telecom providers, Free Basics offered free access to a limited set of low-bandwidth websites—most notably, Facebook. But the initiative sparked controversy, as Facebook's ability to choose the accessible sites violated the principles of net neutrality. India's regulators banned Free Basics in 2016. Meanwhile, Facebook pursued more ambitious connectivity solutions. The solar-powered Aquila drone promised to beam the internet to remote areas from the stratosphere. Google's similar initiative, Project Loon, aimed to achieve the same goal with high-altitude balloons. These schemes embodied the techno-utopian ethos: Universal connectivity was a matter of engineering, not policy or infrastructure.

The reality was less inspiring. Facebook's first test flight of Aquila ended in a crash, despite claims to *The Verge* of a successful landing. Months later, a SpaceX rocket carrying an internet.org satellite exploded on the launchpad. By 2018, Facebook had quietly abandoned Aquila, following Google's decision to shut down its own drone aircraft experiment, Project Titan. Project Loon worked very well as science but not as a business. Google's parent company, Alphabet, closed it in 2021.

No revolutionary technological discovery was needed to get India online. In 2016, telecommunications giant Reliance Jio made 4G data free, sparking a surge of new users. After this shift, the new median internet user for global online activity was Indian. While 2016's top Google searches included "Pokémon Go," "iPhone 7," and "Donald Trump," by 2021, the top three were "Australia vs India," "India vs England," and "IPL"—all cricket-related phrases.

In developing countries, the arrival of the internet had darker consequences. In 2016, Myanmar's military exploited Facebook to incite violence against the Muslim Rohingya minority, creating fake accounts to spread propaganda and stoke fear. The resulting ethnic cleansing killed twenty-five thousand and displaced over a million. In India, viral WhatsApp rumors about child abductions led to mob lynchings. For Facebook, the solution to these problems was more technology. The company launched a $50,000 contest to find technological fixes for misinformation on WhatsApp.

On February 19, 2017, twenty-five-year-old engineer Susan Fowler published an essay about a "very, very strange year" at Uber, the ride-sharing company that had redefined urban transportation and symbolized the new app economy. Just three years earlier, Uber had raised $1.2 billion in funding and boasted the largest valuation for a private tech company in history. By pairing GPS-enabled smartphones with an army of freelance drivers, Uber promised consumers convenience and cashless transactions.

Fowler found a dark culture inside Uber. Weeks into her tenure, she received chat messages from her manager soliciting a sexual relationship. When she reported the incident to HR, she was told the manager wouldn't face serious consequences because it was his "first offense."

As she changed teams, Fowler discovered that her manager had a long history of such behavior—one that HR had deliberately ignored. Her essay also detailed broader dysfunction at Uber: "It was an organization in complete, unrelenting chaos." Fowler, like many other women, left the company. As the scandal unfolded, Uber fired twenty employees, and a media firestorm led the company's top investors to oust CEO and cofounder Travis Kalanick.

Fowler's essay became one of the most impactful pieces of twenty-first-century whistleblowing and made it difficult to fully swallow Silicon Valley's self-styled narrative of benevolent capitalism. For years, tech companies had reimagined the workplace as a private utopia. They offered free meals, spacious gyms, and even nap pods, rejecting traditional hierarchies for "flat" structures designed to empower employees. These companies positioned themselves as mission-driven entities dedicated to connecting the world and delighting consumers. Yet Uber's toxic culture tore apart this illusion. The new face of Silicon Valley was Kalanick, a leader who favored aggressive bellicosity over collaborative innovation.

Uber's rise hinged on exploiting regulatory loopholes and waging all-out war on local governments. Kalanick motivated his workforce with frat-house bravado. In a 2013 memo sent ahead of a Miami party that opened with "You better read this or I'll kick your ass," he outlined rules for the evening that included: "Do not have sex with another employee UNLESS a) you have asked that person for that privilege and they have responded with an emphatic 'YES! I will have sex with you' AND b) the two (or more) of you do not work in the same chain of command." His own guidelines led Kalanick to conclude that he would be "celibate on this trip," adding the hashtag "#FML."

In a time of ZIRP (zero-interest-rate policy), Uber leveraged cheap capital to subsidize rides, undercutting traditional taxis and capturing a massive user base. The company hemorrhaged money on every ride but promised investors a bright future—a monopoly that would allow it to raise prices. However, Uber underestimated the competition. Lyft, its gentler rival, gained ground with quirky branding, such as furry pink mustaches adorning its cars. Uber's ambitions in China also collapsed after burning a billion dollars in a price war with local rival DiDi, forcing a sale of its China operations in 2016. Finally, Uber's dream of self-driving cars unraveled after its autonomous vehicle killed a pedestrian in Tempe, Arizona, in 2018. (Two years later, Uber would quietly shutter its self-driving unit.)

Despite these failures, the company rushed toward its IPO in May 2019. Kalanick and his banking partners aimed for a $120 billion valuation but settled for $69 billion. When the bell rang, Kalanick had made himself $5.4 billion for this creation, while early investors like Tim Ferriss of *The 4-Hour Workweek* reaped enormous rewards.

Beyond its toxic work culture and headline-grabbing failures, Uber exemplified the inequities of modern capitalism. The company's inability to post a profit until 2023 did little to deter the massive enrichment of its original investors. Meanwhile, Uber drivers—who were some of the first blue-collar workers to interface with Big Tech—faced dwindling pay and instability. The company's refusal to classify drivers as employees allowed it to avoid paying health care and other benefits. Days before the IPO, Uber further slashed driver revenue shares, fueling anger and skepticism about whether the gig economy offered meaningful improvements over traditional labor.

Uber also marked the twilight of the internet as an automated money machine for investors. Unlike Google's AdWords, which generated immense profits almost immediately, Uber's business model relied on finding ethical lines to cross rather than true technological innovation. After Uber, Big Tech could no longer be seen as detached from societal issues, as its business models seemingly worked against the public's best interests.

In an episode of HBO comedy series *Silicon Valley*, fictional CEO Gavin Belson laments, "I don't want to live in a world where someone else makes the world a better place—better than we do." By the mid-2010s, reverence for Silicon Valley's innovation had been replaced with mockery of its self-importance. Created by Mike Judge, of *Office Space*, *Idiocracy*, and *Beavis and Butt-Head* fame, *Silicon Valley* cast tech workers' quirks—productivity hacks, psychedelics, identical fleece vests—as laughable delusions rather than noble eccentricities. After the show, the industry's grandiose mission statements and buzzwords like "local, mobile, social" began to ring hollow, their idealism reduced to wallpaper for profit-driven ventures.

By 2016, tech wasn't just losing its mystique; it was losing its cool. Smartphones, once sleek and expensive status symbols, had become ubiquitous. With more than 70 percent of the US population owning a device, the novelty of pocket-size black rectangles had faded into mundanity. Silicon Valley's promises of the future—self-driving cars, airborne internet drones, seamless "wearables"—had failed to change our lives. Cars still had steering wheels, connections still relied on Wi-Fi and cell towers, and once-breakthrough devices now stagnated in small, incremental updates.

The rise and fall of Google Glass mirrored this faltering vision. Google debuted an early prototype at its annual developer conference, where a skydiver with Glass jumped from a blimp onto the Moscone Center in San Francisco; BMX bikers and rappelers then delivered the unit to Sergey Brin onstage. Journalist Nick Bilton recalled, "It was considered the Gadget, yearned after by everyone from nerds and chief executives, to chefs and fashionistas." Fashion designer Diane von Furstenberg dressed runway models in Glass, and partnerships with companies like EssilorLuxottica—owner of Ray-Ban and Oakley—hinted at its mainstream potential. But the core promise—delivering texts, emails, and notifications directly into users' vision—became less appealing as consumers grew overwhelmed by digital noise. Early adopters, like blogger Robert Scoble famously wearing Glass in the shower, made them "nerd goggles." Worse, the camera's constant recording, with no indication that it was filming, unnerved passersby. By early 2015, Google pulled Glass from the consumer market, pivoting to enterprise applications like warehouse management, before quietly discontinuing the product altogether.

Similarly, the Internet of Things (IoT) trend offered little beyond novelty. "Smart" home devices such as Amazon Echo and Google Home promised a new age of "ambient computing" operated by voice but rarely extended beyond basic functions like setting kitchen timers and telling preprogrammed jokes. And now basic kitchen appliances required firmware updates. The Apple Watch, launched in 2015, proved to be very profitable but only added marginal improvements, such as fitness tracking. Meanwhile, virtual reality headsets like Oculus promised immersive experiences but induced nausea for many users and never culminated in a meaningful cultural movement.

While innovation in consumer tech slowed, opportunities for moneymaking flourished. Even after the IPOs of the most famous companies, hundreds of start-ups promised white-collar workers the chance to strike it rich. A few years in the trenches could translate into millions, and if that didn't pan out, Big Tech provided thousands of middle-management jobs with jaw-dropping salaries, bonuses, and stock options.

This promise of wealth drew new faces to Silicon Valley, including Hollywood celebrities. Ashton Kutcher, fresh off playing Steve Jobs in a panned 2013 biopic, became a successful venture capitalist with investments in Uber, Spotify, SoundCloud, and Airbnb. Tech's expansion into media also created lucrative partnerships. Apple Music, Spotify, and Google Play Music All Access paid billions to the music industry, providing a lifeline in the streaming era. In 2014, Apple's $3 billion acquisition of Beats headphones capped Jimmy Iovine's long history of wrangling pop culture icons to be his personal marketing team. Teens desired Beats for their exaggerated bass, and they had a nice heft thanks to the intentional insertion of nonfunctional weights.

On his quest toward billionaire status, Jay-Z also entered the tech game. In 2015, he acquired Tidal, an obscure Norwegian rival of Spotify, for $56 million and branded it the first artist-owned music platform. Despite limited user adoption, the venture paid off when Twitter cofounder Jack Dorsey bought Tidal for $297 million in 2021. Critics panned the deal as a "$300 million bar tab to hang out with Jay-Z," but it showcased how tech could turn even floundering projects into windfalls for the well connected.

While tech breathed new life into music, traditional publishing continued its decline. *Vice*, which expanded from print to video to online content, fell far short of CEO Shane Smith's ambitious prediction of a $50 billion valuation by 2020. Rupert Murdoch's $70 million investment in 2013, valuing *Vice* at $1 billion, still proved too optimistic. *Vice* may have won over older millennials, but the next generation hated it. A 2017 survey among teens found *Vice* to be the second-least-cool brand, even lower than Yahoo!.

Jonah Peretti's years working to understand the mechanics of virality finally paid off in 2015. *BuzzFeed* won the internet for a day with "the Dress," an optical illusion that sparked debate over its colors: Was it blue and black or white and gold? There was no additional depth to the story, yet as former

BuzzFeed News editor in chief Ben Smith recalled, "The Dress was an unmitigated triumph for *BuzzFeed* and for Jonah. The kind of social content he'd hoped would define us." A year later, *BuzzFeed* again captured the zeitgeist by live-streaming two employees placing rubber bands around a watermelon until it exploded. *BuzzFeed*'s last major viral moment came in 2017 with the *News* team's release of the Steele dossier, filled with unverified claims about Trump's ties to Russia. Smith recalled, "I loved the traffic. . . . My news operation, always jealously eyeing the clicks that came from silly lists and quizzes, finally had its version of the Dress."

Much of *Buzzfeed*'s success, however, was ultimately the success of its hosts, Facebook and YouTube. These platforms, not individual websites, had become the backbone of the internet, reshaping the logic of cultural creation. After brief experiments in elite curation, platforms embraced a laissez-faire approach, prioritizing user numbers and "watch time" over quality content. The twentieth-century content industry's former strategy of investments in auteurs and innovators as the potential hitmakers of tomorrow gave way to full algorithmic optimization. Teenagers were filming amateur videos in their bedrooms that repeatedly drew larger audiences than the work of professional studios. And so there was no need to invest in the creation of content; platforms only had to pay creators *after* the video was a hit. This invited a flood of bland, search-optimized materials from speculators with little interest in art or culture. Content farms like Famous Birthdays, which cataloged celebrities' personal details, outperformed legacy institutions like *Entertainment Weekly* and *Teen Vogue*.

The abandonment of even basic gatekeeping welcomed a rash of sinister content. The "Elsagate" scandal in 2017 involved content farms creating kids' videos for YouTube with lewd and disturbing themes, including Spider-Man and Elsa from *Frozen* in "bizarre situations involving cheating spouses or public urination." Outraged advertisers briefly boycotted YouTube, but Alphabet's bottom line barely wavered. The real money on the internet didn't depend on marquee brands; it thrived on aggregating mid-tier advertisers at scale. This shift eroded another avenue for non–tech elites to shape culture.

The techno-optimistic worldview had promised a renaissance of creativity, in which niche creators could flourish and global connections would expand human knowledge. By the late 2010s, the opposite had occurred: Platforms incentivized people with little interest in culture to clog public spaces with low-quality, ad-driven content. Rather than a hub of innovation, the internet had become an engine for mediocrity.

Peter Thiel's Founders Fund famously lamented, "We wanted flying cars, instead we got 140 characters." Yet those 140 characters—and the rise of short-form content—became powerful vectors for a new kind of culture: fleeting entertainment, get-rich-quick schemes, and venomous propaganda. By 2010, digital advocate Douglas Rushkoff noted that *Boing Boing*, once a defining voice of internet culture, had instead become its "counterculture." A decade later, it was even more marginal than that. Nearly everyone had flocked to the internet on the promise of circumventing the particular norms they disliked—now including the ones we once considered essential to a functional society.

ULTRAPOPTIMISM

A New Cultural Democracy of Global Idols and Digital Natives

n her *Pitchfork* review of Taylor Swift's surprise 2020 indie-inflected album, *Folklore*, critic Jill Mapes offered line after line of effusive praise: "Her biggest strength is her storytelling, her well-honed songwriting craft meeting the vivid whimsy of her imagination." Mapes called the third track, "The Last Great American Dynasty," an "all-timer" and an "instant classic" with "textural and tastefully majestic" qualities and "Fitzgerald-esque lines." *Pitchfork* awarded the album an 8.0—a very good score, much higher than the 6.5 given to Swift's 2017 album, *Reputation*, and the 7.1 given to 2019's *Lover*.

But for Taylor Swift's dedicated "Swifties," this was treachery. Within minutes of the review's publication, they vented their fury across social media, blaming the 8.0 rating (which Mapes didn't personally assign) for lowering *Folklore*'s overall score from 90 to 89 on ranking aggregator Metacritic. In what *The Guardian*'s music editor, Ben Beaumont-Thomas, called "this brutally quantified world," such an incremental downgrade was treated as an unforgivable affront. Swifties mobilized for war.

One fan uploaded an image of Swift with demonic black eyes, accompanied by a warning in Amharic: "Anyone who comes after the Dark Queen, Taylor Swift, dies alone and will be burned forever." Others posted Mapes's personal information, including her home address and telephone number, sparking a campaign of harassment. On Twitter, Mapes wrote, "I've gotten too many emails saying some version of, 'you are an ugly fat bitch who is clearly jealous of Taylor, plz die.'" Mapes survived the onslaught, but the Swifties sent a clear message: There would be serious consequences for anyone who lightly criticized their icon.

The grand irony of the Swiftie uproar was that *Pitchfork*'s 8.0 score was the latest step of its turn to poptimism—the belief that the most commercially minded music is the most important. For most of its early existence, *Pitchfork* was a bastion of indie elitism, favoring obscure rock bands and ignoring pop stars like Swift. Under founder and editor in chief Ryan Schreiber in the early 2000s, only 5 to 7 percent of their reviews could be classified as pop releases. But just as Condé Nast acquired *Pitchfork* in 2015, the site shifted to broader, more inclusive coverage. By 2018, pop albums made up 12 percent of reviews. The following year, the site celebrated "Taylor Swift Day" by reviewing her first five albums to make up for years of neglect.

This transformation was partly driven by an overdue diversification of *Pitchfork*'s staff, expanding beyond its initial core of "white, indie rock dudes." But the shift was also a matter of survival. Staff writer Cat Zhang later noted, "There was no mandate that was like, you had to give Taylor an 8," but *Pitchfork*'s editors couldn't ignore the economic realities of the digital marketplace. "As music media corporatizes and has to think about SEO," she explained, "the more you have to run a review of the Taylor Swift re-recording. You have to write a news item about Taylor Swift." In this sense, poptimism was not just an ideological direction but a pragmatic adaptation to the demands of a competitive marketplace.

Rival publications had already gone full poptimist long before. As cultural historian Saul Austerlitz noted in 2014, *The New Yorker* praised Britney Spears's comeback album, and *Slate*'s annual Music Club devoted most of its essays to *Billboard* Hot 100 artists. "Obsessive coverage of stars like Drake and Justin Bieber," Austerlitz explained, "drives Web traffic in a way that more judicious, varied coverage of the likes of, say, the Tuareg guitar wizard Bombino generally cannot." Critics once understood their role as teaching young devotees about good taste, but this no longer made sense when no one wanted to be a pupil.

The online mob defending *Folklore*, however, demonstrated that the first wave of poptimism was no longer enough. This was an era of *ultrapoptimism*, which posited that popularity itself was the ultimate measure of value. For ultrapoptimists, platforms like YouTube, Spotify, and Twitter represented perfect cultural democracies: a level playing field where the best music could naturally rise to the top. Author Kaitlyn Tiffany wrote in her book on One Direction fandom, "We know that our political system is horribly broken, and so maybe we develop a sense that our true representatives are not those elevated to power at the ballot box, but the ones we have elected far more democratically." By this logic, Taylor Swift's popularity was proof of her superiority, and critics who challenged that narrative became enemies of the people.

This attitude marked a dramatic shift from traditional ideas of criticism and fandom. Fans no longer accepted the possibility of creative missteps. Critic Mark Fisher saw previous notions of fandom as full of ups and downs: "the expectations and the disappointments are part of the masochistic reel/real of being a popfan." By contrast, twenty-first-century fans, connected to millions of others online, refused to admit the possibility of failure. Under ultrapoptimism, every release was a masterpiece. The critics who refused to offer blanket praise burst these palliative bubbles. One Lady Gaga fan explained to *The New York Times*, "You see yourself in your favorite artists . . . when someone insults your favorite artist, you take that as a personal insult." Returning to French theorist Gilles Lipovetsky's prescient idea of the need for *hyper-recognition* in the twenty-first century, pop music fans demanded not just tolerance for their taste but deference to it. Only after leaving the fan community did writer Haaniyah Angus have an epiphany: "Critical consumption doesn't negate enjoyment. I and many others are perfectly able to spot the problematic aspects of music, writing and film whilst still having fun with it."

But inside the fan community, these sentiments were those of wicked apostates. When Nicki Minaj fan Wanna Thompson tweeted a suggestion that Minaj explore more mature themes, the backlash was immediate and brutal. Thompson received so many death threats that her phone crashed, and someone from Minaj's official account joined the pile-on, allegedly messaging Thompson, "Eat a dick u hating ass hoe." *Fanatic*, derived from the sixteenth-century word for religious devotion, no longer felt metaphorical.

Most mainstream twentieth-century pop stars had loyal followers but also needed to win over ad hoc coalitions of fickle consumers. Alanis Morissette's *Jagged Little Pill* sold over thirty million copies worldwide, while its follow-up sold just seven million. In contrast, twenty-first-century fan groups became the entire game, wielding their aggregated buying power and frenzied streaming to dominate the charts without relying on casual listeners. The *Billboard* charts transformed into a "capture the flag" contest. In this chaotic civil war, roaming partisans adopted names for their gangs: Justin Bieber's Beliebers, Lady Gaga's Little Monsters, Ariana Grande's Arianators, One Direction's Directioners, Katy Perry's KatyCats, and Beyoncé's BeyHive. The military metaphors—BTS Army, Rihanna Navy—felt apt.

Like other subcultures, these groups provided a positive refuge for marginalized or bored teens, priding themselves on inclusivity as long as members expressed undying devotion to their idols and joined various support missions. With inclusivity at its core, the ideology of fan culture overlapped with the identity politics of what author Angela Nagle labeled the "Tumblr left." Fan pages on social media sites, as academic Alexander Cho wrote, cultivated "an explicitly anti-heteronormative, anti–white supremacist politics." Amanda Montell, a writer on cults, observed that "pop idols' queer stans are sometimes their most zealous." Even when an artist like Taylor Swift played in explicit heteronormative tropes, queer fans projected hopes and dreams for sapphic desires. "Whether she is conscious of it or not," wrote Anna Marks in *The New York Times*, "Ms. Swift signals to queer people—in the language we use to communicate with one another—that she has some affinity for queer identity."

Yet pseudonymous accounts, while fostering belonging, also encouraged antisocial actions in defense of idols. Fans rebranded themselves as *stans*, inspired by Eminem's song about a psychopathic "stalker + fan." Unlike *locals* (casual fans), stans engaged in campaigns such as buying multiple copies of albums, strategically looping songs on playlists to inflate streaming numbers, and sabotaging rival groups. In one instance, Little Monsters shared links to leaked Ariana Grande tracks to undermine her album release. "Pop fandom," wrote Joe Coscarelli in *The New York Times* in 2020, became "competitive, arcane, sales-obsessed, sometimes pointless, chaotic, adversarial, amusing and a little frightening."

Despite their chaotic nature, stans contributed significantly to online culture. As Kaitlyn Tiffany noted, "Fans became, almost as a rule, the first to adopt new platforms and to invent new features of the internet—a habit molded by the fact that they were the people with the most obvious·incentive to do so." Fan fiction flourished; *Fifty Shades of Grey*, which originated from *Twilight* slash fiction, became a global phenomenon.

Stan culture, however, marked a serious departure from earlier subcultures. Tiffany argued that fan cultures are legitimate heirs to the Teddy Boys, mods, and punks. But instead of inventing rebellious aesthetics or pushing boundaries, stans celebrated preexisting mainstream culture with uncritical devotion. This mirrored millennials' paradoxical embrace of capitalism: apprehensive about its flaws but eager to find identity within its frameworks. A BTS fan in Indonesia told *The New York Times*, "It feels like we're promoting BTS, but we are also promoting our own voices, our own struggles, our own hope for a better world." Yet this activism enriched BTS's management company and record label, which were organized to produce music for financial incentive.

In a fractured media landscape, stans helped consolidate hegemonic cultural power around a few top artists. To stay at the top, stars no longer needed mass majorities, just passionate pluralities. Stans' dedication and overconsumption made these artists safe bets for major tours, TV show appearances, and product sponsorships. By propping up established artists over newcomers, stans contributed to cultural inertia. Madonna reinvented her sound and style to maintain relevance in the 1980s and 1990s. Taylor Swift, buoyed by loyal Swifties, achieved lasting pop dominance from 2012's *Red* with only cosmetic stylistic changes atop her established songwriting formula.

From one perspective, stans helped diversify global pop culture. In 2018, the BTS Army propelled *Love Yourself: Tear* to the number-one slot on *Billboard*—a landmark achievement for K-pop. This success opened the door to acts like K-pop girl group Blackpink, who went from making their Coachella debut in 2019 to headlining it four years later. Yet, despite these mainstream victories, stan culture largely concentrated on glossy, highly produced acts, with only a handful of nations, like Korea, producing music that fit the mold.

In their vanguard usage of online platforms, stans were destined for even more influence on global culture. But herein lay another paradox: Just as they shaped the consumer market through their strong group adhesion, these subcultural dynamics made many of their creative acts inexplicable to the outside world. Stans loved to compose fanfic, imagining fantastical scenarios for their idols—some erotic, some mundane. One Direction fans popularized the "Larry" theory, claiming Harry Styles and Louis Tomlinson were secret lovers, even creating images of Styles pregnant with their imagined child. When a BBC documentary covered the phenomenon, chaos erupted, with false rumors of fan suicides causing a schism within the community. The deeper fans delved into conspiracies, the more isolating their devotion became. At the same time, Kaitlyn Tiffany observed that many stans "achieved utter and irrevocable financial precarity" by spending excessively on tickets and merchandise, often becoming "incomprehensible to their friends and family because of the degree to which they speak and think in fandom references and memes." While fandom offered refuge and connection, its insularity also created the potential for shared delusions.

Unlike Pearl Jam's ambivalence about their mainstream fans in the nineties, the idols mostly loved their cults. Lady Gaga embraced her Little Monsters with public declarations of solidarity: "To every little monster on the planet who feels different," she posted to her Instagram. "So do I. And we have each other. Forever." Swift, meanwhile, weaponized Swiftie devotion for market leverage when she went to war with Scooter Braun in 2019. That year he partnered with a private equity firm to pay $330 million for the master recordings of her first six albums.

Swift was furious about being outbid but also loathed Braun personally due to his work with Kanye West. In 2016, West released the song "Famous," which featured the lyric "I feel like me and Taylor might still have sex / Why? I made that bitch famous." (The video featured an outrageous wax sculpture of a topless Swift in bed sleeping next to West, Kim Kardashian, West's ex-girlfriend Amber Rose, and a variety of other celebrities.) When Swift and her fans complained about the song, Kanye claimed to have gotten the singer's permission. At the Grammy Awards, Swift obliquely blasted West in her acceptance speech for Album of the Year: "I want to say to all the young women out there, there are going to be people along the way who will try to undercut your success or take credit for your accomplishments or your fame." Kim Kardashian then leaked a surreptitiously recorded phone call of Swift giving tacit approval to Kanye. The ensuing negativity in the press cycle, Swift later revealed, felt like "career death."

Upon hearing the news that Braun purchased her masters, Swift posted on her official Tumblr account that she had endured "incessant, manipulative bullying" from him over the years. The "Famous" video was "revenge porn." Swifties mobilized into action, harassing Braun through online channels, including the message, "Why don't you just die with your children? I will buy a gun [tomorrow] and then shoot you all in the head." Within a year, Braun sold the masters to the Disney family for $405 million. Swift then made an unprecedented next chess move: She rerecorded her early albums as "Taylor's Version" soundalikes, effectively devaluing the original masters. Each rerecorded album topped the *Billboard* charts and became the canonical version within the Swiftie community. Swift's act of defiance demonstrated how an artist, backed by a devoted fan base, could challenge entrenched industry norms and regain control over their narrative.

This was the state of pop culture in the twenty-first century: artists and fans joining forces united in one corner of a corporate rivalry between multimillionaires, battling over rights management as a means of securing long-term passive income streams.

The "Taylor's Version" solution fit neatly within the entrepreneurial ethos championed by figures like Jay-Z, in which capital accumulation was framed as an act of heroism. In this ultrapoptimist worldview, wealth creation wasn't just a goal but a measure of democratic and cultural success. Fans eagerly joined their idols in the quest for financial domination, viewing their loyalty and spending as a form of empowerment. As money became synonymous with popularity, industry executives achieved parity with the artists they represented.

The 2017 documentary *The Defiant Ones* reflected this shift. Directed by *Menace II Society* cocreator Allen Hughes, the film follows Jimmy Iovine and Dr. Dre as coequal protagonists, culminating in Apple's acquisition of their company, Beats. In the old logic of cool, defiance was a noble act—an artistic stand against authority. But *The Defiant Ones* redefined it, equating N.W.A's culture-bending releases (e.g., "Fuck Tha Police") with Iovine's "greatest hits": coercing Bruce Springsteen and Tom Petty into making radio-friendly singles, peddling the monstrous Marilyn Manson's banal provocations to suburban teens, and turning his entire Interscope artist roster into a marketing team for Beats headphones. *The Defiant Ones* framed industry profiteering as equally valuable as the art it commercialized. And as Taylor Swift continued to show, fans were right there with their idols—cheering on their quest to escape the embarrassment of being mere multimillionaires.

———

There was another paradox at the heart of "democratic" millennial taste: While some teenagers devoted themselves to the polished output of multinational entertainment companies, others idolized "creators" who seemed like friends next door. This tension became evident with a shocking 2014 *Variety* survey revealing teenagers' preference for YouTube stars like Smosh, the Fine Bros., PewDiePie, KSI, and Ryan Higa over mainstream celebrities like Paul Walker, Jennifer Lawrence, and Katy Perry. The report noted that teens valued the "intimate and authentic" connection with YouTube creators and their "lack of filter." While stans elevated pop idols to godlike status, the rising generation of online stars felt accessible and relatable.

This shift reflected yet another major change in the nature of fame, which was historically a costly signal of status, earned through extraordinary feats. Mass media broadcasting could bestow an automatic aura on anyone in the spotlight. Reality TV confused the situation even more. *Survivor* cast normal people as contestants, yet its popularity turned middle-aged corporate management consultant Richard Hatch into a national celebrity. But within the media ecosystem, the reality stars' lack of glamour and mystique knocked them to the D-list. Viewers subconsciously discounted their status.

Then, as internet culture reporter Taylor Lorenz observed, "Social media was practically a fame machine." Teens no longer needed a production studio or storytelling skills to create compelling content. They just needed to document their lives. Bethany Mota's "haul videos"—showing off banal purchases from H&M—captivated audiences with their sheer ordinariness. Everyone, it seemed, could commercialize their own normality.

Instagram accelerated this trend. The site began as an escape from the pressures of status signaling on Facebook, one in which the creative class could delight in posting abstract Polaroid-like snaps. Within a few years, however, it became a launching pad for glossy personal brands. Influencers inserted products into curated snapshots of beautiful yet relatable lives, offering brands an authentic-feeling advertising medium. With enough followers, influencers could command large sums for sponsored posts, become paid "ambassadors," or partner with private-label manufacturers to create their own product lines. Millennials embraced this new model, seeing it as the ultimate dream job: getting paid to be the best version of oneself without answering to a boss.

The Kardashians raised this business model into global prominence. Kendall Jenner earned $26.5 million in 2018 for posting products. The youngest spawn, Kylie Jenner, denied getting cosmetic surgery on her lips for years—a lie. She then turned the controversy into a company, Kylie Cosmetics, that sold twenty-nine-dollar "lip kits." Her brand inked a giant distribution deal with beauty retailer Ulta, and in 2019, *Forbes* honored her as the "youngest-ever self-made billionaire"—beating Zuckerberg by two years. (This was also based on a lie: *Forbes* retracted the title after discovering that Jenner fudged the numbers.)

With so many youths attempting to become creators and influencers, this mobilized an auxiliary workforce: "a cottage industry of photo and video editors, location scouts, and support teams." Men became "Instagram boyfriends/ husbands" who took snaps for women on their quest to become an internet main character. Influencers moved into "hype houses"—gaudy apartments where they partied and supported each other in creating daily content. Photogenic locations became global landmarks, such as the pink wall at fashion boutique Paul Smith in West Hollywood. Entrepreneurs opened entire mini theme parks, such as the Museum of Ice Cream, for aspiring influencers to take colorful shots. Aggregator accounts opened, such as Influencers in the Wild (with the famed pink wall as its avatar), that mocked semi-celebrities filming in public.

Early YouTube stars found fame in being relatable, but Instagram success worked best when influencers were aspirational. Successful accounts needed to show off exceptional consumer choices or the palpable fruits of financial success. This development further incentivized two new kinds of influencers: the rich and the scammers. Trust fund kids flaunted conspicuous consumption, posting documentary shots of private jets, ski chalets, and Hollywood parties. As Amanda Mull explained in *The Atlantic*, "Absent a notable skill or expertise, a passel of ordinary and in many cases insipid people parlay family wealth or a remunerative marriage into a business all its own." This led to aggregator accounts such as Rich Kids of Instagram, chronicling the site's most grotesque displays of wealth, from champagne being poured into a Jacuzzi bath to giving a Starbucks Frappuccino to a pet cheetah. That account then led to a reality TV show in 2014 called *Rich Kids of Beverly Hills.*

Meanwhile, Instagram's quantification of fame in follower counts and "engagement" (numbers of likes, comments, and reposts) created a veneer of objectivity for tracking fame—and new avenues for deceit. Bot farms in Indonesia and China offered thousands of fake followers for a small fee. This led to the December 2014 "Instagram rapture," in which the site deleted a massive number of fraudulent accounts. Justin Bieber alone lost three million "followers" in one day. The broader problem remained, however, that *posing* as a successful influencer was an effective means of becoming one—"fake it till you make it" was a core technique in influencer circles. This spawned new businesses such as Private Jet Studio in Moscow, which charged five thousand rubles an hour to take photos in a Gulfstream G650 private jet parked on the runway.

Yet this emphasis on manufactured perfection stood in stark contrast to another internet-native phenomenon: SoundCloud rappers. While Instagram demanded polish, SoundCloud rewarded rawness. Digital tools made high-fidelity recording accessible to anyone, allowing young musical artists to bypass traditional gatekeepers. These platforms launched a new wave of hip-hop stars—Lil Yachty, Lil Uzi Vert, Lil Pump, Lil Peep, Playboi Carti, XXXTentacion, Juice WRLD, and 6ix9ine.

Most of these rappers preferred the minimalism of Atlanta's trap and Chicago's drill beats to the musical auteur-rap of Kanye or Odd Future. The "pioneering drill sound," writes Jaimie Hodgson, "was forged from a similarly simple recipe, accessible to any kid with a PC and a cracked copy of Fruity-Loops." Aspiring rappers could find a commodity beat online and scream lyrics into their laptop microphones. SoundCloud rappers further embraced rawness through vibrant self-expression, often through face tattoos, rainbow-dyed hair, and unconventional body modifications. Where Justin Bieber sported fifty-six tattoos and Ed Sheeran sixty, Lil Uzi Vert implanted a diamond into his forehead. While the über-normality of YouTube stars fit poorly with the music and film industries, the transgressiveness of SoundCloud rap often lit a path toward acceptance in elite media circles.

The trend of democratized celebrity then fed back into mainstream circles. Figures like former bikini model Chrissy Teigen and producer DJ

Khaled embraced the tactics of lifestyle influencers to cultivate online personas that felt intimate and relatable. Teigen, with her candid and humorous tweets about domestic life with singer John Legend, and Khaled, with his quirky Snapchat mantras about the "keys to success," thrived by blending aspirational and approachable qualities. As *Vanity Fair*'s Josh Duboff observed, Khaled and other celebrities' use of social media created "a connection that feels more real."

This new era of fame was shaped by what sociologist Pierre Bourdieu called *hysteresis*—the lagging effect of old values in a new paradigm. Social media renown required little more than moxie or notoriety, yet audiences still responded to broadcasting as if it carried the same mystique as in previous eras. The logic of ultrapoptimism ultimately blessed notoriety as a pathway to success. Who could question someone else's status when their fame was backed by quantifiable—and therefore objective—metrics?

The participatory nature of social media also elevated fans' own status, as they could now directly interact with "stars." This fueled parasocial relationships, in which fans felt one-sided intimacy with their idols. As Amanda Montell observed, platforms like Instagram and TikTok bridged "the parasocial gap," creating the illusion that a star like Taylor Swift might respond to a fan's comment in the manner of "the almighty saint answering her believer's prayer." This accessibility, however, also opened the door to abuse, allowing fans to hurl insults with little consequence.

The thin line between content creation and commerce raised new legal and ethical challenges, as monetizing one's own fan base became inherent to the social media experience. A study in 2018 found that influencer brothers Jake and Logan Paul told audiences to buy their products 195 times over just fifty videos. Both mainstream celebrities, such as the Kardashians, and emerging online creators engaged in rampant, undeclared product placement. In 2017 the Fair Trade Commission decreed that creators needed to indicate sponsored posts. Instead of diminishing influencer allure, however, the #ad and #sponsored hashtags became status symbols. Engagement often increased on declared paid posts, as it signaled that an influencer had "made it." Lesser-known creators even falsely tagged posts with #ad to appear more successful.

Yet, by the end of the decade, the dream of democratic celebrity began to falter. Established stars like Vin Diesel and Leonardo DiCaprio remained cultural fixtures, while the original YouTube pioneers faded into obscurity. Burnout became rampant. Beauty guru Michelle Phan disappeared for a few years after suffering from poor mental health. Mommy blogger Heather Armstrong, a trailblazer in personal blogging, tragically ended her life after a long struggle with depression. The pressure to produce ever-evolving content under constantly shifting algorithmic rules took a significant toll.

The largest problem among the new generation of online stars, however, was cancellation. Just like with Gavin McInnes and Paris Hilton, many You-Tubers grabbed audience attention through the kind of outrageous behavior that often drifted into pure sociopathy. Top YouTuber PewDiePie's 2017 stunt of paying two men in India to hold up a sign reading "Death to all Jews" cost him a partnership with Disney. PewDiePie was no longer "provocative and irreverent" but "inappropriate." Creator Arya Mosallah took heavy criticism for his "fake acid attack" video. Logan Paul faced widespread condemnation after making jokes about a victim's corpse in Japan's infamous Aokigahara "suicide forest." Similarly, Shane Dawson's blackface videos and pedophilic comments led to his ostracization from the platform. David Dobrik, primed to be the next YouTube icon, was consumed by a rape scandal among his crew. There were so many canceled YouTubers, in fact, that a list was circulated online distinguishing the subtle gradations in the cancellation categories: "Actually needs to be in jail right now" (Shane Dawson) versus "Can't enjoy anything with them in it or made by them" (Logan Paul).

SoundCloud rappers lived and died by menace. XXXTentacion was murdered at age twenty while awaiting trial for domestic violence charges. Juice WRLD and Lil Peep overdosed. And 6ix9ine, who launched his career while on probation for filming group sex with a thirteen-year-old girl for a music video, spent two years in prison for conspiracy to commit murder. (He snitched on his codefendants and got an early release.) The few SoundCloud survivors leaned toward the genre's softer side, most notably Post Malone. White, heavyset, and covered in facial tattoos, he diluted the SoundCloud rap into mainstream appeal, landing Bud Light Super Bowl commercials. "Cosmetically," critic Grant Rindner observed, "the music world doesn't look much different from when SoundCloud rap came to the fore."

Social media also wrecked the careers of more traditional celebrities. Chrissy Teigen, once lauded for her candidness on Twitter, faced widespread backlash after allegations of bullying surfaced. Similarly, influencer and Dwight School graduate Josh Ostrovsky, better known as the Fat Jewish, built a career on absurd stunts like hosting a SoulCycle-style class for homeless people and selling a wine called White Girl Rosé. Then his Comedy Central show fell through, and he headed into obscurity as accusations emerged that he routinely stole jokes from other comedians.

These individual downfalls, however, were less significant than the broader transformation they symbolized. As Taylor Lorenz observed, "We're all now deeply cognizant of our status, our metrics, our potential for microfame or outright celebrity." Fame, once reserved for the select few, became an accessible aspiration for millions, driven by quantifiable engagement data. Even those without the slightest ambition to become internet stars still found themselves obsessing over digital validation.

This shift also reshaped the principles underlying mass media. The new generation of creators flooded public discourse with content that more closely resembled reality television than traditional narrative art. Even in ostensibly creative spaces like SoundCloud rap, the appeal was not particularly *musical*: As Pharrell Williams noted, "There are no hooks. There's just vibes." The spectacle was everything, and this fit seamlessly with the broader trend in digitized youth culture: For both stans and influencers, commerce and celebrity were the obvious focal points. Creative invention was not just an afterthought, but a potential hindrance on the new path toward fame and fortune.

CAPITALIST SURREALISM

Entrepreneurialism Gets a Boost from Magical Thinking

13

E lizabeth Holmes dreamed of reviving the family's fortunes. She was a descendent of the Fleischmann yeast empire, whose grandfather and father had squandered the money. "I want to be a billionaire," Holmes told friends from a young age. In high school, this desire surely intensified when her father lost his job at Enron during the company's historic collapse.

Once at Stanford University, Holmes cultivated the feisty entrepreneurial zeal of a Gates or a Zuckerberg. She dropped out to launch Theranos, a med-tech start-up promising to revolutionize diagnostics with a single drop of blood. She imitated Steve Jobs's uniform of black turtlenecks. And like an inverted Paris Hilton, Holmes took on a gruff masculine timbre in public and only used her high-pitched feminine voice with intimates.

By 2013, Theranos was valued at $9 billion, making Holmes the youngest self-made billionaire woman of her time. With this achievement, she embodied the era's obsession with entrepreneurial heroism. Theranos also represented an additional key aspect of the zeitgeist: It was a complete fraud. And it wasn't even a clever fraud. There were no elaborate financial maneuvers or schemes to weave around regulatory loopholes—she simply claimed that her technology worked, and it didn't.

Holmes's meteoric rise and disastrous fall captivated the public, spawning bestselling books (*Bad Blood*), documentaries (*The Inventor: Out for Blood in Silicon Valley*), and TV dramas (*The Dropout*). Her story symbolized what hedge fund titan Jim Chanos called a "golden age of fraud": "a really fertile field for people to play fast and loose with the truth, and for corporate wrongdoers to get away with it for a long time." Critic Jia Tolentino linked this to the election of Donald Trump: "an incontrovertible, humiliating vindication of scamming as the quintessential American ethos." But the outbreak of fraud was global, from Germany's Wirecard scandal to China's Luckin Coffee collapse. In 2014, young Japanese researcher Haruko Obokata published two articles in *Nature* about major breakthroughs in stem-cell technology based on false data.

Perhaps the internet was to blame, with its ability to invent alternative realities that confidently presented misinformation as fact. The celebrated 2010 documentary *Catfish* examined the new ease with which online personas could be fabricated for seduction and exploitation. But most of the century's infamous frauds eschewed digital trickery for the age-old long con. Elizabeth Holmes didn't need deepfakes or bots to captivate her audience. There was no more seductive story in the era than potential entrepreneurial success, which gave Holmes a near-hypnotic control over her prestigious board members. In the most shocking detail of the Theranos scandal, she convinced former secretary of state George Shultz to side with her over his own whistleblowing grandson.

While true crime narratives often frame these perpetrators as miscreants attempting to dupe the public, many of the fraudsters also conned themselves. Young millennial entrepreneurs like Holmes fell prey to harmful levels of magical thinking, which writer Amanda Montell defines succinctly as "the belief that one's internal thoughts can affect external events." Holmes operated as if everything would somehow work out despite the repeated failure of Theranos's core technology. A more disciplined swindler might have bailed sooner. Even after exposure, Holmes doubled down on CNBC, dismissing a damning *Wall Street Journal* exposé with the kind of motivational aphorism found on dorm room posters: "This is what happens when you work to change things, and first they think you're crazy, then they fight you and then all of a sudden you change the world."

In a post-Zuckerberg era, many young entrepreneurs took on levels of confidence indistinguishable from pathological self-delusion. If the goal was making billions, there was no future in becoming an astronaut or surgeon. Only entrepreneurial success allowed for the highest forms of self-actualization. Yet even as the tech market roared in the 2010s, the viable paths to such fortunes narrowed to proprietary technological breakthroughs (Google), network effects (Facebook), and ruthless business strategies (Uber). This made magical thinking essential for a generation of aspiring young billionaires. Many saw dishonesty as justifiable—even necessary—to buy time to get the technology working. Holmes surely believed the millions she raised on false pretenses were simply a bridge to the future she promised.

Magical thinking didn't just fuel the supply of fraudsters; it also created a ready audience of marks believing they could get rich quick on entrepreneurs' backs. For every aspiring CEO hoping to become a billionaire, dozens of would-be investors hoped to cash in early and reap millions. Each IPO enriched a few capitalists and gave everyone else a new case of FOMO (fear of missing out). This hunger left them more susceptible to threadbare scams. The low-stakes Russian German grifter Anna Sorokin showed up in New York and reinvented herself as Anna Delvey, a supposed heiress to a solar-power fortune. Armed with magical thoughts, she collected a wide range of suckers who believed she would open an art-themed VIP club. Few found her personally alluring, but the prospect of her wealth attracted a host of potential business partners. "If you show them the money," wrote journalist Jessica Pressler, "they will be virtually unable to see anything else." Sorokin's frauds snowballed as potential business partners tried to exploit her supposed riches, only to end up as the losers.

These scams took on such cultural relevance not from their particular audacity but from their ubiquity in modern media. Streaming platforms, podcasts, and nonfiction books needed a constant stream of true crime, while shows like *Shark Tank* blurred the line between business and pop culture. Sorokin's arrest spawned a friend's memoir (*My Friend Anna*), a Netflix show (*Inventing Anna*), and episodes about her on *American Greed* and *Generational Hustle*. While in prison, Sorokin signed a deal with *The Real World* and *The Simple Life* producer Bunim Murray Productions to star in a reality show. Then, on parole, she launched her own podcast and appeared on season 33 of *Dancing with the Stars.*

This dynamic played out repeatedly in the 2010s. Bernie Madoff's decades-long Ponzi scheme, which collapsed during the 2008 financial crisis, was immortalized by Robert De Niro in HBO's *The Wizard of Lies.* In 2013, disgraced cyclist Lance Armstrong chose Oprah for his doping confession, which spawned a wave of documentaries. Aspiring millennial fraudster Billy McFarland first launched a luxury credit card club, Magnises, before organizing the ill-fated Fyre Festival. Using top models like Emily Ratajkowski and Bella Hadid to promote the event, McFarland promised attendees a luxury experience. They arrived to find it more like a refugee camp. The festival's collapse became the subject of two popular documentaries: *Fyre Fraud* and *Fyre: The Greatest Party That Never Happened.*

The young, unscrupulous pharmaceutical executive Martin Shkreli made pop culture news when he paid $2 million at auction for the single existing copy of the Wu-Tang Clan album *Once Upon a Time in Shaolin.* He later went to prison for securities fraud. The paparazzi surely regretted missing a fraudster Holy Trinity moment in the months when Sorokin socialized with Shkreli and camped out in McFarland's townhouse office.

Magical thinking was particularly alluring in an era when conspiracy theories seemed as plausible as the official record. The idea that the US government had long suppressed knowledge of UFOs gained credibility in 2022, when it admitted to possessing secret video evidence of unidentified aerial phenomena. Yet perhaps nothing better captured this dynamic than the life and crimes of Jeffrey Epstein—a billionaire financier whose story suggested there was no way to ever know the truth about elites' lives.

For decades, Epstein was a ghost. Despite the fact that he owned the largest private residence in Manhattan and the biggest home in New Mexico, no one knew much about how he made his money—a fortune supposedly in the billions. His girlfriend appeared to be Ghislaine Maxwell, daughter of the discredited British media baron Robert Maxwell. Unlike typical billionaires, Epstein avoided public events and magazine profiles. In 2000, he joined the board of directors for New York's Rockefeller University, only to quit after six months, reportedly because he hated wearing suits.

Mainstream media started taking an interest in Epstein in 2002, after he flew former president Bill Clinton and actors Kevin Spacey and Chris Tucker around five African countries on his private jet. These early profiles raised more questions than answers. How did this college dropout and former high school math teacher gain the trust of business titans? Why was his client list so secret, other than Les Wexner of The Limited? Even Donald Trump, seemingly unprompted, made a peculiar comment about Epstein to *New York* magazine: "It is even said that he likes beautiful women as much as I do, and many of them are on the younger side."

As journalists dug deeper, Epstein turned to intimidation. When a *Vanity Fair* reporter pursued claims of sexual abuse, Epstein stormed their offices to complain about the article. A bullet appeared outside editor in chief Graydon Carter's apartment, and a severed cat's head was left on his lawn. Allegations about the abuse of two sisters were cut from the final article.

Even as whispers of wrongdoing persisted, Epstein used his wealth and mystique to pull more people into his network. Harvard psychologist Stephen Kosslyn relayed a story about conducting an experiment on Tibetan monks with Epstein in the room, where "Jeff was on his cell phone most of the time— he actually wanted to short the Tibetan market, because he thought the monk was so stupid. He is amazing." (There is no "Tibetan market" to short.) Others, like Harvard cognitive psychologist Steven Pinker, eventually saw through the charade: "He couldn't really or had very little interest in exploring an issue. He'd wisecrack, change subjects, or get bored after a few seconds." And as investigative reporter Gabriel Sherman concluded, "If you actually really engaged this guy, he was full of shit." But he had money, and that was enough for most people to overlook the obvious flimflam.

In 2006, Epstein was arrested in Florida for sexually abusing dozens of teenage girls, but legal and institutional failures allowed him to escape harsh punishment. Federal prosecutors granted him an inexplicably lenient plea deal, and he served minimal time under charitable conditions. Upon release, Epstein returned to his depraved lifestyle, continuing to socialize in elite circles with little consequence. On July 6, 2019, New York federal prosecutors charged him with the sexual trafficking of minors. A month later, Epstein was dead in his jail cell. Officials ruled it a suicide, but the circumstances—sleeping guards, malfunctioning cameras, and other protocol violations—led many to believe it was murder. The conspiracy theory seemed much more plausible than the official explanation, which Attorney General Bill Barr dismissed as a "perfect storm of screw-ups."

In both life and death, Epstein fueled some of the most paranoid fantasies about the global elite: a billionaire with untraceable wealth, who cavorted with presidents, princes, tech moguls, Nobel laureates, and celebrities while operating a real-life sex-trafficking ring on his private island. No child prostitution existed in the basement of a DC pizza parlor, but Epstein ran an actual network of abuse that thrived for decades with near impunity. Questions abounded: Why did Trump appoint Alexander Acosta, the US attorney behind Epstein's secret (and illegal) federal non-prosecution agreement, as his secretary of labor? Did Epstein's extensive wealth derive from blackmail?

Regardless of the conspiracy angles, Epstein's story also revealed how skilled grifters could climb to the very top rungs of contemporary society. And his fortune exempted him from basic societal norms. Elite society accepted his largesse and private jet flights with few questions. Actual billionaire Bill Gates visited Epstein's Manhattan mansion years after his Florida arrest and casually remarked to colleagues, "His lifestyle is very different and kind of intriguing although it would not work for me." (A spokeswoman later clarified that Gates was "referring only to the unique décor of the Epstein residence.")

Yet ignoring morality for money wasn't an exclusively American phenomenon. Japan harbored its own Epstein-like mogul, Johnny Kitagawa, whose talent agency dominated the nation's boy band industry for decades. Kitagawa's music groups were nightly fixtures on television, and he leveraged them to make millions in advertising deals. Fans of these idols were stans before the word existed. Yet behind the glossy exterior, Kitagawa faced persistent allegations of sexually abusing the young men in his charge.

Unlike Epstein, Kitagawa didn't rely on personal charisma but instead employed a cunning financial strategy that spread profits from his boy bands across all the major media conglomerates. The big publishing companies received the rights to print calendars of one of his artists; each record label received one artist for its roster. This financial interdependence created an omertà, in which reporting on Kitagawa's abuse meant risking getting cut out of the cartel. Middle managers kept quiet, because speaking up would hurt their bottom line.

Kitagawa died in 2019 at age eighty-seven. Initially, Japanese media celebrated his influence on postwar culture. But when a BBC documentary corroborated decades of allegations, the omertà cracked. The Japanese media finally reported the long-known truth, and a subsequent internal investigation at Kitagawa's agency uncovered 478 victims, 325 of whom demanded compensation—150 of whom had been company employees.

The lesson was clear: Systems of power and profit could shield predators. As long as revenue kept flowing, institutions were content to look the other way. Money served as the ultimate tool for norm evasion—and for many, that was the core appeal of getting rich.

———

The internet may not have caused the most famous incidents of fraud in the twenty-first century, but its particular business model inured people to low-level scams. Unlike the polished ads of TV and magazines, internet advertising was a free-for-all. Facebook ads weren't just cheap—they were so well-targeted that entire companies were built around their precision, selling niche products like candles that smell like every US state.

The democratization of advertising reshaped industry expectations. Legacy companies buying the back cover of *Vogue* trusted that Anna Wintour would deliver a glossy, high-quality magazine. As *Vanity Fair's* deputy editor Dana Brown believed, "Magazines aren't democracies. Editors in chief are dictators, ruling by decree." Online platforms, by contrast, offered no such assurances. Marketers buying ads on Facebook or Twitter had less control over what content their ads would support. While established businesses might hesitate to risk brand value, lesser-known companies saw this as an opportunity. Cheap search and display advertising offered instant visibility—particularly for grifts and scams. Podcast listeners, meanwhile, grew accustomed to hosts peddling direct-to-consumer mattresses and underwear subscriptions.

In the twentieth century, advertisements were often as memorable as the programs they accompanied. Slogans like "Where's the beef?" became cultural touchstones. Online ads, by contrast, rarely attained such iconic status. Instead, they became vehicles for forgettable, low-quality products that emerged from the fringes of the marketplace. A good example was dietary supplements. Exempt from FDA regulation, these pills promised miraculous results without needing to prove their efficacy. Nutritionists consistently questioned their value for individuals with balanced diets, yet the industry ballooned to $30 billion in the United States.

Tim Ferriss, author of *The 4-Hour Workweek*, launched his career with BrainQuicken, a nootropic pill containing guarana and a proprietary "cognamine" blend that purportedly enhanced cognitive performance. The now-disgraced payment processor Wirecard transitioned from facilitating pornography and gambling transactions to sales of "nutraceuticals." Unlike pharmaceuticals, which require millions in development costs and rigorous testing, selling placebos was practically effortless. While snake oil salesmen may have once earned revenue but little respect, they now recast themselves as genius entrepreneurs. Even if the product was a fraud, they could be lauded for their marketing savvy.

The entire internet media ecosystem relied on dubious products, especially as the core media platforms cared less and less about how they funded their operations. Right-wing pundits propped up their empires with ad revenue from scams involving gold bullion, collectible plates, and dietary supplements. Alex Jones famously bankrolled *Infowars* by selling a nootropic with Bacopa called Brain Force Plus.

At the other end of the cultural spectrum, similar products targeted the upper-middle class with sleeker packaging and a veneer of wellness. Gwyneth Paltrow's Goop sold their Bacopa nootropic as Why Am I So Effing Tired? and another called Nerd Alert. Start-ups like Care/of offered "personalized" vitamin packs with minimalist design reminiscent of the trendy café chain Blue Bottle Coffee. Ritual, a competing vitamin brand, gained traction with aesthetically pleasing capsules featuring beadlets suspended in oil. Its marketing promised "traceable" ingredients and a commitment to "100% sustainable packaging" by 2025. The entire spectrum of politics and tastes found expression in unnecessary, inefficacious pills—all created, distributed, and gobbled up in a collective act of magical thinking and bad faith.

———

There was a curious link between Paris Hilton, Lady Gaga, Insane Clown Posse, and YouTuber Michelle Phan: a book called *The Secret*. This 2006 self-help tome advocated a life strategy called "manifesting": focusing positive thoughts on a desired outcome to make it happen. This worked, according to the book's Australian author, Rhonda Byrne, because of a scientific "Law of Attraction." "Thoughts are magnetic, and thoughts have a frequency," Byrne asserted. "As you think thoughts, they are sent out into the Universe, and they magnetically attract all like things that are on the same frequency." She cited biblical figures such as Abraham, Moses, and Jesus as early adopters of manifesting, claiming that they enjoyed "more affluent lifestyles than many present-day millionaires could conceive of."

For her brave efforts to share this secret knowledge with humanity, Byrne sold thirty-five million copies of her book, inspiring a generation of celebrities, dreamers, and grifters. Paris Hilton discovered *The Secret* in jail when "a compassionate guard played the audiobook on the speaker system so everyone could hear Rhonda Byrne's reassuring words." Violent J of Insane Clown Posse adopted it as a personal creed: "You have to manifest anything you want. I don't care if you have nothing. I don't care if you were born living under a rock. . . . You can still manifest it and make it happen."

A major driver of *The Secret*'s popularity was Oprah Winfrey, who devoted several episodes of her show in 2006 and 2007 to the book's teachings. By then, Oprah had transcended her role as a television personality to become a cultural sage, especially for American women. Her influence reached its peak in those years, topping *Forbes*'s Celebrity 100 list five times. As *Variety*'s Brian Lowry wrote in 2011, Oprah's "signature power is derived from a singular source, stemming from her ability to create a lucrative commodity: experts." Through her platform, she launched the careers of now-famous figures like psychologist Dr. Phil, wellness advocate Dr. Oz, financial guru Suze Orman, and chef Rachael Ray.

Critics frequently questioned the dubious advice espoused by Oprah's protégés. Dr. Oz used his Oprah-produced show to promote "miracle elixirs, homeopathy, imaginary energies, and psychics who communicate with the dead." Even Oprah herself occasionally had to rein in her anointed experts. When her book club recommendation, James Frey's 2003 memoir, *A Million Little Pieces*, was exposed by the Smoking Gun for containing fabrications, Oprah initially defended the work. But as evidence of deceit mounted, she publicly confronted Frey and his publisher on her show, earning widespread praise for her integrity. For this, *Washington Post* columnist Richard Cohen named her "mensch of the year."

During her peak years of fame, Oprah embraced *The Secret* with enthusiasm. At first, the promotion of Byrne's new take on the power of positive thinking seemed harmless. (Although the entire book is pseudoscientific, it also bizarrely includes fabricated quotes from Ralph Waldo Emerson, such as "The secret is the answer to all that has been, all that is, and all that will ever be.") Critics argued that the biggest danger of manifesting was its tendency to discourage proper preparation for negative contingencies, fostering complacency instead of action. The stakes became disturbingly high, however, when a breast cancer patient named Kim wrote to Oprah pledging to stop chemotherapy. She would follow *The Secret*'s advice and just "manifest" her health. Oprah had to then clarify that the Law of Attraction "is just one law. Not the only law."

Overall, however, as Kurt Andersen wrote, "Perhaps more than any other single American, [Oprah] is responsible for giving national platforms and legitimacy to all sorts of magical thinking, from pseudoscientific to purely mystical, fantasies about extraterrestrials, paranormal experience, satanic cults, and more." While she may have stopped Kim's full reliance on pseudoscience, it's unclear how many other Kims might be out there among the book's tens of millions of readers.

Years after the initial *Secret* mania subsided, manifesting surged back into popularity among younger generations, especially on TikTok. Many young women began to diligently write a "manifestation journal" based on the idea that "scripting" a desire makes it more likely to happen. This new faith blended easily with numerology. In one video with two million views, a TikToker recommended the "3x33" method: taking "the sentence [*sic*] I told you" and writing it down thirty-three times in three days.

These New Age practices took on the moniker *woo-woo*, which originated in rationalists' pejorative name for pseudoscience. Such rationalist critiques began to feel as outdated and shrill as the liberal triumphalism of the Obama era. With technocracy delivering nothing but a hypercapitalist economy and the chaos of Trump's presidency, woo-woo emerged as a potential counterbalance. Manifesting, astrology, and other mystical practices offered not just solace but also a sense of agency. Most critically, woo-woo aligned perfectly with capitalism, as magical thinking often became a tool for building profitable personal brands and working toward future fortunes.

After a long lull in mainstream popularity, astrology found new relevance in the Trump years. "There's something that's happened in the last five years that's given it an edginess, a relevance for this time and place, that it hasn't had for a good 35 years," one Los Angeles astrologer told *The Atlantic* in 2018. Platforms like *BuzzFeed* were early adopters, using astrology-based quizzes to drive traffic. Amanda Montell observed, "High-functioning adults in Los Angeles commonly call upon zodiac signs and retrograde star positions to excuse indiscretions from missed appointments to poor texting etiquette."

Astrology also gained celebrity endorsement. Sagittarius Taylor Swift explained her feud with Katy Perry through the stars: "She's like, 'I'm a Scorpio. Scorpios just strike when they feel threatened.' And I was like, 'Well, I'm an archer. We literally stand back, assess the situation, process how we feel about it, raise a bow, pull it back, and fire.'"

Pundits posited millennials' new interest in star signs as a response to the era's political turbulence. "People tend to turn to astrology in times of stress," *The Atlantic*'s Julie Beck explained. Millennials, as "the most stressed generation," found both comfort and empowerment in its cosmic frameworks. Beyond being a coping mechanism, astrology offered a fun, inclusive, and distinctly woo-woo form of feminism. For women and LGBTQ+ communities, it became a way to navigate careers, relationships, and the creation of new identities.

Astrology also fit comfortably into a meme-driven culture, where, as Beck observed, its "symbols and shorthand are often baked into communication." Each zodiac sign became its own meme, complete with its own buzzwords and traits. Millennial astrologers capitalized on a variety of formats to share their insights with a new, tech-savvy audience. Aliza Kelly, for example, served as an in-house astrologer for *The Cut*, wrote a column for *Cosmopolitan*, appeared on Drew Barrymore's show, offered private online chart readings, hosted Soho House events, consulted for the astrology app Sanctuary, and recorded an astrology podcast.

Astrology also proved adaptable to cultural commentary, from celebrity gossip to political analysis. "Woke astrologer" Chani Nicholas used star charts to interpret events like #MeToo and other social phenomena, connecting them to cosmic alignments like "a new moon in Scorpio." In 2019, New York

City astrology students pored over Jeffrey Epstein's chart, noting that he "had his sun in Aquarius and his moon in Aries, so he was used to having his way." One student accurately predicted, "This is not a guy who's going to live long in prison."

At the same time, astrology served many aspiring entrepreneurs well. Astrologist Maren Altman gained millions of followers on TikTok and YouTube through a mix of astrological musings and lifestyle content (as well as bikini-clad photos and artistic nudes on Instagram). As a teen, Altman charged her friends thirty dollars for thirty-minute readings, and now her Astrology Academy commanded a $1,499 fee to aspiring fortune-tellers. Apps like Co-Star, which offered hyper-personalized astrological insights, raised millions in funding. Astrology joined mindfulness as another spiritual tool comfortably embedded in corporate culture. Companies like Aetna, General Mills, and Goldman Sachs provided free meditation training to employees.

The happy marriage of woo-woo and capitalism echoed the seventies' New Age movement, which emerged from the sixties' collective countercultural ideals. But as Tom Wolfe famously wrote, this communal spirituality quickly devolved into the "Me" generation, marked by self-help cults like EST, Synanon, and Scientology. These groups emphasized individual transformation, beginning with "the most delicious look inward" and a heavy dose of narcissism. In the 2010s, this same spirit resurfaced in practices like manifesting, nootropic pills, and astrology—modern self-help tools tailored for the pursuit of personal success. As Kurt Andersen noted, *The Secret* stripped traditional American ideals—"individualism and supernaturalism and belief in belief"—of their religious and moral trappings, reducing them to the pure materialist lust.

While *The Secret* offered the theoretical possibility of manifesting good for society, most readers weren't looking for inspiration to take collectivist action. As podcast host Peter Shamshiri concluded, *The Secret* promoted a destructive worldview: "The book is proposing the tenets of the fall of human civilization. . . . The complete disconnection of every person from every other person, the discarding of all knowledge heretofore acquired. All of it to be replaced by the unfiltered pursuit of our shallowest desires."

Over the twenty-first century, evangelical Christianity also increasingly adopted self-help tropes. By 2006, 17 percent of American Christians adhered to the "prosperity gospel," which equated Christian faith with material success—particularly financial wealth. Rooted in Pentecostal traditions, prosperity preachers offered not just spiritual guidance but practical advice on getting rich, often framed as a divine reward. Parishioners were encouraged to tithe generously as an investment in God's "hundredfold" returns.

One of the most infamous prosperity preachers, Rev. Creflo A. Dollar Jr. (his real name!), rose to prominence in the early 2000s, preaching the virtues of faith-driven wealth accumulation. Dollar himself was a walking advertisement for his message, enjoying God's blessings in the form of "Rolls-Royces, private jets, [a] million-dollar Atlanta home and [a] $2.5 million Manhattan apartment." Despite widespread condemnation of the prosperity gospel as a "blight on the face of Christianity," Dollar's sermons remained popular for their promise of personal transformation and material gain.

Meanwhile, in Houston, Joel Osteen of Lakewood Church took prosperity preaching to an even grander stage. Osteen's services drew such large crowds that he booked out the entire Compaq Center. His messaging, though couched in Christian language, often sounded more like *The Secret* than the Bible: "It's not a focus on money. It's a focus on fulfilling your purpose." Osteen's books, staples of airport gift shops, sold millions of copies. Despite forgoing a salary from his church, he lived in a $12 million mansion, though this opulence also made him a lightning rod for criticism. In 2017, when Hurricane Harvey devastated Houston, Osteen faced public outrage for refusing to open his megachurch to flood victims. His congregation had more important priorities than tending to the needy.

Astrology, manifestation, and pseudoscientific health trends may have been seen as harmless when contained in a cultural space—but what would woo-woo political rebellion look like?

The Trump era began with the Donald descending a golden escalator on June 16, 2015, and it reached a new level of chaos with the riot at the Capitol on January 6, 2021.

2020 was harrowing. The world grappled with a global pandemic, the economy cratered, and the United States erupted in protest after George Floyd's murder. Against this backdrop, former vice president Joe Biden ran against Donald Trump in a bitterly contested election. And despite an endorsement from SoundCloud rapper Lil Pump, Trump lost by over seven million votes. Refusing to concede, Trump, along with his allies, hatched a convoluted plan to overturn the results through "alternative slates of electors." Around one a.m. on January 6, Trump tweeted, "If Vice President @Mike_Pence comes through for us, we will win the Presidency"—implying Pence could use his ceremonial role to decertify Electoral College results and send the election back to the states.

As dawn broke, Trump supporters, including Alex Jones, the Proud Boys, the Oath Keepers live streamer Anthime "Baked Alaska" Gionet, and even *Bob's Burgers* voice actor Jay Johnston, congregated at the Ellipse outside the White House. Trump appeared shortly before noon and delivered a fiery speech: "We fight. We fight like hell and if you don't fight like hell, you're not going to have a country anymore." Around this time, authorities discovered pipe bombs at the Democratic National Committee and Republican National Committee headquarters. Meanwhile, Trump returned to the White House to watch events unfold on Fox News.

By 2:13 p.m., rioters breached the Capitol. Confederate flags mingled with online-right symbols: Pepe the Frog T-shirts, Kekistan and thin blue line flags. Jacob Chansley, the self-styled "QAnon Shaman," was shirtless, wore red, white, and blue face paint and a fur hat with horns, and carried an American flag on a spear. Amid the chaos, QAnon follower Ashli Babbitt was killed. Despite frantic phone calls from politicians begging Trump to intervene, he refused. Two full hours later, he finally released a video urging his supporters to go home, but not before praising them: "We love you. You're very special."

This was America's first televised coup attempt—a counter-counter-cultural Lollapalooza of political delusion. The January 6 planners, in the grip of their own magical thinking, believed a ragtag riot and shoddy legal schemes could keep Trump in the White House. Even archconservative Senate majority leader Mitch McConnell warned that the plan's success would mean "our democracy would enter a death spiral." But like Theranos and the Fyre Festival, the entire scheme collapsed under its own incoherence, driven by unquestioning belief and a total lack of perspicacity. The January 6 effort embodied the chutzpah of the Fyre Festival marketing executive who infamously declared: "Let's just do it and be legends, man."

At 3:32 a.m. on January 7, Congress finished certifying the Electoral College votes, formally confirming Biden's victory. Trump went into exile at Mar-a-Lago. Yet not even stoking an armed insurrection would disqualify Trump from public life. Could there be consequences for such magical thinking when everyone's thoughts were increasingly magical?

Part Four

2020–2025

THE OMNIVORE MONOCULTURE
Stagnation, Similarities, and Mediocrity— and Their Discontents

The Dutch musician Kiowa Roukema caught the entrepreneurial bug as a teenager. He made his first pocket money selling custom backgrounds to YouTubers. Then a friend noticed his knack for computers and gave him a copy of the music-production software FL Studio. Over the next four months, Roukema taught himself how to make hip-hop beats, selling his creations on YouTube under the alias YoungKio. A few early successes allowed him to open a formal account on the beat marketplace BeatStars, where his business took off.

One day, looking to challenge himself creatively, Roukema experimented with an unlikely sample: "Ghosts IV–34," a 2008 track from industrial pop group Nine Inch Nails. Roukema had never heard of them. Ignoring warnings from friends against using this folky banjo hook, he added a trap beat under it and uploaded the result to BeatStars as a "Future Type Beat," in reference to the Atlanta trap star Future.

Weeks later in Atlanta, nineteen-year-old Montero Lamar Hill, who ran a Nicki Minaj stan account on Twitter and recorded as Lil Nas X, purchased Roukema's beat for thirty dollars. He spent an additional twenty at a local studio to record a country-inflected, singsong rap over it. A month later Lil Nas X released it as "Old Town Road."

Lil Nas X's timing was perfect. Months earlier, Twitter user Bri Malandro had launched the Yeehaw Agenda, a campaign to reclaim the heritage of Black cowboys. On TikTok, this evolved into the Yeehaw Challenge, in which users dressed in cowboy outfits while dancing to cowboy-inspired songs. Bearded hipster Michael Pelchat posted his entry to the trend by dancing to "Old Town Road," which he'd discovered on SoundCloud. As his video went viral, so did the song. The explosive number of playbacks of "Old Town Road" sent the song soaring up the *Billboard* charts—under both hip-hop and country.

Billboard responded to Lil Nas X's incredible homegrown feat by kicking the song off the country charts. They explained, "While 'Old Town Road' incorporates references to country and cowboy imagery, it does not embrace enough elements of today's country music to chart in its current version." By this point, however, Lil Nas X had attracted enough industry bigwigs to his corner for a proper counterstrike. A month later, he released a new duet of "Old Town Road" with 1990s country superstar Billy Ray Cyrus—father of pop icon Miley Cyrus—leaning further into the hip-hop–country hybrid. The result shattered records, including a jaw-dropping 143 million streams in a single week.

The success of "Old Town Road"—and the deus ex machina of Billy Ray Cyrus supporting the bedroom rap of a gay Black teen from Atlanta—marked the final step of omnivore tastes becoming an *omnivore monoculture*. The "mainstream" market was now all-inclusive and boundaryless, containing seemingly every possible genre. In previous notions of monoculture, the culture industry permitted only a very narrow set of stylistic conventions. During the late 1950s, for example, almost every pop song pulled from the same handful of chord progressions. In the omnivore monoculture, artists were free to draw from any genre, provided the end result was glossy, marketable pop (with clever digital promotion). This was the culmination of the Neptunes' and Kanye West's fusions of R&B, gospel, streetwear, street art, rock, techno, indie rock, reality TV, and high fashion. But before Lil Nas X, there was one stubborn holdout: country music.

Omnivore tastes were cosmopolitan, and country music was a proud bastion of provincial American tastes. While genre distinctions often function as artistic boundaries, they also serve as shorthand for audiences who want nothing to do with each other. Despite journalist Nadine Smith's observation that hip-hop and country are "the two forms of pop music that speak most directly to the everyday problems of ordinary people struggling to survive," fans of each genre historically despised the other in reflection of a broader social conflict.

Yet country music long borrowed from mainstream pop trends to stay relevant. By the late 2010s, trap-influenced beats began creeping into country tracks in an appeal to Top 40 radio. Bebe Rexha's collaboration with country act Florida Georgia Line, "Meant to Be," used the 808 kicks and snaps of Southern rap. But for such fusions to be embraced as innovative, hip-hop needed to take the lead. This arguably began with Young Thug's 2017 mixtape, *Beautiful Thugger Girls*, but the particularly catchy fusion of country, trap, and alternative in "Old Town Road"—and its rise on TikTok—fueled an especially explosive pop moment.

This welcomed country music inside the omnivore monoculture. In 2022, rapper Lil Durk collaborated with rising country star Morgan Wallen on "Broadway Girls." Country artist Jelly Roll embraced the face tattoos of SoundCloud rappers, while rapper Post Malone explored country music with an entire album. By 2024, country-rap no longer felt controversial: Nigerian American artist Shaboozey topped the *Billboard* country charts with "A Bar Song (Tipsy)," a genre-blending hit that reworked J-Kwon's 2004 rap classic, "Tipsy."

By the 2020s, as music journalist Amanda Petrusich noted, "Genre feels increasingly irrelevant to the way we think about, create, and consume art." Enforcing genre divisions felt elitist, or worse. In early 2020, Tyler, the Creator criticized the Grammy category of "urban" music, calling it "a politically correct way to say the N-word." The Grammys dropped the term shortly afterward.

But the total freedom of genre ironically engendered a profound sense of stagnancy. Pioneering Black artists had already blended nearly every genre that could be blended. The omnivore monoculture felt complete. By including every possible style, there were no more obvious future avenues for unexpected experimentation or exploration. And with poptimism long discouraging

younger artists from pursuing strange, subversive sounds, the culture industry had few exciting subcultures from which to steal.

Moreover, the omnivore monoculture created steep barriers to entry for
younger artists. In the past, distinct genres allowed emerging musicians to
build followings in niche scenes before attempting to cross over into the
mainstream. Underground movements often developed sounds that made
established artists seem outdated—but those ecosystems had largely disappeared. Instead, new artists were forced to compete directly with established
stars, using the same playbook but with fewer resources. And poptimist critics only took notice once newcomers had already made it big. A rising artist
might land a spot on a popular Spotify playlist, but few listeners bothered to
learn their name. This explained why breaking a new artist cost labels more
than $1 million.

These dynamics further solidified the dominance of monopoly artists,
whose stature only grew. Taylor Swift first rose to prominence in the aughts
as a country-pop sensation, and by the 2020s, she was a superstar drawing
comparisons to the Beatles in terms of influence. Surviving the Scooter
Braun drama only made her stronger. After 2020, she had achieved eight
Billboard number-one hits. Her Eras Tour brought in over $2 billion, and its
accompanying film became the highest-grossing concert documentary of all
time. Swift even enjoyed a leading position in the vinyl revival: Six of the top
bestselling records were her albums, despite half of the buyers lacking turntables to play them.

Yet, despite her cultural and commercial dominance, Swift declined to
take the Neptunes' path of experimentation. She saw herself as a business.
"Commerce used to be a dirty word," said music lawyer Cliff Fluet. "Now it's
like, 'I'm an industry, a conglomerate. I'm Taylor Swift Inc.'" This made it difficult to judge her output as *music*. Critics, notably *The New Yorker*'s Sinéad
O'Sullivan, noted flaws in her eleventh studio album, *The Tortured Poets Department*: "the interminable length, the repetitive synth overlays . . . the un-
inspired lyrics." But this was beside the point. "She is not creating standalone
albums," O'Sullivan wrote, "but, rather, a musical franchise." The album's

performance surely satisfied her corporate-level KPIs: *The Tortured Poets Department* broke records with 314.5 million streams on its first day of release.

By 2023, Swift's cultural omnipresence reached new heights when Gannett, the nation's largest newspaper chain, hired a dedicated reporter solely to cover her. A backlash to her preeminence erupted across the political and cultural spectrum. Conservative critic Mark Hemingway lamented that her dominance reflected a debased cultural landscape: "Swift is very, very good at serving an audience that has been conditioned to accept less in terms of musical and lyrical sophistication." High-fashion enthusiasts complained about her unadventurous personal style. Yet, as fashion critic Cathy Horyn noted, Swift's muted sartorial choices were part of her broader business strategy: "She isn't entirely comfortable with high fashion, and maybe that's something she shares with her young fans and why they instinctively relate to her."

Swift's only serious rival was Beyoncé, whose career stretched back to Destiny's Child in the late 1990s. In 2024, Beyoncé was crowned *Billboard*'s "Greatest Pop Star of the 21st Century." She had amassed a record ninety-nine Grammy nominations and won thirty-five. Though her album sales declined after 2013's *Beyoncé*, her critical reputation remained formidable—almost intimidating. In 2020, *The Daily Beast* asked bluntly, "Why Are People So Deathly Afraid of Criticizing Beyoncé?"

Unlike Swift, Beyoncé pushed genre boundaries. She dabbled in country with "Daddy Lessons" (2016), explored bridge-and-tunnel house music on *Renaissance* (2022), and reinterpreted country again with *Cowboy Carter* (2024). Like many twenty-first-century artists, she also expanded into consumer goods, launching the hair care line Cécred and partnering with Moët Hennessy to create a Texas-finished rye whisky, SirDavis.

Beyoncé's and her husband Jay-Z's self-positioning as pop royalty reframed the entire narrative of culture into a story of their destiny. Their 2021 Tiffany & Co. advertising campaign placed them in front of a baby-blue Jean-Michel Basquiat painting, which Tiffany's dubiously claimed was an homage to its blue box. Jay-Z, from the comfort of Maybachs and opulent mansions, positioned his wealth as revolutionary while complaining that any labeling of him as a "capitalist" was akin to a racial epithet.

Hip-hop, which began as the self-expression of extreme outsiders, now provided the backdrop for luxury consumption. This threw the genre into an existential crisis. Rap could not be more mainstream. Kendrick Lamar won a Pulitzer in 2018, and melodic Canadian rapper Drake shattered records with seventy-eight Top 10 hits. Yet, as critic Jason England argued, hip-hop was not conqueror but "conquered": "Hip hop *assimilated*. And that always comes at a cost." Hits were "conservative, white-flattering, and, maybe worst of all, predictable." Blame landed squarely on Jay-Z and his *"Rich Dad Poor Dad* rap albums." "Popular music has sounded—for a long, long time—like prosperity gospel," England wrote, "and too many of the rappers are sounding more like megachurch pastors than artists or insightful street reporters."

Yet aspiring artists looked to Beyoncé and Jay-Z as standard-bearers for industry success. Bronx drill rapper Ice Spice made waves in 2022 with her bawdy girl-power track, "Munch (Feelin' U)." By 2023, she was collaborating with Dunkin' and Ben Affleck on the Ice Spice Munchkins Drink.

This monopolistic aspect of pop music froze the charts into place, as few novice acts could challenge the existing winners. On top of that sense of stagnancy, retromania entered an even more intense phase with a rise in interpolations—hooks and melodies from older hits being repurposed in new songs. While the music industry had always relied on covers, and hip-hop had emerged from sampling, interpolations took recycling to another level. Music publishers organized songwriters into weeklong camps where they attempted to interpolate the company's back catalog. In rare cases, interpolations achieved an elegance in referencing tradition: Ariana Grande's "7 Rings" transformed *The Sound of Music*'s "My Favorite Things" into a trap anthem. For the most part, however, the practice suggested a total creative exhaustion, as though all possible melodies had been written. Pop culture in 2022 could be summed up by the recycling of Peter Bjorn and John's 2006 indie hit, "Young Folks," into OneRepublic's "I Ain't Worried," featured on the *Top Gun: Maverick* soundtrack. Taylor Swift found herself instantly interpolated when Olivia Rodrigo's 2021 song "Deja Vu" reworked Swift's 2019 track "Cruel Summer."

With the influence of the twentieth century so persistent, alternative legends like the Pixies, Pavement, and My Bloody Valentine returned to touring, earning sums that dwarfed their original payouts. Iconic artists performed their most celebrated albums in their entirety, playing them track for track as if frozen in time. Bruce Springsteen revisited *The River*, U2 resurrected *The Joshua Tree*, and Nas brought *Illmatic* back to life onstage.

For many, these performances were thrilling, offering a chance to relive cultural touchstones. But as novelist Peter C. Baker remarked, "They feel like the onward acceleration of a culture industry that is unsettlingly dedicated—not just in our concert halls but on our screens and everywhere else it can reach us—to monetizing our nostalgic attachment to media from the past." The industry now had an entire arsenal of techniques for eking out tiny bits of novelty without ever having to offer anything truly new.

The defining trends of the late 2010s—megastars, interpolations, and a pervasive sense of creative stagnation—reached a new level of monotony during the COVID-19 pandemic. As the world plunged into isolation, billions endured closed borders, lockdowns, and a collective uncertainty about the future. The pandemic claimed millions of lives and reshaped economies. Meanwhile, the professional class made do with ersatz socialization: drinking takeout Negronis on Zoom cocktail parties or holding synchronized TV streaming sessions with friends. Yet the overall mood was one of social isolation. "We're disconnecting from each other even though online we're probably more connected than we've ever been," Pharrell Williams told *i-D* magazine in June 2020.

The pandemic period seemed to intensify trends already in motion. The culture industry doubled down on diversity, equity, and inclusion in the wake of the racial reckoning of 2020, and with Joe Biden's inauguration, there was an opportunity to tone down the culture war. Netflix's adaptation of J. D. Vance's book, *Hillbilly Elegy*, landed with a thud. As film critic A. S. Hamrah wrote, it was considered "one of the worst films of the year by pretty much everybody who saw it."

There was never a singular way to describe "pandemic culture." The closest thing to a defining sound arrived in April 2020 with Fiona Apple's defiant, #MeToo-inflected album, *Fetch the Bolt Cutters*, which earned a rare 10.0 from *Pitchfork*. But like most twenty-first-century discourse, the moment quickly faded. Later that year, Apple TV+'s *Ted Lasso* became a hallmark of the era's "comfort food TV," praised for making us "feel good without asking too much of us." On the other end of the violence spectrum, Netflix scored a global hit in 2021 with *Squid Game*, a dystopian thriller heavily influenced by the Japanese cult film *Battle Royale* and the *Hunger Games* novels.

The pandemic gave everyone more time to explore the seemingly infinite options of available online entertainment, but much of it felt distinctly underwhelming—a sense captured by the new slang *mid*. The streaming services lured in their first customers among educated sophisticates in pursuit of prestige television. But the need for constant growth meant catering to subscribers in less refined taste worlds. Thus began a glut of mediocre TV: a reality show about TikTokers called *Hype House* and the vacuous *Emily in Paris*.

This coincided with the dominance of what writer and consultant Venkatesh Rao described in 2017 as "premium mediocre"—products for which the idea was much glossier than the execution. The canonical example was gourmet cupcakes. As Amanda Mull observed in *The Atlantic*: "I remain unconvinced that anyone ever took genuine pleasure in eating a dry, fist-size Crumbs Bake Shop cupcake topped with a mountain of hardened buttercream." A major source for premium mediocre goods emerged from influencers' monetization strategies. They partnered with private-label manufacturers to slap their name on commodities as cash grabs. One firm, Masteroast, provided beans for over a thousand coffee brands, with the labels simply picking from a series of diagnostic codes to find the right formula.

Mainstream culture may never have been a reliable place to seek out innovation, but in the 2020s, even the culture of the creative class felt stagnant. Artists once energized cities with edgy bars, experimental storefronts, and offbeat gathering places. Now online culture flattened these aesthetics into what critic Kyle Chayka dubbed "AirSpace": identical, polished interiors offering the same cortados, craft beer, and avocado toast served on raw wood tables, surrounded by exposed brick and Edison bulbs. AirSpace catered to digital nomads who flitted between low-cost creative hubs like Tbilisi and Tallinn without ever having to compromise on their faux-artisanal tastes. The accessibility of AirSpace's aesthetics owed much to Chinese-made dupes— convincing knockoffs of high-end furniture and fixtures that allowed proprietors to re-create the look for a fraction of the price.

Global standardization wasn't confined to spaces or objects; it also reshaped bodies. *The New Yorker*'s Jia Tolentino coined the phrase "Instagram face" to describe the homogenized visage proliferating across social media: "a young face . . . with poreless skin and plump, high cheekbones . . . catlike eyes and long, cartoonish lashes . . . a small, neat nose and full, lush lips." The look was the beauty equivalent of the omnivore monoculture; makeup artist Colby Smith described it as "an overly tan skin tone, a South Asian influence with the brows and eye shape, an African-American influence with the lips, a Caucasian influence with the nose, a cheek structure that is predominantly Native American and Middle Eastern."

The "patients zero" for Instagram face were Kim Kardashian West, Kendall Jenner, Bella Hadid, and Emily Ratajkowski. As cosmetic technologies got safer and less intrusive, these procedures became more socially acceptable. Between 2005 and 2019, there was a 90 percent increase in augmentation surgeries, including the controversial Brazilian butt lift. Filters on social media further blurred the line between real and virtual beauty. And once app users saw their faces "ten per cent more conventionally attractive," as Tolentino put it, they often brought these images into consultations for plastic surgery. But they also wanted to look like one person in particular. Celebrity surgeon Dr. Jason Diamond noted, "thirty per cent of people come in bringing a photo of Kim, or someone like Kim."

Just as filtered faces became actual faces, marketing campaigns became the culture itself. In mid-2023, online communities noticed that *Barbie* and *Oppenheimer* were set to release on the same day, spawning "Barbenheimer" memes that juxtaposed and synthesized the two films' wildly different aesthetics. This user-generated marketing frenzy became an online phenomenon, elevating both movies to box-office juggernauts. In the case of *Barbie*, it wasn't enough for the film to be a two-hour commercial for selling large-busted plastic dolls to children; the producers also collaborated with 165 brands for the global marketing campaign. In 2024, *Wicked* set the new bar for collaborations at 400.

Even with cultural fragmentation, Barbenheimer demonstrated the eternal need for communal participation in a centralized cultural conversation. The twin hits underscored a return to "head" culture, defying Chris Anderson's "long tail" theory. Instead of spreading into infinite niches, cultural dialogue focused on a few shared events.

The line between mass culture and mass marketing was always thin, but as it dissolved, this further freed celebrities from having to pretend to be pure-minded artists. Appearance fees in mainstream productions remained profitable yet no longer sufficed for stars' financial ambitions. Actors transitioned from performers to producers to create their own content empires. Reese Witherspoon's companies Pacific Standard and Hello Sunshine produced hits like *Gone Girl* and *The Morning Show*. Jessica Alba launched the household goods supplier the Honest Company. George Clooney sold his cofounded Casamigos tequila brand to multinational beverage company Diageo for up to $1 billion. Ryan Reynolds followed a similar path, investing in Aviation gin in 2018 and selling it to the same company for upwards of $610 million three years later. Reynolds also invested in Mint Mobile, which T-Mobile acquired in 2023 for $1.35 billion. Rihanna, who launched Fenty Beauty in partnership with LVMH in 2017, was declared a billionaire by *Forbes* in 2021.

In the 1990s, top-tier Hollywood talent often resisted product endorsements, agreeing to appear only in Japanese TV commercials, where their involvement was less likely to be noticed. In the twenty-first century, they were no longer just spokespeople but founders and investors. Once they were recast as entrepreneurs, there was no shame in promotional activities. Sydney Sweeney, fresh off bagging a $7.5 million film role, not only appeared in campaigns for high-end brands like Miu Miu and Jimmy Choo but also promoted mass-market products like low-rent sneaker brand HeyDude and men's body wash Dr. Squatch.

This all had a major effect on the cultural ecosystem: pulling people known for their artistic craft into unambiguous business roles, and pushing fans to spend their money not just on media but across a wide range of premium mediocre commodities. In this new paradigm, the culture industry could no longer sustain itself on culture alone. Personal fame was a loss leader to sell stuff.

––––––––

The most popular TikTok video of 2020 was a ten-second clip of Bella Poarch lip-synching and bobbing her head to the 2016 British grime track "M to the B" before crossing her eyes. The video amassed over five hundred million views.

Poarch took up TikTok while stuck at home during the pandemic. The platform soon became her springboard to cultural prominence, establishing her as a leading media icon of Gen Z. This generation, born between 1997 and 2012, grew up in a fully digitized world, with the internet as a constant presence. The oldest members of the cohort navigated their teenage years alongside the rise of smartphones, while younger ones grew up immersed in the virtual landscapes of *Roblox* and *Minecraft*.

If Gen X found their voice through MTV and millennials discovered themselves on YouTube, Gen Z's cultural baptism was TikTok. Unlike earlier platforms requiring users to search and subscribe, TikTok's algorithm fed viewers an endless, personalized playlist of short, vertical videos. Gen Z didn't just watch TikTok; they built its culture from scratch, creating a closed-off, self-referential world ruled by its own arcane conventions. This ecosystem operated largely without the traditional culture industry's influence. And unlike MTV and YouTube, TikTok had e-commerce baked into the platform.

TikTok's emergence marked a seismic shift in cultural production. It ended the long-standing monopoly of nerds—who pursued film and TV careers through years of training and deep study of the medium—on visual storytelling. Now anyone with a smartphone could shoot, edit, and publish their own short films. In this more competitive marketplace, young audiences overwhelmingly gravitated toward the naturally charismatic and conventionally attractive. "My absolute favorite thing about TikTok," said millennial stand-up Taylor Tomlinson, "is all these people working so hard on their videos—only to have a super-hot girl lip-sync their video and they get like a billion likes."

Sophistication took a back seat to the raw and random. TikTok's top content was absurd, amateur, unfiltered, often embracing the strange and surreal: obsessive fandom over a Chinese glycine factory, spinning dances set to Pavement's obscure B-side "Harness Your Hopes," and the enigmatic chaos of #corecore, described as a "mishmash of stimuli" with no clear purpose. Rather than radical aesthetics, extremely juvenile taste served as a moat.

Despite their insular cultural habits, Gen Z didn't spark much worry among parents about being reckless youth. They drank less, smoked less, avoided drugs, and experienced teenage pregnancy at one third the rate of millennials. In fact, they were hard to quite define: tech savvy and environmentally conscious, yet quite cynical. In *The New York Times*, essayist Stephen Marche described his Gen Z son's world as "a dark one—full of corporate triumph and the defeat of public spirit, where systems of meaning are decaying and a lack of clarity is spreading." But they had a sense of humor about it.

One way they rebelled against their elders was by relentlessly mocking them. A favorite Gen Z phrase was "OK boomer"—shorthand for dismissing outdated, bigoted viewpoints. Gen Z skewered their immediate millennial predecessors for overusing the crying-laughing-face emoji and wearing no-show ankle socks. Millennials' performative earnestness had become "cringe," their kitschy taste "cheugy," and their habit of waiting a beat before talking in TikTok videos derided as the "Millennial pause."

Z perhaps had a point: Millennials' long-running collective moaning about structural inequities became harder to take seriously as they prospered in middle age. Generational researcher Jean Twenge concluded in 2023, "Millennials, as a group, are not broke—they are, in fact, thriving economically." By the end of the 2010s, millennial households out-earned previous generations of the same age, even when adjusted for inflation. While home-ownership rates were down, the gap was less dire than the narrative suggested. Moreover, millennials stood poised to inherit a massive wealth transfer from their baby boomer parents. As the evidence for permanent victimization evaporated, millennials lost their entire self-narrative.

Despite mocking millennials, Gen Z shared one of their key ambitions: to get rich through online hustles. It was a quite plausible career path by 2024, when thirteen million Americans—about 7 percent of the workforce—made a living through the creation of social media content. Living completely online, however, gave them skewed expectations about money. In a poll that year, millennials identified $180,900 as the salary required for "financial success," while Gen Z set the bar at $587,800. This explains why another survey found that over half of Gen Z respondents reported feeling as though they lacked the income to live the way they wanted.

Amid the backdrop of aspirational dissatisfaction, Gen Z directed its scrutiny toward another group with built-in advantages: "nepo babies." These were the children of celebrities or well-connected families who came to occupy a significant share of public attention. Cultural critic Nate Jones helped create a taxonomy of the offenders, from offspring of famous actors (Maya Hawke, Lily-Rose Depp, Ava Phillippe), to those with industry-savvy families (Lena Dunham), to "industry babies," like Billie Eilish and Kristen Stewart, who benefited from their parents' expertise. Then there were the standard-issue children of wealth: Taylor Swift's father was a stockbroker at

Merrill Lynch and Lana Del Rey's father made his money in "vertical domain portfolios on the internet." Nepotism wasn't limited to traditional media. Actor John C. Reilly's son, LoveLeo, gained attention on TikTok with his viral hit, "Boyfren." The definition expanded further to include "nepo friends," such as Anastasia "Stassie" Karanikolaou, who parlayed her childhood camaraderie with Kylie Jenner into a successful vodka brand.

With so many children of privilege winning the public's attention, it felt like society was returning to an explicitly aristocratic age. As French economist Thomas Piketty observed, "Inherited wealth comes close to being as decisive at the beginning of the twenty-first century as it was in the age of Balzac's *Père Goriot* [set in 1819]." Beyond financial inheritance, cultural capital—connections, industry fluency, or even an ingrained affability—gave the offspring of elites a decided edge in the crowded media landscape.

While TikTok dominated as the epicenter of Gen Z culture, the mass media made its first discovery of the generation's creatives in a familiar place: downtown New York City. In 2021, former *BuzzFeed News* editor Ben Smith reported for *The New York Times* on "Dimes Square," a pocket of lower Manhattan near the restaurant Dimes where a sliver of Gen Z's creative class congregated with their elder millennial friends. This cohort drew on both hipster and post-hipster aesthetics, a sometimes-uncomfortable mix of woke and transgressive irony, all while embracing commercialism and pop. Young novelist Honor Levy captured their dogma when she quipped: "I totally understand Valerie Solanas. But I'd rather be Andy Warhol than her."

Despite its initial buzz, the Dimes Square scene had a short shelf life. Where Gen X's downtown New York post-9/11 faded within a few years, and Lena Dunham's *Girls*-era New York never overcame the immediate groans, Dimes Square became a punch line upon arrival. In the most damning indictment, the scene failed to inspire much imitation from Gen Z peers outside Manhattan.

The true leaders of Gen Z were the top posters on digital platforms—those who believed the entire point of culture was to create content that garnered millions of views and provided enough revenue to not require taking a normal job. Some added a Gen Z touch by channeling their earnings into altruistic causes. Take MrBeast (Jimmy Donaldson), who became You-Tube's number-one creator with grandiose video stunts, often centered on giving away large sums of money. From building a hundred wells in five countries in Africa and rescuing a hundred dogs, he gained a fan base rival-ing Taylor Swift's and Drake's—all without support from the mainstream culture industry. He, too, leveraged his success into producing low-quality private-label goods. This included the MrBeast Burger chain, which received complaints for serving undercooked meat. And he worked with Logan Paul and Olajide "KSI" Olatunji on Lunchly, a copycat version of Lunchables in which the cheese sometimes molded before its expiration date.

On the surface, Gen Z appeared to accept the values and tenets of the monoculture, but there were quiet murmurs of dissent. Internet culture jour-nalist Ryan Broderick observed that while millennials gravitated toward "re-latable, mass-appeal content," Gen Z seemed "curious about bringing back niche coolness." The problem was that Gen Z didn't know how, nor did any-one, really. Coolness had traditionally thrived on exclusivity and scarcity—two traits obliterated by the internet. One proposed solution was to bring back "gatekeeping," which came to mean refusing to publicize information about your favorite things to keep the knowledge more valuable.

Where millennials such as Odd Future and Lena Dunham redefined cool for their generations by appealing to existing institutions, Gen Z's TikTok-era icons largely built careers outside the formal culture industry. This self-isolation created challenges when they attempted to cross over. Bella Poarch secured a record deal with Warner Records but never scored a hit. Louisiana-born Addison Rae attempted to leverage her TikTok following into a mainstream career, appearing in a Netflix reboot of 1999's *She's All That* called *He's All That*. But her momentum stalled after a "cringe" appear-ance on *The Tonight Show Starring Jimmy Fallon*. She struggled to break through with her initial music releases.

A two-tier celebrity system emerged. Traditional stars like actress Zen-daya and tennis player Naomi Osaka navigated the offline world and won roles as Louis Vuitton spokespeople. In 2021, the establishment dipped their toes in Gen Z waters as TikTokers Addison Rae, Jackie Aina, Nikkie de Jager, and Emma Chamberlain attended the Met Gala. By 2024, the organizers recanted: Only Chamberlain and Wisdom Kaye attended that year.

Chamberlain was one of the few Gen Z internet-born creators to break into mainstream institutions. She first rose to fame as a relatable video diarist, openly discussing her acne and the mundane details of her life. Unlike many of her peers, she avoided the sociopathic antics that defined influencer culture, making her a natural fit when luxury brands became eager to connect with Gen Z. When Louis Vuitton partnered with Chamberlain, *The Face* noted that the collaboration "radically changed the idea of who luxury brands deemed 'acceptable' and what was considered possible for creators." She was goofy, but her face and body were blank enough to be molded to fit any brand's image.

In her book, *Extremely Online*, journalist Taylor Lorenz described social media as a "revolution" that demolished "traditional barriers" and gutted "legacy institutions." But a true revolution involves a reversal of status—one in which outsiders don't just bypass gatekeepers but seize control of the establishment. While Gen Z bypassed traditional gatekeepers with their platforms, they had little influence on mainstream cultural standards. The walls of Hollywood and high fashion never seemed higher. Louis Vuitton may have lowered the ladder for Emma Chamberlain, but her ascent was the exception. Most Gen Z creators found that the low-effort videos that gained them massive online followings could not redefine taste for the era and lacked the glamour required to sway older, wealthier consumers. During the sixties, adults needed to become familiar with youth culture in order to maintain their cultural capital. Balding executives and their wives danced the twist at Peppermint Lounge. In the 2020s, adults gained little by seeming "terminally online." This further trapped Gen Z in their self-made silos. The future of their careers relied on an algorithm rather than older guardian angels.

For the Gen Z stars who did break out, they assumed the entire point of becoming famous was self-enrichment rather than cultural influence. Emma

Chamberlain made the miraculous upgrade from homey bedroom videos to Louis Vuitton fashion shows, and what did she do with her new platform? She worked with her talent agency to open Chamberlain Coffee, a commodity business.

"I'm opposite, I'm on the other side," sings British pop rebel Charli XCX in her 2024 Taylor Swift diss track, "Sympathy Is a Knife." Charli's boyfriend was George Daniel from the band the 1975, and in 2023, Swift began dating the band's lead singer, Matty Healy. Charli confessed in the song, "Don't wanna see her backstage at my boyfriend's show / Fingers crossed behind my back / I hope they break up quick." She also questioned Swift's position in her public brawl with Scooter Braun over master rights: "Like, yeah, [the labels] own my masters—that's a fucking record deal. That's what they're paying for." In 2018, Charli had opened for Swift on tour and described it as "getting up onstage and waving to 5-year-olds."

A major taboo of the poptimist age was criticizing mainstream stars. But by 2024, up-and-coming artists began to reject fealty to the pop aristocratic class. Charli's oblique barbs fit with her "annoying, dirty, hedonistic, bra-less" persona, and in 2024, the world ushered in "Brat Summer" in honor of her zeitgeist-defining album *Brat*. Kim Kardashian was a fan: Brat Summer was "all about embracing your bold, unapologetic self."

Trend analyst Sean Monahan, who had helped create the normcore concept, speculated in 2021 about an impending "vibe shift," predicting a revival of "indie sleaze" aesthetics from the early 2000s. This look—"American Apparel, flash photography at parties, and messy hair and messy makeup"—found its muse in Charli XCX's *Brat*. The music was supported by the Cobrasnake's nostalgic photography and collaborators like Dimes Square musician the Dare, whose persona and sound was a post-9/11 downtown NYC throwback. The result was a culture of retromania feeding on retromania.

At least Charli's rise suggested a simmering backlash against market-tested, edge-free pop hegemony. Describing *Brat* to her label, she said, "I'm going to make a record that you guys think has no commercial hits on it. Or big songs. Or radio songs. Or streaming songs or whatever." This contrasted with Swift, who was less person than product. As critic B. D. McClay observed, "Like Coca-Cola or a hamburger or blue jeans or white wine, Taylor Swift just is. Not cool. Not uncool. Her cultural saturation makes 'uncool' a meaningless label." Meanwhile, her highly publicized romance with NFL star Travis Kelce in 2023 felt as choreographed as a PG-rated Disney film. It was almost so scripted that the right wing concocted loony conspiracies about the pairing's potential anti-Trump motivations.

In 2024, the theatrical Chappell Roan also emerged as a daring new voice, pushing into places that Swift wouldn't dare tread. Roan's lyrics unabashedly embraced her queer identity, and in the media, she loudly rejected the extreme parasocial relationships that had become common in the fan-artist dynamic. Meanwhile, Billie Eilish and Playboi Carti maintained their relevance through raw eccentricity rather than pleading for mass appeal. There was even a brief moment of exciting futuristic aesthetics in the aggro-computer noise of hyperpop, pioneered by transgender artists Sophie and Laura Les of 100 Gecs.

Amid this shake-up, the deference to the megastars began to feel comical. Kids on TikTok began a "Thank you, Beyoncé" meme mocking other celebrities' unbending reverence toward her. Similarly, pop rapper Drake, long a dominant force, saw the bottom fall out in 2024. His multi-song beef with Kendrick Lamar ended with Lamar's total victory in "Not Like Us," a hit that called out Drake's predilection for teenage girls. Drake sued Universal Music Group, accusing the label of manipulating "streaming services and airwaves" in Lamar's favor.

On a larger scale, the long-standing dominance of US pop stars had begun to waver. By 2022, Puerto Rican artist Bad Bunny had become the world's biggest pop star, proving that English was no longer a prerequisite for global success. His synth-infused trap and Caribbean beats defied conventional expectations, while his refusal to pander to English-speaking markets signaled a shift in global pop's center of gravity. "Skeptics and xenophobes take note," proclaimed Isabelia Herrera for NPR, "English-language music is by no means universal or exceptional." Once inside the omnivore monoculture, Bad Bunny promptly began an off-and-on relationship with Kendall Jenner.

These cracks in the monoculture revealed deeper truths about consumer behavior. Some basic cadence of novelty is required to win over even the most passive audiences. The stan mindset of unconditional love is a fringe position. As much as monopolist artists wanted to maintain control of the market forever, their monotony opened up space for competition.

Moreover, the twentieth-century paradigm of cool continued to linger in the ether, as consumers still gravitated to acts of anti-conservative rebellion. Even in a world without subcultures, there remained something seductive about aesthetics created in isolated, authentic communities. This may explain why Black and Latina drag queens arguably had the most influence on American youth slang, bringing terms and expressions like *mother, dusted, spilling the tea, serving cunt,* and *yas, queen* into the vernacular. Much could be traced to the reality show *RuPaul's Drag Race*, which has enjoyed seventeen seasons and a plethora of international spin-offs. Unlike fan communities online hiding behind anonymity, drag queens pursued an identity with real social consequences. Drag slang carried power because there were still stakes to the community's transgression.

That being said, most consumer "rebellions" were still limited to chasing edgier pop stars rather than overturning the entire system. TikTok creators, while innovative, rarely disrupted the power of the entrenched celebrity class. Instead, they filled a new niche: a petite bourgeoisie of middle-class influencers producing palatable, marketable content. In the most extreme examples, they had become commodities themselves, what critic Alex Quicho labeled the "NPC [non-player character] influencer," like Pinkydoll, who was "smiling and spiritually lobotomized, fine-tuned for an increasingly instinctive response to live cash stimulus."

Grassroots cultural activity ultimately posed little threat to the celebrity aristocracy of movies, TV, and supermodels. Only the mainstream seemed to satisfy the eternal need for a shared culture—one that could fuel conversations with friends and interactions with strangers. At best, the monoculture could undergo slight cosmetic changes: a rotating cast of royal houses in the pop aristocracy rather than a true revolution.

TECHNO-NIHILISM

Automated Creativity, Broken Platforms, and Speculator Culture

15

P ope Francis looked stunning—the latest celebrity to undergo a high-fashion glow up. The eighty-six-year-old pontiff finally found a fashion look as contemporary as his take on Catholic doctrine. With the traditional white zucchetto atop his head, he appeared in a sleek, belted white puffer coat—a bespoke masterpiece that could easily have been from Balenciaga or Moncler. And nothing made him look more like a true man of the people than the Starbucks cup in his right hand.

If only the image were real. In early 2023, a thirty-one-year-old Chicago construction worker had made this piece of art while high on psychedelic mushrooms using the generative AI tool Midjourney. He first shared the image in the Facebook group AI Art Universe before posting it to Reddit, where he was quickly banned. By then, it had already gone viral, with many believing it to be an actual photograph. Internet culture critic Ryan Broderick hailed it as "the first real AI-generated hoax."

In the early 2020s, artificial intelligence emerged as the next major frontier in consumer technology, following the mobile revolution and the rise of social media. Companies like Google, Facebook, and Microsoft had quietly been refining AI tools for enterprise and medical applications throughout the 2010s. During this time, tech companies treaded carefully with the term "artificial intelligence" because of its connotations of sci-fi dystopias, from the evil Skynet in *Terminator* to the malevolent robots of *The Matrix*.

But OpenAI, run by Sam Altman, went on a full-out marketing blitz for "generative AI" with the release of the image-generation software DALL-E in early 2021 and large language model ChatGPT in late 2022. Generative AI empowered everyday users to produce stunningly humanlike creations from simple text prompts. As ChatGPT stole the cultural spotlight, the tech world pivoted en masse: Major companies overhauled both their product and market strategies around AI, while venture capital poured into start-ups with even the flimsiest AI angle.

In an AI era, technology didn't just provide new tools or platforms for fostering human creativity: It automated the act of creation itself. Aspiring creators could outsource their writing, illustration, photo editing, and even songwriting to machines. While the technology was far from perfect—large language models often "hallucinated" facts with alarming confidence—it performed enough magic tricks to simultaneously delight and unsettle society.

By this point, however, the public was already skeptical of Big Tech, and its AI-first strategies made companies seem even more determined to steamroll over civilization rather than act in service of its users. Neoliberal economics had already shipped well-paying blue-collar work overseas; now generative AI threatened to replace workers in routine service roles. White-collar fields like law and medicine seemed next in line. More than just displacing jobs, AI had the potential to radically devalue the very concept of labor. Jean Baudrillard's 2001 warning echoed loudly: "When computer technology and the automatism of machines are all that is needed for production, work becomes a useless function."

The fear of AI went further than just taking jobs: It could perhaps seize the entire production of human symbols. In March 2023, *Sapiens* author Yuval Noah Harari, with Tristan Harris and Aza Raskin, warned in *The New York Times* that "A.I. could rapidly eat the whole of human culture—everything we have produced over thousands of years—digest it and begin to gush out a flood of new cultural artifacts. Not just school essays but also political speeches, ideological manifestos, holy books for new cults." If culture shapes how we perceive reality, they argued, AI's flood of pseudo-culture might distort our collective understanding and push civilization toward collapse.

Putting aside the obvious dangers in AI-enhanced disinformation, Harari's fear-mongering misunderstood how artistic culture works. Even without AI, the 2020s already saw a crisis of cultural overproduction. The internet hosted 630 billion words, 14 billion visible YouTube videos (with only 4 percent driving traffic), and 75.9 million musicians uploading 100,000 songs to Spotify *each day*. Far from igniting a creative renaissance, this endless flood of content reinforced the dominance of megastars. Moreover, the early stage of AI-generated art wasn't offering anything very competitive—it merely copied existing tropes, pumping out clichés and stale kitsch at lightning speed. In fact, its greatest contribution was illuminating how creation was the easiest step in the process of cultural invention. Every day, thousands if not millions of people proposed new ideas and practices, but only a tiny sliver ever won recognition, attracted adherents, or forged collective meaning. Those distraught over AI's impact on culture offered little explanation for why computer-created pseudo-art would receive widespread interest and reverence, when 99.99 percent of old-fashioned, human-made symbolic output failed.

Even the early AI-culture breakouts seemed to quickly grow tiresome. In March 2023, a YouTuber named demonflyingfox received accolades for his Balenciaga-inspired high-fashion video parody of the Harry Potter series. But with few technical or creative barriers to producing these videos of "one IP in another style," there was instantly a flood of copies and spin-offs. The charm evaporated within days.

Yet ultrapoptimists found something inspirational in AI. These tools removed all remaining barriers to creativity—money, time, skills—that locked noncreators out of artistic pursuits. National Novel Writing Month organizers refused to reject the use of AI, citing "classist and ableist undertones" to any complaints. The CEO of Suno, a music-generation start-up, pitched AI as a democratizing force: "There's this entire side of music around creating music and enjoying the process of creating that most people just don't have access to, because they don't play an instrument, or they don't know some complicated piece of production software. And what we do is we let everybody make the music that's in their heads." AI companies vowed to end the evil monopoly of pernicious creators who dared take the time to make things with a sense of craft and intention.

By 2024, AI began to create real problems for the internet, as content farms flooded social media with low-quality AI content known as "slop." These posts weren't made out of untapped creative ambition as much as financial opportunism: Platforms like Facebook paid users for successful posts, fueling cottage industries in countries like India, Pakistan, Indonesia, Thailand, and Vietnam. Low-skill workers could be taught to use Midjourney, Stable Diffusion, and Microsoft's AI image creator to churn out cheaply made, often bizarre imagery designed to game engagement algorithms. Popular trends included surreal religious iconography and photorealistic "beautiful cabin crew" portraits of flight attendants with impossible bodies modeled on Japanese adult animation. Journalist Jason Koebler traced the oddness of the images to "prompts that are written in Hindi, Urdu, and Vietnamese, which are underrepresented in large language model training data." He continued: "Other bizarre outcomes arise because people are using Google Translate and speech-to-text to say a prompt aloud in Hindi, translate it to English, and are using that often poorly-translated prompt to generate the images."

This slop soon began to corrode the entire online experience. On platforms like X, users were inundated with AI-generated nonsense replies. Authors on Amazon competed not only with each other, but against AI-written "study guides" to their books filled with auto-generated dummy text. AI researchers used AI tools to write academic papers, turning their entire field into a recursive loop. By 2024, more than half of LinkedIn's long-form posts were AI-enhanced, making professional networking indistinguishable from automated PR. AI even threatened to harm itself, as models trained on synthetic, AI-generated data.

While all this happened, social media platforms—having cemented their dominance over global cultural production—took few concrete steps to prevent AI slop from overtaking the online experience. And during the 2024 US election, AI slop became fodder for political propaganda. Republicans shared an AI-generated image online of a crying girl in a life jacket clutching a puppy amid rising floodwaters, meant as a critique of the Biden administration's supposedly failed response to Hurricane Helene. When pressed about the image's authenticity, Republican activist Amy Kremer admitted, "I don't know where this photo came from and honestly, it doesn't matter."

AI slop further established a growing feeling that the internet was getting worse with every passing day. Google Search, once synonymous with precision, was "broken," partly because search optimization strategies pushed content away from actual human needs. Every online recipe featured thousands of extra words to satisfy Google's algorithm before listing the ingredients and instructions. Once-reliable hubs of information like Quora were inundated with nonsensical queries ("Is Japan owned by China?") and overconfident amateur responses. For many years, a great fear was that internet content was permanent, with many nations passing "right to be forgotten" laws to help citizens expunge articles from Google. By the 2020s, old articles began to disappear without a trace, and Internet Archive, the most important nonprofit for preservation, was under attack.

On Facebook, the decline was even more pronounced. The platform became the "dying Rust Belt city of the internet," overrun with vapid AI-generated clickbait videos promising shocking revelations but delivering literally nothing. Instagram, meanwhile, succeeded in popularizing Stories, copied from Snapchat. Then it tried to steal the mojo of TikTok, stuffing feeds with vertical-video Reels from accounts that the user didn't follow. Zuckerberg launched Threads in 2023 as a competitor to Twitter, reaching 275 million users through engagement hacks. But as tech reporter Katie Notopoulos noted, it did so "without ever having any sort of usefulness, unique culture, or 'moment.'"

But the true Twitter-killer was Elon Musk, whose stewardship of the platform, rebranded as X, exemplified the internet's growing dysfunction. He was once accepted in hip cultural circles, at least enough to partner with beloved indie musician Grimes, with whom he had three unconventionally named children: X Æ A-Xii, Exa Dark Sideræl, and Techno Mechanicus. In 2021, Musk became the world's richest person, drifted from Grimes, and found new spiritual comfort in right-wing meme culture.

Musk purchased Twitter for $44 billion in 2022 and soon embarked on a deliberate campaign to destroy the platform as a home to liberal discourse. He stripped celebrities and media figures of their verified "blue-check" status and allowed anyone to buy verification for eight dollars a month. This worked against the original goal of promoting verified information from trusted sources. Over time, the platform's algorithms instead began amplifying conspiracy theories and right-wing content. By late 2024, *The Atlantic's* Charlie Warzel reported that "heaps of unfiltered posts that plainly celebrate racism, anti-Semitism, and outright Nazism are easily accessible and possibly even promoted."

As Musk became associated with the nihilistic right wing, progressives fell out of love with Tesla; the brand's polygon-shaped Cybertruck became "a culture war on wheels" subject to vandalism. Musk went further right. He began using a stylized Pepe the Frog icon and changed his X handle to Kekius Maximus. He amplified anti-"woke" content on X that echoed Gamergate. By late 2024, coinciding with Musk's full-throated endorsement of Trump, growing discontent among left-leaning users led to a mass migration to alternative platforms like Bluesky.

By the 2020s, the internet no longer resembled the vibrant, user-driven playground it had once been. Platforms like Facebook, Twitter, and Instagram once catered to creatives and professionals. Now they seemed aggressively indifferent, if not hostile, to their original audiences. There was a growing nostalgia for the "old internet," with its serendipitous discovery and niche communities. In *Wired*, Kate Knibbs ascribed this shift to inevitable generational transition: Internet culture was a lot like *Saturday Night Live*, in which people preferred the content "they grew up with and watched during their formative years." Gen Z's fondness for surreal memes, like a blue Grinch bizarrely captioned "That Feeling When Knee Surgery Is Tomorrow," underscored that maybe every new cohort of young people fundamentally loves content that is incomprehensible to older users. "Just because you aren't having fun on the internet doesn't mean the internet itself is broken," she argued.

But maybe it was actually broken. Former *Boing Boing* editor Cory Doctorow coined the term "enshittification" to describe a cycle in which platforms initially offer users value to attract massive audiences, then shift focus to advertisers and suppliers, and finally prioritize their own profits at the expense of everyone else. Amazon drew in third-party sellers, copied their successful products, and then forced them to pay for ad placement to remain visible. According to Doctorow, this process would inevitably lead to users abandoning the platform—but only if there were any viable alternatives.

It also became clear that the reliance on algorithms further compounded the sense of malaise. Platforms like TikTok were built around algorithmic recommendations, which prioritized content that would maximize engagement. While this democratized visibility for some marginalized creators, it flattened culture into a "Filterworld," as Kyle Chayka described in his book of the same name. Algorithmic culture "tends to be accessible, replicable, participatory, and ambient," leading to what Chayka called a pervasive "averageness." "People tend to watch just a sliver of what YouTube has to offer," wrote researcher Ryan McGrady, "and, on the whole, they follow what the algorithm serves to them." In order to succeed on these platforms, creators spent less time making compelling content and more on deciphering the opaque "rules" of the algorithm, a process Doctorow likened to "useless platform Kremlinology."

At the broadest level, the growing reliance on algorithms disrupted traditional pathways for cultural discovery. In the past, young people sought guidance from elders who recommended art, books, and music to expand their horizons. Blogger Matthew Yglesias noted that these recommendations often came with an implicit promise: "Given my understanding of your interests, my belief is that reading this book will help you become a better version of yourself." By contrast, algorithms served up the most broadly appealing content, reinforcing the most common part of users' existing tastes rather than challenging them. For all the early promises of "personalization," algorithmic sites pushed most users into a homogenized experience, contributing to the growing sense of a stagnant monoculture.

Whatever the validity of these complaints, tech companies enjoyed massive profits during the 2010s and steady stock rises during the pandemic. But as people emerged from their home isolation in 2022, the growth began to wane. Companies that had overhired during the pandemic initiated layoffs. For those who remained, the once-legendary perks of Silicon Valley dwindled.

The industry downturn shattered the myth of the ultraefficient tech worker. On TikTok and Instagram, tech employees offered "day in the life" videos in which they spent most of their energy silently attending online meetings and deciding which snacks to eat in the micro-kitchen. The tools meant to streamline work—email, chat, and video calls—had, by 2023, just created more bureaucratic make-work. Microsoft's Jared Spataro noted, "It sometimes seems as if the modern worker spends more time talking about work than actually working." Academic Cal Newport gained traction with his call for "deep work" and "slow productivity," as employees sought to reclaim focus from the chaos of hyperconnected offices. The original tech hacks needed their own counter-hacks.

Start-ups fared no better in the post-pandemic era. Airbnb cofounder Brian Chesky quipped, "It feels like we were in a nightclub and the lights just turned on." The era of zero-interest-rate policy—which fueled a VC-backed gold rush—had ended, leaving start-ups scrambling for capital. While Elizabeth Holmes of Theranos was serving an eleven-year prison sentence, her downfall hardly deterred other magical-thinking fraudsters. The authorities came for Frank's Charlie Javice (who was on the *Forbes* 30 Under 30 list), Outcome Health's Rishi Shah, Ozy Media's Carlos Watson, Slync's Christopher Kirchner, and Nikola's Trevor Milton. WeWork emerged as the Fyre

Festival of start-ups. Its founder Adam Neumann was a "tall, long-haired, barefoot, meat-banning, weed-smoking, tequila-drinking, Kabbalah-studying, experimental school-opening [Gwyneth] Paltrow-cousin-in-law." With backing from Japanese megafund SoftBank and Saudi money, Neumann raised We-Work's valuation to a staggering $47 billion—only for it to drop to $9 billion after going public, then collapse to $270 million before declaring bankruptcy.

The implosion of internet media followed suit. *Gawker* was the first to fall, in 2016, after Peter Thiel funded Hulk Hogan's successful lawsuit against it. The site made a brief comeback in 2021 but was shuttered for good shortly thereafter. *BuzzFeed News*, once a pioneer in digital journalism, shut down in April 2023, leaving the main *BuzzFeed* site to hobble along. *Vice* collapsed a month later. In early 2024, Condé Nast laid off staff at Pitchfork Media and folded the site into *GQ*.

Where the internet once promised to be an entrepreneurial playground, it now resembled a suburban strip mall full of bait-and-switch operations. The deterioration of core sites pushed users into smaller, more private online groups. This balkanization of internet content gave rise to what Kickstarter cofounder Yancey Strickler dubbed the "dark forest" era, when "people turn away from big, open mega-platforms in favor of more private or niche digital spaces, from nonpublic Slack channels to invite-only WeChat groups or special-interest podcasts."

But perhaps this simply ended a peculiar experiment in global culture, in which all tastes—high, middle, and low; cosmopolitan and provincial—coexisted on the same mega-platforms. Rather than a total collapse, this fragmentation signaled a return to the natural order—the splintering of culture into smaller, more insular communities. Regardless, these changes were taken as a catastrophe. The internet felt like a burning building, with users grabbing whatever they could on the way out.

In previous eras, public negativity encouraged many monopolistic industry titans to give back to society in conspicuous ways. The Gates Foundation worked to eradicate diseases. But many of the new Big Tech billionaires showed little sense of noblesse oblige. They privately competed on yacht length and lived out their midlife crises in public. Jeff Bezos bulked up and took on a new romantic partner. Musk challenged Zuckerberg to a "cage match." They seemed fully disinterested in cavorting together within "high society." Peter Thiel used his great wealth to plan a doomsday-ready concrete bunker in New Zealand.

Even the winners of techno-capitalism seemed unhappy. Elon Musk, the richest man in the world, found no peace in his astronomical wealth, using prescription ketamine to treat his depression. Money and power were not enough for him, and he lost interest in winning the kind of broad esteem that accompanies the achievement of concrete improvement to human life. Instead, he seemed to be desperate for only one thing: to be seen as transgressively cool.

———

On November 15, 2021, abstract expressionist Jackson Pollock's monochromatic painting *Number 17, 1951* sold for $61.6 million at Sotheby's New York, far exceeding its expected price of $35 million and setting an auction record for the artist. Yet even this landmark sale was eclipsed by a Christie's auction earlier that year, where forty-year-old Wisconsin-born, South Carolina–based artist Mike Winkelmann, known as Beeple, sold his work *Everydays: The First 5,000 Days* for an astonishing $69.3 million.

Beeple, an outsider to the traditional art world, curated *Everydays* as a montage of five thousand sketches and digital images. It included a "gender-swapped Captain Crunch rebranded as 'Cap'n Bitch'" and graphic renderings of a large-breasted Donald Trump in S&M gear dominating an anthropomorphized COVID virus. One of its buyers, Anand Venkateswaran, admitted he hadn't even looked through the images before purchasing. For Venkateswaran and his partner Vignesh Sundaresan of the Singapore-based cryptocurrency company Metapurse, the content was irrelevant. They saw *Everydays* as a milestone in the burgeoning world of non-fungible tokens (NFTs), a digital format they believed would revolutionize art ownership. "This is going to be a billion-dollar piece someday," Venkateswaran claimed. Thanks to these crypto investors, Beeple joined the ranks of the world's most valuable living artists, alongside Jasper Johns, Jeff Koons, and David Hockney.

NFTs entered global consciousness through the wider craze for cryptocurrency. Back in 2008, the enigmatic "Satoshi Nakamoto" published a white paper proposing Bitcoin, an electronic currency detached from the traditional financial system. Bitcoin's foundations lay in blockchain technology, which used a public ledger to document every transaction. Though initially embraced by a fringe of techno-anarchists, Bitcoin struggled to gain traction without a compelling use case. That changed with the dark-web marketplace Silk Road, where Bitcoin became the currency of choice for purchasing drugs and other illicit services. In April 2013, Tyler and Cameron Winklevoss of *The Social Network* fame bought up 1 percent of the world's Bitcoins. By October, the FBI had shuttered Silk Road, but the attention brought baseball-cap-wearing normies into Bitcoin. Ideologues hailed cryptocurrency as a cure-all for global financial woes, while speculators banked on ever-increasing demand to inflate prices. By 2021, a single Bitcoin hit a high of $68,000, turning the Winklevoss twins into billionaires. (That year they also began playing with their "hard-hitting" band Mars Junction, covering classic nineties songs like Pearl Jam's "Even Flow.")

Yet cryptocurrency remained hard to convert into cash or use for purchasing goods. Enter NFTs: non-fungible tokens that applied blockchain's transaction-tracking capabilities to digital assets. This innovation provided crypto paper millionaires with a new outlet for their earnings. NFTs promised to solve two nagging problems: how to establish ownership over digital files and how to compensate creators for future resales. Moreover, as *The New York Times*' Zachary Small put it, "NFTs were about creating a decentralized society, where users traded digital artworks like money, and about bankrupting the toxic business model of social-media platforms that siphoned their personal data for profit." Enthusiasts argued that NFTs and blockchain heralded a new version of the internet—a Web 3.0.

NFTs were envisioned as crucial for humanity's inevitable migration into the "metaverse"—a shared digital realm where users could interact as avatars in immersive 3D virtual reality. Mark Zuckerberg rebranded Facebook as Meta in October 2021, betting the future of his company on this vision. However, the early results were underwhelming. Investors balked at the money Zuckerberg was pouring into his Oculus virtual reality division, while regular users avoided the metaverse's nausea-inducing headsets and primitive avatar designs that initially lacked legs. ("But seriously," Zuckerberg asserted, "legs are hard.") Apple launched its Apple Vision Pro VR headset in 2024; a few months later, market analysts labeled its momentum "dead."

In a time of perceived economic scarcity, the metaverse had an underlying utopian promise: to create a new world where everyone had access to everything. The "meatspace," or physical world, was constrained by limited resources and endless debates over their distribution; the metaverse could provide humanity with the ultimate egalitarian playground, free from scarcity and inequity. Yet before this virtual utopia could even take shape, the tech industry's first move was to reintroduce scarcity into the system. NFTs became the digital frontier's version of private property, assigning ownership to otherwise infinitely replicable digital goods. With NFTs, anyone could download the same JPEG, but only one person could "own" it.

Visual art became NFTs' first medium, offering collectors the chance to "own" unique artworks or limited-edition profile picture (PFP) collections like Bored Ape Yacht Club, CryptoPunks, and Pudgy Penguins. The frenzy around NFTs mirrored the broader art market's record-breaking auction prices, yet it arrived at a moment when contemporary art itself seemed to lack energy or direction.

Once a hotbed for cultural invention, the avant-garde art world had long since descended into a marketplace of raw speculation. Andy Warhol kicked this off in pushing what he called "Business Art," which merged avant-garde experimentation with celebrity culture and financial capital. Perhaps this was the only trajectory left. Critic Arthur Danto proclaimed the "end of art" in the 1980s, as the great explosion of avant-garde ideas in the early twentieth century exhausted future opportunities for stylistic progress. Contemporary art, he argued, "has no brief against the art of the past, no sense that the past is something from which liberation must be won." By the mid-1990s, theorist Jean Baudrillard complained that contemporary art had become "mediocrity squared," masking its lack of ambition with irony. "It claims to be null—'I am null! I am null!'—*and it truly is null.*"

This had the benefit, however, of making art easier for "philistines" to buy, and the twenty-first-century art market saw an incoming rush of "Russian oligarchs, mysterious collectors in Dubai, Hong Kong, Singapore, India, and South Korea." In 2006, a hedge-fund owner paid $143.5 million for a single Willem de Kooning painting. "The art world used to be a community," remarked New York gallerist Jeffrey Deitch. "But now it's an industry."

Luxury fashion, welcomed into the fold by Andy Warhol's open embrace of commerce, became an equal partner in the art world. Louis Vuitton turned to Stephen Sprouse, Takashi Murakami, and Jeff Koons for handbag designs. Historically, argued scholar Natasha Degen, art provided the "most trenchant critiques against consumer culture" by drawing attention to the fleeting nature of conspicuous consumption. In conquering the art world, "Luxury brands neutralize the inherent challenge [art] poses to fashion. Through patronage, brands see an opportunity to subtly recast art in their image." When Tom Sachs satirized the industry through his works *Prada Deathcamp* and *Prada Toilet*, the brand responded not with lawsuits but by adding him to its roster of collaborators.

As critic Dean Kissick described in 2024, the art world responded to late-2010s politics by prioritizing the amplification of marginalized voices over other concerns: "The ambition to explore every facet of the present was quickly replaced by a devout commitment to questions of equity and accountability." Simultaneously, the energy of the art scene moved from traditional European capitals to party-friendly Miami. Young artists in the "ultracontemporary" space saw big money come their way, only for their prices to crash in 2024.

NFTs initially promised to disrupt the corruption of the art world. As Zachary Small observed, younger generations "embraced NFTs as a symbol of their own rising power in society and a definitive breaking point with older models of cultural production." Where emerging artists once challenged established norms through aesthetics, now they would use technology to fight the system. But the NFT movement's marquee moment—Beeple's $69.3 million sale—epitomized its complete crassness. The transaction was less about creative merit and more about technological novelty. Beeple believed himself to be a true artist, but unlike his predecessors, he refused to learn much about the history of the medium. He admitted to *The New Yorker*, "When you say, 'Abstract Expressionism,' literally, I have no idea what the hell that is."

The rise of NFTs was a stark departure from traditional notions of artistic value. Journalist Rebecca Alter dismissed projects like Bored Ape Yacht Club as having "all the aesthetic complexity of a pissing Calvin bumper sticker." Beeple claimed, like avant-garde artists before him, "I'm just trying to expand people's idea of what art is," but in his case, he was fighting for the dignity of mediocre, tasteless art. Contemporary art had long been tied to speculation and status marking, but NFTs stripped away even the pretense of intellectual or symbolic experimentation, reducing the entire exercise to mere commodification.

Proponents, however, framed NFTs as a democratization of culture. Meme stars like Zoë Roth of Disaster Girl and the owner of the dog Kabosu from the Doge meme used them to monetize their virality. But the NFT boom was, at its core, forged in the cauldron of financial speculation. In this, NFTs embodied the end form of poptimism: Raw commercialization was now treated as culture. The entire appeal of NFTs was in establishing ownership for future profits. This found a receptive audience in a new generation of Zoomer creators, who, as art journalist Hiji Nam put it, "don't want to be broke and obscurely cool artists; they want to be rich and legibly cool entrepreneurs."

NFTs hit the mainstream in mid-2021 as Bored Ape Yacht Club profile pics were snapped up as status symbols. A founder of the avatar project Pudgy Penguins admitted, "The way I describe it to my family members and friends is like, people buy Supreme clothes, or they buy a Rolex." BAYC's creators Yuga Labs worked with Madonna's agent to build the brand through celebrity endorsements. Steph Curry paid $180,000 for Bored Ape #7990, and Justin Bieber owned one worth $1.3 million. The phenomenon spread globally to consumer goods, spawning BAYC-themed products like Ape Water and branding a coconut distributor in Thailand. Universal Music even signed the virtual band Kingship, composed of three Bored Apes and one Mutant Ape. The cultural peak of BAYC came in January 2022, when Paris Hilton and Jimmy Fallon showcased their apes on *The Tonight Show* in an awkward, infomercial-like exchange.

This celebrity support made NFTs appear to be a sure bet. Skeptics were mocked as destined to stay poor, while blockchain-savvy insiders flaunted their ape-head JPEGs as symbols of cultural and financial savvy. Alas, it all began to collapse around the time of the Hilton–Fallon segment. This was as actor Seth Green worked on an ill-fated TV pilot, *White Horse Tavern*, which posited, "What if your friendly neighborhood bartender was Bored Ape Yacht Club #8398?" The show hit a snag when "Fred," as he called the ape, was "literally kidnapped" in a phishing attack.

Status symbols are not just exclusive items but represent an individual's membership in an elite tier of society. This is precisely why NFTs failed. They became too associated with crypto cultists—an outsider group marked by grifters and speculators of questionable taste. Anthony Scaramucci captured the disconnect when he attended a crypto conference: "I'm here in a Brioni, these guys are in Lululemon pants. . . . These are some of the worst-dressed people I ever met in my life." Moreover, the PFPs were not the organic "behavioral residue" of a high-end life but intentionally displayed as part of an obvious high-risk, high-reward investment strategy. By 2024, the market had collapsed; prices for NFTs had plummeted over 90 percent. The BAYC-themed supergroup Kingship never launched, taken out to pasture in an obscure corner of *Roblox*.

In 2009, economist Tyler Cowen predicted that the Great Recession might teach young people financial humility and prudence: "Today's teenagers stand less chance of making foolish decisions in the stock market down the road. They are likely to forgo some good business opportunities, but also to make fewer mistakes." Instead, the collapse of trust in the global financial system drove an entire generation of young people into speculative fervor. Crypto became more than a financial vehicle—it became a lifestyle. Born from techno-anarchist dreams of overthrowing the global financial order, cryptocurrency eventually merged with other twenty-first-century macro-trends: the entrepreneurial hustle of Jay-Z, the scarcity of streetwear, and the magical thinking of woo-woo. To no one's surprise, astrologist Maren Altman often turned her powers of prediction to the price of Bitcoin.

For young people who aspired to get rich quick, crypto was the surest bet—the fattest FIRE. In 2017, Bitcoin shot up from $830 to $19,783, then crossed $100,000 in late 2024. Ethereum went to market at under $1 and, at its peak in 2021, hit over $4,800. Crypto forums exuded a peculiar optimism: The 4chan catchphrase WAGMI, "We're all going to make it," reflected a collective belief in eventual success. Community rituals included exchanging cheerful "gm" (good morning) and "gn" (good night) greetings. The shared hope was that holding ("hodl") crypto assets would drive prices sky-high, making millionaires of everyone involved. Crypto culture appealed particularly to men who "value masculinity highly but feel they aren't traditionally masculine enough," as one research report put it. And like fans rallying around a beleaguered local sports team, there was camaraderie in failure. As enthusiast Patrick Loney recommended, "Invest heavily in crypto, lose your ass, come back for more, make insane money, learn about monetary policy and tech in the process, make incredible friends who share these same experiences." The crypto hero was a "degen" (for "degenerate") who was willing to risk it all in pursuit of financial glory.

As crypto became a cornerstone of internet-driven culture, it also borrowed heavily from meme culture. Alongside Bitcoin and Ethereum came a deluge of "initial coin offerings" (ICOs), many inspired by internet memes like Dogecoin (based on the Doge Shiba Inu) and Pepe Cash (derived from

Pepe the Frog). Despite 80 percent of ICOs turning out to be fraudulent, trading "shitcoins" became a new pastime. Crypto also served as the next career step for online creators who had grown disenchanted with making videos. After makeup tutorial pioneer Michelle Phan returned from self-exile, she pivoted to crypto evangelism: "I'm a proud Bitcoin maxi now. I'm toxic as fuck."

This culture of financial speculation spilled into traditional markets. Reddit thread r/wallstreetbets orchestrated one of the most symbolic events of the 2020s: the GameStop short squeeze. Led by Keith Gill (a.k.a. Roaring Kitty), the group of amateur investors caused massive losses to hedge funds, while Gill allegedly turned a $53,000 position into $48 million.

The film adaptation, *Dumb Money*, celebrated this financial populism but revealed how detached the culture had become from the original human motivations for profit. The protagonists in *The Wolf of Wall Street* spend their ill-procured dollars on sex, drugs, and menace for the audience's vicarious pleasure. The characters in *Dumb Money* spend their time staring at expanding zeros in their accounts but never use the money to do anything glamorous or even practical. Online trading culture revolved around holding at all costs—"diamond hands." All the fun was postponed for the future. "Wen Lambo?" they asked longingly.

The gambling mentality wasn't limited to crypto. Legalized sports betting, following a 2018 Supreme Court decision, became a $10-billion-plus industry by 2023, complete with its own dedicated apps. Platforms like Polymarket extended wagering to political elections and other events. Soon Gamblers Anonymous retooled its programs for a younger clientele.

By 2023, crypto's gentle decline had become a dramatic collapse. The furry-haired, perpetually disheveled Sam Bankman-Fried (SBF) emerged as the poster child of crypto's implosion. As the millennial founder of FTX, a leading cryptocurrency exchange, SBF presented himself as a mogul guided by a philosophical movement called effective altruism. FTX gained mainstream appeal through stadium naming rights, high-profile endorsements from Tom Brady and Gisele Bündchen, and even a Larry David Super Bowl commercial. But when the truth about FTX's shady financial practices surfaced, the empire crumbled and SBF ended up behind bars.

"So many smart people," *Bloomberg* journalist Zeke Faux reflected, "had spent so many thousands of hours working on crypto—and yet shockingly little of use had come of it." Crypto's promises of a transformative Web 3.0 never materialized. Yet, for a time, it stood as a true cultural phenomenon, rivaling music, film, and fashion in its influence. The crypto lifestyle found a transgressive energy in raw finance that rivaled art and culture, for which it received an exuberant "LFG" from a giant swath of youth.

A NEW LUXURY

The Omnivore Monoculture Changes Aspirations in Both East and West

16

I n the middle of a November 2015 Shanghai screening of science-fiction film *The Martian*, the audience erupted in laughter. The film, starring Matt Damon and a host of other Hollywood stars, abruptly shifted to a scene featuring Chinese actors Chen Shu and Eddy Ko in the China National Space Administration speaking in Mandarin. Though the scene appeared in Andy Weir's original novel, its placement in the film came across as another unsubtle attempt to pander to Chinese audiences, like in *2012* and *Transformers: Age of Extinction*. These clumsy efforts to win over China broke the local audience's suspension of disbelief mid-film.

With its meteoric economic rise and growing geopolitical power, China was primed to profoundly shape culture in the twenty-first century. At first, however, the influence manifested only in the background. China's seemingly near-infinite capacity for low-cost, high-quality production gutted factory jobs across high-income nations, fueling the populist backlash that helped propel right-wing leaders like Donald Trump into power. At the same time, rising incomes within China made the market much more appealing to multinational firms. In 2000, China's GDP per capita was just $959—lower than Honduras or Syria. By 2023, that figure had surged to $12,614, giving the Chinese middle class significant purchasing power. China also had the world's second-largest pool of millionaires (more than 6 million) and billionaires (473 in 2024). As international brands began to consider the needs of

Chinese consumers, it affected the underlying logic of what they created and how they marketed it.

International conglomerates would certainly have to make changes. At the beginning of the century, there had been a lingering belief that economic growth would lead China toward democratization—just as blue jeans and Michael Jackson helped bring down the Berlin Wall. But under General Secretary Xi Jinping's long rule, domestic freedoms tightened. Minority Uyghur Muslims were detained in camps. The pro-democracy Umbrella Movement in Hong Kong was crushed, with student leaders facing imprisonment. Dissident artist Ai Weiwei was arrested and sent into exile. By 2020, Beijing had revoked visas for journalists from *The New York Times*, *The Wall Street Journal*, and *The Washington Post*. Even whimsical internet comparisons of Xi to Winnie-the-Pooh resulted in the widespread censorship of Pooh-related memes.

While Japan and Korea deliberately aimed to achieve "soft power" through cultural exports, China understood popular culture to be part of the state order. Its domestic cultural industry either engaged in the creation of overt propaganda or had to navigate strict censorship laws to exercise its creative freedom. (Hollywood also agreed to censorship of its films in China, including the addition of a law-and-order ending to *Fight Club* and the removal of references to Freddie Mercury being gay in *Bohemian Rhapsody*.) This approach hindered the emergence of breakout stars akin to K-pop and J-pop sensations. While the free-flowing internet enabled East Asian culture to seamlessly enter mainstream markets, China's Great Firewall largely prevented its memes and media from reaching people overseas. Censorship also stifled the spread of Western music and films inside China, leaving many Chinese young creators less exposed to the artistic conventions required to make works of global interest. There were plenty of budding rappers, rock bands, fashion designers, and visual artists in China, but only a handful managed to successfully export their creations.

China was also at a market disadvantage in that coolness—the exaltation of individualistic defiance as the supreme virtue—had yet to fully infect Chinese society the way it had in the West. Patriotism and communalism remained strong, often expressed through earnest traditional themes and wholesome group activities. While some disillusioned Chinese youth embraced an unambitious, *tang ping* ("lying flat") lifestyle as a form of silent protest against status-obsessed society, even these acts of withdrawal had yet to result in the kind of countercultural, transgressive artistic expressions that resonate on a global stage.

For such a populous and increasingly affluent country, China's contributions to global pop culture remain surprisingly sparse. Hong Kong accounted for most of the exceptions. In the late 1990s and early 2000s, Hong Kong cinema reached an international peak with John Woo's action movies and Jackie Chan's emergence as a Hollywood star. Writer-director Wong Kar-wai became a global indie film icon with masterpieces like *Chungking Express* and *In the Mood for Love*. On the international stage, *Crouching Tiger, Hidden Dragon*—a China-backed production helmed by Taiwanese director Ang Lee—became an international phenomenon. There was a brief trend among European hipsters around Chinese socialist-chic Feiyue sneakers, and Liu Cixin's sci-fi novel *The Three-Body Problem* won over Obama, Zuckerberg, and George R. R. Martin. Attempts to adapt or capitalize on these successes, however, faltered. Netflix's 2024 adaptation of *The Three-Body Problem* controversially recast the main characters as "ethnically balanced twentysomethings," reducing its distinctiveness to generic Hollywood fare.

But Chinese creators experienced similar struggles inside China. In 2018, the feminist television drama *Story of Yanxi Palace*—a critical and commercial hit about a cunning concubine's rise in the Forbidden City—was denounced by the Chinese Communist Party for "propagating a luxurious and hedonistic lifestyle" and swiftly taken off the air.

China's sophisticated mobile internet infrastructure offered new opportunities for cultural export, but with their own caveats. ByteDance's short-video app Douyin, launched in 2016, was rebranded as TikTok for global markets and quickly became a major media platform for youth worldwide. The app's Chinese origins, however, proved to be a major geopolitical liability. Amid allegations of data harvesting and covert censorship, India banned the app in 2020, and by 2024, the US government demanded that Byte-Dance sell TikTok to a non-Chinese entity. (This resulted in a confusing semi-enforcement in 2025.) Though TikTok revolutionized global digital culture with its vertical-video format, few videos went viral on both Douyin and TikTok. Chinese youth remained loyal to domestic platforms like Weibo and Instagram-like Xiaohongshu, "Little Red Book," which had no significant presence beyond China's borders. (Xiaohongshu had a brief moment in the global spotlight in early 2025 as Americans flocked to it in protest of the TikTok ban.)

Ultrafast-fashion powerhouse Shein, by contrast, made a global splash through its combination of mass production and mobile technology. The company added up to ten thousand new designs daily. The app exploded in popularity in the US during the pandemic, with young poptimists praising the company for making fashion affordable for more people. Critics, however, accused Shein of exploiting laborers, plagiarizing designs, and violating the Uyghur Forced Labor Prevention Act. To counter the negative coverage, Shein flew in a group of Western influencers to tour its facilities in Guangzhou. The influencers' glowing reviews themselves became a PR fiasco as online audiences derided their endorsements: "The gaslighting is CRAZY!"

The real impact of China in the twenty-first century has been less about its direct attempts to shape global culture and more about what is happening behind the scenes, where the enormous consumer power of Chinese youth helped give a new direction to the world's most aspirational products.

———

Wong Kar-wai was a fan of Japanese surrealist romantic author Haruki Murakami, and perhaps the similarity in sentiment is what attracted Japanese audiences in the late 1990s to his films *Days of Being Wild*, *Chungking Express*, *Fallen Angels*, and *Happy Together*. Among his admirers was Nigo, founder of the Japanese streetwear brand A Bathing Ape. Frequent visits to Hong Kong deepened Nigo's connection to the city and to local comedian-actor Eric Kot, who had collaborated on the 1998 Wong tribute film *First Love: The Litter on the Breeze*. Kot convinced Nigo to bring BAPE to Hong Kong, leading to the 1999 opening of the brand's first international boutique—accessible only to members with a Hong Kong passport and a scheduled appointment.

BAPE's Hong Kong launch caused a media frenzy, forever transforming the city's fashion ecosystem. Tokyo supplanted Paris and London as the main source of fashion inspiration for Hong Kong's affluent youth. The local magazine *Milk*, founded by editors with close ties to Tokyo, became a pipeline for information about the Japanese fashion scene. Over the next decade, streetwear became the defining style for youth across Greater China.

This embrace of streetwear gave Hong Kong a head start on the global boom that would later dominate American fashion and shape online media. In 2005, Kevin Ma, a student in Vancouver who moved back to Hong Kong to work for a bank, founded *Hypebeast*, a streetwear blog named after the pejorative term for the clothing's most rabid fans. Inspired by the Japanese fashion magazines he encountered while studying at the University of British Columbia, Ma took advantage of Hong Kong's geographical proximity to create a site that consistently delivered the most up-to-date English coverage of Japanese streetwear. By 2013, *Hypebeast* had grown into a major cultural force, with *Complex* magazine calling Ma "arguably the most important person on the Internet when it comes to dictating which streetwear brands are worth knowing about." He reached second on their streetwear power rankings, trailing only Pharrell Williams.

The influx of mainland tourists to Hong Kong in the early 2000s influenced young people across Greater China to find their style guidance in the city's celebrities and media. Streetwear's straightforward approach made it an ideal entry point for young people getting into the fashion game. Brands like Supreme and A Bathing Ape relied on a single cultural signifier: the logo. This simplicity required no deep familiarity with runway collections or avant-garde design concepts, making it the perfect lingua franca for a new generation of wealth.

In the early 2000s, *Milk*'s editorial page pushed boundaries by mixing

Japanese streetwear brands with European luxury brands, a bold move that initially drew criticism. This helped maintain traditional luxury names like Louis Vuitton and Chanel as the ultimate status symbols. These brands began in the nineteenth and early twentieth centuries as artisanal workshops catering to the European elite: Hermès's horse saddles, Louis Vuitton's travel trunks, Chanel's haute couture for society women. By the late twentieth century, they were mostly consolidated under publicly traded conglomerates like LVMH, Kering, and Richemont. They made goods at price points for all consumers at giant margins, facilitated by moving most production to Chinese factories.

Asian consumers, meanwhile, taught these conglomerates how to tap into middle-class markets. In the mid-1970s, rising incomes and a strong yen encouraged the most wealthy Japanese to travel to Europe, where they snapped up Louis Vuitton bags as souvenirs. Japanese shoppers mobbed Louis Vuitton's Paris flagship, and the company struggled with parallel importers. To address the chaos, Louis Vuitton hired a Japanese consultant who successfully placed Vuitton boutiques in Japan's major department stores. By the early 1980s, there were only two Louis Vuitton stores in France but five in Japan. As Japan's economy flourished, it became the world's largest market for European luxury goods, with East Asian consumers at one point accounting for half of Louis Vuitton's sales. The brand expanded to wherever Japanese travelers went—in particular, duty-free airport shops.

By the twenty-first century, Japanese enthusiasm for luxury goods had waned, but the template was easily adapted to China. By 2009, China had surpassed the United States to become the second-largest market for luxury goods. Chinese consumers accounted for one fifth of global luxury sales, a figure Bain consultants predicted would rise to 40 percent by 2030. As Indonesian Chinese designer Gracia Ventus explained, having grown up in prosperity, the younger generation in China were less inclined to save for the future, while also being taught to signal success through conspicuous consumption. This shift elevated tastes: "The super rich are trading their run-of-the-mill Mercedes for a Maybach, their BAPE for Rick Owens." Domestic tariffs on luxury goods encouraged affluent Chinese shoppers to travel abroad, purchasing handbags, jewelry, and watches in Hong Kong, Japan, and Europe.

By 2015, Louis Vuitton had become so ubiquitous in China that elite customers began to look elsewhere. In a market study, HSBC reported that the average Chinese luxury shopper now believed they "[couldn't] buy Vuitton. . . . It's a brand for secretaries." Luxury goods are different from commodities or electronics: More than any intrinsic value, they sell the fact that other people *don't* possess them. When brands reach too broad of an audience, it destroys the sense of exclusivity that consumers are buying. To solve this, LVMH and other conglomerates developed a clever strategy: cycling brands through phases of mass appeal and exclusivity. As popular labels risked overexposure, their more exclusive lines—among them, Kering's Bottega Veneta and LVMH's Loro Piana, known for their understated craftsmanship—could take center stage. Once brands fell out of favor, they were primed for radical reinvention.

At the same time luxury fashion was expanding to the global middle classes, streetwear was becoming, as *Vogue* noted, "the biggest fashion movement in recent history." The collision between these worlds was inevitable. In 2012, Comme des Garçons collaborated on a capsule collection with Supreme, bridging the gap between high fashion and street authenticity. As Adrian Joffe, president of Comme des Garçons, observed, Supreme's James Jebbia had a "strong, single-minded vision" rooted in his values, which was an appealing attribute for brands desperate for more credibility. By 2015, Kering had hired Demna Gvasalia, the designer behind streetwear brand Vetements, to breathe new life into Balenciaga. Under Demna's direction, Balenciaga redefined luxury by embracing T-shirts, baseball caps, and, most famously, chunky sneakers that became a streetwear staple.

These collaborations picked up steam when Louis Vuitton, under designer Kim Jones, teamed up with Supreme on a collection. Rich kids from Dubai to Shanghai wrapped their Ferraris in the hybrid logo. Even Harlem's Dapper Dan, once shunned by the industry for his creative bootlegs of luxury goods, became an official collaborator, legitimizing the long-standing influence of hip-hop and streetwear on high fashion. The omnivore mono-culture, with its fusion of elite and popular taste, had fully infiltrated the luxury sector.

Then, on March 25, 2018, Louis Vuitton cemented the streetwear-luxury hybridization by appointing Virgil Abloh as its men's artistic director. A Ghanaian American and Kanye West's former creative director, Abloh had gained fame with his streetwear label Off-White. His ascent to the helm of Europe's most prestigious luxury brand marked a historic moment, celebrated as a triumph of Black representation in fashion. Louis Vuitton CEO Michael Burke first met Abloh in 2009 when he and Kanye interned at Fendi for $500 a month.

Abloh used his appointment to intentionally reshape the luxury paradigm. Historically, luxury brands dictated style to the wealthy; under Abloh, they took cues from the streets. "My muse has always been what people actually wear," he remarked, "and I am really excited to make a luxury version of that."

One person was very upset by all this: Abloh's former employer, Kanye West. In the wake of the Abloh appointment, Kanye felt "a lot of pain and jealousy." A self-proclaimed "Louis Vuitton Don" since his debut album in 2004, West believed the position should have been his, especially with his massive success at Yeezy. He claimed that Bernard Arnault, LVMH's chairman, had offered him the role and then retracted it. Hiring West at the height of his MAGA phase, however, posed obvious risks.

At the helm of Louis Vuitton, Abloh's star continued to rise. He designed Hailey Baldwin's wedding dress for her marriage to Justin Bieber and pulled even more streetwear into the luxury fold. In 2020, Abloh collaborated on a capsule collection with his hero, A Bathing Ape founder Nigo. "Me being at Louis Vuitton is directly attributable to work Nigo's done in the past," explained Abloh. Despite selling A Bathing Ape to Hong Kong retailer I.T for a modest $2.8 million due to mounting debts, Nigo's influence endured. "BAPE is like my generation's Chanel," Abloh believed. "To me, what Nigo did to build this brand is something we may never see in our lifetime again.

It represents youth culture, it represents Japanese streetwear aesthetic, it represents American hip-hop." A$AP Rocky agreed, saying, "Nigo is just as important and significant to hip-hop as Pharrell, or Slick Rick, or Kanye." It felt like a logical step in 2021 for LVMH to appoint Nigo the artistic director of Kenzo, formalizing his place in the luxury world.

But streetwear's influence wasn't limited to the high end. In 2017, Supreme sold 50 percent of its shares to private equity firm the Carlyle Group for $500 million. Three years later, VF Corporation—owner of the North Face, Timberland, Dickies, and Vans—acquired Supreme for $2.1 billion. Streetwear collaborations became the norm across the industry. London skate brand Palace partnered with Polo Ralph Lauren in 2018, while the Yeezy-Gap partnership followed two years later. By 2023, even McDonald's had joined the fray, teaming up with Palace, Vetements, and rapper Travis Scott's Cactus Jack label. Guram Gvasalia of Vetements told *The New York Times*, "McDonald's is an incredible brand. It's the Louis Vuitton of food."

The blending of European luxury houses and mass consumer brands with hip-hop and streetwear was another inevitable endpoint for the omnivore monoculture. Luxury brands that once represented the refined elegance of suits and ball gowns now trafficked in casual, logo-laden garments. As fashion journalist Vanessa Friedman observed, "Hoodies and sneakers and T-shirts have become so fully absorbed by the high fashion establishment that the line between streetwear and fashion has effectively disappeared." This merchandising strategy worked particularly well in Asia, as consumers viewed streetwear as the default clothing style.

In 2022, after all the streetwear collaborations, LVMH founder Bernard Arnault once again became the world's richest person—even beating out Elon Musk. The luxury sector found a formula for printing money by extracting incredible margins from low-cost goods. A $2,780 Dior Book Tote cost only $57 to make. The French names and design teams then imbued these goods with almost mystical levels of cachet, masking the reality that many products were made in China and then sold back to Asian customers. But maintaining the image required strategic silence about this fact. Discussing how brands catered to Chinese tastes—or how China's role in production shaped the industry—remained a quiet taboo.

This didn't sit well with Chinese youth, who felt like they were being treated as second-class citizens. The tension erupted in 2018, when Dolce & Gabbana released a controversial video featuring a Chinese model struggling to eat Italian dishes with chopsticks. The video sparked a wave of backlash on Weibo, inspiring a "Boycott Dolce" campaign. Then, muckraking social media account Diet Prada uncovered a series of anti-Chinese messages allegedly from Stefano Gabbana's Instagram account. Although D&G claimed Gabbana was hacked, the scandal erupted into a full-fledged brand meltdown. The fallout included the cancellation of a major fashion show and a public apology on Weibo. Angelica Cheung, editor in chief of *Vogue China*, concluded, "Instead of dictating everything from head office, they would gain a lot from listening to the opinions and insights of their Chinese teams." The scandal underscored a hard truth: Failure in China could be fatal for a luxury brand, which explains why D&G's subsequent defamation lawsuit against Diet Prada demanded $665 million in damages.

Friction between European brands and Chinese consumers continued. In 2022, Christian Dior faced criticism over a garment that Chinese netizens claimed resembled a traditional Song dynasty mamian qun ("horse-face skirt"). While some brands stumbled, others took steps to foster earnest cultural dialogue. Louis Vuitton collaborated with Beijing-based artist Sun Yitian, a postmodernist painter who used the partnership as a proof point in her college thesis about postmodernism.

On November 28, 2021, Abloh died suddenly after a private battle with cardiac angiosarcoma. His untimely death left a void at Louis Vuitton, and in February 2023, the brand announced his replacement: musician and style icon Pharrell Williams. The appointment surprised many, given Pharrell's lack of formal design experience. But Louis Vuitton noted that Pharrell had long been a trendsetter: a "visionary whose creative universes expand from music to art, and to fashion." He pioneered one of the first streetwear-luxury crossovers with his LV Millionaires sunglasses in the early 2000s. And he had the power to make specific items come back into style—most famously, reviving global interest in Vivienne Westwood's eighties brown derby hat in 2014. His first LV collection wrapped Paris's Pont Neuf in gold, which drew over a billion online views. He proposed a true "millionaire" version of the Speedy bag that actually cost $1 million. LV then staged a pre–fall 2024 show in Hong Kong, followed by Pharrell's three-day tour in China, which featured an inflatable sculpture of his red Speedy handbag floating down the river in Shanghai's iconic Bund district.

Despite this cultural momentum, 2024 brought troubling signs for the luxury sector. A downturn in Chinese sales led to plummeting stock prices for the major conglomerates. Kering saw its shares fall from a peak of €798 in 2021 to under €230 in early 2025. The luxury-streetwear merger also began to cause narrative confusion. A Chinese consumer complained that Gucci "turned itself into a streetwear brand for a while, then tried to shift back to a high-end brand. Now I don't know who it wants to target." Despite steps to rationalize the luxury sector, brands never completely solved the fundamental paradox of maintaining exclusivity while selling at mass scale. But if there were ever a question about the role of China in the luxury market, the stock price drops made it clear that the industry badly needed Chinese consumers to increase shareholder value.

Meanwhile, streetwear's absorption into the mainstream weakened its claims to authenticity. Even in 2019, Virgil Abloh had predicted its decline: "I would definitely say [streetwear]'s gonna die, you know? Like, its time will be up." Certainly, it was no longer from the streets. London-based brand founder Jehu-cal Emmanuel Enemokwu noted that at its peak, "Streetwear became almost like a rich man's fetish." A major data point for the genre's collapse was VF Corporation's 2024 sale of Supreme to eyewear conglomerate EssilorLuxottica for $1.5 billion—significantly less than its 2020 purchase price. Meanwhile, the highest-end consumers were beginning to resent the proliferation of logos and instead reached for the "quiet luxury" (or "stealth wealth") of craft-driven brands like Loro Piana and Brunello Cucinelli.

Despite such temporary stumbles, the conglomerates' entire financial existence depended on making status symbols accessible to everyone, and there was no going back to being small-scale, artisanal companies for a select clientele. They also couldn't return to exclusively outfitting the wealthy in formal clothing, as the world's elite had lost interest in decorum. When Silicon Valley finally decided to dress up, the tech elite also flocked to streetwear. At age forty, Mark Zuckerberg abandoned his dull gray hoodies and T-shirts for "the imperialist phase of his glow-up": trendy "broccoli perm" hair, a single thin gold chain, and exclusive T-shirts made with LA designer Mike Amiri with the Latin phrase "aut Zuck, aut nihil" (a reference to the expression "either a Caesar or nothing"). He teased that a "limited drop" of this gear was in the works. (Bluesky CEO Jay Graber later sold a parody shirt that read MUNDUS SINE CAESARIBUS—"a world without Caesars.")

Here, the traditional barriers between Old Money and New Money continued to erode. Historically, cultural capital had served as a divider between aristocratic estates and upstarts; knowing how to dress, speak, and socialize in elite circles was as critical as wealth itself. But the twenty-first-century elite demanded the obliteration of such barriers, insisting that money alone should afford access to everything. In these years, Hermès bucked most of the luxury trends and kept its brand image focused on made-in-France craft. Its stores limited sales of its Birkin bag to top customers, forcing shoppers to become regulars before gaining access to the stock. This made the Birkin bag the world's most desired item: "My baby want a Birkin / She's been tellin' me all night long" is the first line of Shaboozey's "A Bar Song (Tipsy)." But its sales exclusivity angered two wealthy customers, who sued Hermès in 2024 claiming a violation of antitrust law.

The original idea of luxury goods was that only the richest, most established families possessed the resources to purchase high-quality items from artisanal creators. Now the industry factory-produced products for the millions of millionaires, while the lower and middle classes snapped up "entry-level" diffusion lines and street counterfeits. In late 2024, a Reuters headline noted, with no irony: "Luxury labels bulk up on lower-priced goods to appeal to middle-class shoppers." Craft no longer mattered. Fashion critic Katharine

K. Zarrella complained in *The New York Times*, "As costs climb, quality hasn't. In fact, it's largely declined."

The twenty-first-century luxury business provided the clearest example yet of Jean Baudrillard's famed idea of simulation. Luxury goods first arrived as actual artifacts from a rarefied lifestyle, and then their logos became symbols of those symbols. Now, as the logos were attached to T-shirts and tote bags, the globe's status symbols were even further removed from the entire point—they were just a series of artificial stand-ins for wealth created to be artificial stand-ins for wealth with only the loosest connection to the social order.

This shift ultimately demonstrated how shareholder capitalism changes the artifacts that make up our world. To meet the demands of global markets, luxury goods needed to be stripped of their cultural specificity. Taste, after all, was particular; money was universal. The result was a homogenization of style under the omnivore monoculture, in which numerical aspiration, rather than tradition, defined fashion.

Another clear example was the fate of "preppy"—an American Old Money style that originated as the organic uniform of teens at New England boarding schools such as Choate Rosemary Hall and Phillips Exeter. In the twenty-first century, Gen Z no longer understood preppy style as something based in L.L.Bean and J. Press (that's "cottagecore"). When asked about preppy clothes, a Gen Z teenager explained that the style was "people who wear Nirvana shirts." Another teen on Instagram agreed: "Nirvana is my favorite clothing brand btw," to which a commenter added, "my fav clothing brands are nirvana,queen,metallica,kiss and guns n' roses."

BOYS GONE WILD

The Counter-Counterculture Takes Power
Through Alternative Media

17

F rank A. Garbutt made his first fortune inventing equipment for oil drilling before turning to Hollywood, where he helped establish Paramount Pictures. In 1928, he moved into a concrete mansion overlooking Silver Lake Reservoir—a fitting palace for America's new aristocracy. Nearly eight decades later, in 2006, Dov Charney, the disgraced founder of American Apparel, purchased the house at the height of his indie sleaze empire. He promptly installed a sculpture of a middle finger flipping off Los Angeles.

By 2024, after American Apparel's bankruptcy, the courts ordered Charney to sell the mansion to pay off his debts. This meant evicting his roommates: disgraced *Breitbart* provocateur Milo Yiannopoulos and several staffers of the equally disgraced Kanye West—now known as Ye.

After being ousted from *Breitbart* in 2017 over pro-pedophilia comments, Yiannopoulos seemed intent on compounding his ostracization. Twitter banned him for calling Black actress Leslie Jones "barely literate," and Australia denied him entry over anti-Islamic comments tied to New Zealand's Christchurch mosque massacre. He later claimed to have undergone "gay conversion therapy" and pledged allegiance to the Catholic Church.

By 2024, Yiannopoulos had reinvented himself yet again—this time as the founder of a talent management and consulting company for the canceled: Dov Charney, jailed pharma-bro Martin Shkreli, erratic pro-Trump rapper Azealia Banks, and former *Pitchfork* darling turned January 6 insurrectionist Ariel Pink. He also worked with QAnon-supporting Congress-woman Marjorie Taylor Greene, who once suggested the Rothschilds used space lasers to start California wildfires.

At some point in the 2020s, Yiannopoulos maneuvered his way into Ye's orbit as his chief of staff, tasked with "solving mysteries and fixing problems where others have failed." One of those "problems" was helping Ye stage another presidential campaign after his disastrous 2020 bid. On November 22, 2022, Yiannopoulos orchestrated a meeting between Ye and Donald Trump at Mar-a-Lago, bringing along a surprise guest: white nationalist and Holocaust denier Nick Fuentes. "I wanted to show Trump the kind of talent that he's missing out on by allowing his terrible handlers to dictate who he can and can't hang out with," Yiannopoulos later gloated. During dinner, Ye suggested that Trump should serve as his vice-presidential running mate. Trump was not amused.

Afterward, Trump tried to downplay the dinner. "[Ye and I] got along great, he expressed no anti-Semitism, & I appreciated all of the nice things he said about me on 'Tucker Carlson.'" But the damage was done: Headlines blared that Trump had been "dining with Nazis."

Ye's presidential campaign quickly unraveled, and by May 2024, Yiannopoulos had severed ties with him—reportedly over Ye's plans to produce a line of pornographic videos with Mike Moz, the creator of the interracial sex website blacked.com. (Moz, notably, had once been married to Stormy Daniels, the adult film star at the center of Donald Trump's hush-money scandal.) Later that year, Yiannopoulos claimed that Ye was suffering from brain damage due to excessive use of nitrous oxide—a drug Ye had credited in 2015 with giving him a "completely new attitude on everything."

By the early 2020s, the #MeToo movement and a broader push for social accountability had toppled a wide range of male entertainers, though with varying degrees of consequence. Harvey Weinstein, Bill Cosby, and R. Kelly faced legal reckonings. Others were simply branded with a scarlet hashtag, cut off from mainstream platforms and corporate partnerships. But in the age of digital media, there were always ways to work around exile. By the mid-2020s, the counter-counterculture had grown into a thriving industry, offering a lucrative second life to men once cast aside.

In a pre-internet age, Yiannopoulos, Charney, and Ye would have had little in common. They weren't natural allies in traditional conservative politics—none seemed particularly invested in national security, tax policy, or the pro-life movement. But they could bond over their shared contempt for liberal decency. Like any good alternative status group, their new clique defined itself in opposition to the mainstream, embracing a spectrum that ranged from bro-ey misogyny to outright antisemitism. Audiences rewarded them for their "bravery" in making bigoted statements.

The more the canceled proved they could make a living outside traditional gatekeepers, the weaker the concept of cancellation became. "There is no point," *The Atlantic*'s Graeme Wood wrote, "in yelling 'racist' at someone who is already yelling racial epithets at full volume." In the early twenty-first century, "fuck-you money" described a fortune large enough to exempt its owner from social norms. The canceled twisted that logic into a business model: making a living by saying "fuck you" to everyone, all the time.

This pivot worked because transgressiveness had become the most aspirational human virtue across the political spectrum (outside of wealth, of course). And there was money to be made in edgelording: "deliberately engaging in shocking or controversial behavior online to elicit strong reactions from others or to appear edgy and nonconformist."

After admitting to sexual misconduct, comedian Louis C.K. lost his TV deal with FX and an estimated $35 million in income. Yet just months later, he made a surprise return to New York's famed Comedy Cellar and received an ovation. By 2022, he was able to bypass traditional distribution entirely, releasing an independent pay-per-view special that won a Grammy. Many fans framed their support of the canceled as a defense of free speech. In practice, it was both a spiritual and financial endorsement of people saying offensive things directly to their enemies. As *Comedy Book* author Jesse David Fox explains, "You can make a career of offending crowds, saying whatever you want, and your audience will eventually be made up of exclusively the people who like what others find offensive."

This market shift may have encouraged Ye to double down on his outrageous antics. Despite his full-throated support of Trump in an era of corporate wokeness, Yeezy continued generating billions for Adidas. But he soon moved from mere instability to full ideological malice.

In 2018, Ye stopped taking his medication for bipolar disorder and reportedly considered naming his eighth album *Hitler*. The following year, he launched Sunday Service, a gospel-inflected revival choir, and cozied up to prosperity preacher Joel Osteen. His behavior spiraled further after his failed 2020 presidential bid and subsequent divorce from Kim Kardashian. By 2022, he was praising Hitler on *Infowars*, wearing a "White Lives Matter" shirt to Paris Fashion Week, and sporting merch from Burzum, a Norwegian metal band whose front man was both a neo-Nazi organizer and convicted murderer.

Ye reportedly told a Jewish Adidas employee to kiss a photo of Hitler daily. He then married architect Bianca Censori, who often appeared with him in near-nude outfits. He bought a $57.3 million Malibu beachfront home designed by Japanese architectural legend Tadao Ando—only to strip it down into a concrete shell without electricity. Despite China's usual reluctance to host Western entertainers—both Justin Bieber and Lady Gaga had been denied—Ye was oddly allowed to perform for forty-two thousand fans on the island of Hainan in 2024. Soon after, he relocated to Tokyo.

None of this erratic behavior deterred his most devoted fans. His *Vultures* albums topped the *Billboard* charts in 2024, and he remained a fixture in the right-wing cultural sphere. From his very first album, Ye had indulged in a victimization narrative, but now, as *Washington Post* critic Chris Richards noted, his grievances aligned perfectly with "the paranoiac selfishness of today's most unfathomably wealthy and the triumph of the sore winner."

But Ye was hardly the only controversial figure of the new right. After Kyle Rittenhouse's acquittal for killing Black Lives Matter protesters, he received a standing ovation at Turning Point USA's AmericaFest in 2021. "You're a hero to millions," the group's leader, Charlie Kirk, told him. "It's an honor to be able to have you."

British comedian Russell Brand, once a self-styled antiestablishment leftist, pivoted to full MAGA allegiance after accusations surfaced of sexual abuse and grooming underage women. By 2024, he had undergone an evangelical rebirth, baptized in the Thames by *Man vs. Wild* host Bear Grylls. As a newly devout man of God, he became the spokesperson for Aires Tech's $240 "magical amulet," marketed as protection from "evil energies" such as Wi-Fi. (In 2025 he faced charges of sexual assault in the UK.)

The canceled right, which was an overwhelmingly male demographic, overlapped neatly with the "manosphere"—a loose web of gender-traditionalist influencers who coached young men on how to dominate women. As women's educational and economic gains accelerated, a subset of men refused to adapt, instead seeking refuge in like-minded online communities. What began with the Gamergate movement in 2014 metastasized into a broader network of "men's rights activists," pickup artists, and self-proclaimed alpha males. As novelist and essayist Peter C. Baker put it, the manosphere is an "amorphous, fractious constellation of online men's groups united in their belief that feminism is ruining the world."

The manosphere's most brazen figure was Andrew Tate, a former kickboxer who built his brand on explicit misogyny. His first brush with notoriety came when he was expelled from the reality show *Big Brother* after a video surfaced of him hitting a woman with a belt. From there, he built Hustlers University, a subscription-based tutorial promising to help young men "escape the matrix" of feminist society. "There's no way you can be rooted in reality and not be sexist," Tate declared. His real fortune, however, came from a Romania-based webcam business, where he matched lonely men with women who read from a script of tragic tales to manipulate them into handing over cash. Tate, pocketing the profits, invested in crypto and a fleet of thirty-three luxury cars. In 2022, Romanian authorities arrested him and his brother on charges of human trafficking and rape.

Meanwhile, those seeking a more intellectual veneer for the manosphere found a hero in Jordan Peterson, a Canadian psychologist who urged men to reclaim a world he feared had been overtaken by radical leftism. His 2018 bestseller, *12 Rules for Life,* dispensed cryptic advice such as "Stand up straight with your shoulders back" and "Do not bother children when they are skateboarding."

His meteoric rise was derailed by a series of medical crises. After adopting an all-meat diet at the urging of his daughter, he suffered an extreme reaction to a sip of apple cider containing sulfites, triggering what he described as "an overwhelming sense of impending doom." Sleepless for twenty-five days, he was prescribed clonazepam, developed a dependency, and sought an experimental detox treatment in Russia that involved an induced eight-day coma—after which he temporarily lost the ability to speak or write.

As angry men looked for ways to unmoor society from its liberal tenets of inclusivity, a market emerged for a range of once-discredited ideologies. While Peterson introduced young men to Jungian mysticism, the New Right found inspiration in the aristocratic, antidemocratic rhetoric of Romanian American Costin Alamariu, better known as Bronze Age Pervert (BAP). His philosophy, gilded with racism and misogyny, championed a return to classical Greek ideals of the strong dominating the weak. "The only right government," he declared, "is military government, and every other form is both hypocritical and destructive of true freedom."

His ideas extended beyond the fringes. Billionaire Peter Thiel referenced BAP in speeches; Senator J. D. Vance followed him on Twitter. Senior national security adviser (and menswear blogger) Michael Anton warned, "In the spiritual war for the hearts and minds of the disaffected youth on the right, conservatism is losing. BAPism is winning." *The Atlantic*'s Graeme Wood saw BAP's ascendance as the return of "a gnarly virus that had lain dormant for decades in circles of philosophers and their unread books."

Despite its influence among reactionary elites, the New Right still grappled with a fundamental contradiction: Could it ever be cool? Would it fulfill Gavin McInnes's prediction of merging with the creative class? One early experiment in bridging that gap was Praxis, a libertarian start-up that aspired to build "an autonomous, high-tech nation" on an island in the Mediterranean. Founded by Dryden Brown, a twentysomething college dropout and former hedge-fund employee with a taste for Balenciaga, Praxis raised $19.2 million from crypto investors and Thiel-adjacent financiers. With a supposed membership of sixty-two thousand, Brown set out to infiltrate downtown New York's hipster scene by hiring Kaitlin Phillips, the publicist who had boosted the Dimes Square scene.

In 2024, Praxis launched an eponymous magazine, styling itself with *Vice*-like snark. One caption read: "Fifteen years ago, these girls would have been following [The Strokes'] Julian Casablancas around on tour. Instead, they were born too late and have to pretend to care about things like AI and crypto in order to sleep around." Despite its performative irreverence, *Praxis* failed to achieve real cultural cachet. Where *Vice* had thrived by serving its anti-liberalism as an amuse-bouche of a standard menu of youthful debauchery, Praxis presented its politics as a full meal for crypto-fascist dorks. The project bled naturally into other forms of pseudo-spiritual hokum: One former *Praxis* employee left to start a company producing "halo-shaped wearables that use 'neurostimulation' to try to induce lucid dreams."

If the manosphere's promise of hypermasculine dominance was meant to help men succeed with the opposite sex, in practice it often had the reverse effect. Increasingly isolated from career-oriented women, many gravitated toward the idealized fantasy of the "trad wife": "women who spend their days taking care of their homes and families and documenting their activities on social media." Trad wives ranged from Orthodox Jewish homemaker Abby Roth (sister of political pundit Ben Shapiro) to nonpolitical domesticity influencers like Alena Kate Pettitt. TikTok star Nara Smith, the wife of blond Mormon model Lucky Blue Smith, rose to fame posting artisanal cooking videos with soothing voice-overs. One widely parodied clip showed the couple making their own toothpaste from scratch.

To professor Kelsey Kramer McGinnis, the trad-wife movement was less a serious political position than an aestheticized form of magical thinking and prosperity gospel: "If you live this lifestyle, if you do this thing that God is calling you to [do] as a woman, he will provide. And not only will he provide, he will provide beautifully. He will provide a beautiful family, a beautiful home, beautiful surroundings, a beautiful body."

Milo Yiannopoulos praised Ye's partner Bianca Censori as "a traditionally-minded wife (notwithstanding the outfits) who honors, obeys and defers to her man." The rising fascination with trad wives made it an obvious space for opportunists. Gwen Swinarton, once an ASMR YouTuber who later turned to OnlyFans, eventually found God—and Jordan Peterson. Reinventing herself as "Gwen the Milkmaid" on TikTok, she delivered viral sound bites about subservience to men.

Fierce partisanship against liberalism also emboldened some country music stars to push back against the encroachment of omnivore monoculture into their provincial sound. Jason Aldean's 2023 hit single "Try That in a Small Town" championed rural vigilantism against social justice protesters. Its video was filmed in front of the Columbia, Tennessee, courthouse where a white mob lynched eighteen-year-old Henry Choate in 1927. (Aldean denied any historical allusion.) Republican candidates played it at rallies, positioning it as a culture-war anthem.

Meanwhile, another unlikely hit—Oliver Anthony's "Rich Men North of Richmond"—mined economic frustration with raw, folky populism. The song took aim at Jeffrey Epstein (looking out for "minors on an island somewhere") and food stamp recipients ("God, if you're five foot three and you're 300 pounds / taxes ought not to pay for your bags of fudge rounds"). The online right quickly embraced it, though Anthony later distanced himself from partisanship, describing the song as broadly antiestablishment.

As 4chan's casual misogyny and racism seeped further into mainstream discourse, fringe internet cultures pushed toward new extremes to set themselves apart. One disturbing avenue was the growing fandom surrounding Columbine shooters Eric Harris and Dylan Klebold. In adjacent online spaces, mass murderers—from Adam Lanza (Sandy Hook) to Randy Stair (Weis Markets)—were idolized like K-pop stars, complete with dedicated stan armies producing fan art and fiction. As Katherine Dee observed, these killers were "depicted in an anime, 'chibi' style, decorated with hearts and glitter, or 'slash' pics that imagine shooters in homosexual pairings with one another." The worship of mass murderers extended to a reappraisal of the Unabomber's *Industrial Society and Its Future* manifesto, which found new admirers among digital-age antimodernists. One such fan, Luigi Mangione, seemingly took the rhetoric offline when he assassinated a health-care CEO on the streets of Manhattan in December 2024.

The best part of any superhero movie is the origin story. One night in the summer of 2024, the hosts of the online show *Tim & Dee TV* were cruising the streets of Nashville, Tennessee, conducting Girls Gone Wild–lite interviews—flirting with women on camera, tossing out heavy sexual innuendo, then angling for their phone numbers. Midway through the episode, they stumbled upon a twenty-one-year-old blonde named Haliey Welch. Dressed in a tight black dress and white go-go boots, Welch was visibly intoxicated, repeatedly wandering off camera to yell at friends across the street. DeArius "Dee" Marlow eventually reeled her back in frame and hit her with his stock question: "What's one move in bed that makes a man go crazy every time?" Welch, in a thick Tennessee drawl, leaned in and delivered an instant classic: "Ah, you gotta give 'em that *hawk tuah* and spit on that thing. You get me?"

The video went viral, and within days, Welch was known across the internet as Hawk Tuah Girl. Pornhub reported 4.7 million searches for "hawk tuah."

Welch moved quickly to capitalize on her fame, including a Spirit Halloween costume collaboration. A debate ignited over whether she was pro-Trump or anti-Trump after she dismissed him as an old "granddaddy" unworthy of a hawk tuah. When *New York* magazine writer Ej Dickson declared that Welch had "at best, 1-2 more days left in the news cycle," she promptly signed with Nashville talent agency the Penthouse. *Rolling Stone* anointed her "a charming Gen Z Dolly Parton who's rightfully becoming

America's Sweetheart." She quit her job at a spring factory, judged a bikini contest at Florida's Seminole Hard Rock Hotel & Casino, then jetted off to speak at Korea Blockchain Week. By fall, YouTuber-boxer Jake Paul's production company, Betr, launched her podcast, *Talk Tuah*, which rose to the third most popular in the country. Later that year, she introduced a meme coin called Hawk, which reached a $490 million market capitalization before collapsing by 95 percent in an alleged "rug-pull." Facing criticism and legal scrutiny, Welch disappeared for weeks, issued a statement in stiff legalese, and went back into hiding.

Welch's fame was largely confined to the "barstool conservative" corners of the internet—what critic Max Read dubbed the "Zynternet," after the Zyn nicotine pouches favored by its denizens. The Zynternet wasn't explicitly ideological or anti-liberal, but its biggest personalities were "'edgy,' trollish, hedonistic, attention-seeking"—or, as Read put it more bluntly, "dipshits." Podcasting had started as a left-leaning medium, but in an increasingly subliterate society, it became the perfect delivery system for dudes talking to dudes about dude stuff. The audience, as internet critic Ryan Broderick put it, was full of "stinky guys" who spent their days vaping in sparsely decorated apartments, gambling on sports, playing *Call of Duty*, and funneling cash into parasocial bonds with OnlyFans models.

This was the Lumpenproletariat strain of the counter-counterculture. In Broderick's view, it represented "a flattening of digital media, internet drama, and sex work, where all of it just ends up as more content on our timelines." The hard-right manosphere remained niche, but once in solidarity with the Zynternet and the canceled celebrities, the counter-counterculture had become arguably the loudest and most influential nonmainstream force in American culture. This was what "alternative" now looked like in the twenty-first century: a loosely affiliated swarm of men trying to reassemble the remnants of twentieth-century gender norms by force.

The undisputed king of the Zynternet was Joe Rogan, a former actor, comedian, and *Fear Factor* host who reinvented himself as the world's most influential podcaster. As the "male Oprah," he conducted long, rambling interviews that thrived on the illusion of pure, unfiltered curiosity—"just asking questions" that poked at conventional wisdom. Though not explicitly right-wing, Rogan's brand of conspiracy-minded skepticism provided a platform for a long list of the canceled and near-canceled, from anti-vaccine crusaders to Elon Musk and Alex Jones.

Political analyst John Ganz argued that Rogan's appeal stemmed from "the appearance of open inquiry" in contrast to a growing sense of enforced liberal dogma: "The main feature tying together the shows that young right-leaning men watch and listen to now is *curiosity*. They include discussions and debates; their hosts might not be particularly knowledgeable and they are open about it, so they ask what might seem like dumb questions without shame." In a world that told them they were wrong about everything they believed, open inquiry gave them some hope they could be right about *something*.

One unifying thread across these male-oriented ecosystems was a hunger for self-improvement, whether that meant success with women, making money, or sculpting the ideal physique. Despite Gen Z's efforts to differentiate themselves from millennials, one belief remained intact: entrepreneurial heroism. A particularly attractive get-rich-quick scheme among Zynternet bros was "dropshipping": a frictionless e-commerce hustle that involved sourcing cheap production from Chinese manufacturers, marketing them aggressively on social media, and only placing bulk orders once sales were locked in. The most successful dropshippers pocketed a 15 to 20 percent margin while operating their businesses from suburban bedrooms, coffee shops, or the beaches of Bali.

With no college degree required, dropshipping also became a way for teens to strike it rich. Fourteen-year-old Londoner Alex Philip profited $5,000 a month from his Shopify store, crediting his entrepreneurial destiny to childhood quirks: "Whenever I found loose change anywhere my dad would say it was a sign that I would make loads of money." Aaron Grant, another junior capitalist wunderkind, started out selling candy at his high school before launching DropshipVenture. For his eighteenth birthday, he bought himself a $100,000 BMW M4. The ultimate dropshipper flex, however, wasn't just getting rich—it was monetizing wisdom. With *The 4-Hour Workweek* maven Tim Ferriss serving as our century's Richard Branson, the real play was to parlay a tiny bit of success into an even bigger business of coaching others. YouTube was flooded with self-proclaimed "ecom experts" offering dubious mentorship programs. One of the biggest names, Mike Vestil, built his brand by posing shirtless on exotic beaches, branding himself as the leader of a new movement of "freedom fighters" escaping the nine-to-five grind.

With its revanchist views on masculinity and power, the extended Zynternet had a natural synergy with pornography. Joe Rogan's first major sponsor was the Fleshlight masturbatory aid. In the early 2000s, Paris Hilton had fought to distance herself from the humiliation of her leaked sex tape, and Kim Kardashian still denies engineering her own leak. But porn found a seat at the table in the counter-counterculture. David Choe, who made hundreds of millions from painting an office mural for a pre-IPO Facebook, ran a podcast with adult film actress Asa Akira. Others straddled street culture and the adult industry, like face-tattooed BMX blogger turned podcast mogul Adam Grandmaison, a.k.a. Adam22. He first built an influential music platform that helped launch SoundCloud rappers like 6ix9ine. Then, he pivoted: He and his wife, adult film actress Lena the Plug, filmed their own pornographic videos and cohosted *Plug Talk*, a sex videocast that fused influencer marketing with the mechanics of adult entertainment.

All of this followed from the logic of the internet economy: "People are just trying to get attention by any means," Grandmaison explained. "That's really what's going to be the thing that decides if you're successful or not. And it's kind of all about if you really want to play that game or not." In a world where money reigned supreme and norms no longer constrained behavior, there was no downside to chasing the most extreme forms of provocation. Shame was just another roadblock to profit.

By 2024, the Zynternet's increasing dominance made the entire internet feel fractured for everyone else. When Joe Rogan declared Hawk Tuah Girl "the most famous person on the planet" during the first weeks of her rise, most people had no idea who she was.

This strange dynamic also applied to "the Costco Guys"—former wrestler Andrew "A.J." Befumo, his son Eric, and a child influencer known as "the Rizzler." After years of failed attempts at stardom, including a "a web show about being a MAN," Befumo finally cracked the code with TikTok. Their videos pulled massive numbers but existed in a weird limbo. As Max Read asked: "Are there 'real' or 'authentic' fans of the Costco Guys out there? Or is their presence in my field of vision entirely the product of an unspoken collective agreement to ironically follow them closely as you would a 'real' celebrity, because it allows you to make funny jokes on X?" When they appeared on Jimmy Fallon's late-night show, Fallon was clearly annoyed that he had to make small talk with these internet nobodies.

The absurdity of online microfame was crystallized in a 2023 meme: "Is Baby Gronk the new Drip King? Or is Livvy just using him for clout?" Understanding this sentence required not only fluency in Gen Z slang but familiarity with an entire cast of minor online figures: Baby Gronk, a preteen football prodigy; Livvy, a blond LSU gymnast turned influencer; and the Drip King, a UMass lacrosse player who briefly trended for his over-the-top fashion sense.

By late 2024, however, Zynternet culture found a successful pathway into the mainstream through sheer cynical spectacle. The boxing match between Jake Paul and fifty-eight-year-old retired champion Mike Tyson demonstrated that male-dominated online culture, for all its irony and self-referential absurdity, could now command an enormous audience. Netflix streamed the fight to sixty million households.

Jake Paul had begun his career making Vine videos with his brother before pivoting to a lucrative empire built on controversy, bro-ey energy drinks, NFTs, and Betr, his attempt at a "TikTok of gambling." Boxing became his most successful grift—part sport, part WWE-style entertainment. He "inspires a lot of vitriol," noted Gen Z analyst Kelsey Weekman. "He is the villain in every single matchup—but people tune in specifically to see him get punched."

And yet, the Paul–Tyson fight itself felt too openly like a sham. The much-hyped bout featured Paul pulling his punches and Tyson carefully pacing himself, ensuring the fight was less a genuine competition than a carefully staged pantomime of violence. Novelist Will Leitch summarized the letdown: "It's one thing to watch a farcical fight; it's another entirely when farcical fights are all that are left."

"Who would have guessed going into this year's RNC and DNC," tweeted journalist Nick Gillespie, "that aesthetically the Dems would have presented as more @WonderBreadUSA, church-and-family-loving, mom-and-apple pie & the GOP was like a JV version of the Gathering of Juggalos?" The 2024 Republican National Convention, held just days after an assassination attempt on Trump, was a counter-countercultural variety show. One guest speaker was Amber Rose—Ye's ex, known for her shaved head and forehead tattoo of her sons' names. Russell Brand was there to support the cause. Meanwhile, the Democratic ticket of Kamala Harris and Tim Walz ran on the premise that Republicans had become extremely "weird," which convinced the GOP to lean in and make weird its defining aesthetic.

Throughout the campaign, Trump again rejected every rule of traditional politics. He openly insulted his own constituents. At one rally, instead of taking questions, he swayed in place for thirty-nine minutes to music. In speeches, he inexplicably praised "the late, great Hannibal Lecter" from *The Silence of the Lambs*, a fictional serial killer who never died in the films. During his debate with Harris, he pushed a bizarre, baseless claim that Haitian immigrants were "eating the dogs . . . they're eating the cats."

Harris allied with the omnivore monoculture, winning an early endorsement from Charli XCX, who declared, "Kamala IS brat." Trump, meanwhile, made the rounds on Joe Rogan, Logan Paul, Adin Ross, Theo Von, and the Nelk Boys. "Trump sat with all of them," wrote journalist Brian Barrett, "reaching millions of conservative or apolitical people, cementing his status as one of them, a sigma, a guy with clout, and the apex of a model of masculinity that prioritizes fame as a virtue unto itself." Trump's iconoclastic behavior may have helped activate young male voters who rarely turned out to the polls.

He had another wind at his back: tech billionaires. Elon Musk poured more than $270 million into his campaign and weaponized X as a political force. Silicon Valley power players Marc Andreessen and Ben Horowitz endorsed him. The crypto world saw him as a guardian angel. Tech turned toward the right. Palmer Luckey—the Oculus founder once exiled from tech for supporting Trump in 2016—was no longer an outlier but instead re-emerged as a sage-like "American Vulcan" running the defense tech giant Anduril.

Trump won the election. The media had dismissed his 2016 victory as a fluke—with a handful of votes in a few swing states tipping the Electoral College. But in 2024, Trump won the popular vote. Almost every part of the country shifted toward him, even big cities.

French scholar Olivier Roy wrote that the globalized world had left the provincial white majority in a state of "cultural anxiety"—a loss of identity, an inability to define *their* culture. The right found its solution in embracing the digital counter-counterculture and bringing that energy directly into the mainstream conservative movement. And with Trump's victory in November, the onetime-fringe weirdos were proclaimed the new cultural leaders. After the election, Ian Ward at *Politico* stated, "It's not cool or subversive right now to be a Democratic partisan, who are seen as defenders of the status quo. There's a certain subversiveness to being MAGA."

Trump's triumph at the polls encouraged America's economic leaders to fully genuflect, although they didn't seem to need much convincing. In 2025, Amazon, Apple, Google, Meta, Microsoft, Uber, and OpenAI CEO Sam Altman all donated to Trump's inauguration fund. At one inauguration event, Elon Musk threw a stiff-armed Nazi-style salute. Amazon paid Melania Trump a $40 million licensing fee for the right to make a documentary about her. When the Trump administration mobilized against DEI in its first week, Facebook and Google publicly announced that they had dismantled their own diversity-promotion programs, which had once been central to their corporate values and internal culture.

Under Trump, the crypto community saw immediate gains. Bitcoin prices skyrocketed. Trump and Melania both launched their own meme coins; $Trump had a market cap of $14.5 billion at its peak.

Trump pardoned the January 6 rioters en masse. Their woo-woo rebellion had paid off after all. The Trump administration helped the manosphere's Andrew Tate and his brother escape rape charges in Romania and roam free in the US.

He tasked Elon Musk, the world's richest man, with running the Department of Government Efficiency—known as DOGE in homage to the Shiba Inu meme. His team was made up of young rightists who had gone through what John Ganz called "groyperification." The fringe politics of 4chan were now guiding the people working to dismantle government agencies. The administration defunded watchdogs, scientific research, medical standards, and anything else associated with service-minded members of the professional class.

A few weeks after the inauguration, Ye went on a fascist tirade on X: "I'm a Nazi," he wrote in one post. Another stated, "Hitler was sooooo fresh." During the 2025 Super Bowl, he ran an advertisement, shot on an iPhone from a dentist's chair, pointing viewers toward his online store. It sold a single product: a white T-shirt with a black swastika. In May, he released a new single titled "Heil Hitler."

Conclusion
RESTORING CULTURAL INVENTION

Were you not entertained? Nearly every day of the twenty-first century provided new distractions: viral memes, outrageous statements, celebrity meltdowns, life hacks and horoscopes, leaked album tracks, extremely talented animals. Culture has never contained more *stuff*—an endless reel of words, ideas, games, songs, and videos. There were more gradations of celebrity than ever, with influencers shilling an ever-expanding cornucopia of private-label goods. And thanks to poptimism and entrepreneurial heroism, the culture industry's most successful figures got paid very well for their contributions. Consumers elected a new aristocracy of billionaires and mere multimillionaires: Taylor Swift, Jimmy Iovine, George Clooney, Ryan Reynolds, King Jay-Z, and Queen Bey.

At the same time, culture proved to be a highly effective political tool for both the left and the right. A 2024 study using facial recognition software revealed a sharp increase in the representation of women and people of color in Hollywood films after 2010. Artists and stars who crossed legal, moral, and ethical boundaries lost their careers. Meanwhile, the right found their own formula for political revival in online transgressive anti-liberalism.

Culture has been central to the narrative of the last twenty-five years— but merely as entertainment, commerce, and politics. In reliving the first quarter of the century in these pages, we can feel what's missing—there is a conspicuous *blank space* where art and creativity used to be. For all the energy invested in culture today, little has emerged that feels *new* at a symbolic level. Certainly, nothing radical enough to fully outmode the past. Audrey

Hepburn, Miles Davis, and Joan Didion remain iconic because no one has emerged who can compete with their cool.

Poptimists demanded equal respect for art and kitsch, which was only a short leap from equal respect to the artist and the businessperson. This inevitably crowded out the romantic ideal of making art for art's sake. But as scholar Natasha Degen warns, art without autonomy is indistinguishable from any other commodity. We may be already there. "If [Theodor] Adorno were to look upon the cultural landscape of the twenty-first century," music critic Alex Ross writes, "he might take grim satisfaction in seeing his fondest fears realized. The pop hegemony is all but complete, its superstars dominating the media and wielding the economic might of tycoons."

In his 2022 book, *The Crisis of Culture*, French scholar Olivier Roy argues that we have reached the end of cultural progress—what he calls the "deculturation of cultures." The canon is abandoned, subcultures are reduced to mere "codes of communication," and the marketplace has swallowed everything. The history in these pages bears some of this out, but as a full diagnosis, it feels too pessimistic. *Culture* in the anthropological sense will always exist, and there remain subcultures—just fewer of them. The canon is not *dead*; the problem is that it casts a long shadow over the present. Kurt Cobain would have surely wanted the next generation to kill their idols, including him. Instead, they wear his face on T-shirts and call it "preppy." Still, the lingering reverence toward Cobain suggests a latent respect for the agents of radical cultural change, even in capitalist-realist times. Deep in our hearts, however subconscious, we know that artists—not skilled commodity merchants or financial manipulators—should be our true heroes.

Capitulation to our new commerce-first values would be the easiest route. *New York Times* critic Jason Farago wrote in total exasperation, "Surely it would be healthier—and who knows what might flower—if we accepted and even embraced the end of stylistic progress, and at last took seriously the digital present we are disavowing." Internet culture critic Katherine Dee agreed: "There's a new culture all around us. We just don't register it as 'culture.'" As examples, Dee pointed to new digital forms—Bronze Age Pervert's persona-driven "internet-personality-as-art," TikTok's vaudevillian vertical sketches, and the amorphous aesthetic of "vibe" channels.

But no, we should reject calls for lowering our expectations. Certainly, digital tools offer new canvases for artistic exploration, but Dee's particular examples aren't enough to fill the blank space. What's missing is an artistic *mindset*—the imagination to reject kitsch and pursue artworks that expand the possibilities of human perception. This requires complexity, ambiguity, and formal experimentation. These attributes are not elitist; they power the masterpieces that draw millions of people every year to museums. Why exactly should we feel bad about encouraging more of these beloved artworks? How did advocating for timeless artistry at the expense of shallow commerciality become an "elitist" position?

In my previous book *Status and Culture*, I argued that the easy acquisition of information and goods on the internet destroyed an important source of cultural value and elevated money to the supreme status symbol. Between this structural shift and a full rationalization of the culture industry, the system is certainly stacked against the creation of pure art. But that is no reason to surrender. Capitalism may seem inevitable, yet political parties around the world organize to reform it. Environmentalists don't throw up their hands and say, "Who knows what might flower if we embraced the boiling oceans?"

The real crisis in culture, then, isn't market domination—it's resignation. Neoliberalism didn't just create pernicious economic structures; it provided a set of extremely seductive ideologies that convinced us to stop idolizing artistic progress. So far this has been a century of pop realists who find it harder to imagine the end of Taylor Swift than the end of the world. Meanwhile, the right, in its conquest of the countercultural spirit, repurposed the entire idea of transgression to power agitprop with no artistic pretensions. Even conservative scholar Spencer Klavan conceded that "all conservatives in the arts know that a major sector of the audience they're trying to reach will go in for the most appalling kitsch if it's slathered in red, white, and blue." (Or increasingly, slathered in semi-ironic nods to the Third Reich.)

The first step in reversing cultural stagnation is to accept that artistic invention is a *social good*. And like so many other social goods, we shouldn't expect the market to optimize for its production. We have to make an effort. Creators need to *try* to make radical new forms of culture. Even their failures and half steps will be more interesting than overly market-tested, premium-mediocre pop.

Restoring cultural invention doesn't even require dismantling the entire culture industry—it just needs a small vanguard to get things going. Throughout history, the human race has been blessed with dedicated creative enclaves—bohemianism, the avant-garde, the counterculture, Native Tongues, nineties alternative—that pursued creative invention without the promise of immediate financial rewards. Pearl Jam, in 1992, lived by an honor code that made it easier to resist money and fame. If you're an artist, find peers who share these aspirations. If you're not an artist, encourage aspiring artists to make art, not immediately indulge in commerce. First and foremost, artists crave esteem, and this once gave critics a central role in promoting creativity. Then the poptimists decided to withhold respect from anyone who didn't harbor grand commercial ambitions.

Cultural invention doesn't require government funding or mass persuasion. It begins inside small but influential creative communities. The goal, then, is to create more of these communities and support them. The following five steps aren't a blueprint for guaranteed success, but they point in the right direction.

1. Rebuild and Enforce Social Norms

For over a century, the world's most creative people have viewed social norms with deep suspicion. Norms were, after all, the foundation of middle-class respectability—the very thing that stifled genius. By the midtwentieth century, to be "cool" meant rejecting convention outright. Capitalists agreed: Customs, biases, manners, and taboos were merely obstacles to greater market expansion.

So society chipped away at the entire idea of norms, throwing out the baby with the bathwater. The result was not human liberation but societies in which only money held value. Meanwhile, the erosion of norms left us defenseless against opportunists who learned to hack the system. The media dutifully amplified every calculated outrage, and norm breakers rose as our cultural leaders through sheer volume alone.

Social norms remain one of the most powerful tools we have for fighting against the forces that want to further carve out the blank space. Humans have always used norms to rebalance social rewards and punishments, ensuring that self-interest doesn't erode the collective good. This means we can use norms to reward invention and discourage cynical, exploitative uses of culture. Consider the Mafia's omertà—a code of silence designed to prevent snitching. By threatening dishonor (and worse) to anyone who squeals, the omertà shifts the incentives of the classic prisoner's dilemma, ensuring nobody talks.

Obviously, the Mafia is an odd role model for cultural renewal, but the same logic powered the highly productive twentieth-century taboo against selling out. Artists and subcultures enforced strong norms against commercialism, steering younger creators away from internalizing market goals. Experimentation rarely pays in the short term, so social rewards—status, respect, admiration—became critical for sustaining artists on the path of invention.

Critics play a crucial role in this process. Before poptimism glorified kitsch, critics used their platforms to elevate the most daring, innovative work. Their positive reviews conferred status on artists *and* their fans. Audiences felt a sense of pride in their reverence for cult works, providing a counterweight to mainstream commercialism. Director David Lynch died a cultural legend—because of critical support and cultish fandom, not the rewards of the marketplace.

If we want to restore cultural invention, we must first become comfortable again enforcing norms around things we care about. Reinstituting nonfinancial values would not only bolster genuine artistic creation—it would also help expel the grifters who have overrun culture. We owe no deference to faux artists who clog up the media with moneymaking rackets disguised as creativity. There are plenty of DJs who can pick up the slack once Paris Hilton and David Solomon are exiled. ·

2. Treat Culture as an Ecosystem

Poptimism gained traction in the early 2000s by framing complex, experimental culture as inherently elitist—a tool used by the educated to make everyone else feel inferior. In this view, the criticism of mass-produced pop culture wasn't just snobbery; it denied "the people" their right to take pleasure. But in focusing too much attention on the most popular cultural output, poptimism treated culture like it was sports, in which only the major leagues mattered. Everything else was ignorable as the minor leagues.

But culture isn't sports. The minor leagues of marginalized communities, niche subcultures, and experimental creators have always been the most important crucible of innovation. While the mainstream occasionally produces something original, it mostly feeds on ideas generated outside its walls. Artists, subcultures, and countercultures are intrinsically motivated to break conventions, and the industry relies on them for fresh ideas to commercialize later. Even the most passive consumers, those indifferent to "high art," may not actively seek out experimental work, but they instinctively grow bored with repetition. Hip-hop's longevity comes from its ability to follow the lead of its vanguard, resulting in a long chain of stylistic evolution from drum machines to soul samples to synthesized trap beats.

By denying this central principle of cultural dynamics, we've created a cultural landscape that feels increasingly stagnant. Poptimists thought they were liberating the world from taste, but celebrating Ashlee Simpson's lip-synching opened the door for Kim Kardashian and Jake Paul. As Mark Fisher observed, "The media class's refusal to be paternalistic has not produced a bottom-up culture of breathtaking diversity, but one that is increasingly infantilized."

Worse, the poptimist logic is quite patronizing—it assumes marginalized communities need to be rewarded for kitsch, when in reality, so many of the past century's most enduring cultural breakthroughs have come from out-casts and outsiders.

A cultural ecosystem approach is more inclusive than poptimism. When innovative artists are supported and taken seriously, the entire system thrives. Critics and tastemakers play an essential role—not by acting as obstinate gatekeepers, but by assuming that audiences are capable of engaging "with cultural products that are complex and intellectually demanding," as Fisher writes. And by fostering a deep reservoir of creative ideas, we ensure that even mainstream pop culture remains vibrant and dynamic, rather than end-lessly recycling its own past.

3. Break Off into Smaller Communities

Every enduring cultural movement—hip-hop, rock, punk, streetwear—began as an insular, tightly knit community of like-minded peers. These groups were driven by dissatisfaction with the mainstream and a deep desire to create something new. Historically, these subcultures existed in real-world spaces—clubs, skate parks, dive bars, DIY venues—where ideas evolved organically.

Today such subcultures have largely migrated online. While digital spaces allow people to find their niches more easily, they do not create adequate so-cial distance for the isolation that fosters invention. And the omnipresence of mainstream culture means that many subcultures are now just fan commu-nities devoted to existing mass-market entertainment. The omnivore mono-culture's inclusiveness created the odd situation in which the most fervent, distinct subcultures exist on the political right. Yet because these groups are largely motivated by revanchist nostalgia rather than forward-thinking crea-tivity, their cultural influence is stunted. Right-wing memes like Rare Pepes are toxic rather than generative.

Where non-right-wing subcultures exist, they tend to be largely invisible. As critic Caroline Busta pointed out, today's counter-hegemonic culture is "not particularly interested in being seen—at least not in person." This shift has diminished the essential laboratories where cultural experimentation happens. Subcultures operating in the old model—such as drag queens, Chicago drill, and Atlanta trap—have profoundly reshaped the culture. Consumers still crave the energy of subcultural innovation and enjoy seeing underground ideas fused with commercial styles. But we've nearly exhausted the existing places to pull from. Reviving culture requires a new generation of outsiders willing to create their own movements from scratch.

Unfortunately, the current media ecosystem discourages this. The internet makes it far too easy for creators to chase virality rather than cultivate smaller, self-sustaining communities. Multinational brands tease lucrative deals to emerging artists and micro-influencers, reinforcing the idea that "getting the bag" is the ultimate goal. As art critic Jerry Saltz observed, "Nowadays these avant-gardes are instantly either eclipsed, calcified into hipness, absorbed, bought up, spit out, resold, recycled, and erased by the wider culture. It's almost impossible for fragile underground scenes to grow, get nurtured, and take root, especially when we move at light speed." Ice Spice came up in the intimate drill scene and faced little pushback for taking money from Big Donut. In an era where we live as "personal brands," every life decision is made to increase our own shareholder value.

Those who want to create something lasting must resist the pull of instant exposure and early buyouts. We need creators to disappear into their own worlds for a while, developing ideas away from corporate influence and mainstream assimilation. Not everyone will have the discipline to do this— but those who do will shape the future of culture.

4. Learn the Canon So Well That It Becomes Boring

There is no official cultural canon. It's a shifting, contested collection of the greatest symbolic experiments—works that have endured because they reshaped the way people think, create, and interpret the world. In the past, conservatives treated the canon as a sacred and complete archive, something to be preserved rather than expanded. This is precisely why the avant-garde sought to destroy it: Too much reverence for dead white men became an obstacle to creative liberation. But in truth, even the avant-garde needed the canon. The only way to invent something new was to fully understand what came before.

If we want true cultural invention beyond fleeting novelties, we need to reengage with the past—not as stultifying nostalgia but as building blocks. Right now, we're in a strange limbo: Knowledge of the canon is no longer required, yet its presence is inescapable. The bold experimentation of the twentieth century still feels more thrilling than most of today's cultural output. The canon has become a crutch for those bored with the present. The moment we tire of Addison Rae and Baby Gronk, we reach back into the archives for something stimulating. The solution is paradoxical: To move forward, we need to study the past, so thoroughly that it becomes boring—as boredom is one of the most reliable catalysts for innovation. The goal should be a disciplined engagement with historical works, paired with a futurist drive to forge entirely new creative pathways.

5. Don't Give the People What They Want

Relying too heavily on data to shape creative decisions misunderstands the nature of culture. Whether it's entertainment or art, humans seek culture for stimulation, not just familiarity. Data can reveal what people enjoy now, but by the time trends are replicated, audiences have already numbed to the same stimuli. The role of true creative inventors is not to follow tastes but to invent what will excite and challenge people next.

There is nothing elitist about resisting the immediate desires of the audience; in fact, it serves the public better in the long run. The great auteurs of the past—every single person we still revere—trusted their intuition, not audience analytics. If we want more lasting art, we must give creators the freedom to ignore the data and dream big. The best works have always been high-risk, high-reward—exactly the kind of creation that data-driven systems are programmed to suppress.

———

Much of the culture of the past twenty-five years was disposable and transitory. Early memes are already forgotten, and viral stars have faded into obscurity (or are picking up the pieces of their shattered lives). Once-popular influencers will spend their later years chasing attention like aging rock stars on the state fair circuit.

Some artworks from the early twenty-first century will endure, but the greatest value of this time period may be its role as a grand social experiment. We asked the question: What happens when we greet the tidal wave of postmodernism—the dreaded cultural logic of late capitalism—with open arms and put up no resistance?

Now we have our answer: We created a blank space. And now that we can see it, it's time to rebuild.

CREDITS

EDITOR: Ibrahim Ahmad (Viking Books)

AGENT: Mollie Glick (CAA)

FACT-CHECKERS: Sejla Rizvic, Conor McCann, Amy van den Berg, Sara Carminati

COVER ART: Andrew Kuo

COVER DESIGN: Dave Litman

INTERIOR DESIGN: Nerylsa Dijol

PUBLICIST: Julia Rickard

MARKETER: Molly Fessenden

SUBRIGHTS: Bridget Gilleran

PRODUCTION EDITOR: Anna Dobbin

EDITORIAL ASSISTANCE: Kriti Iyer Basaiawmoit, Elizabeth Pham Janowski

UNION SUPPORT: WGAE, URTU

EARLY READERS: Josh Lambert, Morris Marx, Connor Shepherd, Nick Sylvester

WITNESSES: Dana Brown, Jian DeLeon, Ben Dietz, Dan Frommer, Ann Liu, Emily Liu, Paul Mittleman, Jordan Schneider, Lauren Sherman, among many others

Thank you so much for making this book possible

NOTES

INTRODUCTION

1 **top-selling rock album of 1992:** Chuck Philips, "Cyrus, Brooks Give Their All to Record Sales," *Los Angeles Times*, January 5, 1993, https://www.latimes.com/archives/la -xpm-1993-01-05-ca-1031-story.html.

1 **"With any more popularity":** Mark Yarm, *Everybody Loves Our Town: An Oral History of Grunge* (Three Rivers Press, 2011), 374.

1 **took an early slot:** Yarm, *Everybody Loves Our Town*, 340.

1 **Vedder told *Spin*:** Jonathan Rowe, "Our Lollapalooza Guide from '92 Was a Tribute to an Age of Grunge Innocence," *Spin*, July 28, 2022, https://www.spin.com/2022/07 /our-lollapalooza-guide-from-92-was -a-tribute-to-an-age-of-grunge-innocence.

1 **"scathing critique of conformist":** Steven Hyden, "A Lion Unleashed: The Enduring Legacy of Pearl Jam's 'Jeremy,'" *Ringer*, September 27, 2022, https://www.theringer .com/music/2022/9/27/23374148/jeremy -pearl-jam-long-road-steven-hyden.

2 **"The concept of 'selling out'":** Chuck Klosterman, *The Nineties* (Penguin Press, 2022), 20.

2 **as "corporate puppets":** Craig Jenkins, "Pearl Jam Isn't Cool, but That Doesn't Mean They're Not Great," *Slate*, April 20, 2017, https://slate.com/culture/2017/04 /pearl-jam-may-not-be-cool-but-they-re -great.html.

2 **no longer produce music videos:** They held this promise for five years, through their career peak.

2 **"I immediately knew":** Yarm, *Everybody Loves Our Town*, 426.

2 **Vedder promptly cut:** "Better Man" was

released on their third album, *Vitalogy*, and was a number-one hit.

2 **first-week album sales:** Chuck Philips, "One Band 'Vs.' the Rest: No Contest: Pop Music: Pearl Jam's New Album Sets a First-Week Sales Record with an Estimated 950,000 Copies Sold," *Los Angeles Times*, October 28, 1993, https://www.lat imes.com/archives/la-xpm-1993-10-28 -ca-50571-story.html.

3 **Solomon's professional résumé:** Kate Kelly, "Inside the Race for the Top Job on Wall Street," *New York Times*, November 22, 2017, https://www.nytimes.com/2017 /11/22/business/goldman-sachs-harvey -schwartz-david-solomon.html.

3 **Goldman's Gulfstream G650:** Lisa Ryan, "Staffers Say Goldman Sachs CEO David Solomon Has Asked Them to Help with His DJ Account," *Business Insider*, September 22, 2022, https://www.businessinsider .com/goldman-sachs-david-solomon-dj -wall-street-staffers-2022-9.

3 **"spun remixes of ABBA":** Althea Legaspi, Nina Corcoran, and Joshua Klein, "Lollapalooza 2022 Day Two: Dua Lipa Levitates, MGK Brings Out Avril Lavigne, Wet Leg Buzz," *Rolling Stone*, July 30, 2022, https://www .rollingstone.com/music/music-features/lol lapalooza-2022-day-two-review-dua-lipa -machine-gun-kelly-wet-leg-1386905.

4 **"Culture appears more monolithic":** Alex Ross, "The Naysayers," *New Yorker*, September 8, 2014, https://www.newyorker .com/magazine/2014/09/15/naysayers.

4 **"come to a standstill":** Jason Farago, "Why Culture Has Come to a Standstill." *New York Times Magazine*, October 10,

2023, https://www.nytimes.com/2023/10/10/magazine/stale-culture.html.

5   **"cancellation of the future":** Franco Berardi, *After the Future* (AK Press, 2011), 18.

5   **"paradoxical combination of speed":** Simon Reynolds, *Retromania: Pop Culture's Addiction to Its Own Past* (Farrar, Straus and Giroux, 2011), 427.

5   **"absence of novelty":** Leonard B. Meyer, *Music, the Arts, and Ideas* (University of Chicago Press, 1967), 102.

5   **"culture crash":** Scott Timberg, *Culture Crash: The Killing of the Creative Class* (Yale University Press, 2015).

5   **"flattening" culture:** Kyle Chayka, *Filterworld: How Algorithms Flattened Culture* (Doubleday, 2024).

7   **"impudently embracing the language":** David Harvey, *The Condition of Postmodernity* (Blackwell, 1990), 7.

7   **"cultural logic of late capitalism":** Fredric Jameson, *Postmodernism, or, the Cultural Logic of Late Capitalism* (Duke University Press, 1991).

7   **small cadre:** Daniel Bell, *Communitarianism and Its Critics* (Oxford University Press, 1993), 37.

7   **where there is no honor:** Kwame Anthony Appiah, *The Honor Code: How Moral Revolutions Happen* (W. W. Norton, 2010), 177.

PART ONE:
2001–2008

CHAPTER 1:
DOWNTOWN NEW YORK AFTER 9/11

13   **sensational cover:** Brian Goedde, "The Coup's Bomb," *Stranger*, September 20, 2001, https://www.thestranger.com/music/2001/09/20/8708/the-coups-bomb.

13   **an autumn release:** Garrett Blanton, "The Coup Party Music: 9/11 a Decade Later," *Rap Music Guide* (blog), September 11, 2012, https://www.rapmusicguide.com/blog/the-coup-party-music-911-a-decade-later.

13   **Progressive Labor Party:** Alex N. Press, "Boots Riley: 'The Only Answer Is Organizing on the Job,'" *Jacobin*, November 5, 2023, https://jacobin.com/2023/11/boots-riley-hollywood-gaza-class-struggle-wga-art.

13   **"metaphor for destroying capitalism":** Goedde, "The Coup's Bomb."

13   **guitar tuner:** The particular model is the TU-70 Boss Guitar and Bass Auto Tuner.

13   **morning of September 11, 2001:** Joanna Glasner, "Eerie Image Pulled from CD," *Wired*, September 13, 2001, https://www.wired.com/2001/09/eerie-image-pulled-from-cd.

13   **"The 21st century began":** Douglas Coupland, "Douglas Coupland: God, No-God," *Financial Times*, August 29, 2014, https://www.ft.com/content/672802f2-2e3f-11e4-b760-00144feabdc0. In *The Nineties* (Penguin Press, 2022, 337), Chuck Klosterman marks 9/11 in a similar way: "The nineties collapsed with the skyscrapers."

14   **"We are At War now":** Hunter S. Thompson, "Fear & Loathing in America," Hey Rube, ESPN.com Page 2, September 12, 2001, https://www.espn.com/espn/page2/story?id=1250751.

14   **90 percent approval rating:** Gallup, "Presidential Approval Ratings—George W. Bush," https://news.gallup.com/poll/116500/presidential-approval-ratings-george-bush.aspx.

14   **hard-line conservatives:** Julian Borger, "Bush Finalises His Mixed Bag of a Cabinet," *Guardian*, January 2, 2001, https://www.theguardian.com/world/2001/jan/03/uselections2000.usa1.

14   **shadowy influence:** Nicholas Lemann, "The Quiet Man," *New Yorker*, April 30, 2001, https://www.newyorker.com/magazine/2001/05/07/the-quiet-man-nicholas-lemann.

14   **Media conglomerate Clear Channel:** Gil Kaufman, "Filter's Richard Patrick, Don McLean, Drowning Pool, Saliva & More Talk Post-9/11 Clear Channel Radio Scrub," *Billboard*, September 9, 2021, https://www.billboard.com/music/rock/9-11-radio-scrub-anniversary-stories-9626045.

14   ***Tokion* pulled its anti-Bush T-shirts:** I worked as an intern at *Tokion* at this time and recommended that we take the T-shirt out of the store. Surprisingly, a Scottish man came a week later hoping to buy it.

14   **Riley expressed his "deepest sympathy":** Goedde, "The Coup's Bomb."

14   **flaming martini glass:** The Coup's *Party Music* went on to be named the best rap album of 2001 by *Rolling Stone* and best album of 2001 by *The Washington Post*.

14   **Susan Sontag received:** Susan Sontag, "Tuesday, and After," *New Yorker*, September 16, 2001, https://www.newyorker.com/magazine/2001/09/24/tuesday-and-after-talk-of-the-town.

14   **Bill Maher's *Politically Incorrect*:** "In What Sense Are Terrorists Cowards?,"

Slate, September 11, 2001, https://slate.com /news-and-politics/2001/09/in-what -sense-are-terrorists-cowards.html.

14 **"greatest work of art"**: "Attacks Called Great Art," *New York Times*, September 19, 2001, https://www.nytimes.com/2001 /09/19/arts/attacks-called-great-art .html.

14 **"People have to watch"**: Bill Carter and Felicity Barringer, "A Nation Challenged: Speech and Expression; in Patriotic Time, Dissent Is Muted," *New York Times*, September 28, 2001, https://www.nytimes .com/2001/09/28/us/a-nation-challenged -speech-and-expression-in-patriotic-time -dissent-is-muted.html.

15 **"Fly and enjoy"**: Office of the Press Secretary, "At O'Hare, President Says 'Get On Board,'" George W. Bush White House Archives, September 27, 2001, https:// georgewbush-whitehouse.archives.gov /news/releases/2001/09/20010927-1.html.

15 **"age of irony"**: Eric Randall, "The 'Death of Irony,' and Its Many Reincarnations," *Atlantic*, September 9, 2011, https://www .theatlantic.com/national/archive/2011 /09/death-irony-and-its-many-reincarna tions/338114.

15 **"For some 30 years"**: Roger Rosenblatt, "The Age of Irony Comes to an End," *Time*, September 24, 2001, https://content .time.com/time/subscriber/article/0,33 009,1000893,00.html.

15 **their first New York issue**: Brian Van-Hooker, "An Oral History of The Onion's 9/11 Issue," *MEL Magazine*, June 29, 2020, https://melmagazine.com/en-us/story/on ion-911-issue-oral-history.

15 **"righteous anger"**: VanHooker, "An Oral History."

15 **the headlines blared**: James Dasilva, "The Onion's 9/11 Issue, 20 Years Later," *The Onion: 20 Years Later* (Substack), September 26, 2021, https://onion20.substack .com/p/the-onions-911-issue-20-years -later.

15 **"thick as a phone book"**: VanHooker, "An Oral History."

16 **Crime rates plummeted**: George L. Kelling, "How New York Became Safe: The Full Story," *City Journal*, 2009, https:// www.city-journal.org/article/how-new -york-became-safe-the-full-story.

16 **"To this day"**: Maddie Camplese, "Becoming Carrie Bradshaw," *MGC* (blog), June 27, 2022, https://www.maddiecamplese .com/post/becoming-carrie-bradshaw.

16 **"built on the carcass"**: Lizzy Goodman,

Meet Me in the Bathroom: Rebirth and Rock and Roll in New York City 2001–2011 (Dey Street Books, 2018), 7.

16 **like *Total Request Live***: John Seabrook, *The Song Machine: Inside the Hit Factory* (W. W. Norton, 2015), 97.

17 **Casablancas first encountered**: Goodman, *Meet Me in the Bathroom*, 113.

17 **Hammond's father bought them**: Goodman, *Meet Me in the Bathroom*, 124.

17 **Père Casablancas's agency**: Goodman, *Meet Me in the Bathroom*, 123.

17 **fashion mag *V***: Goodman, *Meet Me in the Bathroom*, 125.

17 **"band that's seen enough publicity"**: Ryan Schreiber, "The Strokes: Is This It," *Pitchfork*, October 14, 2001, https://pitch fork.com/reviews/albums/7537-is-this-it.

17 **obscure performance art project**: Goodman, *Meet Me in the Bathroom*, 103.

18 **"last real rock stars"**: Goodman, *Meet Me in the Bathroom*, 591.

18 **Electroclash fizzled**: Goodman, *Meet Me in the Bathroom*, 104.

18 **"Seven Nation Army"**: Rick Karr, "Why 'Seven Nation Army' Is the One Jock Jam to Rule Them All," NPR, July 11, 2018, https://www.npr.org/2018/07/11/626 288758/american-anthem-world-cup -white-stripes-seven-nation-army.

18 **"Mr. Brightside"**: Andrew Kahn, "How 'Mr. Brightside' by the Killers Became a Michigan Stadium Tradition," *MLive*, October 21, 2021, https://www.mlive.com /wolverines/2021/10/how-mr-brightside -by-the-killers-became-a-michigan -stadium-tradition.html.

18 **"cocaine era of New York"**: Goodman, *Meet Me in the Bathroom*, 92.

19 **coolness was traditionally defined**: Joel Dinerstein, *The Origins of Cool in Postwar America* (University of Chicago, 2017), 228.

19 **"Why has everything moral"**: Jean Baudrillard, *The Conspiracy of Art* (Semio-text(e), 2005), 30.

19 **"hamster nests"**: Grace Linden, "New York's Downtown in Dan Colen's and Dash Snow's 'Nests,'" *Burlington Contemporary*, June 2020, https://contemporary .burlington.org.uk/journal/journal/new -yorks-downtown-in-dan-colens-and -dash-snows-nests.

19 **Terry grew up amid**: Benjamin Wallace, "Is Terry Richardson an Artist or a Predator?," *The Cut*, June 15, 2014, https://www .thecut.com/2014/06/terry-richardson -interview.html.

20 **exposing the models' pubic hair:** Sean O'Hagan, "Good Clean Fun?," *Guardian*, October 16, 2004, https://www.theguardian.com/film/2004/oct/17/photography.art.

20 **"I like sex and I like women":** Josh Sims, "Raw Talent," *Guardian*, November 24, 2000, https://www.theguardian.com/lifeandstyle/2000/nov/24/fashion.

20 **"sleazy energy and aesthetic":** Ariel Levy, *Female Chauvinist Pigs: Women and the Rise of Raunch Culture* (Free Press, 2005), 26.

20 **"greased" poses:** Levy, *Female Chauvinist Pigs*, 2.

20 **"Things got very repressed":** Phoebe Eaton, "Terry Richardson's Dark Room," *Observer*, September 20, 2004, https://observer.com/2004/09/terry-richardsons-dark-room.

21 **"At first, the girls":** Arty Nelson, "It's Terry's World and You're Just Afraid of It," *LA Weekly*, October 28, 2004, https://www.laweekly.com/its-terrys-world-and-youre-just-afraid-of-it.

21 **4.5 million units:** Amy Wallace, "Guy Gone Wild," *Los Angeles Magazine*, December 2002, 54.

21 **Francis claimed Eminem:** Joe Francis, "Personal Bio," Meet Joe Francis, https://www.meetjoefrancis.com/biography-page-3.

21 **"has a smell for":** Wallace, "Guy Gone Wild," 58.

21 **"feminists love us":** Wallace, "Guy Gone Wild," 62.

21 **"Only one of those":** Rachel Shukert, "Dirty Pictures I Didn't Want Taken," *Salon*, April 24, 2010, https://www.salon.com/2010/04/24/dirty_pictures_of_me.

21 **rebellion from his staff:** Eaton, "Terry Richardson's Dark Room."

22 **"Terry was in deep shit":** Eaton, "Terry Richardson's Dark Room."

22 **"We were in a community":** Goodman, *Meet Me in the Bathroom*, 99.

22 **Pakistani Canadian professors:** Adam Leith Gollner, "The Secret History of Gavin McInnes," *Vanity Fair*, June 29, 2021, https://www.vanityfair.com/news/2021/06/the-secret-history-of-gavin-mcinnes.

22 **nonprofit Haitian community:** Lucas Wisenthal and Sheldon Gordon, "Uncommon Reading Material," *McGill News*, May 11, 2016, https://web.archive.org/web/20160511161351/http://publications.mcgill.ca/mcgillnews/2012/07/30/uncommon-reading-material.

22 **illegally arbitraging currency:** Gollner, "Secret History of Gavin McInnes."

22 **was so high on LSD:** Gollner, "Secret History of Gavin McInnes."

22 **"blend of outright fabrication":** Gollner, "Secret History of Gavin McInnes."

22 **"That's why we're here":** Gavin McInnes, "Party Hard," *Dazed and Confused*, July 2002.

23 **Blue-collar chic:** Vanessa Grigoriadis, "The Edge of Hip: Vice, the Brand," *New York Times*, September 28, 2003, https://www.nytimes.com/2003/09/28/style/the-edge-of-hip-vice-the-brand.html.

23 **defended himself well:** Les Borsai, "Music Critics Suck!," *Spin*, July 26, 2024, https://www.spin.com/2024/07/music-critics-suck.

23 **"mindless fun":** McInnes, "Party Hard."

23 **"juvenile and naïve":** Grigoriadis, "Edge of Hip."

23 **"When you see":** Adam Heimlich, "Vice-Rising: Why Corporate Media Is Sniffing the Butt of the Magazine World," *New York Press*, October 2, 2002, https://web.archive.org/web/20021001185902/http://www.nypress.com/15/40/news&columns/feature.cfm.

23 **crossed-out swastikas:** Gollner, "Secret History of Gavin McInnes."

23 **tattoo on his back:** Grigoriadis, "Edge of Hip."

23 **Redneck Manifesto:** Gollner, "Secret History of Gavin McInnes."

23 **"Western chauvinist":** Gollner, "Secret History of Gavin McInnes."

23 **"largely an extension":** Gollner, "Secret History of Gavin McInnes."

24 **"want to be dominated":** Grigoriadis, "Edge of Hip."

24 **"big dorm":** Heimlich, "ViceRising."

24 **"If you think Vice":** Grigoriadis, "Edge of Hip."

24 **interviewed the editor:** Gollner, "Secret History of Gavin McInnes."

24 **"cooler to be conservative":** Gavin McInnes, "Hip to Be Square," *American Conservative*, August 11, 2003, https://web.archive.org/web/20031008080551/http://www.amconmag.com/08_11_03/feature.html.

24 **"dumb community's days":** McInnes, "Hip to Be Square."

24 **"rebel subculture":** Mark Greif, "What Was the Hipster?" *New York*, October 24, 2010, https://nymag.com/news/features/69129.

24 **Hipster fashion:** Grigoriadis, "Edge of Hip."

25   "two people leaping": *Nathan Barley,*
      episode 2, "Episode #1.2," written by
      Charlie Brooker and Christopher Morris,
      directed by Christopher Morris, aired
      February 18, 2005.

25   "without the revolutionary core": Greif,
      "What Was the Hipster?"

CHAPTER 2:
HIP-HOP HYBRIDIZATION

26   Inspiration struck Murphy: Lizzy Good-
      man, *Meet Me in the Bathroom: Rebirth
      and Rock and Roll in New York City 2001–
      2011* (Dey Street Books, 2018), 286.

26   43 percent of US radio: Simon Hatten-
      stone, "Pharrell Williams: 'My Music Is So
      Much Bigger Than Me, and What I Am,'"
      Guardian, March 8, 2014, https://www
      .theguardian.com/music/2014/mar/08
      /pharrell-williams-interview-daft-punk.

26   "music industry's mandate": Hua Hsu,
      "Their So-Called Life," *Slate,* March 30,
      2004, https://slate.com/culture/2004/03
      /n-e-r-d-s-adolescent-fly-or-die-really-is
      -adolescent.html.

26   "hybrid-minded compositions": Hsu,
      "Their So-Called Life."

27   navy brat: Jeff Mao, "In Search of Chad
      Hugo," *GQ,* May 12, 2022, https://www.gq
      .com/story/chad-hugo-neptunes-profile.

27   Baptist and Pentecostal services: Gavin
      Edwards, "Q&A: Pharrell Williams of
      N.E.R.D.," *Rolling Stone,* July 4, 2002,
      https://www.rollingstone.com/music/mu
      sic-news/qa-pharrell-williams-of-n-e-r
      -d-55924.

27   white skateboarding scene: John Ar-
      lidge, "My Sporting Life," *Guardian,*
      November 22, 2008, https://www.the
      guardian.com/sport/2008/nov/23/phar
      rell-williams-neptunes-sport.

27   "billion parts cut": Pharrell Williams,
      Pharrell-isms, ed. Larry Warsh (Princeton
      University Press, 2023), 3.

27   middle school band camp: Alphonse
      Pierre, "The Neptunes' Chad Hugo on the
      Music That Made Him," *Pitchfork,* June
      14, 2022, https://pitchfork.com/features
      /5-10-15-20/the-music-that-made-the
      -neptunes-chad-hugo.

27   award-winning drum lines: Mia Naza-
      reno, "What's Next For Chad Hugo? 'It's
      Time for the Spinoff,'" *Vogue Philippines,*
      June 23, 2023, https://vogue.ph/lifestyle
      /whats-next-after-chad-hugo.

27   recording songs in Hugo's attic: Mao,
      "In Search of Chad Hugo."

27   such as A Tribe Called Quest: Pharrell
      Williams, "Transcript: Pharrell Williams
      in Conversation with NYU Tisch & NPR
      Music," interview by Jason King, NPR,
      October 23, 2015, https://www.npr.org
      /about-npr/452953953/transcript-pharrell
      -williams-in-conversation-with-nyu-tisch
      -npr-music.

27   "ahead of their time": Chris Williams,
      "Interview: Teddy Riley on His Virginia
      Years," Red Bull Music Academy, April 8,
      2015, https://daily.redbullmusicacademy
      .com/2015/04/teddy-riley-interview.

28   Dropping out of Northwestern: Alexan-
      der Hernandez Gonzalez, "Pharrell Wil-
      liams Takes Louis Vuitton to the Rodeo
      During Paris Fashion Week," *Daily North-
      western,* January 29, 2024, http://dailynorth
      western.com/2024/01/29/ae/pharrell-wil
      liams-takes-louis-vuitton-to-the-rodeo
      -during-paris-fashion-week.

28   "We were trying to reach": Craig Jen-
      kins, "The Humble Hitmaker," *Vulture,*
      May 19, 2022, https://www.vulture.com
      /2022/05/producer-chad-hugo-neptunes
      -interview-pharrell.html.

28   pseudo–Middle Eastern clavichord:
      "Transcript: Pharrell Williams."

28   Blondie-inspired vocal hook: Jenkins,
      "Humble Hitmaker."

28   "I dumbed down": Michael Eric Dyson,
      Jay-Z: Made in America (St. Martin's Press,
      2019), 66.

28   "I can't help the poor": Dyson, *Jay-Z,* 68.

28   "Everybody else is doing": Edwards,
      "Q&A: Pharrell Williams."

28   penned "Rock Your Body": Sean Mi-
      chaels, "Justin Timberlake Says His Solo
      Career Is Owed to Michael Jackson,"
      Guardian, May 7, 2014, https://www.the
      guardian.com/music/2014/may/07/justin
      -timberlake-career-michael-jackson.

28   Chuck Brown's 1979 go-go track: Katie
      Moulton, "The Middle of Everywherre:
      Katie Moulton on How Nelly's 'Hot in
      Herre' Defines Millennial Dance Pop,"
      Marchxness, March 2024, https://marchx
      ness.com/1strd-nellyvsaplusd.

28   "late-'90s throwback tunefulness":
      Moulton, "Middle of Everywherre."

29   car-door-slam-like: Alexis Petridis,
      "Pharrell Williams's 30 Greatest Songs—
      Ranked!," *Guardian,* March 10, 2022,
      https://www.theguardian.com/culture
      /2022/mar/10/pharrell-williamss-30
      -greatest-songs-ranked.

29   struggled to comprehend: Insanul
      Ahmed, "Knowledge Drop: Pharrell

Threatened to Give the Beat to Clipse's 'Grindin' to Jay-Z." *Genius*, August 22, 2020, https://genius.com/amp/a/pharrell-threatened-to-give-the-beat-to-clipse-s-grindin-to-jay-z.

29 **"most popular rap song":** Alexis Petridis, "Pharrell Williams's 30 Greatest Songs—Ranked!," *Guardian*, March 10, 2022, https://www.theguardian.com/culture/2022/mar/10/pharrell-williamss-30-greatest-songs-ranked.

29 **local drug dealers:** Sowmya Krishnamurthy, *Fashion Killa: How Hip-Hop Revolutionized High Fashion* (Gallery Books, 2023), 24.

29 **"artist starter pack":** Krishnamurthy, *Fashion Killa*, 150.

30 **weren't its "target customer":** Alysha Webb, "How Hip Hop's Love of the Iconic Yellow Workboot Helped Make Timberland a Billion-Dollar Company," CNBC, December 20, 2020, https://www.cnbc.com/2020/12/20/how-timberland-became-billion-dollar-company.html.

30 *The Oprah Winfrey Show:* Lakshmi Gopalkrishnan, "Dirty Linen," *Slate*, April 11, 1997, https://slate.com/culture/1997/04/dirty-linen.html. Spike Lee satirized Hilfiger in his 2000 film *Bamboozled*, with a parody commercial for "Timmi Hilln****r."

30 **"We have no desire":** Rose Apodaca, "Sportswear Designer Stussy Is Prospering Partly by Limiting His Outlets," *Los Angeles Times*, July 12, 1992, https://www.latimes.com/archives/la-xpm-1992-07-12-fi-4334-story.html.

31 **anchored his personal style:** "Transcript: Pharrell Williams."

31 **"brand label whore":** "Transcript: Pharrell Williams."

31 **Nigo grew BAPE:** W. David Marx, *Ametora: How Japan Saved American Style* (Basic Books, 2015).

31 **Nigo found his canvas:** Joyce Li, "Pharrell Shares How Jacob the Jeweler Introduced Him to NIGO," *Hypebeast*, November 16, 2023, https://hypebeast.com/2023/11/joopiter-pharrell-how-jacob-the-jeweler-introduced-him-to-nigo-explanation.

31 **"most amazing thing":** Kadia Blagrove, Joe La Puma, and Jian DeLeon, "The Oral History of Billionaire Boys Club and Icecream," *Complex*, December 3, 2013, https://www.complex.com/style/a/kadia-blagrove/oral-history-bbc-icecream.

32 **Billionaire Boys Club (BBC):** Blagrove et al., "Oral History."

32 **composed for Prince:** Paula Rogo, "Pharrell Williams Reveals He Initially Wrote 'Frontin' for Prince," *Essence*, October 23, 2020, https://www.essence.com/celebrity/pharrell-williams-frontin-prince.

32 **"most influential music video":** Cam Wolf, "The Story of the Most Influential Music Video in Menswear History," *GQ*, October 27, 2021, https://www.gq.com/story/pharrell-jay-z-frontin-video-style-influence.

32 **long-running feud:** Krishnamurthy, *Fashion Killa*, 174.

32 **hiring streetwear legends:** This includes bringing on Hiroshi Fujiwara as an adviser and hiring Fraser Cooke from Hit and Run.

32 **sunglasses for Louis Vuitton:** Kristopher Fraser, "Pharrell Williams's 2004 Millionaire Louis Vuitton Sunglasses Spike in Search Interest," *WWD*, February 14, 2023, https://wwd.com/pop-culture/culture-news/pharrell-millionaire-louis-vuitton-spike-search-interest-1235527393.

32 **"nobody ever used to line up":** Nigo, "Nigo and Pharrell on Sneaker Drops and Bootleggers," interview by Pharrell Williams, *Interview*, June 2005, https://www.interviewmagazine.com/fashion/from-the-vault-nigo-and-pharell-on-sneaker-drops-and-bootleggers.

33 **"from pop radio":** Rob Mitchum, "The College Dropout," *Pitchfork*, February 20, 2004, https://pitchfork.com/reviews/albums/8767-the-college-dropout.

33 **Kanye was raised:** Touré, "Kanye West: Head of the Class," *Rolling Stone*, April 29, 2004.

33 **"Living in Chicago":** "Pharrell Williams: 'Faith Is About What You Feel,'" *i-D*, June 10, 2020, https://i-d.co/article/pharrell-williams-interview-i-d-magazine.

34 **his orthodontic retainers:** *Jeen-yuhs: A Kanye Trilogy*, directed by Chike Ozah and Coodie Simmons (Creative Control, Leah Natasha Productions, and Time Studios, 2022).

34 **"Every motherfucker told me":** Kanye West, "Last Call," track 21 on *The College Dropout*, Roc-A-Fella Records, 2004.

34 **reluctantly signed Kanye:** *Jeen-yuhs*.

34 **"bridge the gap":** *Jeen-yuhs*.

34 **modeled on the Polo Bear:** Krishnamurthy, *Fashion Killa*, 162.

34 **over two million copies:** Kelefa Sanneh, "Kanye West's Argument with Himself," *New York Times*, July 24, 2005, https://www.nytimes.com/2005/07/24/arts/music/kanye-wests-argument-with-himself.html.

34 **Pazz & Jop poll:** "The 2004 Pazz & Jop Critics Poll," Robert Christgau, https://www.robertchristgau.com/xg/pnj/pjres04.php.

34 **"best-dressed man":** "The 21 Best Dressed Men in the World 2005," *Esquire*, September 1, 2005, https://classic.esquire.com/article/2005/9/1/the-21-best-dressed-men-in-the-world-2005.

34 **inspired Kanye to adopt:** "Pharrell Williams: 'Faith Is About.'"

34 **first met backstage:** *Jeen-yuhs*.

35 **"rap version" of Fiona Apple:** Fiona Apple, "Kanye West," *Interview*, October 2005.

35 **worked at A Bathing Ape:** Karizza Sanchez, "Kid Cudi & NIGO®: The Originators," *Complex*, 2019, https://www.complex.com/style/kid-cudi-nigo-2019-cover-story.

CHAPTER 3:
POP, IDOLS, AND CELEBRITY

36 **wrote a defense of Simpson:** Kelefa Sanneh, "The Rap Against Rockism," *New York Times*, October 31, 2004, https://www.nytimes.com/2004/10/31/arts/music/the-rap-against-rockism.html.

36 **"idolizing the authentic old legend":** Sanneh, "Rap Against Rockism."

37 **"Carey's neo-disco?":** Sanneh, "Rap Against Rockism."

37 **became known as "poptimism":** British music writers such as Simon Reynolds first used the word *poptimism* to describe English rock bands on independent labels with a bouncy sound. Its modern usage starts in the early 2000s, when Reynolds, alongside theorist Mark Fisher, revived the term as part of debates raging in primitive internet music forums.

37 **"postmodernism is the consumption":** Fredric Jameson, *Postmodernism, or, the Cultural Logic of Late Capitalism* (Duke University Press, 1991).

37 **"incoherent, corporate-financed":** Sanneh, "Rap Against Rockism."

38 **website: Pitchfork Media:** Dan Kois, Nitish Pahwa, and Luke Winkie, "The Oral History of Pitchfork," *Slate*, March 19, 2024, https://slate.com/culture/2024/03/pitchfork-oral-history-music-festival-conde-nast-review.html.

38 **Sonic Youth and Liz Phair:** Kois et al., "Oral History of Pitchfork."

38 **The Pitchfork Effect:** Ryan Dombal, Anna Gaca, Jayson Greene, et al., "The History of Pitchfork's Reviews Section in 38 Reviews," *Pitchfork*, May 25, 2021, https://pitchfork.com/features/lists-and-guides/the-history-of-the-pitchfork-reviews-section-in-38-important-reviews.

38 **"The writer for *Spin*":** Hillary Frey, "Pitchforkmedia.com Music Dudes Dictate Culture from Chicago," *Observer*, November 29, 2004, https://observer.com/2004/11/pitchforkmediacom-music-dudes-dictate-culture-from-chicago.

38 **"responsibility of the music press":** Jon Caramanica, host, *Popcast*, podcast, episode 461, "Pitchfork, the Early Years," New York Times, January 24, 2024, https://www.nytimes.com/2024/01/24/arts/music/popcast-pitchfork.html.

38 **"stages at Union Park":** Kelefa Sanneh, "Indie Bands That Made the Grade in Webland," *New York Times*, July 19, 2005, https://www.nytimes.com/2005/07/19/arts/music/indie-bands-that-made-the-grade-in-webland.html.

39 **dominant mode of:** Jody Rosen, "The Perils of Poptimism," *Slate*, May 9, 2006, https://slate.com/culture/2006/05/does-hating-rock-make-you-a-music-critic.html.

40 **"A Stroke of Genius":** Dorian Lynskey, "When Christina Met the Strokes: The Song That Defines the Decade," *Guardian*, November 26, 2009, https://www.theguardian.com/music/2009/nov/26/songs-of-the-decade-a-stroke-of-genius.

42 **"stars into ordinary people":** Emily Nussbaum, *Cue the Sun! The Invention of Reality TV* (Random House, 2024), 284.

42 **album debuted at number five:** Billboard Staff, "Lopez Bows at No. 1; O-Town, Dream Debut High5," *Billboard*, January 31, 2001, https://www.billboard.com/music/music-news/lopez-bows-at-no-1-o-town-dream-debut-high5-80647.

42 **"essentially unthinkable":** John Seabrook, *The Song Machine: Inside the Hit Factory* (W. W. Norton, 2015), 126.

42 **only two champions:** There were a few losing *Idol* contestants who prospered, most notably Jennifer Hudson.

42 **music sales plummeted:** "Global Recorded Music Industry Revenues (2001–2019)," Evidence Hub, https://evidencehub.net/chart/global-recorded-music-industry-revenues-2001-2019-169.0.

43 **"man's name was not apt":** Daniel J. Boorstin, *The Image* (Penguin Books, 1961), 56.

43 **"a person who is known":** Boorstin, *Image*, 67.

43 **her great-grandfather Conrad Hilton:** Nancy Jo Sales, "Hip-Hop Debs," *Vanity Fair,* September 1, 2000, https://www.vanityfair.com/culture/2000/09/hiltons200009.

44 **Hilton's early years:** Paris Hilton, *Paris: The Memoir* (Dey Street Books, 2023).

44 **"New York City-based heiress":** Radar Staff, "More Than a Decade in Paris: The History of Paris Hilton's Infamous Sex Tape," *Radar,* March 23 2020, https://radaronline.com/exclusives/2019/01/the-history-of-paris-hiltons-infamous-sex-tape.

44 **"I want to be famous":** Hilton, *Paris,* 255.

44 *Sweetie Pie:* Sales, "Hip-Hop Debs."

44 **Trump's modeling agency:** Charlie Porter, "Is This Article Going to Trash Me?," *Guardian,* February 16, 2001, https://www.theguardian.com/lifeandstyle/2001/feb/16/fashion2.

44 **"I wanted to model":** Porter, "Is This Article."

44 **$1 million in gambling chips:** David Strow, "Huge Crowd Flocks to New Resort," *Las Vegas Sun,* November 16, 2001, https://lasvegassun.com/news/2001/nov/16/huge-crowd-flocks-new-resort.

45 **"ticket to financial freedom":** Hilton, *Paris,* 283.

45 **"character I played":** Hilton, *Paris,* 283.

45 **"for a regular person":** Hilton, *Paris,* 213.

45 **"life was over":** Hilton, *Paris,* 240.

45 **expert Dan Klores:** Guy Martin, "Downloads Are a Girl's Best Friend," *Guardian,* June 19, 2004, https://www.theguardian.com/theobserver/2004/jun/20/features.magazine57.

45 **self-deprecating appearance:** Reuters, "Paris Hilton 'Directed' Sex Video," CNN, February 24, 2004, https://web.archive.org/web/20040405192117/https://www.cnn.com/2004/SHOWBIZ/02/24/hilton.sextape.reut/index.html.

45 **"some disgraced exile":** Ariel Levy, *Female Chauvinist Pigs: Women and the Rise of Raunch Culture* (Free Press, 2005), 28

45 **most "overrated" celebrity:** "Paris Hilton, World Record Winner," *TMZ,* August 15, 2006, https://www.tmz.com/2006/08/15/paris-hilton-world-record-winner.

46 **FCC imposed hefty fines:** Skyler Caruso, "A Look Back at Janet Jackson and Justin Timberlake's Super Bowl Halftime Controversy 20 Years Later," *People,* February 1, 2024, https://people.com/music/janet-jackson-justin-timberlake-super-bowl-halftime-controversy-timeline.

46 **discussed lurid sexual preferences:** Owen Gibson, "Stern Sacked in US Radio Crackdown," *Guardian,* February 26, 2004, https://www.theguardian.com/media/2004/feb/26/radio.

46 **Japanese street photo magazine:** Jocelyn Silver, "The Return of the Misshapes," *Dazed Digital,* June 21, 2017, https://www.dazeddigital.com/music/article/36428/1/the-return-of-the-misshapes-new-york-nightlife.

47 **"watching reality TV":** Lizzy Goodman, *Meet Me in the Bathroom: Rebirth and Rock and Roll in New York City 2001–2011* (Dey Street Books, 2018), 476.

47 **surprise visit to Misshapes:** Tricia Romano, "Celebrity Spin," *Village Voice,* February 07, 2006, https://web.archive.org/web/20100531092207/https://www.villagevoice.com/content/printVersion/200630.

47 **first breakout star:** Lori Kozlowski, "Cobra Snake Is Young, Making Money and Still Using Coupons," *Los Angeles Times,* September 3, 2009, https://web.archive.org/web/20221225105928/https://www.latimes.com/archives/blogs/all-the-rage/story/2009-09-03/cobra-snake-is-young-making-money-and-still-using-coupons.

47 **girlfriend Cory Kennedy:** Brock Colyar, "Cory Kennedy Was the Internet's First 'It' Girl," *Cut,* April 24, 2023, https://www.thecut.com/article/cory-kennedy-new-york-it-girl.html.

47 **"People sweating, running around":** Colyar, "Cory Kennedy."

47 **Von Dutch was the nickname:** Andrew Fiouzi, "The Nazi-Sympathizing Pinstriper Who Inspired the 'Von Dutch' Trucker Hat," *Mel,* 2020, https://melmagazine.com/en-us/story/von-dutch-trucker-hat-racist-origins.

47 **"world's first-ever":** Britney Spears, *The Woman in Me* (Gallery Books, 2023), 138.

47 **"One of the people":** Spears, *Woman in Me,* 141.

48 **blunting her depression:** Spears, *Woman in Me,* 142.

48 **"I'm glad I got":** Lola Ogunnaike, "Paris Inc.," *New York Times,* May 2, 2005, https://www.nytimes.com/2005/05/02/arts/paris-inc.html.

48 **particular business heroes:** Ogunnaike, "Paris Inc."

48 **"this whole empire":** Ogunnaike, "Paris Inc."

48 **arrested in 2023:** Decca Muldowney, "Inside Paris Hilton's Ex Biz Partner's Wild

Murder-for-Hire Plot," *Daily Beast*, June 23, 2023, https://www.thedailybeast.com/paris-hiltons-former-business-partner-fereidoun-fred-khalilian-wild-murder-for-hire-plot.

48   **editor at *In Touch Weekly*:** Oli Coleman, "The Kim Kardashian Sex Tape: An Oral History," Page Six, March 27, 2017, https://pagesix.com/2017/03/27/the-kim-kardashian-sex-tape-an-oral-history.

49   **gum-smacking:** Benjamin Wallace, "What Will the Fashion World Do with Kim Kardashian?," *Cut*, August 12, 2012, https://www.thecut.com/2012/08/kim-kardashian-fashion-world.html.

49   **broker the deal:** Claire Cohen, "Regardless of Whether She Leaked It or Not, Does Anyone Have a Right to Judge Kim Kardashian for Her Sex Tape?," *British Vogue*, October 8, 2023, https://www.vogue.co.uk/article/house-of-kardashian-review.

49   **her own reality show:** Louise Randell, "Kardashians Only Landed Reality Show When Lindsay Lohan's Series Stalled After Arrest," *Mirror*, June 4, 2021, https://web.archive.org/web/20211026124826/https://www.mirror.co.uk/3am/celebrity-news/kardashians-only-landed-reality-show-24249166.

49   **announced a new reality show:** Katie Baker, "The Kardashians' Climb Is Far from Over, Even If Their Show Is," *Ringer*, June 11, 2021, https://www.theringer.com/tv/2021/6/11/22528998/keeping-up-with-the-kardashians-finale-kris-jenner-kim.

CHAPTER 4:
THE NERD INTERNET

50   **began with Stewart Brand:** John Markoff, *Whole Earth: The Many Lives of Stewart Brand* (Penguin Press, 2022).

50   **"next thing after acid":** Markoff, *Whole Earth*, 156.

50   **"Google in paperback form":** Carole Cadwalladr, "Stewart Brand's Whole Earth Catalog, the Book That Changed the World," *Guardian*, May 4, 2013, https://www.theguardian.com/books/2013/may/05/stewart-brand-whole-earth-catalog.

50   **He attended Burning Man:** Markoff, *Whole Earth*, 328.

50   **first TED conference:** Markoff, *Whole Earth*, 262.

50   **phrase "Information wants to be free":** Markoff, *Whole Earth*, 269; it's worth noting that Brand's words were taken out of context.

50   **alternative zine called *Boing Boing*:** Mark Frauenfelder, "Boing Boing Is 20 (or 33) Years Old Today," Boing Boing, January 21, 2020, https://boingboing.net/2020/01/21/boing-boing-is-20-or-33-year.html; also see Michael Szul, "A History of Boing Boing," Codepunk, July 3, 2021, https://codepunk.io/apotheosis/a-history-of-boing-boing.

50   **"cyberpunk science fiction":** Mark Frauenfelder, "Boing Boing: Free Collection from the Print Zine, 1989–1997," *Boing Boing* (blog), May 18, 2011, https://boingboing.net/2011/05/18/boing-boing-free-col.html.

50   **distributors went bankrupt:** Frauenfelder, "Boing Boing Is 20."

50   **fledgling company called Blogger:** Rob Walker, "Inside the Wild, Wacky, Profitable World of Boing Boing," *Fast Company*, November 30, 2010, https://www.fastcompany.com/1702167/inside-wild-wacky-profitable-world-boing-boing.

51   **began to pester Frauenfelder:** Frauenfelder, "Boing Boing Is 20."

51   **seven posts a *day*:** Cory Doctorow, "Hey, Mark Made Me A," Boing Boing, January 13, 2001, https://boingboing.net/2001/01/13/hey-mark-made-me-a.html.

51   **"Web's most popular blog":** "VCs See Opportunity in Blogosphere," CNET, August 21, 2006, https://www.cnet.com/culture/vcs-see-opportunity-in-blogosphere.

51   **Creative Commons license:** Cory Doctorow, "Giving It Away," *Forbes*, December 1, 2006, https://www.forbes.com/2006/11/30/cory-doctorow-copyright-tech-media_cz_cd_books06_1201doctorow.html.

51   **ran *Boing Boing* as a passion project:** Walker, "Inside the Wild."

51   **Google, *Wired*, and O'Reilly:** Walker, "Inside the Wild."

51   **361 million people:** "The Incredible Growth of the Internet Since 2000," SolarWinds, October 22, 2010, https://www.pingdom.com/blog/incredible-growth-of-the-internet-since-2000.

52   **utopian visions:** Wagner James Au, "There Will Never Be Another Second Life," *Atlantic*, June 26, 2023, https://www.theatlantic.com/technology/archive/2023/06/second-life-virtual-reality-platform-longevity/674533.

52   **"Many residents of Second Life":** Leslie Jamison, "The Digital Ruins of a Forgotten Future," *Atlantic*, December 2017,

https://www.theatlantic.com/magazine/ar chive/2017/12/second-life-leslie-jamison /544149.

52   **"n00b," "ZOMG," "pwned":** The exact origin is unclear, but their proliferation has been attributed to *Warcraft*.

52   **$1 billion a year:** Elizabeth Harper, "World of Warcraft Earns Over $1 Billion a Year," Engadget, July 21, 2014, https://www .engadget.com/2014-07-21-world -of-warcraft-earns-over-1-billion-a-year .html.

52   **"Our culture and economy":** Chris Anderson, *The Longer Long Tail* (Hyperion, 2008), 52.

53   **without underwear:** Paparazzi took these photos in late 2003; they're referenced in Tim Goodman, "Loveliness of Paris Seems Sadly Vacuous," *SF Gate*, December 1, 2003, https://www.sfgate.com/en tertainment/article/Loveliness-of-Paris -seems-sadly-vacuous-2547342.php.

53   **"Giving people the things":** Ben Smith, *Traffic: Genius, Rivalry, and Delusion in the Billion-Dollar Race to Go Viral* (Penguin Press, 2023), 63.

53   **flamboyant alter ego:** Tyler Gray, "Pop Goes Perez," *Radar*, September 28, 2006, https://web.archive.org/web/2008020 7225531/http://www.radaronline.com/fea tures/2006/09/perez_hilton_blogger _baron.php.

54   **"Postings may contain":** Gray, "Pop Goes Perez."

54   **LA Coffee Bean:** Gray, "Pop Goes Perez."

54   **"I want to sell out":** Gray, "Pop Goes Perez."

54   **launch of TMZ:** Anne Helen Petersen, "The Down and Dirty History of TMZ," *BuzzFeed*, July 24, 2014, https://www.buzz feed.com/annehelenpetersen/the-down -and-dirty-history-of-tmz.

54   **video of a car crash:** Petersen, "Down and Dirty History."

54   **"important media organization":** Petersen, "Down and Dirty History."

54   **white middle-aged male:** Petersen, "Down and Dirty History."

54   **"Chicken McNugget":** Paris Hilton, *Paris: The Memoir* (Dey Street Books, 2023), 230.

54   **coined the term *Web 2.0*:** Darcy DiNucci, "Fragmented Future," *Print*, April 1999, 32.

55   **Web 2.0 conference:** Richard MacManus, "The First Web 2.0 Conference in 2004," Cybercultural, November 8, 2023, https://cybercultural.com/p/003-the-first -web-20-conference-2004.

55   **"Back Dorm Boys":** Limor Shifman, *Memes in Digital Culture* (MIT Press, 2014), 106.

55   **"Star Wars Kid" was:** Philip Drost, "Man Who Became Famous 20 Years Ago as the 'Star Wars Kid' Says Your Digital Shadow Shouldn't Define You," CBC Radio, April 1, 2022, https://www.cbc.ca/radio/thecur rent/the-current-for-march-31-2022-1 .6403614/man-who-became-famous-20 -years-ago-as-the-star-wars-kid-says-your - digital-shadow-shouldn-t-define-you -1.6404089.

56   **forbade unsigned posting:** Markoff, *Whole Earth*, 266.

56   **dubbed "Afro Ninja":** Will Wei, "Where Are They Now? 'Afro Ninja' Picked Himself Up and Made a Movie Based on His Viral Video," *Business Insider*, August 24, 2010, https://www.businessinsider.com/where -are-they-now-afro-ninja-picked-himself -up-and-made-a-movie-based-on-his-viral -video-2010-8.

56   **"If I had a choice to do it":** Wei, "Where Are They Now?"

56   **forced to leave school:** Drost, "Man Who Became Famous."

56   **opened Something Awful:** Taylor Wofford, "Fuck You and Die: An Oral History of Something Awful," *Vice*, April 5, 2017, https://www.vice.com/en/article/fuck-you -and-die-an-oral-history-of-something -awful.

56   **"Everybody was talking":** Wofford, "Fuck You and Die."

56   **Twitter comedian @dril:** Wofford, "Fuck You and Die."

56   **documentary *Loose Change*:** Kevin Roose, "How a Viral Video Bent Reality," *New York Times*, September 8, 2021, https://www.nytimes.com/2021/09/08 /technology/loose-change-9-11-video.html.

57   **including filmmakers:** John McDermott, "A Comprehensive History of 'Loose Change'—and the Seeds It Planted in Our Politics," *Esquire*, September 10, 2020, https://www.esquire.com/news-politics /a33971104/loose-change-9-11-cons piracy-documentary-history-interview.

57   **"social epidemics":** Malcolm Gladwell, *The Tipping Point* (Back Bay Books, 2000), 7.

57   **Mike Godwin adapted a term:** Mike Godwin, "Meme, Counter-Meme," *Wired*, October 1, 1994, https://www.wired.com /1994/10/godwin-if-2.

58   **"group of digital items":** Shifman, *Memes in Digital Culture*, 41.

58 **mischaracterized the mechanics:** Richard Dawkins, *The Selfish Gene: New Edition* (Oxford University Press, 1989), 11–12.

58 **"dark broadcasters":** Derek Thompson, *Hit Makers: The Science of Popularity in an Age of Distraction* (Penguin Press, 2017), 194.

58 **rapid declines:** Smith, *Traffic*, 72.

59 **gray British shorthair:** David Britton, "Almost 10 Years Ago, This Cat Asked for a Cheeseburger—and Changed the Internet Forever," *Daily Dot*, October 28, 2024.

59 **eponymous website:** Will Wei, "'Cheezburger' Network Acquires 'Know Your Meme' for 7-Figures," *Business Insider*, March 28, 2011, https://www.businessinsider.com/cheezburger-buys-know-your-meme-2011-3.

59 **B-movie called *Snakes on a Plane*:** Mark Brown, "Snakes on a Plane Leaves Critics Flying Blind," *Guardian*, August 18, 2006, https://www.theguardian.com/uk/2006/aug/18/film.filmnews.

59 **box office disappointment:** Sharon Waxman, "After Hype Online, 'Snakes on a Plane' Is Letdown at Box Office," *New York Times*, August 21, 2006, https://www.nytimes.com/2006/08/21/movies/21box.html.

59 **"interest in a movie":** Waxman, "After Hype Online."

60 **Verizon and American Express:** Walker, "Inside the Wild."

60 **never attempted a major:** Walker, "Inside the Wild."

60 **counterweight to the Drudge Report:** Walker, "Inside the Wild."

60 **public wasn't clamoring:** Walker, "Inside the Wild."

61 **"concerned with taste":** Walker, "Inside the Wild."

61 **search engine optimization:** Walker, "Inside the Wild."

61 **thanks to celebrity endorsements:** Tricia Duryee, "T-Mobile Uses Celebrity Buzz to Market Its Sidekick," *Seattle Times*, December 12, 2005, https://archive.seattletimes.com/archive/20051212/sidekick12/t-mobile-uses-celebrity-buzz-to-market-its-sidekick.

62 **"email machine":** Graham Rapier, "Steve Ballmer Famously Slammed the iPhone—Here Are 12 Other Times Bosses Got It Wrong on New Tech," *Business Insider*, June 29, 2017, https://www.businessinsider.com/iphone-steve-ballmer-bosses-mocked-new-technology-and-got-it-wrong-2017-6.

62 **"Online politics":** Smith, *Traffic*, 102.

62 **Terry Richardson photographed:** Sonia Zjawinski, "Terry Richardson Shoots Obama," *Wired*, July 30, 2007, https://www.wired.com/2007/07/terry-richardso.

62 **earned $222 million:** "Fahrenheit 9/11," Box Office Mojo, https://www.boxofficemojo.com/release/rl2672854529.

62 **"Bush doesn't care":** Morgan Parker, "I Think About This a Lot: Kanye West at the Katrina Telethon," *Cut*, March 12, 2018, https://www.thecut.com/2018/03/i-think-about-this-a-lot-kanye-west-at-the-katrina-telethon.html.

62 **named both "top hero":** Associated Press, "Bush Picked as Top Villain AND Hero of '06 in Poll," *Gainesville Sun*, December 28, 2006, https://www.gainesville.com/story/news/2006/12/29/bush-picked-as-top-villain-and-hero-of-06-in-poll/31506994007.

63 **"Raining McCain":** Sean L. McCarthy, "The Men Behind the McCain Girls," *Comic's Comic*, April 10, 2008.

PART TWO: 2009–2015

CHAPTER 5: THANKS, OBAMA

67 **after his inauguration:** Robert E. Terrill, "An Uneasy Peace: Barack Obama's Nobel Peace Prize Lecture," *Rhetoric and Public Affairs* 14, no. 4 (2011): 761–79.

67 **"what he stands for":** Terrill, "An Uneasy Peace."

67 **fierce Republican opposition:** George Packer, *The Unwinding: An Inner History of the New America* (Farrar, Straus and Giroux, 2013), 319.

67 **"putting in Cracker Jacks":** Terrill, "An Uneasy Peace."

67 **wiped out $19 trillion:** Sarah Childress, "How Much Did the Financial Crisis Cost?," PBS, May 31, 2012, https://www.pbs.org/wgbh/frontline/article/how-much-did-the-financial-crisis-cost.

67 **"earnest, optimistic, energized":** Nate Jones, "That Feeling You Recognize? Obamacore," *Vulture*, August 20, 2024, https://www.vulture.com/article/obama core-list-obama-era-tv-movies-music-pop-culture.html.

68 **CNBC coined *recession pop*:** Jessica Dickler and Ana Teresa Solá, "'Recession

Pop' Is In: Why So Many Listeners Are Returning to Music from Darker Economic Times," CNBC, July 21 2024, https://www.cnbc.com/2024/07/21/recession-pop-explained-how-music-collides-with-economic-trends.html.

68 **"more unequal, less vibrant":** Annie Lowrey, "The Great Recession Is Still with Us," *Atlantic*, December 1, 2017, https://www.theatlantic.com/business/archive/2017/12/great-recession-still-with-us/547268.

68 **"People were dripping":** Eliza Brooke, "How the Great Recession Influenced a Decade of Design," *Vox*, December 27, 2018, https://www.vox.com/the-goods/2018/12/27/18156431/recession-fashion-design-minimalism.

68 **luxury brand Hermès:** Brooke, "How the Great Recession Influenced."

68 **hunted for bargains:** Jonathan Birchall, "Gilt Groupe Shines amid Worldwide Slump," *Financial Times*, February 14, 2010, https://www.ft.com/content/c7bceb3a-19bf-11df-af3e-00144feab49a.

68 **Warby Parker's:** Brooke, "How the Great Recession Influenced."

68 **particularly for sports:** Bill Shea, "Sports Economists Weigh In on How Another Recession Could Prove Costly for the Industry," *Athletic*, August 19, 2019, https://www.nytimes.com/athletic/1147279/2019/08/19/sports-economists-weigh-in-on-how-another-recession-could-prove-costly-for-the-industry.

69 **"popular culture's catering":** Tyler Cowen, "Recession Can Change a Way of Life," *New York Times*, January 31, 2009, https://www.nytimes.com/2009/02/01/business/01view.html.

69 **"like a speed bump":** Packer, *Unwinding*, 356.

69 **elevating prescient voices:** Stephen Mihm, "Dr. Doom," *New York Times*, August 15, 2008, https://www.nytimes.com/2008/08/17/magazine/17pessimist-t.html.

69 **"black swan" theory:** Edward Helmore, "The New Sage of Wall Street," *Guardian*, September 27, 2008, https://www.theguardian.com/books/2008/sep/28/businessandfinance.philosophy.

69 **fast-tracked his adaptation:** Gareth Rubin, "The Hollywood Recession . . . It Still Has a Happy Ending," *Guardian*, December 27, 2008, https://www.theguardian.com/film/2008/dec/28/hollywood-recession-luhrmann-great-gatsby.

69 **$20 million budget:** "Capitalism: A Love Story," Box Office Mojo, https://www.boxofficemojo.com/release/rl3110241793.

69 **reshaping Hollywood:** Rebecca Winters Keegan, "Financial Crisis Puts Squeeze on Hollywood," *Time*, September 18, 2008, https://time.com/archive/6904552/financial-crisis-puts-squeeze-on-hollywood.

69 **major banks began:** Keegan, "Financial Crisis Puts Squeeze on Hollywood."

69 **Their "best bet":** Daniel Bessner, "The Life and Death of Hollywood," *Harper's Magazine*, May 2024, https://harpers.org/archive/2024/05/the-life-and-death-of-hollywood-daniel-bessner.

70 **lone exception:** "2011 Worldwide Box Office," Box Office Mojo, https://www.boxofficemojo.com/year/world/2011.

70 **"Low-revenue arthouse films":** Rubin, "Hollywood Recession."

70 **it left little cultural impact:** David Haglund, "Why People Don't Care About *Avatar*," *Slate*, August 5, 2013, https://slate.com/culture/2013/08/avatar-sequels-three-no-one-cares-here-s-why.html.

70 *Saturday Night Live* **sketch:** Dana Schwartz, "Best of 2017 (Behind the Scenes): SNL Writer Julio Torres Breaks Down His Avatar Sketch, 'Papyrus,'" *Entertainment Weekly*, December 19, 2017, https://ew.com/tv/2017/12/19/snl-writer-julio-torres-avatar-sketch.

70 **joke stuck:** Jake Kring-Schreifels, "The Intertwining History of the 'Avatar' Papyrus Font and the 'SNL' Sketch That Spoofed It," *Ringer*, December 14, 2022, https://www.theringer.com/movies/2022/12/14/23507513/saturday-night-live-papyrus-sketch-avatar-james-cameron.

70 **"part that went viral":** Kring-Schreifels, "Intertwining History."

70 **Occupy Wall Street (OWS):** Packer, *Unwinding*, 224.

71 **beats of drum circles:** Megan McArdle, "Occupy Wall Street vs. the Drum Circle," *Atlantic*, October 25, 2011, https://www.theatlantic.com/business/archive/2011/10/occupy-wall-street-vs-the-drum-circle/247366.

71 **economist Joseph Stiglitz:** Andrew Anthony, "'We Showed It Was Possible to Create a Movement from Almost Nothing': Occupy Wall Street 10 Years On," *Guardian*, September 12, 2021, https://www.theguardian.com/us-news/2021/sep/12/occupy-wall-street-10-years-on.

71 **"meritocratic values":** Thomas Piketty, *Capital in the Twenty-First Century*, trans.

Arthur Goldhammer (Belknap Press, 2014), 1.

71 **definitions of "elites":** Beverly Gage, "How 'Elites' Became One of the Nastiest Epithets in American Politics," *New York Times*, January 3, 2017, https://www.ny times.com/2017/01/03/magazine/how -elites-became-one-of-the-nastiest -epithets-in-american-politics.html.

71 **anarchistic governance structures:** Anthony, "'We Showed It Was Possible.'"

71 **"Two hours is too little":** "The Trouble with Drums at Wall Street's Occupation," *Wall Street Journal*, October 26, 2011, https://www.wsj.com/video/the-trouble -with-drums-at-wall-street-occupation /67A1E734-ACC5-4854-89A5-592 C444129B8.

71 **commentators praised OWS:** Michael Levitin, "Occupy Wall Street Did More Than You Think," *Atlantic*, September 14, 2021; Anthony, "'We Showed It Was Possible.'"

72 **"asterisk in the history":** Andrew Ross Sorkin, "Occupy Wall Street: A Frenzy That Fizzled," *New York Times*, September 17, 2012, https://archive.nytimes.com/deal book.nytimes.com/2012/09/17/occupy -wall-street-a-frenzy-that-fizzled.

72 **idea of "capitalist realism":** Mark Fisher, *Capitalist Realism: Is There No Alternative?* (Zero Books, 2022), 2.

72 **"ally with whites":** Stacey Patton, "Why African Americans Aren't Embracing Occupy Wall Street," *Washington Post*, November 26, 2011, https://web.archive .org/web/20191025045125/https://www .washingtonpost.com/opinions/why -blacks-arent-embracing-occupy-wall -street/2011/11/16/gIQAwc3FwN_print .html.

72 **"almost every day":** "Russell Simmons Calls Out Jay-Z over 'Occupy Wall Street,'" *Vibe*, September 10, 2012, https:// www.vibe.com/news/entertainment/rus sell-simmons-calls-out-jay-z-over-occupy -wall-street-110771.

72 **Zuccotti Park's cleanup:** Julia La Roche, "Russell Simmons Just Offered Mayor Bloomberg to Pay for Zuccotti Park Cleanup," *Business Insider*, October 13, 2011, https://web.archive.org/web/2011111 6081849/http://www.businessinsider .com/russell-simmons-just-offered-mayor -bloomberg-to-pay-for-zuccotti-park -cleanup-2011-10.

72 **make any statements:** Eckardt, "How Celebrities Protest."

72 **"marvel of affluenza":** Hua Hsu, "Watch the Throne: Let Them Eat Cake," *Grantland*, August 24, 2011, https://grantland .com/features/let-eat-cake.

72 **"Rarely has an album":** Hsu, "Watch the Throne: Let Them Eat Cake."

72 **$450 million:** Rachel Kaadzi Ghansah, "He Shall Overcome: Jay-Z Is $450 M Beyond the Marcy Projects. Where Does He Go from Here?," *Observer*, December 1, 2010, https://observer.com/2010/12/he-shall -overcome-jayz-is-450-m-beyond-the -marcy-projects-where-does-he-go-from -here.

72 OCCUPY ALL STREETS: This slogan is said to have been first used at Berlin's SlutWalk protests earlier that year.

72 **no intention of sharing profits:** Packer, *Unwinding*, 372.

72 **"1 percent that's robbing":** Zadie Smith, "The House That Hova Built," *T Magazine*, September 6, 2012, https://www.ny times.com/2012/09/09/t-magazine/the -house-that-hova-built.html.

73 **"aggressively unapologetic":** Conor Friedersdorf, "Unapologetic Millionaire Jay-Z to Sell 'Occupy All Streets' T-Shirts," *Atlantic*, November 12, 2011, https://www .theatlantic.com/entertainment/archive /2011/11/unapologetic-millionaire-jay -z-to-sell-occupy-all-streets-t-shirts /248369.

73 **"the luxury goods, the art":** Hsu, "Watch the Throne."

73 **"agent of social change":** Greg Tate, "Hiphop Turns 30" *Village Voice*, December 28, 2004, https://www.villagevoice.com /hiphop-turns-30.

73 **outfit his Maybach:** Alex Pappademas, "Men of the Year 2011: King: Jay-Z," *GQ*, November 13, 2011: https://web.archive .org/web/20150929005538/https://www .gq.com/story/jay-z-gq-men-of-the-year -issue.

73 **"black-tie event":** "Kegel-ing Up with the Kardashians: Kris Jenner Turns Her Incontinence into a Money Spinner," *Daily Mail*, August 1, 2011, https://www.daily mail.co.uk/tvshowbiz/article-2020989 /Keeping-Up-Kardashians-Kris-Jenner -turns-incontinence-problem-money -spinner.html.

73 **"make it a problem":** "Kegel-ing Up with the Kardashians."

73 **"simply self-absorbed":** Roxana Hadadi, "Real Dumb: 'Keeping Up with the Kardashians,'" *Washington Post*, October 8, 2008, https://www.washingtonpost.com

/express/wp/2008/10/08/real_dumb
_keeping_up_with_the_kardashian.

73 **"seems to understand"**: Ginia Bella-fante, "The All-Too-Easy Route to Star-dom," *New York Times*, October 13, 2007, https://www.nytimes.com/2007/10/13/arts/television/13bell.html.

74 **Kim posing for *Playboy***: Maria Yagoda, "7 Things You Totally Forgot About Sea-son 1 of 'KUWTK,'" *People*, June 10, 2021, https://people.com/tv/keeping-up-with-the-kardashians-episodes-photos.

74 **pulled over for a DUI**: Yagoda, "7 Things You Totally Forgot."

74 **calling in from jail**: Gia Marcos, "Here's How Controversial Girls Gone Wild Founder Joe Francis Is Connected to the Kardashians," TheThings, December 8, 2024, https://www.thethings.com/girls-gone-wild-joe-francis-kardashians.

74 **Reality TV's explosion**: Emily Nussbaum, *Cue the Sun! The Invention of Reality TV* (Random House, 2024), 184–85.

74 **Swedish program *Expedition***: Nussbaum, *Cue the Sun!*, 182.

74 **fifty-one million Americans**: Bill Carter, "Survival of the Pushiest," *New York Times*, January 28, 2001, https://www.nytimes.com/2001/01/28/magazine/survival-of-the-pushiest.html.

74 **2001 hit with "Survivor"**: Chris Malone, "Lip Sync Herstory: 5 Things You Didn't Know About Destiny's Child's 'Survivor,'" *Billboard*, June 8, 2020, https://www.billboard.com/culture/pride/destinys-child-survivor-lip-sync-herstory-93978.

74 **cinematographer Randall Einhorn**: Nussbaum, *Cue the Sun!*, 232.

74 **"appearance of products"**: Carter, "Survival of the Pushiest."

75 **"dramality"**: Carter, "Survival of the Pushiest."

75 **"do-overs"**: Nussbaum, *Cue the Sun!*, 232.

75 **"sweet-and-lows"**: Nussbaum, *Cue the Sun!*, 232.

75 **developer Donald Trump**: Kelsey Mc-Kinney, "The Mythmaker," *Ringer*, January 2, 2017, https://www.theringer.com/2017/1/2/16040412/mark-burnett-donald-trump-the-celebrity-apprentice-5b1a80ad189c.

75 **Burnett developed a show**: Nussbaum, *Cue the Sun!*, 36.

75 **"tough-but-fair executive"**: McKay Cop-pins, "The Most Consequential TV Show in History," *Atlantic*, June 5, 2024, https://www.theatlantic.com/politics/archive
/2024/06/trump-apprentice-in-wonder land-reality-tv/678601.

75 **Trump a "soul mate"**: McKinney, "The Mythmaker."

75 **success in *Shark Tank***: McKinney, "The Mythmaker."

75 **"offered something authentic"**: Nuss-baum, *Cue the Sun!*, xv.

75 **"any other cultural product"**: Nuss-baum, *Cue the Sun!*, xv.

76 **paid appearances**: Nussbaum, *Cue the Sun!*, 229.

76 **"extreme sport"**: Nussbaum, *Cue the Sun!*, 391.

76 **"here to make friends"**: Nussbaum, *Cue the Sun!*, 309.

76 **their business ventures**: Styles Desk, "How 'Keeping Up with the Kardashians' Changed Everything," *New York Times*, September 9, 2020, https://www.nytimes.com/2020/09/09/style/kardashians-ending-takeaways.html.

76 **endless brand collaborations**: Styles Desk, "How 'Keeping Up With the Kar-dashians.'"

76 **"Family turmoil feeds"**: Amy Chozick, "Keeping Up with the Kardashian Cash Flow," *New York Times*, March 30, 2019, https://www.nytimes.com/2019/03/30/style/kardashians-interview.html.

76 **"I really do believe"**: Eric Wilson, "Kim Kardashian Inc.," *New York Times*, No-vember 17, 2010, https://www.nytimes.com/2010/11/18/fashion/18KIM.html.

76 **"appears to 'have it all'"**: Safy-Hallan Farah, "The Alienation and Fantasy of Modern Femininity," *Document*, January 26, 2022, https://www.documentjournal.com/2022/01/the-alienation-and-fantasy-of-modern-femininity.

76 **"as my friends"**: Jamie Valentino, "The Everlasting Appeal of the Real House-wives," *Observer*, February 8, 2024, https://observer.com/2024/02/the-ever lasting-appeal-of-the-real-housewives.

77 **her event fees quintupled**: Maureen O'Connor, "The Rising Price of Snooki: A Comparative Analysis of *Jersey Shore* Ap-pearance Fees," *Gawker*, January 13, 2010, https://web.archive.org/web/201002 05081011/https://gawker.com/5446943 /the-rising-price-of-snooki-a-comparative -analysis-of-jersey-shore-appearance-fees.

77 **Kim guest-starred**: Coppins, "The Most Consequential TV Show in History."

77 **woman with autism**: "Susan Boyle Says Asperger's Diagnosis Was a Relief," *Flor-*

ida Times-Union, December 9, 2013, https://www.jacksonville.com/story/enter tainment/local/2013/12/09/susan-boyle -says-aspergers-diagnosis-was-relief /15806293007.

77 *The Tigers of Money:* Robyn Klingler-Vidra, "How Japan Pioneered the Global Phenomenon of Entrepreneur Pitch Shows like Dragons' Den," *Conversation*, January 2, 2025, https://theconversation .com/how-japan-pioneered-the-global -phenomenon-of-entrepreneur-pitch -shows-like-dragons-den-245873.

77 *Warsaw Shore:* Issy Sampson, "Shore Thing: Did You Know There Are FIVE Other Versions of Geordie Shore and Jersey Shore Around the World—and They're Even More Outrageous Than Ours," *Sun*, July 27, 2018, https://www.thesun.co.uk /tvandshowbiz/6880607/geordie-shore -jersey-warsaw-acapulco-super-gandia -shore/.

77 most important sources: Anne Helen Petersen, "The Down and Dirty History of TMZ," *BuzzFeed*, July 24, 2014, https:// www.buzzfeed.com/annehelenpetersen /the-down-and-dirty-history-of-tmz.

78 stormed the stage: Mandi Bierly, "Kanye West: How Do You Say 'Sore Loser' in Danish?," *Entertainment Weekly*, November 3, 2006, https://ew.com/article/2006 /11/03/kanye.

78 Obama called West: Constance Grady, "How the Taylor Swift–Kanye West VMAs Scandal Became a Perfect American Morality Tale," *Vox*, August 26, 2019, https://www.vox.com/culture/2019/8/26 /20828559/taylor-swift-kanye-west-2009 -mtv-vmas-explained.

78 "Mariana Trench–like depths": Taylor Clark, "The Strokes' *Is This It*," *Slate*, October 10, 2011, https://slate.com/culture /2011/10/the-strokes-is-this-it-anniversary -why-it-s-the-best-album-of-the-past -decade.html.

78 "high-decibel energy": Calvin Tomkins, "A Fool for Art," *New Yorker*, November 4, 2007, https://www.newyorker.com/maga zine/2007/11/12/a-fool-for-art.

78 cocaine-induced heart attack: Melena Ryzik, "Cocaine: Hidden in Plain Sight," *New York Times*, June 10, 2007, https:// www.nytimes.com/2007/06/10/fashion /10cocaine.html.

78 disappeared from runways: Matthew Schneier, "Death of a Downtown Icon: Remembering Benjamin Cho," *New York Times*, June 11, 2017, https://www.nytimes .com/2017/06/11/fashion/death-of-a -downtown-icon-benjamin-cho.html.

78 "Luxury Reborn" ads: Gemma Sieff, "Photo Ops," *n+1*, Spring 2011, https:// www.nplusonemag.com/issue-11/essays /photo-ops/.

78 Germanotta, better known: Rachel Syme, "The Shape Shifter," *New York Times Magazine*, October 3, 2018, https://www .nytimes.com/interactive/2018/10 /03/magazine/lady-gaga-movie -star-is-born.html.

79 absorbed its aesthetics: Vanessa Grigoriadis, "Growing Up Gaga," *New York Magazine*, March 26, 2010, https://nymag .com/arts/popmusic/features/65127.

79 "Italian girl with brown hair": *The Defiant Ones*, season 1, episode 4, "Part 4," written by Allen Hughes, Lasse Järvi, and Doug Pray, directed by Allen Hughes, aired July 12, 2017.

79 Moroccan Swedish producer: Grigoriadis, "Growing Up Gaga."

79 aesthetic of drag culture: Grigoriadis, "Growing Up Gaga."

80 "Everything about Gaga": Simon Reynolds, "The 1980s Revival That Lasted an Entire Decade," *Guardian*, January 22, 2010, https://www.theguardian.com/music /musicblog/2010/jan/22/eighties-revival -decade.

80 "noughties pop": Reynolds, "The 1980s Revival."

80 now-iconic image of her: "Lady Gaga for Supreme in Purple Fashion by Terry Richardson Full Look," Hypebeast, February 13, 2011, https://hypebeast.com/2011/2 /lady-gaga-for-supreme-in-purple -fashion-by-terry-richardson-full-look.

80 pop artist Jeff Koons: Natasha Degen, *Merchants of Style: Art and Fashion After Warhol* (Reaktion Books, 2023), 109.

80 artist Marina Abramović: Degen, *Merchants of Style*, 110.

80 radical inclusivity: Syme, "Shape Shifter."

80 "new or innovative": Liz Jones, "Lady Contrick: To Her Fans Lady Gaga Is a Cutting Edge Style Icon. But Is She Really Just a Shameless Plagiarist?," *Daily Mail*, September 17, 2010, https://www.daily mail.co.uk/femail/article-1313107/Lady -Contrick-To-fans-Lady-Gaga-cutting -edge-style-icon-But-really-just-shame less-plagiarist.html.

80 "chimerical sprite" persona: Syme, "Shape Shifter."

81 **"Plastic Ono Band meets"**: Patrck Darcy, "Perry Farrell: Gaga Is Lolla's 'Centerpiece,'" *Spin*, July 16, 2010, https://www.spin.com/2010/07/perry-farrell-gaga-lollas-centerpiece.

81 **"opened the doors for"**: Syme, "Shape Shifter."

81 **meat dress**: Christopher Knight, "Lady Gaga, Meat Jana Sterbak," *Los Angeles Times*, September 13, 2010, https://www.latimes.com/archives/blogs/culture-monster-blog/story/2010-09-13/lady-gaga-meat-jana-sterbak.

81 **"past into future"**: Reynolds, "The 1980s Revival."

81 **blatant rip-off**: Brian Hiatt, "Madonna Tells All: 'This Is What a 56-Year-Old Ass Looks Like!'" *Rolling Stone*, March 12, 2015, https://www.rollingstone.com/music/music-features/madonna-cover-story-rebel-heart-interview-1234793509.

81 **partnered with Oreo**: Rob LeDonne, "Lady Gaga's Chromatica Oreos: The Story Behind the Cookie Collaboration," *Variety*, February 17, 2021, https://variety.com/2021/music/news/lady-gagas-oreos-chromatica-1234908489.

81 **"claims high-art cachet"**: Degen, *Merchants of Style*, 103.

81 **out of Mr. Brainwash**: Banksy, dir., *Exit Through the Gift Shop*, Paranoid Pictures, 2010.

CHAPTER 6:
TECHNO-OPTIMISM

83 **fruit and vegetable vendor**: Kareem Fahim, "Slap to a Man's Pride Set Off Tumult in Tunisia," *New York Times*, January 21, 2011, https://www.nytimes.com/2011/01/22/world/africa/22sidi.html.

83 **"Facebook revolutions"**: Haythem Guesmi, "The Social Media Myth About the Arab Spring," *Aljazeera*, January 27, 2021, https://www.aljazeera.com/opinions/2021/1/27/the-social-media-myth-about-the-arab-spring.

84 **"Facebook to schedule"**: Maeve Shearlaw, "Egypt Five Years On: Was It Ever a 'Social Media Revolution'?," *Guardian*, January 25, 2016, https://www.theguardian.com/world/2016/jan/25/egypt-5-years-on-was-it-ever-a-social-media-revolution.

84 **"They forced everyone"**: Harry Smith, "Wael Ghonim and Egypt's New Age Revolution," CBS News, February 16, 2011, https://www.cbsnews.com/news/wael-ghonim-and-egypts-new-age-revolution.

84 **"particularly important role"**: Sam Gregory and Olivia Ma, "A New Human Rights Channel on YouTube," *YouTube Official Blog*, May 24, 2012, https://blog.youtube/news-and-events/new-human-rights-channel-on-youtube.

84 **"It was good that"**: Smith, "Wael Ghonim."

84 **The Wisdom of Crowds**: Scott McLemee, "'The Wisdom of Crowds': Problem Solving Is a Team Sport," *New York Times*, May 22, 2004, https://www.nytimes.com/2004/05/22/books/review/the-wisdom-of-crowds-problem-solving-is-a-team-sport.html.

84 **quick decisions**: Malcolm Gladwell, *Blink: The Power of Thinking Without Thinking* (Back Bay Books, 2007), 14.

85 **"What can we put"**: Elisa Lipsky-Karasz, "Mr. Know-It-All," *W*, August 31, 2008, https://www.wmagazine.com/story/jimmy-wales.

85 **beloved across**: Amy Chozick, "Jimmy Wales Is Not an Internet Billionaire," *New York Times*, June 27, 2013, https://www.nytimes.com/2013/06/30/magazine/jimmy-wales-is-not-an-internet-billionaire.html.

85 **"knowledge is power"**: Lipsky-Karasz, "Mr. Know-It-All."

85 **"censored material"**: Jonathan Zittrain and Molly Sauter, "Everything You Need to Know About Wikileaks," *MIT Technology Review*, December 9, 2010, https://www.technologyreview.com/2010/12/09/120156/everything-you-need-to-know-about-wikileaks.

85 **anti-war left**: Sean Wilentz, "Would You Feel Differently About Snowden, Greenwald, and Assange If You Knew What They Really Thought?," *New Republic*, January 19, 2014, https://newrepublic.com/article/116253/edward-snowden-glenn-greenwald-julian-assange-what-they-believe.

85 **hacktivist group Anonymous**: Quinn Norton, "Anonymous 101: Introduction to the Lulz," *Wired*, November 8, 2011, https://www.wired.com/2011/11/anonymous-101.

85 **host Hal Turner**: David Kravets, "Lawyer: FBI Paid Right-Wing Blogger Charged with Threats," *Wired*, August 19, 2009, https://www.wired.com/2009/08/lawyer-fbi-paid-right-wing-blogger-charged-with-threats.

85 **Project Chanology**: Norton, "Anonymous 101."

86 **V for Vendetta**: Arthur Jones and Giorgio Angelini, dir., *The Antisocial Network: Memes to Mayhem* (Netflix, 2024).

86 **Iran's 2009 elections:** Noah Shachtman, "Activists Launch Hack Attacks on Tehran Regime," *Wired*, June 15, 2009, https://www.wired.com/2009/06/activists-launch-hack-attacks-on-tehran-regime.

86 **PayPal's websites:** Quinn Norton, "Anonymous 101 Part Deux: Morals Triumph over Lulz," *Wired*, December 30, 2011, https://www.wired.com/2011/12/anonymous-101-part-deux.

86 **Mexican drug cartel:** Norton, "Anonymous 101."

86 **Tunisian president's website:** David Kushner, "The Masked Avengers," *New Yorker*, September 1, 2014, https://www.newyorker.com/magazine/2014/09/08/masked-avengers.

86 **"Freedom Ops":** Quinn Norton, "2011: The Year Anonymous Took On Cops, Dictators and Existential Dread," *Wired*, January 11, 2012, https://www.wired.com/2012/01/anonymous-dicators-existential-dread.

86 **libertarian from Alabama:** Lipsky-Karasz, "Mr. Know-It-All."

86 **idolized Yippie Abbie Hoffman:** Kushner, "Masked Avengers."

86 **"individual versus institution":** Peter Ludlow, "WikiLeaks and Hacktivist Culture," *Nation*, September 15, 2010, https://www.thenation.com/article/archive/wikileaks-and-hacktivist-culture.

86 **supporting Occupy Wall Street:** Norton, "2011: The Year Anonymous"; Andrew Anthony, "'We Showed It Was Possible to Create a Movement from Almost Nothing': Occupy Wall Street 10 Years On," *Guardian*, September 12, 2021, https://www.theguardian.com/us-news/2021/sep/12/occupy-wall-street-10-years-on.

86 **used homophobic slurs:** Ethan Case, "The Dark Side of Anonymous: Everything You Never Knew About the Hacktivist Group," *Mic*, January 3, 2012, https://www.mic.com/articles/3106/the-dark-side-of-anonymous-everything-you-never-knew-about-the-hacktivist-group.

86 **online game *Habbo:*** Ryan Singel, "Palin Hacker Group's All-Time Greatest Hits," *Wired*, September 19, 2008, https://www.wired.com/2008/09/palin-hacker-gr-2.

86 **harassing grieving families:** Singel, "Palin Hacker."

86 **targeting epileptics:** Kushner, "Masked Avengers."

86 **Sieg Heil salutes:** *The Antisocial Network.*

87 **"failed attempt to bottle":** Michael Cieply and Miguel Helft, "Facebook Feels Unfriendly Toward Film It Inspired," *New York Times*, August 20, 2010, https://www.nytimes.com/2010/08/21/business/media/21facebook.html.

87 **"They just can't wrap":** Margaret Lyons, "Mark Zuckerberg says 'The Social Network' Got His Clothing Exactly Right," *Entertainment Weekly*, October 18, 2010, https://ew.com/article/2010/10/18/mark-zuckerberg-social-network.

88 **"problem with Microsoft":** David Streitfeld, "Defending Life's Work with Words of a Tyrant," *New York Times*, October 6, 2011, https://www.nytimes.com/2011/10/07/technology/steve-jobs-defended-his-work-with-a-barbed-tongue.html.

88 **captured 72 percent:** Pavel Alpeyev and Yoshinori Eki, "Apple IPhone Captures 72% of Japan Smartphone Market," *Bloomberg*, April 22, 2010, https://www.bloomberg.com/news/articles/2010-04-23/apple-ships-1-69-million-iphones-in-japan-gets-72-of-market-group-says.

88 **"not a conventional company":** Larry Page and Sergey Brin, "A Letter from Larry and Sergey," Google, December 3, 2019, https://blog.google/alphabet/letter-from-larry-and-sergey.

88 **been to Burning Man:** Steven Kotler and Jamie Wheal, "What Google Found at Burning Man: A CEO and the Art of Flow," NBC News, February 22, 2017, https://www.nbcnews.com/better/careers/what-google-found-burning-man-ceo-art-flow-n723856.

88 **ballooned to $200 million:** Lynn Farah, "7 of the Richest Artists Alive—Net Worths, Ranked: From Damien Hirst's Formaldehyde Animals to Jeff Koons' Most Expensive, US$9 Million Work, and Anish Kapoor—but Who's a Billionaire?," *South China Morning Post*, March 28, 2024, https://www.scmp.com/magazines/style/entertainment/article/3257009/7-richest-artists-alive-net-worths-ranked-damien-hirsts-formaldehyde-animals-jeff-koons-most.

88 **media darling:** Lisa Miller, "Can Marissa Mayer Really Have It All?," *Cut*, October 7, 2012, https://www.thecut.com/2012/10/marissa-mayer-yahoo-ceo.html.

89 **"sex on wheels":** Chuck Squatriglia, "Driven (Finally): Tesla Roadster," *Wired*, March 4, 2009, https://www.wired.com/2009/03/driven-finally.

89 **drew celebrity fans:** Stephen Markley, "Tesla Delivers 100th Roadster," Cars.com, March 5, 2015, https://www.cars

.com/articles/tesla-delivers-100th-roadster-1420663262120.

89 **brought casual photography:** Jenna Wortham, "A Stream of Postcards, Shot by Phone," *New York Times*, June 3, 2011, https://www.nytimes.com/2011/06/04/technology/04photosharing.html.

89 **double rainbow appeared:** I witnessed this personally on the 101 at the time his death was announced, and I corroborated my memory with this post: Satomi Ichimura, "Double Rainbow over Silicon Valley Following Steve Jobs' Death," *Long Tail World* (blog), October 6, 2011, https://longtailworld.blogspot.com/2011/10/double-rainbow-over-silicon-valley.html.

89 **Issey Miyake turtlenecks:** Vanessa Friedman, "Why Steve Jobs Chose This Designer's Turtlenecks," *New York Times*, August 10, 2022, https://www.nytimes.com/2022/08/10/style/issey-miyake-steve-jobs-black-turtleneck.html.

89 **most valuable company:** Tripp Mickle and Karen Weise, "Microsoft Tops Apple to Become Most Valuable Public Company," *New York Times*, January 12, 2024, https://www.nytimes.com/2024/01/12/technology/microsoft-apple-most-valuable-company.html.

89 **"attacked by some idiot":** Shira Lazar, "'Bed Intruder' YouTube Star Antoine Dodson Exclusive: I Was Rape Victim," CBS News, August 19, 2010, https://web.archive.org/web/20110818083732/http://www.cbsnews.com/8301-504464_162-20014008-504464.html.

90 **"I didn't want":** Lazar, "'Bed Intruder.'"

90 **Reddit and *BuzzFeed*:** Chris Watson, "Antoine Dodson / Bed Intruder," Know Your Meme, https://knowyourmeme.com/memes/antoine-dodson-bed-intruder.

90 **reached the Gregory Brothers:** Dave Itzkoff, "The Gregory Brothers Auto-Tune the Internet," *New York Times Magazine*, August 11, 2011, https://www.nytimes.com/2011/08/14/magazine/the-gregory-brothers-auto-tune-the-internet.html.

90 **Within two days:** Itzkoff, "Gregory Brothers Auto-Tune."

90 **most-watched YouTube video:** Mark Memmott, "'Bed Intruder Song' Tops YouTube's Most-Watched List in 2010," NPR, December 13, 2010, https://www.npr.org/sections/thetwo-way/2010/12/13/132027922/-bed-intruder-song-tops-youtube-s-most-watched-list-in-2010.

90 **fueled by iTunes downloads:** Itzkoff, "Gregory Brothers Auto-Tune."

90 **enabling them to move:** Lazar, "'Bed Intruder.'"

90 **BET Hip Hop Awards:** Brad Wete, "'Bed Intruder Song' Singer Antoine Dodson Performs at 2010 BET Hip-Hop Awards," *Entertainment Weekly*, October 13, 2010, https://ew.com/article/2010/10/13/antoine-dodson-2010-bet-hip-hop-awards.

90 **"Blessings come in disguise":** Lazar, "'Bed Intruder.'"

90 **trivialized a serious crime:** Andy Carvin, "'Bed Intruder' Meme: A Perfect Storm of Race, Music, Comedy and Celebrity," NPR, August 5, 2010, https://www.npr.org/sections/alltechconsidered/2010/08/05/129005122/youtube-bed-intruder-meme.

90 **"aesthetics of Black poverty":** Zoe Chace, "'Bed Intruder Song' Climbs the Charts," NPR, August 13, 2010, https://www.npr.org/sections/therecord/2010/08/13/129178815/bed-intruder-song-climbs-the-charts.

90 **"got mad and bipolar":** John Corrigan, "The Bedroom Intruder That Made Antoine Dodson Famous Tells His Side Before Their Celebrity Fight on Sunday," *AL.com*, October 31, 2014, https://www.al.com/news/huntsville/2014/10/the_bedroom_intruder_that_made.html.

90 **denied this account:** John Corrigan, "Antoine Dodson Responds to the Bedroom Intruder, Reveals Which Celebrity He'd Fight Next After This Sunday's Boxing Match," AL.com, October 31, 2014, https://www.al.com/news/huntsville/2014/10/antoine_dodson_responds_to_the.html.

90 **video froze:** Paul Huggins, "Antoine Dodson Beats the Intruder in First Round of Celebrity Boxing Match; See Brief Video," AL.com, November 3, 2014, https://www.al.com/entertainment/2014/11/antoine_dodson_vs_the_intruder.html.

91 **YouTube Partner Program:** "YouTube Launches Revenue Sharing Partners Program, but No Pre-Rolls," *TechCrunch*, May 4, 2007, https://techcrunch.com/2007/05/04/youtube-launches-revenue-sharing-partners-program-but-no-pre-rolls.

91 **"In one fell swoop":** Itzkoff, "Gregory Brothers Auto-Tune."

91 **tackled taboo topics:** Taylor Lorenz, *Extremely Online: The Untold Story of Fame, Influence, and Power on the Internet* (Simon & Schuster, 2023), 20.

91 **only 7 percent:** Jens Manuel Krogstad and Carolyne Im, "Key Facts About Asians in the U.S.," Pew Research Center,

May 1, 2025, https://www.pewresearch
.org/short-reads/2025/05/01/key-facts
-about-asians-in-the-us.

91 **Makeup artist Michelle Phan:** Kathleen
Hou, "Michelle Phan Was YouTube's Biggest Beauty Star. Then She Vanished,"
Cut, September 26, 2019, https://www
.thecut.com/2019/09/michelle-phan-you
tube-beauty-star-on-why-she-left.html.

91 **Black Twitter emerged:** Jason Parham, "A
People's History of Black Twitter, Part I,"
Wired, July 15, 2021, https://www.wired
.com/story/black-twitter-oral-history
-part-i-coming-together.

91 **Ice Bucket Challenge:** Karen Weintraub,
"ALS Ice Bucket Challenge Turns 10:
Much Achieved, but Much Work Remains," *USA Today*, July 31, 2024, https://
www.usatoday.com/story/news/health
/2024/07/31/als-ice-bucket-challenge
-10th-anniversary/74474349007.

91 **Adam Nyerere Bahner:** Jay Boller,
"'Chocolate Rain' at 15: A 4,000-Word Interview with Tay Zonday About . . . Everything," *Racket*, April 6, 2022, https://
racketmn.com/tay-zonday-chocolate-rain
-youtube-minneapolis.

91 **forums like 4chan:** Lorenz, *Extremely
Online*, 68.

91 **Dr Pepper paid him:** Jenna Wortham,
"New 'Cherry Chocolate Rain' Remix
Pushes Dr Pepper," *Wired*, November 29,
2007, https://www.wired.com/2007/11/new
-cherry-choc.

91 **"worst band of all time":** Louis Pattison,
"Insane Clown Posse: A Magnet for Ignorance," *Guardian*, August 18, 2010,
https://www.theguardian.com/music/mu
sicblog/2010/aug/18/insane-clown-posse.

92 **widely disparaged lyric:** Dave Itzkoff,
"Fools' Gold: An Oral History of the Insane Clown Posse Parodies," *New York
Times*, April 26, 2010, https://archive.ny
times.com/artsbeat.blogs.nytimes.com
/2010/04/26/fools-gold-an-oral-history-of
-the-insane-clown-posse-parodies.

92 **"honest affection for":** Sean Fennessey,
"The /b/ Boys: Odd Future and the Swag
Generation," *Pitchfork*, October 18, 2010,
https://web.archive.org/web/2010
1020081559/https://pitchfork.com/fea
tures/articles/7863-the-b-boys-odd
-future-and-the-swag-generation.

92 ***Washington Post** and **Slate**:* Sridhar
Pappu, "Washington's New Brat Pack
Masters Media," *New York Times*, March
25, 2011, https://www.nytimes.com/2011
/03/27/fashion/27YOUNGPUNDITS

.html; Cutline, "Slate Hires Matthew Yglesias After Dismissing His Writing on Twitter," Yahoo! News, November 10, 2011,
https://www.yahoo.com/news/blogs/cut
line/slate-hires-matthew-yglesias-dismiss
ing-writing-twitter-231446176.html.

92 **mommy bloggers moved:** Lorenz, *Extremely Online*, 22–23.

92 **twelve-year-old Justin Bieber:** Jan Hoffman, "Justin Bieber Is Living the Dream,"
New York Times, December 31, 2009,
https://www.nytimes.com/2010/01/03
/fashion/03bieber.html.

92 **R&B ballad "So Sick":** Dan Schawbel, "Inside the Brand of Justin Bieber: An Interview with Manager Scooter Braun," *Forbes*,
February 11, 2011, https://www.forbes.com
/sites/danschawbel/2011/02/11/inside-the
-brand-of-justin-bieber-an-interview-with
-manager-scooter-braun.

93 **attention of Scooter Braun:** Hoffman,
"Justin Bieber Is Living."

93 **"God, you don't want this":** Hoffman,
"Justin Bieber Is Living."

93 **rival Justin Timberlake:** Hoffman, "Justin
Bieber Is Living."

93 **performing for President Obama:** Hoffman, "Justin Bieber Is Living."

93 **YouTube history:** "Bieber's Baby Breaks
YouTube Record," CBC, July 16, 2010,
https://www.cbc.ca/news/entertainment
/bieber-s-baby-breaks-youtube-record
-1.933329.

93 **all Twitter traffic:** Jon Ronson, "Justin
Bieber: One Day with the Most Googled
Name on the Planet," *Guardian*, November 12, 2010, https://www.theguardian
.com/music/2010/nov/13/justin-bieber
-interview.

93 **viral marketing campaign:** Lizzie Widdicombe, "Teen Titan," *New Yorker*, August 27, 2012, https://www.newyorker
.com/magazine/2012/09/03/teen-titan;
Derek Thompson, *Hit Makers: The Science of Popularity in an Age of Distraction*
(Penguin Press, 2017), 34; Kyle Anderson,
"It's a 'Call Me Maybe' World," *Entertainment Weekly*, June 22, 2012, https://ew
.com/article/2012/06/22/its-call-me
-maybe-world.

94 **birthday present:** "Rebecca Black's Friday removed from YouTube," *BBC News*,
June 20, 2011, https://www.bbc.com/news
/newsbeat-13839127.

94 **turned it into a meme:** Lyndsey Parker,
"Is YouTube Sensation Rebecca Black's
'Friday' the Worst Song Ever?," Yahoo!
Music Blogs, March 14, 2011, https://web

.archive.org/web/20110322133013/http://
new.music.yahoo.com/blogs/videogaga
/71429/is-youtube-sensation-rebecca
-blacks-friday-the-worst-song-ever.

94   "so unbelievably BAD": Parker, "Is You-
Tube Sensation."

94   Bieber's view counts: Dan Whitworth,
"Justin Bieber Loses YouTube Crown to
Rebecca Black," BBC News, April 18,
2011, https://www.bbc.com/news/newsbeat
-13117539.

94   Boston in 1996: Jim Edwards, "What It
Was Like to Be Psy's Roommate When He
Was Dropout at Boston University in
1996," Business Insider, April 19, 2013,
https://www.businessinsider.com/when
-psy-lived-in-boston-2013-4.

95   Further scandal erupted: Seabrook,
Song Machine, 167.

95   marijuana possession: Max Fisher,
"Gangnam Style, Dissected: The Subversive Message Within South Korea's Music
Video Sensation," Atlantic, August 23,
2012, https://www.theatlantic.com/inter
national/archive/2012/08/gangnam-style
-dissected-the-subversive-message-within
-south-koreas-music-video-sensation
/261462.

95   entirely in Korean: Kirsten Acuna,
"Here's the English Translation of 'Gangnam Style,'" Business Insider, September
19, 2012, https://www.businessinsider.com
/gangnam-style-translation-2012-9.

95   nuanced class commentary: Fisher,
"Gangnam Style."

95   "cannot even describe": Fisher, "Gangnam Style."

95   Dance Cam: Randall Roberts, "K-Pop's
PSY Hits Dodgers Stadium with Viral
Song 'Gangnam Style,'" LA Times, August
21, 2012, https://web.archive.org/web
/20200304160603/https://www.latimes
.com/entertainment/music/la-xpm-2012
-aug-21-la-et-ms-psy-dodgers-stadium
-gangnam-style-20120821-story.
html.

95   "There is one reason": Billy Nilles, "The
Making of a Pop Star: How One Man Created Justin Bieber and Ariana Grande's
Careers out of Scratch." E!, July 17, 2018,
https://www.eonline.com/news/952516
/the-making-of-a-pop-star-how-one-man
-created-justin-bieber-and-ariana
-grande-s-careers-out-of-scratch.

95   spreading K-pop globally: C. Custer,
"Korean Government Awards Google for
Helping Spread Korean Culture," Tech in
Asia, December 13, 2012, https://www.tech

inasia.com/korean-government-awards
-google-helping-spread-korean-culture.

95   two billion views: "Gangnam Video First
to Hit Two Billion Views on YouTube,"
BBC News, May 31, 2014, https://www.bbc
.com/news/newsbeat-27647802.

96   endorsements from Oprah: Emma Madden, "'Kony 2012,' 10 Years Later," New
York Times, March 8, 2022, http://www
.nytimes.com/2022/03/08/style/kony
-2012-invisible-children.html.

96   a hundred million views: Madden,
"'Kony 2012.'"

96   "masturbating in public": Jordan Zakarin,
"Jason Russell, Kony 2012 Filmmaker,
Arrested for Allegedly Masturbating in
Public in San Diego," Hollywood Reporter,
March 16 2012, http://www.hollywoodre
porter.com/news/general-news/jason
-russell-kony-2012-arrested-masturba
tion-public-invisible-children-301236.

96   "dehydration and malnutrition": Zakarin, "Jason Russell."

96   #Horny2012 replaced #Kony2012: Madden, "'Kony 2012.'"

96   $32 million: Sam Sanders, "The 'Kony 2012'
Effect: Recovering from a Viral Sensation,"
NPR, June 14, 2014, http://www.npr.org
/2014/06/14/321853244/the-kony-2012
-effect-recovering-from-a-viral-sensation.

CHAPTER 7:
MILLENNIALS

97   dark gray hoodie: At this point, Zuckerberg wore the same gray sweatshirt and
jeans every day. See Jay Yarow, "It's True!
Mark Zuckerberg Wears the Same Thing
Every Day," Business Insider, October 3,
2012, https://www.businessinsider.com
/mark-zuckerberg-wears-the-same-thing
-every-day-photos-2012-10.

97   Menlo Park headquarters: Khadeeja
Safdar, "Facebook, One Year Later: What
Really Happened in the Biggest IPO Flop
Ever," Atlantic, May 20, 2013, https://
www.theatlantic.com/business/archive
/2013/05/facebook-one-year-later-what
-really-happened-in-the-biggest-ipo-flop
-ever/275987.

97   worth $19 billion: Evelyn M. Rusli and Pe-
ter Eavis, "Facebook Raises $16 Billion in
I.P.O.," New York Times, May 17, 2012,
https://archive.nytimes.com/dealbook.ny
times.com/2012/05/17/facebook
-raises-16-billion-in-i-p-o.

97   Harvard crew: Alyson Shontell, "Meet
the 10 Billionaires of the Facebook IPO,"

Business Insider, May 18, 2012, https://www.businessinsider.com/meet-the-10-billionaires-of-the-facebook-ipo-2012-5.

97   **self-made billionaires:** Thomas Stewart, "Who Gives a Hoot About Gen Y?," CBS News, March 1, 2011, https://www.cbsnews.com/news/who-gives-a-hoot-about-gen-y.

97   **"Very few of us":** Anne Helen Petersen, *Can't Even: How Millennials Became the Burnout Generation* (Houghton Mifflin Harcourt, 2020), viii.

97   **into the "precariat":** Petersen, *Can't Even*, 96.

97   **"doomed to be the first":** Hunter S. Thompson, "When War Drums Roll," ESPN.com Page 2, September 17, 2001, https://www.espn.com/page2/s/thompson/010918.html.

98   **Only 33 percent of Americans:** "Chapter 3. Inequality and Economic Mobility," May 23, 2013, Pew Research Center, https://www.pewresearch.org/global/2013/05/23/chapter-3-inequality-and-economic-mobility.

98   **scientific validity:** David Costanza, "Can We Please Stop Talking About Generations As If They Are a Thing?," *Slate*, April 13, 2018, https://slate.com/technology/2018/04/the-evidence-behind-generations-is-lacking.html.

98   **"unluckiest generation":** Andrew Van Dam, "The Unluckiest Generation in U.S. History," *Washington Post*, June 5, 2020, https://www.washingtonpost.com/business/2020/05/27/millennial-recession-covid.

98   **"saddled with debt":** Annie Lowrey, "Millennials Don't Stand a Chance," *Atlantic*, April 13, 2020, https://www.theatlantic.com/ideas/archive/2020/04/millennials-are-new-lost-generation/609832.

98   **"success in life":** Bruce Stokes, "U.S. and European Millennials Differ on Their Views of Fate, Future," Pew Research Center, February 10, 2015, https://www.pewresearch.org/short-reads/2015/02/10/u-s-and-european-millennials-differ-on-their-views-of-fate-future; Bruce Stokes, "Who Are Europe's Millennials?," Pew Research Center, February 9, 2015, https://www.pewresearch.org/short-reads/2015/02/09/who-are-europes-millennials.

98   **high school in 2000:** Samantha Sharf, "What Is a 'Millennial' Anyway? Meet the Man Who Coined the Phrase," *Forbes*, August 24, 2015, https://www.forbes.com/sites/samanthasharf/2015/08/24/what-is-a-millennial-anyway-meet-the-man-who-coined-the-phrase.

98   **Time's 2013 cover story:** Joel Stein, "The Me Me Me Generation," *Time*, May 20, 2013, https://time.com/247/millennials-the-me-me-me-generation.

98   **largest generation:** Dorothy Neufeld, "There Are 1.8 Billion Millennials on Earth. Here's Where They Live," World Economic Forum, November 8, 2021, https://www.weforum.org/stories/2021/11/millennials-world-regional-breakdown.

98   **helped elect Barack Obama:** Tom Rosentiel, "Young Voters in the 2008 Election," Pew Research Center, November 13, 2008, https://www.pewresearch.org/politics/2008/11/13/young-voters-in-the-2008-election.

98   **markers of adulthood:** Chloe Bryan, "RIP: Here Are 70 Things Millennials Have Killed," Mashable, July 31, 2017, https://mashable.com/article/things-millennials-have-killed.

98   **cars, casual sex:** Martha Henriques, "Millennials Are Ruining America's Sex Life," *International Business Times UK*, March 7, 2017, https://www.ibtimes.co.uk/millennials-are-ruining-americas-sex-life-1610203.

98   **"millennial whoop":** Patrick Metzger, "The Millennial Whoop: A Glorious Obsession with the Melodic Alternation Between the Fifth and the Third," The Patterning, August 20, 2016, https://thepatterning.com/2016/08/20/the-millennial-whoop-a-glorious-obsession-with-the-melodic-alternation-between-the-fifth-and-the-third.

98   **"apricotty salmon":** "'Millennial Pink' Is the Colour of Now—but What Exactly Is It?," *Guardian*, March 22, 2017, https://www.theguardian.com/artanddesign/shortcuts/2017/mar/22/millennial-pink-is-the-colour-of-now-but-what-exactly-is-it.

99   **"relative deprivation":** Jean M. Twenge, "The Myth of the Broke Millennial," *Atlantic*, April 17, 2023, https://www.theatlantic.com/magazine/archive/2023/05/millennial-generation-financial-issues-income-homeowners/673485.

99   **"I'm CEO, bitch":** MG Siegler, "Card Designer: The Inspiration for Zuckerberg's 'I'm CEO, Bitch'? Steve Jobs," *TechCrunch*, June 25, 2011, https://techcrunch.com/2011/06/25/im-ceo-bitch.

99   **"human capital":** Malcolm Harris, *Kids These Days: Human Capital and the Making of Millennials* (Little, Brown, 2017), 5.

99 **"lazy, entitled narcissists"**: Stein, "The Me Me Me Generation"; Emily Crockett and StudentNation, "Why Millennials Aren't Lazy, Entitled Narcissists," *Nation*, May 16, 2013, https://www.thenation.com /article/archive/why-millennials-arent -lazy-entitled-narcissists.

99 **unambitious, itinerant hipster**: Kyle Chayka, "Why Did We Stop Saying 'Hipster'?," *One Thing* (Substack), March 28, 2024, https://onethingnewsletter.substack .com/p/why-did-we-stop-saying-hipster.

99 **"infected by the conviction"**: David Infante, "The Hipster Is Dead, and You Might Not Like Who Comes Next," Mashable, June 9, 2015, https://web.archive.org/web /20150623195912/http://mashable.com /2015/06/09/post-hipster-yuccie.

99 **"getting rich quick"**: Infante, "Hipster Is Dead."

99 **"coordinating #sponsored"**: Infante, "Hipster Is Dead."

99 **"brogrammers hawking Uber"**: Infante, "Hipster Is Dead."

99 **"need to find"**: Petersen, *Can't Even*, 68.

100 **coined the term *adulting***: Kathryn Jezer-Morton, "What We've Learned from a Decade of *Adulting*," *Cut*, December 26, 2022, https://www.thecut.com/2022/12 /adulting-book-10-years-later.html.

100 **"*adulting* sums up"**: Kathryn Jezer-Morton, "Brooding: Was 'Adulting' Actually Good for Us?," *Cut*, December 26, 2022, https://www.thecut.com/2022/12/adult ing-book-10-years-later.html.

100 **"award for fulfilling"**: Madeleine Davies, "You're Not 'Adulting,' You're Acting Your Fucking Age," *Jezebel*, December 8, 2015, https://www.jezebel.com/youre-not -adulting-youre-acting-your-fucking-age -1746878718.

100 **"nobility in poverty"**: There's a popular Instagram account, @and.i.choose.rich, that mostly just recycles this clip.

101 **"passion and perseverance"**: "FAQ," Angela Duckworth, https://angeladuckworth .com/qa.

101 **avocado toast and lattes**: Roshan Abraham, "The Original 'Avocado Toast' Millionaire Is Back, and He Wants 'Pain in the Economy,'" *Vice*, September 12, 2023, https://www.vice.com/en/article/the-origi nal-avocado-toast-millionaire-is-back -and-he-wants-pain-in-the-economy.

101 **"my first business"**: Sam Levin, "Millionaire Tells Millennials: If You Want a House, Stop Buying Avocado Toast," *Guardian*, May 15, 2017, https://www.the guardian.com/lifeandstyle/2017/may/15 /australian-millionaire-millennials-avo cado-toast-house.

101 **Texas Christian University**: "How Many Times Have We Been Ripped Off?," Red Productions, July 29, 2014, https://redpro ductions.com/how-many-times-have-we -been-ripped-off.

101 **tweets per minute**: Reuben Fischer-Baum, "When and Where Do Americans 'Rise and Grind'?," *Deadspin*, July 2, 2014, https://deadspin.com/when-and-where -do-americans-rise-and-grind-1598227991.

101 **famously attributed**: Chris Matyszczyk, "Marissa Mayer Says the Secret of Success Is Working 130 Hours a Week," CNET, August 4, 2016, https://www.cnet.com /culture/marissa-mayer-says-the-secret-of -success-is-working-130-hours-a-week.

101 **"If you go in on a Saturday afternoon"**: Matyszczyk, "Marissa Mayer Says."

101 **1980s archetype**: A good example is the cover of 1983's *The Official Silicon Valley Guy Handbook*.

101 **North Face vests**: "29 Memes Roasting Silicon Valley and Its Tech-Bro Culture, Chosen by a Former Valley-Dweller," *Business Insider India*, September 6, 2019, https://www.businessinsider.in/slide shows/miscellaneous/29-memes-roasting -silicon-valley-and-its-tech-bro-culture -chosen-by-a-former-valley-dweller/slidel ist/71012867.cms.

102 **cognitive supplements**: Rebecca Mead, "Better, Faster, Stronger," *New Yorker*, August 29, 2011, https://www.newyorker .com/magazine/2011/09/05/better-faster -stronger.

102 **"Tim is a total fraud"**: Mead, "Better, Faster, Stronger."

102 **"kind of hyperkinetic entrepreneurial-ism"**: Mead, "Better, Faster, Stronger."

102 **Ferriss's "New Rich"**: "This is why everyone is working 14-hour days in the first place: to strike it rich and cash out." Alex Williams, "Too Much Information? Ignore It," *New York Times*, November 11, 2007, https://www.nytimes.com/2007/11/11 /fashion/11guru.html.

103 **Harvard's Kirkland House**: Marguerite Ward, "Mark Zuckerberg Returns to the Harvard Dorm Room Where Facebook Was Born," CNBC, May 25, 2017, https:// www.cnbc.com/2017/05/25/mark -zuckerberg-returns-to-the-harvard-dorm -where-facebook-was-born.html.

103 **seventeen-acre estate**: Diana Shaman, "In the Region/Long Island; For a Bridge-

hampton Project, It's Back to the Future," *New York Times*, August 14, 1994, https://www.nytimes.com/1994/08/14/realestate/in-the-regionlong-island-for-a-bridgehampton-project-its-back-to.html.

103 **St. Paul's School:** Richard Feloni and Daniel Richards, "'The 4-Hour Workweek' Author Tim Ferriss Reveals What He's Learned After a Difficult Year of Introspection, and How He Built a Passionate Fanbase of Millions," *Business Insider*, November 18, 2017, https://www.businessinsider.com/tim-ferriss-explains-how-he-built-a-fanbase-of-millions-2017-11.

103 **Taiwanese gyms:** Feloni and Richards, "'The 4-Hour Workweek.'"

103 **Seventy-three percent:** Stokes, "U.S. and European Millennials."

103 **"financial independence, retire early":** Amy X. Wang, "Your Neighbors Are Retiring in Their 30s. Why Can't You?," *New York Times Magazine*, May 7, 2024, https://www.nytimes.com/2024/05/07/magazine/retire-early-saving.html.

103 **subsisting on beans:** Wang, "Your Neighbors Are Retiring."

103 **strain became "FatFIRE":** Wang, "Your Neighbors Are Retiring."

103 **"when an individual woman":** Jia Tolentino, "The Case Against Contemporary Feminism," *New Yorker*, February 8, 2017, https://www.newyorker.com/books/page-turner/the-case-against-contemporary-feminism.

103 **"mediagenic female founders":** Marisa Meltzer, "Where Have All the Girlbosses Gone?," *Vanity Fair*, September 6, 2023, https://www.vanityfair.com/style/2023/09/where-have-all-the-girlbosses-gone.

104 *Teen Vogue* **internship:** Amy Odell, "How Emily Weiss Started One of the Fashion Media's Most-Respected Beauty Sites," *BuzzFeed*, June 3, 2013, https://www.buzzfeed.com/amyodell/how-emily-weiss-started-one-of-the-fashion-medias-most-respe.

104 **$1 billion valuation:** Victoria Turk, "How Glossier Turned Itself into a Billion-Dollar Beauty Brand," *Wired*, February 6, 2020, https://www.wired.com/story/how-to-build-a-brand-glossier.

104 **relationship with Terry Richardson:** Allison P. Davis, "Audrey Gelman Is No Longer Doing PR for Terry Richardson," *Cut*, December 19, 2013, https://www.thecut.com/2013/12/audrey-gelman-and-terry-richardson-split.html.

104 **"captured the imagination of":** Meltzer, "Where Have All the Girlbosses Gone?"

104 **"hipster dynamo dream girl":** Erin Gloria Ryan, "Women at Work," *New York Times*, May 16, 2014, https://www.nytimes.com/2014/05/18/books/review/sophia-amorusos-girlboss-and-more.html.

104 **launched Nasty Gal on eBay:** Nicole Perlroth, "Naughty in Name Only," *New York Times*, March 24, 2013, https://www.nytimes.com/2013/03/25/technology/nasty-gal-an-online-start-up-is-a-fast-growing-retailer.html.

104 **$300 million in annual sales:** Valeriya Safronova, "Nasty Gal's Path to Bankruptcy," *New York Times*, November 11, 2016, https://www.nytimes.com/2016/11/11/fashion/nasty-gal-sophia-amoruso-bankruptcy.html.

104 **Nasty Gal went bankrupt:** Safronova, "Nasty Gal's Path."

104 **shut its doors:** Katherine Rosman, "The Wing Shuts Down," *New York Times*, August 31, 2022, https://www.nytimes.com/2022/08/31/style/the-wing-shuts-down.html.

104 **Weiss stepped down:** Alisha Haridasani Gupta, "The Sunsetting of the Girlboss Is Nearly Complete," *New York Times*, May 26, 2022, https://www.nytimes.com/2022/05/26/style/glossier-emily-weiss.html.

104 **"truly terrible show":** Laura Bradley, "Was *Girlboss* Netflix's First Truly Terrible Show?," *Vanity Fair*, June 26, 2017, https://www.vanityfair.com/hollywood/2017/06/girlboss-netflix-canceled-one-season.

104 **support of publicists:** Meltzer, "Where Have All the Girlbosses Gone?"

105 **Virgin Records logo:** Perlroth, "Naughty in Name Only."

105 **"entrepreneurial good luck":** "Sir Richard Branson Gives a Shout Out to Fans with Virgin Tattoos," *Hope Blog*, November 21, 2012, https://hopegallery.wordpress.com/2012/11/21/sir-richard-branson-gives-a-shout-out-to-fans-with-virgin-tattoos.

105 **spent his early years:** Grant Wahl, "Ahead of His Class," *Sports Illustrated*, February 18, 2002, https://vault.si.com/vault/2002/02/18/ahead-of-his-class-ohio-high-school-junior-lebron-james-is-so-good-that-hes-already-being-mentioned-as-the-heir-to-air-jordan.

105 **anointed "King James":** Leon F. Seltzer, "LeBron James: The Making of a Narcissist (Part 1 of 2)," *Psychology Today*, July 12, 2010, https://www.psychologytoday.com/intl

/blog/evolution-the-self/201007/lebron-james-the-making-narcissist-part-1-2.

105 **Nike contract dwarfed:** Seltzer, "LeBron James."

105 **including a napping Kanye:** Chris Chase, "Kanye West Fell Asleep at The Decision," For the Win, July 9, 2013, https://ftw.usatoday.com/2013/07/kanye-west-fell-asleep-at-the-decision.

106 **called him a "coward":** Jake Simpson, "The Older, Wiser LeBron James," *Atlantic*, July 11, 2014, https://www.theatlantic.com/entertainment/archive/2014/07/lebrons-all-grown-up-now/374324.

106 **"if not as an outright":** Ian Crouch, "LeBron James: You Are Loved," *New Yorker*, March 1, 2013, https://www.newyorker.com/sports/sporting-scene/lebron-james-you-are-loved.

106 **"no more egomaniacal":** David Cho, "LeBron James: Ultimate Millennial," Medium, July 9, 2010, https://medium.com/the-awl/lebron-james-ultimate-millennial-23bc398a4736.

106 **"generation that's been told":** Cho, "LeBron James."

106 **"what many Millennials":** "LeBron James Is Such a Millennial," *Ebony*, July 16, 2014, https://www.ebony.com/lebron-james-is-such-a-millenial-405.

106 **"looking for *meaningful work*":** John Gorman, "LeBron James: Living the Millennial Dream," Medium, June 30, 2015, https://the-cauldron.com/lebron-james-living-the-millennial-dream-f38b59da7727.

106 **read Malcolm Gladwell:** Reeves Wiedeman, "Liking LeBron," *New Yorker*, June 21, 2012, https://www.newyorker.com/sports/sporting-scene/liking-lebron.

106 **from Warren Buffett:** Cho, "LeBron James."

106 **comedy *Trainwreck*:** Ananth Pandian, "An All-Around Star: Movie Critics Think LeBron Is Hilarious in 'Trainwreck,'" CBS Sports, July 22, 2015, https://www.cbssports.com/nba/news/an-all-around-star-movie-critics-think-lebron-is-hilarious-in-trainwreck.

106 **His ultimate goal:** Eric Lach, "The Exchange: Buzz Bissinger," *New Yorker*, November 5, 2009, https://www.newyorker.com/books/page-turner/the-exchange-buzz-bissinger.

106 **lifetime Nike contract:** Michael Pavitt, "Inside Cristiano Ronaldo's Vast Business Empire: How Star Boasts a Growing Hotel Chain and Even a Media Company—but His Hair Transplant Clinics Are Facing a Tax Probe in Spain," *Mail Online*, November 18, 2023, https://www.dailymail.co.uk/sport/football/article-12751897/cristiano-ronaldo-business-empire.html.

107 **"and a great player":** Jamie Jackson, "Cristiano Ronaldo: I'm Booed Because I'm Rich, Handsome and Brilliant," *Guardian*, September 15, 2011, https://www.theguardian.com/football/2011/sep/15/cristiano-ronaldo-booed-rich-handsome.

107 **"incidence of narcissistic":** Stein, "The Me Me Me Generation."

107 **"on a pandemic level":** Brooke Lea Foster, "The Persistent Myth of the Narcissistic Millennial," *Atlantic*, November 19, 2014, https://www.theatlantic.com/health/archive/2014/11/the-persistent-myth-of-the-narcissistic-millennial/382565.

107 **debunked the idea:** Costanza, "Can We Please Stop Talking."

107 **millennials simply adapted:** Foster, "The Persistent Myth."

107 **"22 Rule":** Reeves Wiedeman, "A Company Built on a Bluff," *New York*, June 10, 2018, https://nymag.com/intelligencer/2018/06/inside-vice-media-shane-smith.html.

107 **filmmaker Spike Jonze:** Matthew Garrahan, "Lunch with the FT: Shane Smith," *Financial Times*, December 28, 2012, https://www.ft.com/content/61c51d64-4a9c-11e2-968a-00144feab49a.

107 **gonzo-style documentaries:** Wiedeman, "A Company Built on a Bluff."

107 **invested $25 million:** Wiedeman, "A Company Built on a Bluff."

108 **"synonymous with authenticity":** Joel Dinerstein, *The Origins of Cool in Postwar America* (University of Chicago, 2017), 4.

108 **"mask of cool":** Dinerstein, *The Origins of Cool in Postwar America*, 11.

108 **"toughness and self-mastery":** Dinerstein, *Origins of Cool*, 11.

108 **dulled down coolness:** Dinerstein, *Origins of Cool*, 441.

108 **"too white for the Black kids":** Logan Murdock, "Walking Paradox: How Tyler, the Creator Grew into the Rebel He Always Wanted to Be," *Ringer*, May 10, 2021, https://www.theringer.com/2021/05/10/music/tyler-the-creator-10th-anniversary.

108 ***In My Mind*:** Insanul Ahmed, "Knowledge Drop: How Pharrell's 'In My Mind' Inspired Tyler, the Creator to Start Odd Future," Genius, July 25, 2020, https://genius.com/a/how-pharrell-s-in-my-mind-inspired-tyler-the-creator-to-start-odd-future.

108 **"complete fucking failure":** Ahmed, "Knowledge Drop."

108 **rapper Earl Sweatshirt:** Kelefa Sanneh, "Where's Earl?," *New Yorker*, May 16, 2011, https://www.newyorker.com/magazine/2011/05/23/wheres-earl.

108 **mixtapes and albums:** Jon Caramanica, "Young, Gifted and Outrageous: Can Odd Future Survive Popularity?," *New York Times*, November 12, 2010, https://www.nytimes.com/2010/11/13/arts/music/13odd.html.

108 **"skinny white kids":** Sanneh, "Where's Earl?"

109 **about sexual violence:** Zach Baron, "On Odd Future, Rape and Murder, and Why We Sometimes Like the Things That Repel Us," *Village Voice*, November 10, 2010, https://www.villagevoice.com/on-odd-future-rape-and-murder-and-why-we-sometimes-like-the-things-that-repel-us.

109 **shout-outs to Hitler:** Tom Breihan, "Odd Future Mixtapes," *Pitchfork*, March 13, 2011, https://pitchfork.com/features/article/7940-odd-future-mixtapes.

109 **"societal representations":** Briana Younger, "Found Family: How Odd Future Changed Everything," *Pitchfork*, July 31, 2018, https://pitchfork.com/thepitch/found-family-how-odd-future-changed-everything.

109 **most celebrated works:** "The 200 Best Albums of the 2010s," *Pitchfork*, October 8, 2019, https://pitchfork.com/features/lists-and-guides/the-200-best-albums-of-the-2010s.

109 **"racially diverse generation":** Bruce Drake, "6 New Findings About Millennials," Pew Research Center, March 7, 2014, https://www.pewresearch.org/short-reads/2014/03/07/6-new-findings-about-millennials.

109 **"massive Strokes fans":** Lizzy Goodman, *Meet Me in the Bathroom: Rebirth and Rock and Roll in New York City 2001–2011* (Dey Street Books, 2018), 532.

109 **"new kind of guitar identity":** Goodman, *Meet Me in the Bathroom*, 532.

110 **"lack of hesitation":** Simon Reynolds, *Retromania: Pop Culture's Addiction to Its Own Past* (Farrar, Straus and Giroux, 2011), 414.

110 **"They didn't give a shit":** Andy Greenwald, "Vampire Weekend: The Graduates," *Spin*, February 25, 2008, https://www.spin.com/2008/02/vampire-weekend-graduates.

110 *Spin* **cover story:** Greenwald, "Vampire Weekend."

110 *Contra,* **debuted at:** Harvilla, "The Only Living Band."

110 **like "The Fountain":** Rebecca Mead, "Downtown's Daughter," *New Yorker*, November 7, 2010, https://www.newyorker.com/magazine/2010/11/15/downtowns-daughter.

110 **New York's art-world elite:** Mead, "Downtown's Daughter."

110 **"voice of . . . a generation":** *Girls*, season 1, episode 1, "Pilot," written and directed by Lena Dunham, aired April 15, 2012, on HBO.

111 **gentrified Greenpoint:** Matthew Schuerman, "Books: When Gentrification Came to Greenpoint," CityLimits, November 8, 2019, https://citylimits.org/2019/11/08/books-when-gentrification-came-to-greenpoint.

111 **"that would be Facebook":** Scott Stinson, "From Girls' Twentysomethings to Veep's West Wing," *National Post*, April 12, 2012, https://nationalpost.com/entertainment/from-girls-twentysomethings-to-veeps-west-wing.

111 **Progressive critics lambasted:** Eva Wiseman, "'I Stopped Being a Person I Liked': Lena Dunham on Time Out, Rehab and Marriage," *Guardian*, September 25, 2022, https://www.theguardian.com/culture/2022/sep/25/i-stopped-being-a-person-i-liked-lena-dunham-on-time-out-rehab-and-marriage.

111 **millennial degeneracy:** Wiseman, "'I Stopped Being a Person I Liked.'"

111 **who abandoned irony:** Joe Bish, "What Will Replace the Hipster?," *Vice*, December 18, 2015, https://www.vice.com/en/article/nne5qm/hw-what-will-replace-the-hipster-245.

112 **they are "all minorities":** Lauren Garafano, "18 'Glee' Moments That I'm Still Suffering Secondhand Embarrassment From," *BuzzFeed*, September 5, 2020, https://www.buzzfeed.com/laurengarafano/cringiest-moments-on-glee.

112 **actors with Down syndrome:** June Thomas, "In Its Final Season, *Glee* Was the Gayest Show That's Ever Been on Television," *Slate*, March 19, 2015, https://slate.com/human-interest/2015/03/glee-finale-in-its-final-season-glee-was-the-gayest-show-that-s-ever-been-on-television.html.

112 **"normalize homosexuality":** Thomas, "In Its Final Season."

112 **73 percent of millennials:** "Support for Same-Sex Marriage at Record High, but

Key Segments Remain Opposed," Pew Research Center, June 8, 2015, https://www.pewresearch.org/politics/2015/06/08/section-1-changing-views-of-same-sex-marriage.

113 **"borderline aristocratic"**: Willa Paskin, "The New *Gossip Girl* Adds the Wrong Ingredient," *Slate*, July 7, 2021, https://slate.com/culture/2021/07/gossip-girl-hbo-reboot-review.html.

113 **"how many rules"**: Lana Cooper, "Gossip Girl's Class and Gender Warfare," *Pop Matters*, May 13, 2012, https://www.popmatters.com/gossip-girl-class-gender-warfare.

113 **"Everyone on *Gossip Girl*"**: David Klion, "XOXO, Ruling Class," *Drift*, September 14, 2021, https://www.thedriftmag.com/xoxo-ruling-class.

113 **"neat summation"**: Paskin, "New *Gossip Girl* Adds."

CHAPTER 8:
KIMYE

114 **model Kate Upton**: Amy Odell, "The Untold Story of Vogue Embracing Kim Kardashian," *Bustle*, February 20, 2024, https://www.bustle.com/style/anna-wintour-biography-excerpt-kim-kardashian-vogue-cover.

114 **"KW and KK"**: Anonymous source.

114 **"most talked about" couple**: "Kardashian's Vogue Cover Sparks Angry Calls to Boycott Magazine," The-Latest.com, March 24, 2014, https://www.the-latest.com/kardashians-vogue-cover-sparks-angry-calls-boycott-magazine.

114 **Lanvin wedding gown**: Hamish Bowles, "Kim Kardashian and Kanye West: Keeping up with Kimye," *Vogue*, March 24, 2014, https://www.vogue.com/article/kim-kardashian-and-kanye-west-keeping-up-with-kimye.

114 **watershed moment**: Hilary Lewis, "Kim Kardashian 'Honored' to Be on Vogue Cover Despite Criticism (Video)," *Hollywood Reporter*, March 26, 2014, https://www.hollywoodreporter.com/tv/tv-news/kim-kardashian-honored-be-vogue-691285.

114 **dating in April 2012**: Grace Gavilanes and Christopher McKittrick, "Kim Kardashian and Kanye West's Relationship Timeline," *People*, June 29, 2023, https://people.com/tv/kim-kardashian-kanye-west-relationship-history-ups-downs.

114 **The brevity of that union**: Andrea Peyser, "For Richer, or Richer: Inevitable Collapse of a Scam Marriage," *New York Post*, November 1, 2011, https://nypost.com/2011/11/01/for-richer-or-richer-inevitable-collapse-of-a-scam-marriage.

114 **surfaced in his lyrics**: Gavilanes and McKittrick, "Kim Kardashian and Kanye West's."

114 **sleeping with other women**: "Kanye Watched Kim K Sex Tape While Bedding Other Women: Report," Page Six, September 10, 2012, https://pagesix.com/2012/09/10/kanye-watched-kim-k-sex-tape-while-bedding-other-women-report.

114 **AT&T Park**: Gavilanes and McKittrick, "Kim Kardashian and Kanye West's."

114 **"Young and Beautiful"**: Peter Gicas, "Inside Kanye West's $3.3 Million Proposal to Kim Kardashian—Get All the Lavish Details!," E! News, October 22, 2013, https://www.eonline.com/news/472922/inside-kanye-west-s-3-3-million-proposal-to-kim-kardashian-get-all-the-lavish-details.

115 **second engagement of Kim's**: "Kim Kardashian's Engagement to Be Filmed for TV," *Hollywood Reporter*, May 25, 2011, https://www.hollywoodreporter.com/news/general-news/kim-kardashians-engagement-be-filmed-192289.

115 **neo-preppy aesthetic**: Em Whitney, "Kanye West, Enamored with Band of Outsiders, Tries to Give the Daily Transom the Slip," *Observer*, February 16, 2009, https://observer.com/2009/02/kanye-west-enamored-with-band-of-outsiders-tries-to-give-the-daily-transom-the-slip.

115 **crash the front row**: Benjamin Wallace, "What Will the Fashion World Do with Kim Kardashian?," *Cut*, August 12, 2012, https://www.thecut.com/2012/08/kim-kardashian-fashion-world.html.

115 **dismissed her curves**: Wallace, "What Will the Fashion World Do."

115 **"unofficial ban"**: Dana Brown, *Dilettante: True Tales of Excess, Triumph, and Disaster* (Ballantine, 2022), 237.

116 **introspective, singsong rappers**: Benj Salking, "The Forgotten Legacy of '808s and Heartbreak,'" *Occidental*, January 1, 2016, https://theoccidentalnews.com/culture/2016/01/01/the-forgotten-legacy-of-808s-and-heartbreak-2/2884432.

116 **visual transformation**: Jake Woolf, "Kanye West's Greatest *808s & Heartbreak*–Era Style Swerves," *GQ*, November 24,

2015, https://www.gq.com/gallery/kanye -west-808s-heartbreak-style-haircut.

116 **own fashion label:** Sowmya Krishnamur-thy, *Fashion Killa: How Hip-Hop Revolu-tionized High Fashion* (Gallery Books, 2023), 167.

116 **hit sneaker collaboration:** Krishnamur-thy, *Fashion Killa*, 164.

116 **from many collections:** Trace William Cowen and Karizza Sanchez, "Virgil Abloh on Iconic PFW Photo with Kanye: 'What May Seemingly Be Impossible Is Possible,'" *Complex*, January 24, 2019, https://www .complex.com/style/a/tracewilliamcowen /virgil-abloh-on-paris-fashion-week-2009 -photo-kanye-west-tommy-ton.

116 **photographer Tommy Ton:** Brooke Bobb, "Remember When Kanye West Carried a Goyard Briefcase to Paris Fashion Week?," *Vogue*, February 28, 2017, https://www .vogue.com/article/fashion-runway-kanye -went-paris-fashion-week-ready-to-wear -2017.

116 **"They say I was":** "Power," by Kanye West, track 3 on *My Beautiful Dark Twisted Fan-tasy*, Roc-A-Fella, 2010.

116 **"small masterpiece":** Allison Stewart, "Album Review: Taylor Swift, 'Speak Now,'" *Washington Post*, October 24, 2010, https://web.archive.org/web/201308 12201835/http://blog.washingtonpost .com/clicktrack/2010/10/album_review _taylor_swift_spea.html.

116 **intern at Fendi:** Francesco Martino, "The Story of the Internship of Kanye West and Virgil Abloh at Fendi," *NSS Magazine*, No-vember 29, 2021, https://www.nssmag.com /en/fashion/25226/kanye-west-virgil -abloh-stage-fendi.

116 **Hawaii studio:** Charles Holmes, "Seclu-sion in Hawaii, Elton John, and Musical 'Survivor': Inside the Making of 'My Beau-tiful Dark Twisted Fantasy,'" *Ringer*, No-vember 23, 2020, https://www.theringer .com/2020/11/23/music/making-of-my -beautiful-dark-twisted-fantasy-elton -john-podcast.

117 **Released on November 22:** Jacob Ganz, "New Albums from Kanye West and Nicki Minaj Top Chart," NPR, December 1, 2010, https://www.npr.org/sections/there cord/2010/12/01/131726212/new-albums -from-kanye-west-and-nicki-minaj-top -chart.

117 **perfect 10.0:** Ryan Dombal, "My Beauti-ful Dark Twisted Fantasy: Kanye West," *Pitchfork*, November 22, 2010, https://pitch

fork.com/reviews/albums/14880-my -beautiful-dark-twisted-fantasy.

117 **his best work:** Brett Schewitz, "#17 Kanye West, 'My Beautiful Dark Twisted Fan-tasy' (2010)," Rolling Stone 500 Greatest Albums of All Time, June 25, 2021, https: //www.rs500albums.com/50-1/17.

117 **decade's defining albums:** Damien Scott, "Kanye West's 'My Beautiful Dark Twisted Fantasy' Is the Best Album of the Decade," *Complex*, November 22, 2019, https://www.complex.com/music/a /damien-scott/kanye-west-my-beautiful -dark-twisted-fantasy-best-album-of-the -2010s.

117 **the best rap of 2008–2013:** Lauren Nos-tro, Dave Bry, Ornah, et al., "The 25 Best Rap Verses of the Last 5 Years," *Complex*, May 29, 2013, https://www.complex.com /music/a/lauren-nostro/best-rap-verses -of-the-last-5-years.

117 **thirty-four-minute:** Will Dean, "Kanye West's Runaway: Purple Rain or Bird Brains?," *Guardian*, October 25, 2010, https://www.theguardian.com/music/mu sicblog/2010/oct/25/kanye-west-runaway.

117 **Greek mythology:** Nitsuh Abebe, "Filthy, Rich: Kanye West's Royal *Fantasy*," *Vul-ture*, November 12, 2010, https://www .vulture.com/2010/11/filthy_rich_kanye _wests_royal.html.

117 **like Sarah Andelman:** Tina Isaac-Goizé, "In Paris, the Two Women Who Are Co-lette," *New York Times*, March 3, 2017, https://www.nytimes.com/2017/03/03 /fashion/paris-boutique-colette.html.

117 **casual brand A.P.C.:** Jake Woolf, "The GQ Guide to A.P.C. Kanye," *GQ*, July 16, 2014, https://www.gq.com/gallery/the-gq -guide-to-a-p-c-kanye.

117 **revamped Kim's wardrobe:** Krish-namurthy, *Fashion Killa*, 168.

117 **"Back in the day":** Amy Woodyatt, "Kim Kardashian Praises Ex Kanye West for In-troducing Her to Fashion," CNN, Decem-ber 8, 2021, https://edition.cnn.com/style /article/kim-kardashian-west-peoples -choice-intl-scli/index.html.

117 **Kim to the Met Gala:** Kristin Contino, "A History of Kim Kardashian at the Met Gala: Her Outfits Through the Years," Page Six, May 8, 2025, https://pagesix .com/article/kim-kardashian-met-gala -outfits-through-the-years.

117 **"I didn't know anyone":** Sarah Spellings, "Kim Kardashian West Cried After Her First Met Gala," *Cut*, May 6, 2019, https://

www.thecut.com/2019/05/kim-kardashian-west-cried-at-her-first-met-gala.html.

117 **"really, really, *really*"**: Lou Reed, "Lou Reed on Kanye West's Yeezus: 'It Brings Tears to My Eyes,'" *Guardian*, July 3, 2013, https://www.theguardian.com/music/2013/jul/03/lou-reed-kanye-west-yeezus.

117 **no additional beats**: "It's Not Kanye, It's Me," Alex Castle, November 27, 2013, https://alexcastle.net/2013/11/27/its-not-kanye-its-me.

117 **reached instant infamy**: Jerry Saltz, "Jerry Saltz on Kanye, Kim, and 'the New Uncanny,'" *Vulture*, November 25, 2013, https://www.vulture.com/2013/11/jerry-saltz-on-kanye-west-kim-kardashian-bound-2.html.

118 **performed a new track**: Jerry Saltz, "'Picasso Baby' Live: Jerry Saltz Goes Face-to-Face with Jay-Z," *Vulture*, July 11, 2013, https://www.vulture.com/2013/07/jerry-saltz-face-to-face-with-jay-z.html.

118 **"cultural cringe"**: Jonathan Jones, "Jay Z v Marina Abramović They Both Used Each Other," *Guardian*, May 20, 2015, https://www.theguardian.com/artanddesign/shortcuts/2015/may/20/marina-baramovic-says-shell-never-work-with-jay-z-again.

118 **retracted her comments**: Lanre Bakare, "Marina Abramović Institute Apologises to Jay Z," *Guardian*, May 20, 2015, https://www.theguardian.com/artanddesign/2015/may/20/jay-z-substantial-donation-maria-abramovic.

118 **#BoycottVogue trended**: Hannah Marriott, "Why Kim Kardashian Deserves to Be on the Cover of Vogue," *Guardian*, March 24, 2014, https://www.theguardian.com/fashion/2014/mar/24/why-kim-kardashian-deserves-to-be-on-the-cover-of-vogue.

118 **Nikki Finke suggested**: "Kardashian's Vogue Cover Sparks Angry Calls."

118 **canceling her subscription**: "Kardashian's Vogue Cover Sparks Angry Calls."

118 **"if we just remain"**: Cheryl Wischhover, "Anna Wintour Implies Kim and Kanye Are Not 'Tasteful,'" *Fashionista*, November 18, 2014, https://fashionista.com/2014/11/anna-wintour-kim-kardashian-vogue-cover.

118 **"arbiters of taste"**: Brown, *Dilettante*, 9–10.

118 **the "New Establishment"**: Brown, *Dilettante*, 91.

119 **"than (on) celebrity"**: Amy Larocca, "Why Are People Being Snobs About Kim Kardashian on the Cover of Vogue?," *Cut*, March 26, 2014, https://www.thecut.com/2014/03/stop-being-snobs-about-the-kimye-cover.html.

119 **"puritanical self-righteousness"**: Larocca, "Why Are People."

119 **"Culture was shifting"**: Allison P. Davis, "The End of Kimye's Wild Ride," *Vulture*, April 26, 2021, https://www.vulture.com/article/kim-kardashian-kanye-west-divorce.html.

119 **"broke the internet"**: David Hershkovits, "How Kim Kardashian Broke the Internet with Her Butt," *Guardian*, December 17, 2014, https://www.theguardian.com/lifeandstyle/2014/dec/17/kim-kardashian-butt-break-the-internet-paper-magazine.

119 **"self-created, self-aware"**: Jerry Saltz and David Wallace-Wells, "Jerry Saltz: How and Why We Started Taking Kim Kardashian Seriously (and What She Teaches Us About the State of Criticism)," *Vulture*, May 20, 2015, https://www.vulture.com/2015/05/saltz-how-kim-kardashian-became-important.html.

119 **"spent her life"**: Laura Bennett, "Self-Publishing," *Slate*, May 6, 2015, https://slate.com/culture/2015/05/selfish-kim-kardashian-wests-book-of-selfies-reviewed.html.

119 **"in her way"**: Megan Garber, "You Win, Kim Kardashian," *Atlantic*, May 13, 2015, https://www.theatlantic.com/entertainment/archive/2015/05/kim-kardashian-selfish/393113.

119 **Kris Jenner, attended**: Vanessa Friedman, "Met Gala 2015," *New York Times*, June 17, 2015, https://www.nytimes.com/interactive/projects/cp/red-carpet-watch/met-gala-2015/kris-jenner.

120 **model in the world**: Courtney Mason, "These Are the Highest-Paid Models in the World," L'Officiel USA, August 31, 2024, https://www.lofficielusa.com/fashion/highest-paid-models-in-the-world-kendall-jenner-gisele-bundchen.

120 **sneaker empire**: Megan Twohey, "Kanye and Adidas: Money, Misconduct and the Price of Appeasement," *New York Times*, October 27, 2023, https://www.nytimes.com/2023/10/27/business/kanye-west-adidas-yeezy.html.

120 **Wintour snuck out**: Sam Reed, "Anna Wintour Got Lost in the Basement of MSG, Cried," *Hollywood Reporter*, April 13, 2016, https://www.hollywoodreporter.com/lifestyle/style/anna-wintour-got-lost-basement-883462.

CHAPTER 9:
BLURRED TIMELINES

121 **the theme songs:** "The Facts of Life, Diff'rent Strokes, Wheel of Fortune," Canadian Songwriters Hall of Fame, September 28, 2020, https://www.cshf.ca/song/the-facts-of-life-diffrent-strokes-wheel-of-fortune.

121 **become a musician:** James C. McKinley Jr., "Robin Thicke, a Romantic, Has a Naughty Hit," *New York Times*, July 19, 2013, https://www.nytimes.com/2013/07/21/arts/music/robin-thicke-a-romantic-has-a-naughty-hit.html.

121 **impressed Jimmy Iovine:** McKinley, "Robin Thicke, a Romantic."

121 **introduced him to Pharrell:** "The Evolution of Robin Thicke," Vancouver Public Library, https://vpl.bibliocommons.com/v2/record/S38C1516498.

121 **topped the R&B charts:** Kelefa Sanneh, "An R&B Star Who Doesn't Look Like One," *New York Times*, March 17, 2007, https://www.nytimes.com/2007/03/17/arts/music/17thic.html.

121 **official story:** Jayson Greene, "'Blurred Lines,' Harbinger of Doom," *Pitchfork*, March 29, 2023, https://pitchfork.com/features/article/robin-thicke-blurred-lines-10-years-later.

121 **Vicodin and alcohol:** Greene, "'Blurred Lines.'"

121 **effectively written everything:** Eriq Gardner, "Robin Thicke Admits Drug Abuse, Lying to Media in Wild 'Blurred Lines' Deposition (Exclusive)," *Hollywood Reporter*, September 15, 2014, https://www.hollywoodreporter.com/business/business-news/robin-thicke-admits-drug-abuse-732783.

121 **ten million copies:** Hugh McIntyre, "Robin Thicke, Pharrell and T.I.'s Controversial Single 'Blurred Lines' Has Been Certified Diamond," *Forbes*, June 8, 2018, https://www.forbes.com/sites/hughmcintyre/2018/06/08/robin-thicke-pharrell-and-t-i-s-controversial-single-blurred-lines-has-been-certified-diamond.

121 **song of the summer:** Phoebe Robinson, "The 20 Best Songs That Represent Summer 2013," *Glamour*, August 29, 2013, https://www.glamour.com/story/the-songs-of-the-summer-2013-e.

121 **homage to Terry Richardson:** Greene, "'Blurred Lines.'"

121 **model Emily Ratajkowski:** Bee Shapiro, "For Emily Ratajkowski, 'Blurred Lines'

Brings a Career Path into Focus," *New York Times*, October 23, 2013, https://www.nytimes.com/2013/10/24/fashion/for-emily-ratajkowski-robin-thickes-blurred-lines-video-brings-a-career-path-into-focus.html.

122 **"unrated" version:** Greene, "'Blurred Lines.'"

122 **Ratajkowski later alleged:** Greene, "'Blurred Lines.'"

122 **no-means-yes lyrics:** Greene, "'Blurred Lines.'"

122 **its female director:** Greene, "'Blurred Lines.'"

122 **accused the song:** Ben Sisario and Noah Smith, "'Blurred Lines' Infringed on Marvin Gaye Copyright, Jury Rules," *New York Times*, March 10, 2015, https://www.nytimes.com/2015/03/11/business/media/blurred-lines-infringed-on-marvin-gaye-copyright-jury-rules.html.

122 **"distinctive and significant":** Greene, "'Blurred Lines.'"

122 **jury unanimously ruled:** "Robin Thicke, Pharrell Williams Copied from Marvin Gaye in Blurred Lines, Court Confirms," *ABC News*, March 22, 2018, https://www.abc.net.au/news/2018-03-22/court-rules-with-gaye-family-in-blurred-lines-case/9576518.

122 **"Recorded popular music":** Agnès Gayraud, *Dialectic of Pop* (Urbanomic, 2019), 8.

122 **17 percent of royalties:** Nate Jones, "Mark Ronson and Bruno Mars Legally Admit That 'Uptown Funk' Sounds a Lot like a 1979 Funk Classic," *Vulture*, May 1, 2015, https://www.vulture.com/2015/05/ronson-gap-band-settle-uptown-funk-claim.html.

122 **was quietly settled:** Noah Yoo, "Mark Ronson Settles 'Uptown Funk' Zapp Copyright Lawsuit," *Pitchfork*, July 2, 2018, https://pitchfork.com/news/mark-ronson-settles-uptown-funk-zapp-copyright-lawsuit.

123 **"sensation of moving forward":** Simon Reynolds, *Retromania: Pop Culture's Addiction to Its Own Past* (Farrar, Straus and Giroux, 2011), x.

123 **sounded especially groundbreaking:** Reynolds, *Retromania*, 405.

123 **meaningless jargon:** *The Simpsons*, season 8, episode 14, "The Itchy & Scratchy & Poochie Show," written by Matt Groening, James L. Brooks, Al Jean, et al., directed by Steven Dean Moore, aired February 7, 1997, on Fox.

123 **macro-values:** Young Back Choi, *Paradigms and Conventions* (University of Michigan Press, 1993), 7–8.

124 **bestselling album of the decade:** "Hudson Hosts Holiday Special; Beatles Have Decade's Top Selling Album," Voice of America, December 15, 2009, https://www.voanews.com/a/beatles-have-decades-top-selling-album-79297047/416447.html.

124 **ran for eighteen years:** John Katsilometes, "'A State of Shock': The Beatles' 'Love' Bows Out After 18 Years," *Las Vegas Review-Journal*, July 7, 2024, https://www.reviewjournal.com/entertainment/entertainment-columns/kats/a-state-of-shock-the-beatles-love-bows-out-after-18-years-3081776.

124 **"There has never before":** Reynolds, *Retromania*, xxi.

124 **decades-old shows:** I was the exact age in which these shows were part of my viewing habits.

124 **began to outsell:** Ted Gioia, "Is Old Music Killing New Music?," Honest Broker, January 19, 2022, https://www.honest-broker.com/p/is-old-music-killing-new-music.

125 **once derided disco:** Ben Myers, "Why 'Disco Sucks!' Sucked," *Guardian*, June 18, 2009, https://www.theguardian.com/music/musicblog/2009/jun/18/disco-sucks.

125 **racist and homophobic:** Myers, "Why 'Disco Sucks!' Sucked."

125 **"Nothing seems to wither":** Reynolds, *Retromania*, 407.

125 **Volkswagen won accolades:** *Wired* notes it was a "clever ad." Ethan Gilsdorf, "Why the New Star Wars Volkswagen Super Bowl Ad Is a Travesty," *Wired*, February 4, 2012, https://www.wired.com/2012/02/volkswagen-travesty.

125 **Brisk iced tea ads:** Gilsdorf, "Why the New Star Wars."

125 **$4.05 billion purchase:** "Disney Buys Star Wars Maker Lucasfilm from George Lucas," *BBC News*, October 31, 2012, https://www.bbc.com/news/business-20146942.

125 **Billions of dollars poured:** Caroline Reid, "Disney Reveals $645 Million Spending on Star Wars Show 'Andor,'" *Forbes*, December 22, 2024, https://www.forbes.com/sites/carolinereid/2024/12/22/disney-reveals-645-million-spending-on-star-wars-show-andor.

125 **live-instrument disco:** Paul Tingen, "Recording Random Access Memories | Daft Punk," Sound on Sound, July 2013, https://www.soundonsound.com/people/recording-random-access-memories-daft-punk.

125 **"push pop music forward":** "Pitchfork Reviews: Rescored," *Pitchfork*, October 5, 2021, https://pitchfork.com/features/lists-and-guides/pitchfork-reviews-rescored.

126 **became a global sensation:** Kyle Denis, "Pharrell Williams Reflects on 10 Years of Daft Punk's 'Get Lucky': 'I Thought I Was Writing for Someone Else,'" *Billboard*, October 11, 2023, https://www.billboard.com/music/pop/pharrell-williams-reflects-on-get-lucky-daft-punk-memory-tapes-random-access-memories-1235439845.

126 **bestselling song of 2014:** Ayomikun Adekaiyero, "Pharrell Williams Says Writing 'Happy' Broke Him. It Went on to Become One of the Biggest Songs of the 2010s," *Business Insider*, October 11, 2024, https://www.businessinsider.com/pharrell-williams-happy-broke-him-dispicable-me-soundtrack-2024-10.

126 **"R&B instruments":** Harriet Gibsone, "How Pharrell Williams Captured the Essence of Happiness," *Guardian*, April 8, 2014, https://www.theguardian.com/music/musicblog/2014/apr/08/pharrell-williams-happy-single.

126 **fans everywhere:** Pharrell Williams, "Happiness Matters," *New York Times*, December 4, 2014, https://www.nytimes.com/2014/12/04/opinion/pharrell-williams-on-the-happy-phenomenon.html.

126 **Atlanta's drug trade:** Joe Coscarelli, *Rap Capital: An Atlanta Story* (Simon & Schuster, 2022).

126 **chopped and looped:** Coscarelli, *Rap Capital*, 135–36.

126 **the triplet flow:** Coscarelli, *Rap Capital*, 70.

127 **twenty minutes:** Coscarelli, *Rap Capital*, 244.

127 **"If they really take":** Coscarelli, *Rap Capital*, 244.

127 **"We're playing spaceman!":** *Mad Men*, season 1, episode 2, "Ladies Room," written by Matthew Weiner, directed by Alan Taylor, aired July 26, 2007, on AMC.

127 **business casual reigned:** Richard Feloni, "How Levi's Made 'Business Casual' the Standard in American Workplaces," *Business Insider*, August 12, 2014, https://www.businessinsider.com/levis-helped-define-business-casual-2014-8.

128 **"Marc Jacobs' new collection!":** *Glee*, season 1, episode 1, "Pilot," written by Ryan Murphy, Brad Falchuk, and Ian Brennan, directed by Ryan Murphy, aired May 19, 2009, on Fox.

128 **Dior Homme suits:** Jonathan Heaf and

Lauren Cochrane, "How Mad Men Changed the Way Men Dress," *Guardian*, April 15, 2014, https://www.theguardian.com/fashion/2014/apr/15/mad-men-changed-way-men-dress-don-draper.

128 **"No TV show"**: Finlay Renwick, "15 Years On from *Mad Men*, the Don Draper Effect Is Dead in Menswear," *British GQ*, July 25, 2022, https://www.gq-magazine.co.uk/fashion/article/mad-men-anniversary-don-draper-suit.

128 **"too-tailored suits"**: Renwick, "15 Years On from Mad Men."

128 **boxy gray wool suits**: Alex Pappademas, "Designer of the Year: The Incredible Suit-Shrinking Man," *GQ*, October 31, 2008, https://www.gq.com/story/designer-of-the-year-thom-browne-menswear.

128 **Hollywood and K-pop**: Amina Ayoud, "NCT's Johnny & Shinee's Taemin Go Classic in Oxfords for Thom Browne's 20th Anniversary Celebration in Seoul," *Footwear News*, October 24, 2023, https://footwearnews.com/fashion/celebrity-style/ncts-johnny-shinees-taemin-thom-brownes-20th-anniversary-1203544524; "Remaking Fashion for 20 Years: Thom Browne," Samsung C&T Newsroom, November 14, 2023, https://news.samsungcnt.com/en/features/fashion/2023-11-remaking-fashion-for-20-years-thom-browne.

128 **to LeBron James**: Samuel Hine, "How Thom Browne's Radical Suit Found Its Way to LeBron James," *GQ*, September 4, 2019, https://www.gq.com/story/thom-browne-lebron-james-suit.

129 **series *The Sartorialist***: Alex Pappademas, "Up from the Streets," *GQ*, June 2012, https://web.archive.org/web/20120524042924/http://www.gq.com/style/profiles/201206/scott-schuman-sartorialist-gq-june-2012-interview.

129 **rose to global fame**: Jenna Sauers, "How Fashion Blogger BryanBoy Became a Front-Row Fixture," *Observer*, February 8, 2012, https://observer.com/2012/02/bryanboy-new-york-fashion-week-anna-win tour-karl-lagerfeld-marc-jacobs.

129 **boxer Manny Pacquiao**: Sauers, "How Fashion Blogger BryanBoy."

129 **renamed it "BB"**: Sauers, "How Fashion Blogger BryanBoy."

129 **sit in the front row**: Tyler McCall, "Bryanboy Hasn't Missed a Fashion Week in over a Decade," *Cut*, February 12, 2024, https://www.thecut.com/article/bryanboy-fashion-week-front-row.html.

129 **Bryanboy's seat**: Pappademas, "Up from the Streets."

129 **thirteen-year-old Tavi Gevinson**: Michael Schulman, "The Oracle of Girl World," *New York Times*, July 27, 2012, https://www.nytimes.com/2012/07/29/fashion/tavi-gevinson-the-oracle-of-girl-world.html.

129 **"eye on some kid"**: Eric Wilson, "Bloggers Crash Fashion's Front Row," *New York Times*, December 24, 2009, https://www.nytimes.com/2009/12/27/fashion/27BLOGGERS.html.

129 **Gevinson's giant bow**: Schulman, "Oracle of Girl World."

129 **loaner laptops to bloggers**: Pappademas, "Up from the Streets."

130 **over 160 times**: Coscarelli, *Rap Capital*, 82.

130 **collaboration with Bloomingdale's**: Coscarelli, *Rap Capital*, 244.

130 **online streetwear forums**: Kelefa Sanneh, "Where's Earl?," *New Yorker*, May 16, 2011, https://www.newyorker.com/magazine/2011/05/23/wheres-earl.

130 **"invent a camera"**: Pappademas, "Up from the Streets."

130 **"Ninety percent of my clothes"**: Sowmya Krishnamurthy, *Fashion Killa: How Hip-Hop Revolutionized High Fashion* (Gallery Books, 2023), 185.

130 **"We used to save up"**: Allyson Shiffman, "What Jeremy Scott Means to A$AP Rocky," *Interview*, September 9, 2013, https://www.interviewmagazine.com/fashion/asap-rocky-x-jeremy-scott.

130 **rejection of omnivore tastes**: K-Hole, *Youth Mode: A Report on Freedom*, October 2013, https://khole.net/issues/youth-mode.

130 **"Blank clothes"**: Fiona Duncan, "Normcore: Fashion for Those Who Realize They're One in 7 Billion," *Cut*, February 26, 2014, https://www.thecut.com/2014/02/normcore-fashion-trend.html.

131 **less "hip or chic"**: Lauren Sherman, "Why the 'Normcore' Phenomenon Is a Fraud," *Elle*, March 4, 2014, https://www.elle.com/fashion/news/a15307/probably-cant-pull-off-normcore.

131 **"contemporary normcore styles"**: Duncan, "Normcore: Fashion for Those."

131 **more than tripled**: From 42.81 on January 30, 2009, to 143.50 at the end of January 2015.

131 **"president did yesterday"**: Eileen Cartter, "It Happened: President Biden Wore a Tan Suit," *GQ*, August 6, 2021, https://www.gq.com/story/joe-biden-khaki-suit.

131   **84 percent in France:** Richard Wike, Jacob Poushter, and Hani Zainulbhai, *As Obama Years Draw to Close, President and U.S. Seen Favorably in Europe and Asia* (Pew Research Center, 2016), 22, https://www.pewresearch.org/global/wp-content/uploads/sites/2/2016/06/Pew-Research-Center-Balance-of-Power-Report-FINAL-June-29-2016.pdf.

132   **legal same-sex unions:** Frank Newport and Andrew Dugan, "5 Ways America Changed During the Obama Years," Gallup, January 27, 2017, https://news.gallup.com/opinion/polling-matters/203123/america-changed-during-obama-years.aspx.

132   **Jenner's public transition:** Dana Brown, *Dilettante: True Tales of Excess, Triumph, and Disaster* (Ballantine, 2022), 241.

132   **identified as "socially liberal":** Newport and Dugan, "5 Ways America Changed."

132   **religious right:** Gregory A. Smith, "About Three-in-Ten U.S. Adults Are Now Religiously Unaffiliated," Pew Research Center, December 14, 2021, https://www.pewresearch.org/religion/2021/12/14/about-three-in-ten-u-s-adults-are-now-religiously-unaffiliated.

132   **"to dislike it":** Jesse Green, "Theater Review: Lin-Manuel Miranda's Hamilton Is Worth Way More Than $10," *Vulture*, February 17, 2015, https://www.vulture.com/2015/02/theater-review-lin-manuel-mirandas-hamilton.html.

132   **astronomical sums:** N. Gregory Mankiw, "I Paid $2,500 for a 'Hamilton' Ticket. I'm Happy About It," *New York Times*, October 21, 2016, https://www.nytimes.com/2016/10/23/upshot/i-paid-2500-for-a-hamilton-ticket-im-happy-about-it.html.

132   **mentioned *Hamilton* twice:** Kevin McFarland, "Relax, Haters. Hillary Clinton Knows Hamilton Better Than You," *Wired*, July 29, 2016, https://www.wired.com/2016/07/hillary-clinton-really-does-love-hamilton.

132   **Obama frequently referenced:** Matt Lewis, "Obama Loves Martin Luther King's Great Quote—but He Uses It Incorrectly," *Daily Beast*, January 16, 2017, https://www.thedailybeast.com/obama-loves-martin-luther-kings-great-quotebut-he-uses-it-incorrectly.

132   **wrote Ta-Nehisi Coates:** Ta-Nehisi Coates, *Between the World and Me* (One World, 2015), 103.

132   **"permanent Democratic majority":** Rick Perlstein, "Why a Permanent Democratic Majority Is Not a Demographic Inevitability (Part One: Antecedents)," *Nation*, February 4, 2013, https://www.thenation.com/article/archive/why-permanent-democratic-majority-not-demographic-inevitability-part-one-antecedents.

**PART THREE:
2016–2019**

**CHAPTER 10:
REVANCHISM AND RESISTANCE**

137   **"Donald Trump is here":** "Public Papers of the Presidents of the United States: Barack Obama (2011, Book I)," GovInfo, 2011, https://www.govinfo.gov/app/details/PPP-2011-book1/PPP-2011-book1-doc-pg478.

137   **released the full document:** Dan Pfeiffer, "President Obama's Long Form Birth Certificate," White House, April 27, 2011, https://obamawhitehouse.archives.gov/blog/2011/04/27/president-obamas-long-form-birth-certificate.

138   **"humiliation was as absolute":** Adam Gopnik, "Trump and Obama: A Night to Remember," *New Yorker*, September 12, 2015, https://www.newyorker.com/news/daily-comment/trump-and-obama-a-night-to-remember.

138   **pinpointed this moment:** Roxanne Roberts, "I Sat Next to Donald Trump at the Infamous 2011 White House Correspondents' Dinner," *Washington Post*, April 28, 2016, https://www.washingtonpost.com/lifestyle/style/i-sat-next-to-donald-trump-at-the-infamous-2011-white-house-correspondents-dinner/2016/04/27/5cf46b74-0bea-11e6-8ab8-9ad050f76d7d_story.html; Maggie Haberman and Alexander Burns, "Donald Trump's Presidential Run Began in an Effort to Gain Stature," *New York Times*, March 12, 2016, https://www.nytimes.com/2016/03/13/us/politics/donald-trump-campaign.html.

138   **doesn't quite align:** Edward Helmore, "How Trump's Political Playbook Evolved Since He First Ran for President in 2000," *Guardian*, February 5, 2017, https://www.theguardian.com/us-news/2017/feb/05/donald-trump-reform-party-2000-president; Michael Kruse, "The True Story of Donald Trump's First Campaign Speech—in 1987," *Politico*, February 5, 2016, https://www.politico.com/magazine

/story/2016/02/donald-trump-first-cam paign-speech-new-hampshire-1987-213595.

138 **"short-fingered vulgarian":** Jon Kelly, "How Donald Trump Became 'the Short-Fingered Vulgarian,'" *Vanity Fair*, March 7, 2016, https://www.vanityfair.com/news /2016/03/how-donald-trump-became-the -short-fingered-vulgarian.

138 *Home Alone 2*: Thomas LeGro, "Watch Donald Trump as Donald Trump in His Movie and TV Show Cameos," *Washington Post*, January 14, 2016, https://www.wash ingtonpost.com/video/politics/watch -donald-trump-as-donald-trump-in-his -movie-and-tv-show-cameos/2016/01/14 /6ac2b4ac-bad9-11e5-85cd-5ad59bc 19432_video.html.

138 **six bankruptcies:** Michelle Lee, "Fact Check: Has Trump Declared Bankruptcy Four or Six Times?," *Washington Post*, September 26, 2016, https://www.washington post.com/politics/2016/live-updates/gen eral-election/real-time-fact-checking-and -analysis-of-the-first-presidential-debate /fact-check-has-trump-declared-bank ruptcy-four-or-six-times.

139 **2000 episode of** *The Simpsons*: *The Simpsons*, season 11, episode 17, "Bart to the Future," written by Dan Greaney, directed by Jim Reardon and Michael Marcantel, aired March 19, 2000, on Fox.

139 **image makeover:** McKay Coppins, "The Most Consequential TV Show in History," *Atlantic*, June 5, 2024, https://www.theat lantic.com/politics/archive/2024/06 /trump-apprentice-in-wonderland -reality-tv/678601.

139 **"American maverick tycoon":** Emily Nussbaum, *Cue the Sun! The Invention of Reality TV* (Random House, 2024), 382.

139 **half of Republicans:** Andy Barr, "51% of GOP Voters: Obama Foreign," *Politico*, February 15, 2011, https://www.politico .com/story/2011/02/51-of-gop-voters -obama-foreign-049554.

139 **"burlesque house":** Coppins, "Most Consequential TV Show."

139 **Operation Neptune Spear:** Garrett M. Graff, "'I'd Never Been Involved in Anything as Secret as This,'" *Politico*, April 30, 2021, https://www.politico.com/news/maga zine/2021/04/30/osama-bin-laden-death -white-house-oral-history-484793.

140 **over 50 percent:** Gallup, "Presidential Approval Ratings—Barack Obama," Gallup, April 21, 2016, https://news.gallup.com /poll/116479/barack-obama-presidential -job-approval.aspx.

140 **"When Mexico sends":** "What Donald Trump Has Said About Mexico and Vice Versa," ABC News, August 31, 2016, https://abcnews.go.com/Politics/donald -trump-mexico-vice-versa/story?id= 41767704.

140 **"they let you do it":** Jane C. Timm, "Trump on Hot Mic: 'When You're a Star . . . You Can Do Anything' to Women," NBC News, October 7, 2016, https://www.nbcnews.com/politics/2016 -election/trump-hot-mic-when-you-re -star-you-can-do-n662116.

140 **mocking a disabled reporter:** Irin Carmon, "Donald Trump's Worst Offense? Mocking Disabled Reporter, Poll Finds," NBC News, August 10, 2016, https://www .nbcnews.com/politics/2016-election /trump-s-worst-offense-mocking -disabled-reporter-poll-finds-n627736.

140 **pro-Hillary rap video:** Allison P. Davis, "'Yeah, I'm Not for Everyone.' Lena Dunham Comes to Terms with Herself," *Cut*, November 25, 2018, https://www.thecut .com/2018/11/lena-dunham-comes-to -terms-with-herself.html.

140 **"political 9/11":** François Bonnet, "Donald Trump's Victory, a 'Political 9/11,'" Mediapart, November 9, 2016, https://www .mediapart.fr/en/journal/international /091116/donald-trumps-victory-political -911.

140 **fundamentalist Christians:** Emma Green, "The Evangelical Reckoning over Donald Trump," *Atlantic*, November 10, 2016, https://www.theatlantic.com/politics/ar chive/2016/11/the-evangelical-reckoning -on-trump/507161.

141 **"(Obama) a socialist":** George Packer, *The Unwinding: An Inner History of the New America* (Farrar, Straus and Giroux, 2013), 317.

141 **start a TV network:** Stephen Battaglio, "If Donald Trump Loses the Election, Launching a TV Network Won't Be an Easy Plan B," *Los Angeles Times*, September 21, 2016, https://www.latimes.com /entertainment/envelope/cotown/la-et-ct -trump-tv-20160916-snap-story.html; Sarah Ellison, "Exclusive: Is Donald Trump's Endgame the Launch of Trump News?," *Vanity Fair*, June 16, 2016, https://www .vanityfair.com/news/2016/06/donald -trump-tv-network.

141 **within the Republican Party:** Nash Jenkins, "Fighting Donald Trump Cost Jeff Flake His Job. But He's Not Going Quietly," *Time*, November 30, 2017, https://

time.com/5042705/donald-trump-jeff
-flake-not-going-quietly.

141 **refused to dismantle:** Coppins, "Most Consequential TV Show."

141 **voters despised Clinton:** Matthew Yglesias, "Trump Won by Running as a Moderate Republican," *Vox*, July 11, 2017, https://www.vox.com/policy-and-politics/2017/7/11/15941846/trump-moderate-republican.

141 **as a "jobs guy":** Coppins, "Most Consequential TV Show."

141 **White animosity:** Toby Buckle, "A Disease of Affluence," Liberal Currents, November 20, 2024, https://www.liberalcurrents.com/a-disease-of-affluence.

141 **outcome to racism:** Ramesh Ponnuru, "Trump Didn't Win Because of Racism," *Bloomberg*, November 8, 2016, https://www.bloomberg.com/opinion/articles/2016-11-09/trump-didn-t-win-because-of-racism.

141 **"economic anxiety":** Derek Thompson, "Donald Trump and 'Economic Anxiety,'" *Atlantic*, August 18, 2016, https://www.theatlantic.com/business/archive/2016/08/donald-trump-and-economic-anxiety/496385.

141 **new media cliché:** Doug Mack, "Why Are Journalists Always Visiting Diners in Trump Country?," *Counter*, October 22, 2020, https://thecounter.org/trump-rust-belt-diner-presidential-race-election-2020; Katherine J. Cramer, "For Years, I've Been Watching Anti-Elite Fury Build in Wisconsin. Then Came Trump," *Vox*, November 16, 2016, https://www.vox.com/the-big-idea/2016/11/16/13645116/rural-resentment-elites-trump.

141 **"We liberals bear":** Thomas Frank, "Millions of Ordinary Americans Support Donald Trump. Here's Why," *Guardian*, March 7, 2016, https://www.theguardian.com/commentisfree/2016/mar/07/donald-trump-why-americans-support.

142 **idyllic heartland:** Nicholas Gilmore, "The Heartland and the Myth of the 'Real' America," *Saturday Evening Post*, June 24, 2020, https://www.saturdayeveningpost.com/2020/06/the-heartland-and-the-myth-of-the-real-america.

142 **imported hams:** David Brooks, "How We Are Ruining America," *New York Times*, July 11, 2017, https://www.nytimes.com/2017/07/11/opinion/how-we-are-ruining-america.html.

142 **"Kids were dying":** Sam Quinones, *Dreamland: The True Tale of America's Opiate Epidemic* (Bloomsbury, 2015), 7.

142 **self-made petite bourgeoisie:** Patrick Wyman, "American Gentry," *Atlantic*, September 23, 2021, https://www.theatlantic.com/ideas/archive/2021/09/trump-american-gentry-wyman-elites/620151.

142 **lens of taste:** Olivier Roy, *The Crisis of Culture*, trans. Cynthia Schoch and Trista Selous (Oxford University Press, 2023), 87.

142 **"social class (that) sees":** Gopnik, "Trump and Obama."

142 **General Motors built factories:** The Ford River Rouge complex in Dearborn, Michigan, was the largest in the world.

143 **increasingly favored women:** Hanna Rosin, "The End of Men," *Atlantic*, August 15, 2010, https://www.theatlantic.com/magazine/archive/2010/07/the-end-of-men/308135.

143 **leaned decisively liberal:** Constance Grady, "Why So Much Obama-Era Pop Culture Feels So Cringe Now," *Vox*, December 27, 2021, https://www.vox.com/22641501/hamilton-parks-rec-harry-potter-cringe-obama-era-pop-culture.

143 **"his debates, his interviews":** John Hendrickson, "Trump's WWE Theory of Politics," *Atlantic*, March 31, 2023, https://www.theatlantic.com/newsletters/archive/2023/03/how-wrestling-made-trump/673597.

144 **Judith Shklar defined liberals:** Richard Rorty, *Contingency, Irony, and Solidarity* (Cambridge University Press, 1989), xv.

144 **"It makes them feel good":** Adam Serwer, "The Cruelty Is the Point," *Atlantic*, October 3, 2018, https://www.theatlantic.com/ideas/archive/2018/10/the-cruelty-is-the-point/572104.

144 **nuanced explanation:** "Examining Trump's Appeal to Voters," NPR, November 9, 2016, https://www.npr.org/2016/11/09/501382657/author-j-d-vance-explains-trumps-appeal-to-voters.

144 **by making Kaepernick:** Kevin Draper and Julie Creswell, "Colin Kaepernick 'Dream Crazy' Ad Wins Nike an Emmy," *New York Times*, September 16, 2019, https://www.nytimes.com/2019/09/16/sports/football/colin-kaepernick-nike-emmy.html.

144 **Ted Nugent, and Kid Rock:** John Lynch, Anjelica Oswald, and Meryl Gottlieb, "31 Celebrities Who Have Publicly Supported Donald Trump," *Business Insider*, April 4, 2018, https://www.businessinsider.com/celebrities-who-support-trump-2016-11.

144 **of _Duck Dynasty_:** "'Duck Dynasty' Star Willie Robertson Backs Trump, Saying 'I Do Like Me Some Trump,'" ABC News, September 26, 2015, https://abcnews.go.com/Politics/duck-dynasty-star-willie-robertson-backs-trump-trump/story?id=34057394.

145 **voted for Trump:** Curtis M. Wong, "Paris Hilton Continues to Walk Back Previous Praise for Donald Trump," _HuffPost_, March 14, 2023, https://www.huffpost.com/entry/paris-hilton-pretended-to-vote-for-trump-2016_n_64109632e4b0cfde25c1448d.

145 **"Bed Intruder" fame:** Chris Illuminati, "15 Interesting Facts About Antoine Dodson," Daily Dot, May 23, 2021, https://www.dailydot.com/unclick/antoine-dodson-hide-yo-kids-hide-yo-wife.

145 **"MY FUCKING HERO":** Joe Price, "Azealia Banks on Trump: 'I Am TRULY Inspired by This and Feel Deep Amounts of Vindication,'" _Complex_, November 9, 2016, https://www.complex.com/pigeons-and-planes/a/backwoodsaltar/azealia-banks-praises-trump-win.

145 **from Tila Tequila:** "DC Eatery Sorry for Inadvertently Hosting Alt-Right Party, to Donate Money to ADL," _Times of Israel_, November 23, 2016, https://www.timesofisrael.com/dc-eatery-sorry-for-inadvertently-hosting-alt-right-party-to-donate-money-to-adl.

145 **"Hitler Part I":** Anne Cohen, "Tila Tequila Banned from Facebook," _Forward_, December 14, 2013, https://forward.com/schmooze/189282/tila-tequila-banned-from-facebook.

145 **disjointed monologue:** Dee Lockett, "Kanye Should Win an Emmy for His Epic Rant on _Ellen_," _Vulture_, May 19, 2016, https://www.vulture.com/2016/05/kanye-epic-rant-on-ellen.html.

145 **"ideas that can make":** Snuga, "Kanye West Went on a Passionate Rant About Changing the World on 'Ellen,'" _Complex_, May 19, 2016, https://www.complex.com/music/a/suzannah-weiss/kanye-west-passionate-rant-changing-world-ellen.

145 **he donated money:** Kenzie Bryant, "An Incomplete History of Kanye West's Political Views," _Vanity Fair_, April 26, 2018, https://www.vanityfair.com/style/2018/04/kanye-west-political-views-history.

145 **"If I would have voted":** Bryant, "An Incomplete History."

145 **"psychiatric emergency":** Joe Coscarelli, "Kanye West Is Hospitalized for 'Psychiatric Emergency' Hours After Canceling Tour," _New York Times_, November 21, 2016, https://www.nytimes.com/2016/11/21/arts/music/kanye-west-hospitalized-exhaustion.html.

145 **diagnosed with bipolar disorder:** Erica Schwiegershausen, "We Still Don't Know How to Talk About Kanye," _Cut_, February 25, 2022, https://www.thecut.com/2022/02/kanye-west-bipolar-disorder.html.

145 **"We discussed life":** Katie Rogers, "Kanye West Visits Donald Trump," _New York Times_, December 13, 2016, https://www.nytimes.com/2016/12/13/us/politics/kanye-trump-tower-visit.html.

145 **red MAGA cap:** Bryant, "An Incomplete History."

146 **political trickster:** "Who Is Roger Stone?," NPR, January 26, 2019, https://www.npr.org/2019/01/26/689063642/who-is-roger-stone.

146 **for his extreme views:** Josh Harkinson, "Meet the White Nationalist Trying to Ride the Trump Train to Lasting Power," _Mother Jones_, October 27, 2016, https://www.motherjones.com/politics/2016/10/richard-spencer-trump-alt-right-white-nationalist.

146 **credit for inventing:** Graeme Wood, "His Kampf," _Atlantic_, June 2017, https://www.theatlantic.com/magazine/archive/2017/06/his-kampf/524505.

146 **such as rapper Macklemore:** Winston Cook-Wilson, "Macklemore Renounces His (Former) Hitler Youth Haircut," _Billboard_, August 15, 2017, https://www.billboard.com/music/rb-hip-hop/macklemore-renounces-hitler-youth-nazi-trump-haircut-7905066.

146 **sucker-punched him:** Wood, "His Kampf."

146 **button-down dress shirts:** Olivia Nuzzi, "Here's Why Steve Bannon Wears So Many Shirts," _Cut_, September 15, 2017, https://www.thecut.com/2017/09/why-steve-bannon-wears-so-many-shirts.html.

146 **Goldman Sachs banker:** Elisha Fieldstadt, "A Crash Course on Steve Bannon," CBS News, January 5, 2018, https://www.cbsnews.com/pictures/steve-bannon-crash-course.

146 **"downstream of culture":** Wil S. Hylton, "Down the Breitbart Hole," _New York Times Magazine_, August 16, 2017, https://www.nytimes.com/2017/08/16/magazine/breitbart-alt-right-steve-bannon.html.

146 **section on "Black crime":** Hylton, "Down the Breitbart Hole."

146 *globalist* as a slur: Hylton, "Down the Breitbart Hole."

147 hired Milo Yiannopoulos: "Milo Yiannopoulos: Who Is the Alt-Right Writer and Provocateur?," *BBC News*, February 21, 2017, https://www.bbc.com/news/world-us-canada-39026870.

147 "ethics in game journalism": Caitlin Dewey, "The Only Guide to Gamergate You Will Ever Need to Read," *Washington Post*, October 14, 2014, https://www.washingtonpost.com/news/the-intersect/wp/2014/10/14/the-only-guide-to-gamergate-you-will-ever-need-to-read.

147 "very little social capital": Zack Beauchamp, "Milo Yiannopoulos: Breitbart's Star Provocateur and Trump Champion, Explained," *Vox*, February 20, 2017, https://www.vox.com/2016/4/4/11355876/milo-yiannopoulos.

147 his idol Paris Hilton: Angela Nagle, *Kill All Normies: Online Culture Wars from 4chan and Tumblr to Trump and the Alt-Right* (Zero Books, 2017), 102.

147 came to an abrupt halt: Jeremy W. Peters, Alexandra Alter, and Michael M. Grynbaum, "Milo Yiannopoulos's Pedophilia Comments Cost Him CPAC Role and Book Deal," *New York Times*, February 20, 2017, https://www.nytimes.com/2017/02/20/us/politics/cpac-milo-yiannopoulos.html.

147 resigned from Breitbart: Rebecca Hersher, "After Comments on Pedophilia, Breitbart Editor Milo Yiannopoulos Resigns," NPR, February 21, 2017, https://www.npr.org/sections/thetwo-way/2017/02/21/516473521/after-comments-on-pedophilia-breitbart-editor-milo-yiannopoulos-resigns.

147 "want to be punk": Beauchamp, "Milo Yiannopoulos."

147 alienated his colleagues: Adam Leith Gollner, "The Secret History of Gavin McInnes," *Vanity Fair*, June 29, 2021, https://www.vanityfair.com/news/2021/06/the-secret-history-of-gavin-mcinnes.

147 *Taki's Magazine*: Gollner, "Secret History of Gavin McInnes."

147 version of Disney's *Aladdin*: "How Extremists Weaponize Irony to Spread Hate," NPR, April 26, 2021, https://www.npr.org/transcripts/990274685.

148 "maximum freedom": Nagle, *Kill All Normies*, 95.

148 a Fred Perry polo shirt: Gollner, "Secret History of Gavin McInnes."

148 "state of exuberance": Nagle, *Kill All Normies*, 90.

148 "walk into the White House": Gollner, "Secret History of Gavin McInnes."

148 "stand back and stand by": Kathleen Ronayne and Michael Kunzelman, "Trump to Far-Right Extremists: 'Stand Back and Stand By,'" Associated Press, September 30, 2020, https://apnews.com/article/election-2020-joe-biden-race-and-ethnicity-donald-trump-chris-wallace-0b32339da25fbc9e8b7c7c7066a1db0f.

148 resigning days after: Jason Wilson, "Proud Boys Founder Gavin McInnes Quits 'Extremist' Far-Right Group," *Guardian*, November 22, 2018, https://www.theguardian.com/world/2018/nov/22/proud-boys-founder-gavin-mcinnes-quits-far-right-group.

148 "an extremist group": Molly Solomon, "FBI Categorizes Proud Boys as Extremist Group with Ties to White Nationalism," NPR, November 20, 2018, https://www.npr.org/2018/11/20/669761157/fbi-categorizes-proud-boys-as-extremist-group-with-ties-to-white-nationalism.

148 "crisis actors": Shannon Bond, "How Alex Jones Helped Mainstream Conspiracy Theories into American Life," NPR, August 6, 2022, https://www.npr.org/2022/08/06/1115936712/how-alex-jones-helped-mainstream-conspiracy-theories-into-american-life.

148 "Your reputation is amazing": Eric Bradner, "Trump Praises 9/11 Truther's 'Amazing' Reputation," CNN, December 2, 2015, https://edition.cnn.com/2015/12/02/politics/donald-trump-praises-9-11-truther-alex-jones; William Finnegan, "Donald Trump and the 'Amazing' Alex Jones," *New Yorker*, June 23, 2016, https://www.newyorker.com/news/daily-comment/donald-trump-and-the-amazing-alex-jones.

148 repeat *Infowars* staples: Finnegan, "Donald Trump and the 'Amazing.'"

148 promoted by Alex Jones: James Doubek, "Conspiracy Theorist Alex Jones Apologizes for Promoting 'Pizzagate,'" NPR, March 26, 2017, https://www.npr.org/sections/thetwo-way/2017/03/26/521545788/conspiracy-theorist-alex-jones-apologizes-for-promoting-pizzagate.

148 "The intel on this": Hank Sanders, "Man Convicted in Pizzagate Shooting Is Killed in Confrontation with Police," *New York Times*, January 9, 2025, https://www

.nytimes.com/2025/01/09/us/pizzagate-shooter-killed-police.html.

149 "against white people": Don Gonyea, "Majority of White Americans Say They Believe Whites Face Discrimination," NPR, October 24, 2017, https://www.npr.org/2017/10/24/559604836/majority-of-white-americans-think-theyre-discriminated-against.

149 Red Pill subreddit: Nagle, *Kill All Normies*, 88.

149 "the left can't meme": Ed West, "Why the Left Can't Meme," UnHerd, August 14, 2021, https://unherd.com/2021/08/why-the-left-cant-meme.

149 co-opted by 4chan trolls: "Pepe the Frog," Anti-Defamation League, https://www.adl.org/resources/hate-symbol/pepe-frog.

149 "Rare Pepe" memes: Charles Bramesco, "Feels Good Man: The Disturbing Story Behind the Rise of Pepe the Frog," *Guardian*, August 31, 2020, https://www.theguardian.com/film/2020/aug/31/feels-good-man-pepe-frog-4chan-documentary-film.

149 "general hate symbol": "Pepe the Frog," Anti-Defamation League.

149 titled *The Deplorables*: Jessica Roy, "How 'Pepe the Frog' Went from Harmless to Hate Symbol," *Los Angeles Times*, October 11, 2016, https://www.latimes.com/politics/la-na-pol-pepe-the-frog-hate-symbol-20161011-snap-htmlstory.html.

149 called themselves Groypers: "Groyper Army and 'America First,'" Anti-Defamation League, March 17, 2020, https://www.adl.org/resources/backgrounder/groyper-army-and-america-first.

149 "memed Donald Trump": Andrew Marantz, "Trump Supporters at the Deplora-Ball," *New Yorker*, January 29, 2017, https://www.newyorker.com/magazine/2017/02/06/trump-supporters-at-the-deploraball.

150 wore Pepe the Frog: Marantz, "Trump Supporters at the DeploraBall."

150 "Jews will not replace us": Adam Gabbatt, "'Jews Will Not Replace Us': Vice Film Lays Bare Horror of Neo-Nazis in America," *Guardian*, August 16, 2017, https://www.theguardian.com/us-news/2017/aug/16/charlottesville-neo-nazis-vice-news-hbo.

150 chants of "White lives matter": Ta Arr, "Unite the Right Pre Game Torch March," YouTube video, 8:16, April 17, 2018, https://youtu.be/HPPQScy9Z7M.

150 car into a crowd: "Charlottesville Attacker Apologises as He Is Jailed for Life," *BBC News*, June 28, 2019, https://www.bbc.com/news/world-us-canada-48806265.

150 "very fine people": Rosie Gray, "Trump Defends White-Nationalist Protesters: 'Some Very Fine People on Both Sides,'" *Atlantic*, August 15, 2017, https://www.theatlantic.com/politics/archive/2017/08/trump-defends-white-nationalist-protesters-some-very-fine-people-on-both-sides/537012.

150 "Satan-worshiping pedophiles": Kevin Roose, "What Is QAnon, the Viral Pro-Trump Conspiracy Theory?," *New York Times*, September 3, 2021, https://www.nytimes.com/article/what-is-qanon.html.

150 blogger Paul Furber: Brandy Zadrozny and Ben Collins, "Like the Fringe Conspiracy Theory Qanon? There's Plenty of Merch for Sale on Amazon," NBC News, July 18, 2018, https://www.nbcnews.com/business/business-news/fringe-conspiracy-theory-qanon-there-s-plenty-merch-sale-amazon-n892561.

150 believing its core tenets: Mallory Newall, "More Than 1 in 3 Americans Believe a 'Deep State' Is Working to Undermine Trump," Ipsos, December 30, 2020, https://www.ipsos.com/en-us/news-polls/npr-misinformation-123020.

150 emblazoned their slogans: Zadrozny and Collins, "Like the Fringe Conspiracy."

150 outspoken QAnon believer: Alex Rogers, "QAnon Promoter Marjorie Taylor Greene Wins Seat in Congress," CNN, November 3, 2020, https://edition.cnn.com/2020/11/03/politics/marjorie-taylor-greene-wins.

150 politically charged video: Syreeta McFadden, "Beyoncé's Formation Reclaims Black America's Narrative from the Margins," *Guardian*, February 8, 2016, https://www.theguardian.com/commentisfree/2016/feb/08/beyonce-formation-black-american-narrative-the-margins.

150 year's best song: Including *Time* and *Entertainment Weekly*; ABC Radio, "'EW's' Best & Worst Songs of 2016 Include Beyonce, Fifth Harmony, Drake, Britney & More," Live 96.1 & 98.3, December 9, 2016, https://www.live999radio.com/ews-best-worst-songs-of-2016-include-beyonce-fifth-harmony-drake-britney-more.

150 "video of all time": Brian Hiatt, "Why Is Beyonce's 'Formation' the Greatest Music Video of All Time?," *Rolling Stone*, August 21, 2021, https://www.rollingstone

.com/music/music-news/best-music-videos-podcast-beyonce-1214967.

151 **Jay-Z's infidelity:** Ijeoma Oluo, "Beyoncé's Lemonade Is About Much More Than Infidelity and Jay Z," *Guardian*, April 26, 2016, https://www.theguardian.com/commentisfree/2016/apr/25/beyonce-lemonade-jay-z-infidelity-emotional-project-depths.

151 **Associated Press named it:** Mesfin Fekadu, "'Lemonade' by Beyoncé Is Named the AP's Album of the Decade," Associated Press, December 12, 2019, https://apnews.com/article/d66d82c5f7182b087f88b4e787e33073.

151 **Hillary Clinton's campaign:** Sabrina Siddiqui, "Hillary Clinton Backed by Beyoncé and Jay Z in Battleground State of Ohio," *Guardian*, November 5, 2016, https://www.theguardian.com/us-news/2016/nov/05/im-with-her-beyonce-and-jay-z-back-hillary-clinton-in-battleground-state-of-ohio.

151 **"get in formation":** "The 200 Best Songs of the 2010s," *Pitchfork*, October 7, 2019, https://pitchfork.com/features/lists-and-guides/the-200-best-songs-of-the-2010s.

151 **single-day protest:** Anna North, "The Women's March Changed the American Left. Now Anti-Semitism Allegations Threaten the Group's Future," *Vox*, December 21, 2018, https://www.vox.com/identities/2018/12/21/18145176/feminism-womens-march-2018-2019-farrakhan-intersectionality.

151 **hand-crocheted "pussyhat":** Kristen Jordan Shamus, "Pink Pussyhats: The Reason Feminists Are Ditching Them," *Detroit Free Press*, January 10, 2018, https://www.freep.com/story/news/2018/01/10/pink-pussyhats-feminists-hats-womens-march/1013630001.

151 **known as the Resistance:** Beverly Gage, "A 'Resistance' Stands Against Trump. But What Will It Stand For?," *New York Times*, January 31, 2017, https://www.nytimes.com/2017/01/31/magazine/a-resistance-stands-against-trump-but-what-will-it-stand-for.html.

151 **"For both Yiannopoulos":** Nagle, *Kill All Normies*, 54.

151 **demand for "hyper-recognition":** Gilles Lipovetsky, *Hypermodern Times*, trans. Andrew Brown (Polity Press, 2005), 65.

151 **Erykah Badu's recording:** Domenico Montanaro, "What Does the Word 'Woke' Really Mean, and Where Does It Come From?," NPR, July 19, 2023, https://www.npr.org/2023/07/19/1188543449/what-does-the-word-woke-really-mean-and-where-does-it-come-from.

151 **Black Lives Matter movement:** Montanaro, "What Does the Word."

152 **"no grand distinction":** Julia Carrie Wong (@joolia.bsky.social), Bluesky, December 16, 2024, https://bsky.app/profile/joolia.bsky.social/post/3ldgkz34byk2p.

152 **became a bestseller:** Daniel Bergner, "'White Fragility' Is Everywhere. But Does Antiracism Training Work?," *New York Times Magazine*, July 15, 2020, https://www.nytimes.com/2020/07/15/magazine/white-fragility-robin-diangelo.html.

152 **increase opportunities for:** Mike Roe and Tyler Wayne, "In Screenwriting, 'Significant' Gains for Women and People of Color since 2010," LAist, April 7, 2022, https://laist.com/news/arts-and-entertainment/in-screenwriting-significant-gains-for-women-and-people-of-color-since-2010.

152 **hired sensitivity readers:** Lucy Knight, "Sensitivity Readers: What Publishing's Most Polarising Role Is Really About," *Guardian*, March 15, 2023, https://www.theguardian.com/books/2023/mar/15/sensitivity-readers-what-publishings-most-polarising-role-is-really-about.

152 **platforms like Tumblr:** Nagle, *Kill All Normies*, 69.

152 **fragile "snowflakes":** Rebecca Nicholson, "'Poor Little Snowflake'—the Defining Insult of 2016," *Guardian*, November 28, 2016, https://www.theguardian.com/science/2016/nov/28/snowflake-insult-disdain-young-people.

152 **"checking your privilege":** Nagle, *Kill All Normies*, 69.

152 **"sorted by category":** Heather Wilhelm, "Women's March Morphs into Intersectional Torture Chamber," *National Review*, January 11, 2017, https://www.nationalreview.com/2017/01/womens-march-feminists-oppose-donald-trump-struggle-agree-how.

153 **Critical race theory:** Jacey Fortin, "Critical Race Theory: A Brief History," *New York Times*, November 8, 2021, https://www.nytimes.com/article/what-is-critical-race-theory.html.

153 **concept of intersectionality:** Jane Coaston, "The Intersectionality Wars," *Vox*, May 28, 2019, https://www.vox.com/the-highlight/2019/5/20/18542843/intersec

tionality-conservatism-law-race-gender
-discrimination.

153 **introduced the term** *BIPOC*: Constance Grady, "Why the Term 'BIPOC' Is So Complicated, Explained by Linguists," *Vox*, June 30, 2020, https://www.vox.com /2020/6/30/21300294/bipoc-what -does-it-mean-critical-race-linguistics -jonathan-rosa-deandra-miles-hercules.

153 **expanded its scope:** Megan Lasher and Leah Campano, "A Brief History of the LGBTQ Acronym," *Seventeen*, April 5, 2023, https://www.seventeen.com/life /a18209179/lgbtq-meaning.

153 **infighting among groups:** Farah Stockman, "Women's March Roiled by Accusations of Anti-Semitism," *New York Times*, December 23, 2018, https://www.nytimes .com/2018/12/23/us/womens-march-anti -semitism.html.

153 **Tamika Mallory attended a speech:** Stockman, "Women's March Roiled."

153 **wear the pink pussyhat:** Shamus, "Pink Pussyhats."

153 **"choose the color":** Shamus, "Pink Pussyhats."

153 **Caitlyn Jenner's 2015 transition:** Dana Brown, *Dilettante: True Tales of Excess, Triumph, and Disaster* (Ballantine, 2022), 241.

153 **hashtag #OscarsSoWhite:** Reggie Ugwu, "The Hashtag That Changed the Oscars: An Oral History," *New York Times*, February 6, 2020, https://www.nytimes.com /2020/02/06/movies/oscarssowhite -history.html.

153 **all-female cast:** Alissa Wilkinson, "In 2016, the Ghostbusters Reboot Didn't Change Movies. But the Backlash Was a Bad Omen," *Vox*, December 30, 2019, https://www.vox.com/culture/2019/12/30 /21037815/ghostbusters-backlash-decade -black-panther-captain-marvel.

153 **Kelly Marie Tran:** Kelly Marie Tran, "I Won't Be Marginalized by Online Harassment," *New York Times*, August 21, 2018, https://www.nytimes.com/2018/08/21 /movies/kelly-marie-tran.html.

154 **earned over $1 billion:** Yohana Desta, "*Black Panther* Is Officially a $1 Billion Hit," *Vanity Fair*, March 11, 2018, https:// www.vanityfair.com/hollywood/2018/03 /black-panther-box-office-billion-dollars -china-marvel.

154 **"most political movie":** Jamelle Bouie, "*Black Panther* Is a Marvel Movie Superpowered by Its Ideas," *Slate*, February 15, 2018, https://slate.com/culture/2018/02

/black-panther-the-new-marvel-movie -reviewed.html.

154 **#MeToo campaign:** Alyssa Milano helped popularize the hashtag but it was created by Tarana Burke; see Jason Parham, "A People's History of Black Twitter, Part II," *Wired*, July 22, 2021, https:// www.wired.com/story/black-twitter-oral -history-part-ii-rising-up.

154 **against Miramax producer:** "Harvey Weinstein Timeline: How the Scandal Has Unfolded," *BBC News*, February 24, 2023, https://www.bbc.com/news/entertain ment-arts-41594672.

154 **Cristiano Ronaldo faced:** Ken Ritter and Scott Sonner, "US Appeals Court Hears Arguments over 2010 Hush-Money Settlement of Ronaldo Rape Case in Vegas," Associated Press, October 4, 2023, https://apnews.com/article/ronaldo-rape -lawsuit-vegas-appeal-soccer-935996e9 81e80c5d44c61c6a7f905689.

154 **reshot Spacey's role:** Kyle Buchanan, "Ridley Scott's Very Candid Account of How He Saved *All the Money in the World*," *Vulture*, December 26, 2017, https://www.vulture.com/2017/12/ridley -scott-all-the-money-in-the-world-re shoots.html.

154 **James Franco vanished:** Gwilym Mumford, "James Franco Accused of Sexual Misconduct by Five Women Including Former Students," *Guardian*, January 11, 2018, https://www.theguardian.com/film /2018/jan/11/james-franco-accused-sex ual-misconduct-five-women-students.

154 **admitted to sexual misconduct:** Caroline Framke, "The Sexual Harassment Allegations Against Louis C.K., Explained," *Vox*, November 10, 2017, https://www.vox .com/culture/2017/11/9/16629400/louis -ck-allegations-masturbation.

154 **Charlie Rose and Chris Matthews:** Victoria Bekiempis, "Charlie Rose Turned Studio into a 'Sexual Hunting Ground,' New Lawsuit Alleges," *Guardian*, September 22, 2019, https://www.theguardian.com /world/2019/sep/22/charlie-rose-new -sexual-hunting-ground-lawsuit; Jordan Moreau, "Former 'Hardball' Host Chris Matthews Admits to Inappropriate Behavior," *Variety*, April 26, 2020, https://vari ety.com/2020/tv/news/chris-matthews -hardball-allegations-inappropriate -behavior-1234590218.

154 **McMahon also stepped down:** Hendrickson, "Trump's WWE Theory of Politics."

154 **exile to Mexico:** Melissa Whitworth, "The Rise and Fall of Joe Francis and Girls Gone Wild," *Independent*, December 14, 2022, https://www.independent.co.uk/news/world/americas/crime/joe-francis-jail-girls-gone-wild-founder-b2245424.html.

155 **reckoning finally came:** Jessica Testa, "Terry Richardson Accused of Sexual Assault in Two New Lawsuits," *New York Times*, November 22, 2023, https://www.nytimes.com/2023/11/22/style/terry-richardson-sexual-assault-lawsuit.html.

155 **two models had alleged:** Benjamin Wallace, "Is Terry Richardson an Artist or a Predator?," *Cut*, June 15, 2014, https://www.thecut.com/2014/06/terry-richardson-interview.html.

155 **"exploring sexuality":** Wallace, "Is Terry Richardson an Artist."

155 **Hearst, and Bulgari:** Marlen Komar, "More Magazines Are Refusing to Work with Terry Richardson & It's Hard to Ignore the Timing," *Bustle*, October 28, 2017, https://www.bustle.com/p/more-magazines-are-refusing-to-work-with-terry-richardson-its-hard-to-ignore-the-timing-2980079; Hannah Ellis-Petersen, "Fashion Brands Drop Terry Richardson over Allegations of Abuse on Shoots," *Guardian*, October 24, 2017, https://www.theguardian.com/artanddesign/2017/oct/24/terry-richardson-photographer-dropped-fashion-brands-allegations.

155 **launched an investigation:** Danielle Cohen, "All the Allegations Against Terry Richardson," *Cut*, November 27, 2023, https://www.thecut.com/2023/11/terry-richardson-allegations-sexual-assault.html.

155 **Adult Survivors Act:** Cohen, "All the Allegations Against Terry Richardson."

155 **operated a sex cult:** Jim DeRogatis, "Parents Told Police Their Daughter Is Being Held Against Her Will in R. Kelly's 'Cult,'" *BuzzFeed News*, July 17, 2017, https://www.buzzfeednews.com/article/jimderogatis/parents-told-police-r-kelly-is-keeping-women-in-a-cult.

155 **"Do What U Want":** Spencer Kornhaber, "Lady Gaga's R. Kelly Apology Is a Reminder That Abuse Isn't Provocative," *Atlantic*, January 11, 2019, https://www.theatlantic.com/entertainment/archive/2019/01/lady-gaga-r-kelly-do-what-u-want-apology/580048.

155 **"R. Kelly and I":** Kornhaber, "Lady Gaga's R. Kelly Apology."

155 **"victim of sexual assault":** Kornhaber, "Lady Gaga's R. Kelly Apology."

155 **directed by Terry Richardson:** Stephanie Smith, "Why Lady Gaga Scrapped R. Kelly Duet Video," *Page Six*, June 19, 2014, https://pagesix.com/2014/06/19/lady-gaga-scrapped-r-kelly-duet-video-after-controversies.

156 **"I realized that we":** David Renshaw, "Pharrell Says 'Blurred Lines' Critics Taught Him 'We Live in a Chauvinist Culture,'" *Fader*, October 14, 2019, https://www.thefader.com/2019/10/14/pharrell-blurred-lines-chauvinist-culture.

156 **twenty million Americans:** Larry Buchanan, Quoctrung Bui, and Jugal K. Patel, "Black Lives Matter May Be the Largest Movement in U.S. History," *New York Times*, July 3, 2020, https://www.nytimes.com/interactive/2020/07/03/us/george-floyd-protests-crowd-size.html.

156 **67 percent of Americans:** Juliana Menasce Horowitz, Kiley Hurst, and Dana Braga, "Support for the Black Lives Matter Movement Has Dropped Considerably from Its Peak in 2020," Pew Research Center, June 14, 2023, https://www.pewresearch.org/social-trends/2023/06/14/support-for-the-black-lives-matter-movement-has-dropped-considerably-from-its-peak-in-2020.

157 **seventeen-year-old Kyle Rittenhouse:** Joseph Ax, "Hero or Vigilante? Rittenhouse Verdict Reignites Polarized U.S. Gun Debate," Reuters, November 21, 2021, https://www.reuters.com/world/us/hero-or-vigilante-rittenhouse-verdict-reignites-polarized-us-gun-debate-2021-11-19.

157 **"I know *Vogue* has":** Morwenna Ferrier, "Anna Wintour Apologises for Not Giving Space to Black People at Vogue," *Guardian*, June 10, 2020, https://www.theguardian.com/fashion/2020/jun/10/anna-wintour-apologises-for-not-giving-space-to-black-people-at-vogue.

157 **West donated $2 million:** Chloe Melas, "Kanye West Donates $2 Million, Pays College Tuition for George Floyd's Daughter," CNN, June 4, 2020, https://edition.cnn.com/2020/06/04/entertainment/kanye-west-two-million-dollar-donation/index.html.

157 **Pepsi became a punch line:** Daniel Victor, "Pepsi Pulls Ad Accused of Trivializing Black Lives Matter," *New York Times*, April 5, 2017, https://www.nytimes.com/2017/04/05/business/kendall-jenner-pepsi-ad.html.

157 **"If only Daddy"**: Victor, "Pepsi Pulls Ad."

157 **"member of the dominant culture"**: Ligaya Mishan, "What Does Cultural Appropriation Really Mean?," *New York Times Magazine*, September 30, 2022, https://www.nytimes.com/2022/09/30/t -magazine/cultural-appropriation.html.

158 **celebrities like Miley Cyrus**: Ellie Krupnick, "Miley Cyrus' Dreads Bring Cultural Appropriation Moment to 2015 MTV VMAs Red Carpet," Mic, August 30, 2015, https://www.mic.com/articles /124603/miley-cyrus-dreads-bring -cultural-appropriation-moment-to-2015 -mtv-vmas-red-carpet; Rachel Lubitz, "Justin Bieber's Dreads Get Dragged for Cultural Appropriation on Twitter," Mic, April 4, 2016, https://www.mic.com/arti cles/139708/justin-bieber-s-dreads-get -dragged-for-cultural-appropriation -on-twitter.

158 **term *dreadlocks* itself**: Gabrielle Kwarteng, "Why I Don't Refer to My Hair as 'Dreadlocks,'" *Vogue*, July 16, 2020, https:// www.vogue.com/article/locs-history-hair -discrimination.

158 **"horrible cultural disrespect"**: Vanessa Friedman, "Kim Kardashian West and the Kimono Controversy," *New York Times*, June 27, 2019, https://www.nytimes.com /2019/06/27/fashion/kim-kardashian -west-kimono-cultural-appropriation .html.

158 **"perpetuator of celebrity"**: Cait Munro, "Art Critics Concur: Terry Richardson Is Not an Artist," Artnet, July 8, 2014, https:// news.artnet.com/art-world/art-critics -concur-terry-richardson-is-not-an-artist -57212.

158 **term *culture war***: Pietro S. Nivola, "Thinking About Political Polarization," Brookings, January 1, 2005, https://www .brookings.edu/articles/thinking-about -political-polarization.

158 **"no such thing as art"**: Evan Osnos, *Age of Ambition: Chasing Fortune, Truth, and Faith in the New China* (Farrar, Straus and Giroux, 2014), 94.

CHAPTER 11:
TECHNO-PESSIMISM

159 **delicate porcelain ceramics**: Lalage Harris, "Letter from Veles: The Real Story of Macedonia's Fake News Factory," New East Digital Archive, April 4, 2017, https:// www.new-east-archive.org/features/show /8031/letter-from-veles.

159 **under 50 percent**: Craig Silverman, J. Lester Feder, Saska Cvetkovska, and Aubrey Belford, "The Macedonia Connection," *BuzzFeed News*, July 18, 2018, https:// www.buzzfeednews.com/article/craigsil verman/american-conservatives-fake -news-macedonia-paris-wade-libert.

159 **champagne began to flow**: Silverman et al., "Macedonia Connection."

159 **content farm scam**: Silverman et al., "Macedonia Connection."

159 **make in three days**: "$3,000 per day" vs. average salary of €4,363 per year; Emma Jane Kirby, "The City Getting Rich from Fake News," *BBC News*, December 5, 2016, https://www.bbc.com/news/magazine -38168281.

159 **even fluency in English**: Silverman et al., "Macedonia Connection."

159 **Trajche and Panche**: Silverman et al., "Macedonia Connection."

159 **country-techno band Rednex**: Igor Bosilkovski, "Checking In with the Macedonian Fake News Strategist," *Columbia Journalism Review*, April 16, 2019, https:// www.cjr.org/politics/checking-in-with -the-macedonian-fake-news-strategist.php.

159 **playbook was simple**: Samanth Subramanian, "Inside the Macedonian Fake-News Complex," *Wired*, February 15, 2017, https://www.wired.com/2017/02/veles -macedonia-fake-news.

159 **pope endorsing him**: Subramanian, "Inside the Macedonian."

159 **selling arms to ISIS**: Lorelei Mihala, "'Fake News': What's the Best Way to Tame the Beast?," *BBC News*, July 13, 2017, https:// www.bbc.com/news/business-40575479.

160 **clicked Facebook links**: Huo Jingnan and Shannon Bond, "New Study Shows Just How Facebook's Algorithm Shapes Conservative and Liberal Bubbles," NPR, July 27, 2023, https://www.npr.org/2023 /07/27/1190383104/new-study-shows-just -how-facebooks-algorithm-shapes -conservative-and-liberal-bub.

160 **BuzzFeed News exposed**: Craig Silverman and Lawrence Alexander, "How Teens in the Balkans Are Duping Trump Supporters with Fake News," *Buzzfeed News*, November 3, 2016, https://www .buzzfeednews.com/article/craigsilver man/how-macedonia-became-a-global -hub-for-pro-trump-misinfo.

160 **"guys over in Macedonia"**: Eric Johnson, "Full Transcript: Hillary Clinton at Code 2017," *Vox*, May 31, 2017, https:// www.vox.com/2017/5/31/15722218/hill

ary-clinton-code-conference-transcript -donald-trump-2016-russia-walt-moss berg-kara-swisher.

160 MAN WHO HELPED DONALD: Bosilkovski, "Checking In with the Macedonian."

160 Arsov brothers partnered: Silverman et al., "Macedonia Connection."

160 recruited Alicia Powe: Jim Peters, "CONK! News Engages Investigative Journalist Alicia Powe for Video Podcast," EIN Presswire, May 17, 2022, https:// www.einpresswire.com/article/57190 5692/conk-news-engages-investigative -journalist-alicia-powe-for-video-podcast.

160 "We can't afford anything": Heather C. Hughes and Israel Waismel-Manor, "The Macedonian Fake News Industry and the 2016 US Election," *PS: Political Science & Politics* 54, no. 1 (2021): 19–23, https:// doi.org/10.1017/S1049096520000992.

160 "at the altar": Rick Webb, "My Internet Mea Culpa," Medium, December 26, 2017, https://medium.com/newco/my-inter net-mea-culpa-f3ba77ac3eed.

161 "Social-media operators": Ian Bogost, "The Age of Social Media Is Ending," *Atlantic*, November 10, 2022, https://www .theatlantic.com/technology/archive /2022/11/twitter-facebook-social-media -decline/672074.

161 donated to Democrats: Farai Chideya, "Nearly All of Silicon Valley's Political Dollars Are Going to Hillary Clinton," *FiveThirtyEight*, October 25, 2016, https:// fivethirtyeight.com/features/nearly -all-of-silicon-valleys-political-dollars-are -going-to-hillary-clinton.

161 Hastings endorsed Clinton: Maya Kosoff, "Hillary Clinton Sucks Up to Silicon Valley," *Vanity Fair*, June 29, 2016, https:// www.vanityfair.com/news/2016/06/hill ary-clinton-sucks-up-to-silicon-valley.

161 "ideological diversity": Kate Knibbs, "Lexicon Watch: 'Ideological Diversity,'" *Ringer*, March 16, 2017, https://www.the ringer.com/2017/03/16/uncategorized/lex icon-ideological-diversity-buzzword-mark -zuckerberg-inclusivity-dbc9aff10613.

161 anti-Clinton memes: Natalie Jarvey, "Backlash Brews After Oculus Founder Funds Anti–Hillary Clinton Memes," *Hollywood Reporter*, September 23, 2016, https://www.hollywoodreporter.com/news /general-news/oculus-founder-funds-anti -hillary-932287.

161 "impacting the perception": Matt Kamen, "Palmer Luckey Distances Himself from Nimble America Group," *Wired*, September

26, 2016, https://www.wired.com/story /palmer-luckey-apologises-nimble-amer ica-oculus.

161 leather bikini top: Ben Lang, "In First Interview Since Leaving Oculus, Founder Palmer Luckey Talks VR's Mobile Future, Facebook, and Cosplay," *Road to VR*, May 10, 2017, https://www.roadtovr.com/ocu lus-founder-palmer-luckey-first-interview -since-leaving-oculus-facebook.

161 Academic Evgeny Morozov: Noam Cohen, "The Internet's Verbal Contrarian," *New York Times*, August 14, 2013, https:// www.nytimes.com/2013/08/15/business /media/the-internets-verbal-contrarian.html.

162 "internet does not": Evgeny Morozov, "Two Decades of the Web: A Utopia No Longer," *Prospect*, June 22, 2011, https:// www.prospectmagazine.co.uk/ideas/tech nology/49273/two-decades-of-the-web-a -utopia-no-longer.

162 industry dismissed Morozov: Cohen, "Internet's Verbal Contrarian."

162 "Teflon industry": Evgeny Morozov, "Why We Are Allowed to Hate Silicon Valley," *Frankfurter Allgemeine*, November 11, 2013, https://www.faz.net/aktuell/feuille ton/debatten/the-internet-ideology-why -we-are-allowed-to-hate-silicon-valley -12658406.html.

162 deployed "troll armies": Daniel L. Byman, "How Middle Eastern Conflicts Are Playing Out on Social Media," Brookings, January 20, 2022, https://www.brookings .edu/articles/how-middle-eastern-con flicts-are-playing-out-on-social-media.

162 missing Brown student: James Surowiecki, "The Wise Way to Crowdsource a Manhunt," *New Yorker*, April 23, 2013, https://www.newyorker.com/news/daily -comment/the-wise-way-to-crowdsource -a-manhunt.

162 wrong police officers: David Kushner, "What Anonymous Got Wrong in Ferguson," *New Yorker*, September 5, 2014, https://www.newyorker.com/tech/annals -of-technology/anonymous-got-wrong-fer guson.

162 "The Fappening": Kashimra Gander, "The Fappening: After the Third Wave of Leaked Celebrity Photos, Why Can't We Stop It?," *Independent*, September 30, 2014, https://www.independent.co.uk/tech /the-fappening-after-the-third-wave-of -leaked-celebrity-photos-why-can-t-we -stop-it-9763528.html.

162 "logical end of this": Morozov, "Two Decades of the Web."

163 **"assault on human autonomy"**: Joanna Kavenna, "Shoshana Zuboff: 'Surveillance Capitalism Is an Assault on Human Autonomy,'" *Guardian*, October 4, 2019, https://www.theguardian.com/books/2019/oct/04/shoshana-zuboff-surveillance-capitalism-assault-human-automomy-digital-privacy.

163 **"catalysed awareness"**: "AI and Problems of Scale," Benedict Evans, April 29, 2024, https://www.ben-evans.com/benedictevans/2024/4/29/problems-of-scale-z7mrb.

163 **#DeleteFacebook campaign**: Tiffany Hsu, "For Many Facebook Users, a 'Last Straw' That Led Them to Quit," *The New York Times*, March 21, 2018, https://www.nytimes.com/2018/03/21/technology/users-abandon-facebook.html.

163 **generational exodus**: Olivia Solon, "Teens Are Abandoning Facebook in Dramatic Numbers, Study Finds," *Guardian*, June 1, 2018, https://www.theguardian.com/technology/2018/jun/01/facebook-teens-leaving-instagram-snapchat-study-user-numbers.

164 **"use the internet"**: Leo Mirani, "Millions of Facebook Users Have No Idea They're Using the Internet," *Quartz*, February 9, 2015, https://qz.com/333313/milliions-of-facebook-users-have-no-idea-theyre-using-the-internet.

164 **global messaging app**: Robert McMillan, "You May Not Use WhatsApp, but the Rest of the World Sure Does," *Wired*, February 20, 2014, https://www.wired.com/2014/02/whatsapp-rules-rest-world.

164 **issue of *Time***: Lev Grossman, "The Man Who Wired the World," *Time*, December 4, 2014, https://time.com/magazine/us/3617654/december-15th-2014-vol-184-no-23-u-s.

164 **banned Free Basics**: Rahul Bhatia, "The Inside Story of Facebook's Biggest Setback," *Guardian*, May 12, 2016, https://www.theguardian.com/technology/2016/may/12/facebook-free-basics-india-zuckerberg.

164 **Aquila drone**: Adam Satariano, "Facebook Halts Aquila, Its Internet Drone Project," *New York Times*, June 27, 2018, https://www.nytimes.com/2018/06/27/technology/facebook-drone-internet.html.

164 **claims to *The Verge***: Casey Newton, "Facebook Takes Flight," *Verge*, July 21, 2016, https://www.theverge.com/a/mark-zuckerberg-future-of-facebook/aquila-drone-internet; Jacob Silverman, "Spies,

Lies, and Stonewalling: What It's Like to Report on Facebook," *Columbia Journalism Review*, January 1, 2020, https://www.cjr.org/special_report/reporting-on-facebook.php.

164 **exploded on the launchpad**: Julia Carrie Wong, "SpaceX Rocket Explosion: Mark Zuckerberg Laments Loss of Internet.org Satellite," *Guardian*, September 2, 2016, https://www.theguardian.com/science/2016/sep/01/mark-zuckerberg-spacex-explosion-africa-internet.

164 **quietly abandoned Aquila**: Hanna Kozlowska, "Facebook Is Stepping Back from Its Plan to Bring the Internet to the World via Giant Drones," *Quartz*, June 27, 2018, https://qz.com/1315864/project-aquila-facebook-is-stepping-back-from-its-plan-to-bring-the-internet-to-the-world-via-giant-drones.

164 **Google's similar initiative**: Matt Burgess, "Google Quietly Shut Its Internet Drone Project Last Year," *Wired*, January 12, 2017, https://www.wired.com/story/google-project-titan-web-drones.

164 **Project Loon worked**: Jack Nicas, "Google's Parent Births New Businesses: Balloons and Drones," *New York Times*, July 11, 2018, https://www.nytimes.com/2018/07/11/technology/google-drones-internet-balloons.html.

164 **Alphabet closed it**: Daisuke Wakabayashi, "Google-Linked Balloon Project to Provide Cell Service Will Close," *New York Times*, January 21, 2021, https://www.nytimes.com/2021/01/21/technology/loon-google-balloons.html.

164 **4G data free**: Charles Riley and Medhavi Arora, "India's Richest Man Offers Free 4G to One Billion People," CNN Business, September 6, 2016, https://money.cnn.com/2016/09/06/technology/india-reliance-jio-4g-internet.

164 **top Google searches**: "Year in Search 2016," Google Trends, 2016, https://trends.withgoogle.com/year-in-search/2016.

164 **top three were**: "Google's Year in Search 2021," Google Trends, 2021, https://trends.withgoogle.com/year-in-search/2021.

165 **military exploited Facebook**: Paul Mozur, "A Genocide Incited on Facebook, with Posts from Myanmar's Military," *New York Times*, October 15, 2018, https://www.nytimes.com/2018/10/15/technology/myanmar-facebook-genocide.html.

165 **resulting ethnic cleansing**: Hannah Ellis-Petersen, "Facebook Removes Accounts Associated with Myanmar Military,"

Guardian, August 27, 2018, https://www
.theguardian.com/technology/2018/aug/27
/facebook-removes-accounts-myanmar
-military-un-report-genocide-rohingya.

165 **over a million:** "Rohingya Refugee Crisis
Explained," USA for UNHCR, August 22,
2024, https://www.unrefugees.org/news
/rohingya-refugee-crisis-explained.

165 **led to mob lynchings:** Geeta Anand and
Suhasini Raj, "Rumors on WhatsApp Ig-
nite 2 Mob Attacks in India, Killing 7,"
New York Times, May 25, 2017, https://
www.nytimes.com/2017/05/25/world/asia
/india-vigilante-mob-violence.html.

165 **launched a $50,000 contest:** Prabhjote
Gill, "WhatsApp Is Offering Rewards for
a Solution to Deal with Misinformation in
India," *Business Insider India*, July 6, 2018,
https://www.businessinsider.in/whatsapp
-is-offering-rewards-for-a-solution-to
-deal-with-misinformation-in-india/articles
how/64889026.cms.

165 **"very strange year":** "Reflecting on One
Very, Very Strange Year at Uber," *Susan
Fowler* (blog), February 19, 2017, https://
www.susanjfowler.com/blog/2017/2/19
/reflecting-on-one-very-strange-year-at
-uber.

165 **raised $1.2 billion:** Liz Gannes, "Uber
Valued at $17 Billion in New "Record-
Breaking" Round," *Vox*, June 6, 2014,
https://www.vox.com/2014/6/6/11627710
/uber-valued-at-17-billion-in-new-record
-breaking-round.

165 **"It was an organization":** Fowler, "Reflecting on One."

165 **fired twenty employees:** Olivia Solon,
"Uber Fires More Than 20 Employees
After Sexual Harassment Investigation,"
Guardian, June 6, 2017, https://www.the
guardian.com/technology/2017/jun/06
/uber-fires-employees-sexual-harassment
-investigation.

166 **"Do not have sex":** Kara Swisher and Jo-
hana Bhuiyan, "Uber CEO Kalanick Advised Employees on Sex Rules for a
Company Celebration in 2013 'Miami
Letter,'" *Vox*, June 9, 2017, https://www
.vox.com/2017/6/8/15765514/2013-miami
-letter-uber-ceo-kalanick-employees-sex
-rules-company-celebration.

166 **leveraged cheap capital:** Ranjan Roy,
"ZIRP Explains the World," *Margins*,
March 6, 2020, https://www.readmargins
.com/p/zirp-explains-the-world.

166 **monopoly that would allow:** Jeff Spross,
"Uber Is Basically Promising Investors It
Will Become a Monopoly," *Week*, April 15,

2019, https://theweek.com/articles/834836
/uber-basically-promising-investors
-become-monopoly.

166 **its China operations:** Paul Mozur and
Mike Isaac, "Uber to Sell to Rival Didi
Chuxing and Create New Business in
China," *New York Times*, August 1, 2016,
https://www.nytimes.com/2016/08/02
/business/dealbook/china-uber-didi
-chuxing.html.

166 **pedestrian in Tempe:** Troy Griggs and
Daisuke Wakabayashi, "How a Self-
Driving Uber Killed a Pedestrian in Arizona," *New York Times*, March 21, 2018,
https://www.nytimes.com/interactive
/2018/03/20/us/self-driving-uber
-pedestrian-killed.html.

166 **self-driving unit:** Aarian Marshall, "Uber
Gives Up on the Self-Driving Dream,"
Wired, December 7, 2020, https://www
.wired.com/story/uber-gives-up-self
-driving-dream.

166 **$120 billion valuation:** Mike Isaac, Mi-
chael J. de la Merced, and Andrew Ross
Sorkin, "How the Promise of a $120 Bil-
lion Uber I.P.O. Evaporated," *New York
Times*, May 15, 2019, https://www.ny
times.com/2019/05/15/technology/uber
-ipo-price.html.

166 **himself $5.4 billion:** Rachel Sandler and
Biz Carson, "Uber IPO: Here's Who Stood
to Get Big Payouts," *Forbes*, May 10, 2019,
https://www.forbes.com/sites/rachel
sandler/2019/05/10/uber-ipo-winners
-kalanick-graves.

166 **like Tim Ferriss:** Alexis C. Madrigal, "Why
Silicon Valley Loved Uber More Than Everyone Else," *Atlantic*, May 24, 2019,
https://www.theatlantic.com/technology
/archive/2019/05/why-silicon-valley-loved
-uber-more-everyone-else/590203.

167 **profit until 2023:** Jasper Jolly and Graeme
Wearden, "Landmark Moment as Uber
Unveils First Annual Profit as Limited
Company," *Guardian*, February 7, 2024,
https://www.theguardian.com/technol
ogy/2024/feb/07/landmark-moment-as
-uber-unveils-first-annual-profit-as
-limited-company.

167 **drivers as employees:** Noam Scheiber,
"Is Gig Work a Job? Uber and Others Are
Maneuvering to Shape the Answer," *New
York Times*, March 26, 2019, https://www
.nytimes.com/2019/03/26/business/econ
omy/gig-economy-lobbying.html.

167 **Uber further slashed driver revenue
shares:** Michael Sainato, "'They Treat Us
like Crap': Uber Drivers Feel Poor and

Powerless on Eve of IPO," *Guardian*, May 7, 2019, https://www.theguardian.com/technology/2019/may/07/uber-drivers-feel-poor-powerless-ipo-looms.

167 **"I don't want to live"**: *Silicon Valley*, season 2, episode 1, "Sand Hill Shuffle," written by Clay Tarver, directed by Mike Judge, aired April 12, 2015, on HBO.

167 **"local, mobile, social"**: *Silicon Valley*, season 1, episode 7, "Proof of Concept," written by Clay Tarver, directed by Mike Judge, aired May 18, 2014, on HBO.

168 **fall of Google Glass**: Nick Bilton, "Why Google Glass Broke," *New York Times*, February 4, 2015, https://www.nytimes.com/2015/02/05/style/why-google-glass-broke.html.

168 **skydiver with Glass**: Bilton, "Why Google Glass Broke."

168 **"considered the Gadget"**: Bilton, "Why Google Glass Broke."

168 **models in Glass**: Bilton, "Why Google Glass Broke."

168 **like EssilorLuxottica**: Claire Cain Miller, "Biggest Eyewear Company Signs on with Google Glass," *New York Times*, March 24, 2014, https://www.nytimes.com/2014/03/25/technology/biggest-eyewear-company-signs-on-with-google-glass.html.

168 **blogger Robert Scoble**: Biz Carson, "The Guy Who Ruined Google Glass with a Shower Selfie Is at It Again with Snapchat's Spectacles," Yahoo! Finance, November 17, 2016, https://finance.yahoo.com/news/guy-ruined-google-glass-shower-010819720.html.

168 **"nerd goggles"**: "Snap Inc: It's Snapchat, but Now with Video-Recording 'Spectacles,'" *Guardian*, September 26, 2016, https://www.theguardian.com/technology/shortcuts/2016/sep/26/snap-inc-snapchat-spectacles-video-recording-sunglasses.

168 **that it was filming**: Charles Arthur, "Google Glass: Is It a Threat to Our Privacy?," *Guardian*, March 6, 2013, https://www.theguardian.com/technology/2013/mar/06/google-glass-threat-to-our-privacy.

168 **pulled Glass from**: Ron Miller, "Google Glass Is Alive and Well and Living in the Enterprise," *TechCrunch*, March 4, 2015, https://techcrunch.com/2015/03/04/google-glass-is-alive-and-well-and-living-in-the-enterprise.

168 **quietly discontinuing**: Kif Leswing, "Google Ends Enterprise Sales of Google Glass, Its Augmented Reality Smartglasses," CNBC, March 15, 2023, https://www.cnbc.com/2023/03/15/google-discontinues-google-glass-enterprise-end-to-early-ar-project.html.

168 **nausea for many users**: James Clayton, "Meta: Can the Firm's New Headset Stop Virtual Reality Sickness?," *BBC News*, October 3, 2023, https://www.bbc.com/news/technology-66980483.

169 **playing Steve Jobs**: Nicolas Vega, "Ashton Kutcher's Tech Investments Made Him Millions—Now He Only Takes 'Roles That I Want to Play,'" CNBC, February 2, 2023, https://www.cnbc.com/2023/02/02/ashton-kutcher-made-millions-investing-doesnt-need-a-hollywood-check.html.

169 **acquisition of Beats**: Brian X. Chen, "Apple to Pay $3 Billion to Buy Beats," *New York Times*, May 28, 2014, https://www.nytimes.com/2014/05/29/technology/apple-confirms-its-3-billion-deal-for-beats-electronics.html.

169 **their exaggerated bass**: Vlad Savov, "Embrace the Bass: Beats Headphones Are Popular for a Reason," *Verge*, January 27, 2016, https://www.theverge.com/2016/1/27/10840614/beats-by-dre-headphones-bass.

169 **nonfunctional weights**: Sarah Griffiths, "A Cheap Trick? Teardown Suggests Beats Headphones Contain Metal 'Weights' to Make Them Appear Better Quality," *Mail Online*, June 19, 2015, https://www.dailymail.co.uk/sciencetech/article-3131799/A-cheap-trick-Teardown-suggests-Beats-headphones-contain-metal-weights-make-appear-better-quality.html.

169 **he acquired Tidal**: Peter Kafka, "Why Did Jack Dorsey Buy Jay-Z's Failed Music Service?," *Vox*, March 4, 2021, https://www.vox.com/recode/22313268/tidal-square-jay-z-jack-dorsey-nft-explainer.

169 **$297 million**: Kafka, "Why Did Jack Dorsey Buy."

169 **"$300 million bar tab"**: Caleb Naysmith, "Jack Dorsey's '$300 Million Bar Tab' to Rub Shoulders with Jay-Z Results in Lawsuit," Yahoo! Finance, June 14, 2023, https://finance.yahoo.com/news/jack-dorseys-300-million-bar-145048096.html.

169 **print to video**: Reeves Wiedeman, "A Company Built on a Bluff," *New York*, June 10, 2018, https://nymag.com/intelligencer/2018/06/inside-vice-media-shane-smith.html.

169 **$50 billion valuation**: Wiedeman, "A Company Built on a Bluff."

169 **$70 million investment:** Wiedeman, "A Company Built on a Bluff."

169 **second-least-cool brand:** Wiedeman, "A Company Built on a Bluff."

170 **"Dress was an unmitigated":** Ben Smith, *Traffic: Genius, Rivalry, and Delusion in the Billion-Dollar Race to Go Viral* (Penguin Press, 2023), 210.

170 **around a watermelon:** Dave Mosher, "The Internet Just Lost Its Mind over an Exploding Watermelon," *Business Insider*, April 8, 2016, https://www.businessinsider.com/watermelon-rubberband-explosion-buzzfeed-video-2016-4.

170 **"I loved the traffic":** Smith, *Traffic*, 253.

170 **success of its hosts:** April Glaser, "How BuzzFeed Makes Money from Its Tasty Food Videos," *Vox*, February 16, 2017, https://www.vox.com/2017/2/14/14594782/buzzfeed-makes-money-from-its-tasty-food-videos-facebook.

170 **elite curation:** The *YouTube Play* exhibit at the Guggenheim was one example; see also Mark Bergen, "Just a Few People Crowned Some of YouTube's Earliest Hits," *Atlantic*, September 5, 2022, https://www.theatlantic.com/technology/archive/2022/09/youtube-homepage-editor-google-algorithm-book-excerpt/671339.

170 **outperformed legacy institutions:** Taylor Lorenz, *Extremely Online: The Untold Story of Fame, Influence, and Power on the Internet* (Simon & Schuster, 2023), 248.

170 **"situations involving cheating":** Russell Brandom, "Inside Elsagate, the Conspiracy-Fueled War on Creepy YouTube Kids Videos," *Verge*, December 8, 2017, https://www.theverge.com/2017/12/8/16751206/elsagate-youtube-ids-creepy-conspiracy-theory.

170 **advertisers briefly boycotted:** Todd Spangler, "YouTube Faces Advertiser Boycott over Videos with Kids That Attracted Sexual Predators," *Variety*, November 25, 2017, https://variety.com/2017/digital/news/youtube-ad-boycott-pedophile-sexual-children-videos-1202622790.

171 **"We wanted flying cars":** George Packer, *The Unwinding: An Inner History of the New America* (Farrar, Straus and Giroux, 2013), 384.

171 **become its "counterculture":** Rob Walker, "Inside the Wild, Wacky, Profitable World of Boing Boing," *Fast Company*, November 30, 2010, https://www.fastcompany.com/1702167/inside-wild-wacky-profitable-world-boing-boing.

CHAPTER 12: ULTRAPOPTIMISM

172 **"Her biggest strength":** Jill Mapes, "Folklore," *Pitchfork*, July 27, 2020, https://pitchfork.com/reviews/albums/taylor-swift-folklore.

172 **blaming the 8.0 rating:** Gita Jackson, "Taylor Swift Super Fans Are Furious About a Good Review," *Vice*, July 31, 2020, https://www.vice.com/en/article/v7gpx8/taylor-swift-super-fans-are-furious-about-a-good-review.

172 **didn't personally assign:** Marlene Lenthang, "Taylor Swift Fans Share Music Critic's Address, Phone Numbers and Threaten to Burn Down Her Home Hours After She Gave the Singer's New Album an 8/10 Review That Followers Deemed That Was Not Enough," *Daily Mail*, July 30, 2020, https://www.dailymail.co.uk/news/article-8578931/Taylor-Swift-fans-harass-Pitchfork-editor-published-review-singers-new-album.html.

172 **"brutally quantified world":** Ben Beaumont-Thomas, "Hardcore Pop Fans Are Abusing Critics—and Putting Acclaim Before Art," *Guardian*, August 3, 2020, https://www.theguardian.com/music/2020/aug/03/taylor-swift-folklore-hardcore-pop-fans-abusing-critics-stan.

172 **"Anyone who comes after":** Lenthang, "Taylor Swift Fans Share."

172 **"too many emails":** Laura Bradley, "Taylor Swift Remains Silent as Fans Doxx and Harass Music Critic Over 'Folklore' Review," *Daily Beast*, July 30, 2020, https://www.thedailybeast.com/taylor-swift-remains-silent-as-fans-doxx-and-harass-music-critic-over-folkore-review.

173 **7 percent of their reviews:** Ruby Justice Thelot (@being_on_line), "I cant speak for the NYT, I dont read the Guardian, and Rolling Stone hasnt been relevant in decades, but Pitchfork has gone *Pop*. I took a look at all the reviews from '99 to '18 and the results were clear: more Pop music was reviewed and it was reviewed increasingly favorably," X (formerly Twitter), December 28, 2023, https://x.com/being_on_line/status/1740215917567422784.

173 **Condé Nast acquired *Pitchfork*:** "Pitchfork Acquired by Condé Nast," *Pitchfork*, October 13, 2015, https://pitchfork.com/news/61621-pitchfork-acquired-by-conde-nast.

173 **"Taylor Swift Day"**: Ryan Dombal, Anna Gaca, Jayson Greene, et al., "The History of Pitchfork's Reviews Section in 38 Reviews," *Pitchfork*, May 25, 2021, https://pitchfork.com/features/lists-and-guides/the-history-of-the-pitchfork-reviews-section-in-38-important-reviews.

173 **"white, indie rock dudes"**: Dan Kois, Nitish Pahwa, and Luke Winkie, "The Oral History of Pitchfork," *Slate*, March 19, 2024, https://slate.com/culture/2024/03/pitchfork-oral-history-music-festival-conde-nast-review.html.

173 **"There was no mandate"**: Kois et al., "Oral History of Pitchfork."

173 **most of its essays**: Saul Austerlitz, "The Pernicious Rise of Poptimism," *New York Times Magazine*, April 4, 2014, https://www.nytimes.com/2014/04/06/magazine/the-pernicious-rise-of-poptimism.html.

173 **"coverage of stars"**: Austerlitz, "Pernicious Rise of Poptimism."

174 **"our political system"**: Kaitlyn Tiffany, *Everything I Need I Get from You: How Fangirls Created the Internet as We Know It* (Farrar, Straus and Giroux, 2022), 225.

174 **ups and downs**: Mark Fisher, "Poptimism (Yes, Again)," *K-punk*, February 5, 2004, https://k-punk.org/poptimism-yes-again.

174 **"You see yourself"**: Joe Coscarelli, "How Pop Music Fandom Became Sports, Politics, Religion and All-Out War," *New York Times*, December 25, 2020, https://www.nytimes.com/2020/12/25/arts/music/pop-music-superfans-stans.html.

174 **"consumption doesn't negate"**: Haaniyah Angus, "Why the Normalization of Stan Culture Is Unhealthy," *Medium*, January 27, 2019, https://haaniyah.medium.com/why-the-normalization-of-stan-culture-is-unhealthy-b37fb8024346 (site discontinued).

174 **Wanna Thompson tweeted**: Michael Schulman, "Superfans: A Love Story," *New Yorker*, September 9, 2019, https://www.newyorker.com/magazine/2019/09/16/superfans-a-love-story.

175 **just seven million**: Alan Sculley, "Getting Back the Jagged Edge," *Herald-Tribune*, June 24, 2005, https://www.heraldtribune.com/story/news/2005/06/24/getting-back-the-jagged-edge/28850970007.

175 **"capture the flag"**: Spencer Kornhaber, "Kanye's Creepy Comeback," *Atlantic*, March 18, 2024, https://www.theatlantic.com/culture/archive/2024/03/kanye-west-ty-dolla-sign-carnival-review/677789.

175 **the "Tumblr left"**: Angela Nagle, *Kill All Normies: Online Culture Wars from 4chan and Tumblr to Trump and the Alt-Right* (Zero Books, 2017), 69.

175 **"anti-heteronormative"**: Tiffany, *Everything I Need*, 83.

175 **"pop idols' queer stans"**: Amanda Montell, *The Age of Magical Overthinking: Notes on Modern Irrationality* (Thorsons, 2024), 23.

175 **"Whether she is conscious"**: Anna Marks, "Look What We Made Taylor Swift Do," *New York Times*, January 4, 2024, https://www.nytimes.com/2024/01/04/opinion/taylor-swift-queer.html.

175 **locals (casual fans)**: Tiffany, *Everything I Need*, 95.

176 **Little Monsters shared**: Coscarelli, "How Pop Music Fandom."

176 **"Pop fandom"**: Coscarelli, "How Pop Music Fandom."

176 **"almost as a rule"**: Tiffany, *Everything I Need*, 73.

176 **Twilight slash fiction**: Ewan Morrison, "In the Beginning, There Was Fan Fiction: From the Four Gospels to Fifty Shades," *Guardian*, August 13, 2012, https://www.theguardian.com/books/2012/aug/13/fan-fiction-fifty-shades-grey.

176 **"we're promoting BTS"**: Coscarelli, "How Pop Music Fandom."

177 **BTS Army propelled**: Tamar Herman, "BTS' Army React to 'Love Yourself: Tear' Topping the Billboard 200," *Billboard*, May 27, 2018, https://www.billboard.com/music/pop/bts-army-love-yourself-tear-billboard-200-reactions-8458042.

177 **headlining it four years**: Shim Sun-ah, "Blackpink Performs at Coachella Festival as 1st-Ever Korean Headliner," *Yonhap News Agency*, April 17, 2023, https://en.yna.co.kr/view/AEN20230417002100315.

177 **"Larry" theory**: Tiffany, *Everything I Need*, 194–98.

177 **rumors of fan suicides**: Alexander Abad Santos, "The Internet Is Mourning 42 Suicidal, Potentially Non-Existent One Direction Fans," *Atlantic*, August 16, 2013, https://www.theatlantic.com/culture/archive/2013/08/internet-mourning-42-suicidal-one-direction-fans-might-not-even-exist/312076.

177 **"utter and irrevocable"**: Tiffany, *Everything I Need*, 121.

177 **"To every little monster"**: Lady Gaga (@LadyGaga), Instagram, April 9, 2018, https://www.instagram.com/p/BhVx0RyB1xX.

177 **master recordings:** Tim Ingham, "Reliving the Taylor Swift Catalog Sale Saga (and Following the Money . . .)," *Music Business Worldwide*, June 14, 2023, https://www.musicbusinessworldwide.com/taylor-swift-catalog-sale-following-the-money.

178 **due to his work with Kanye West:** Natalie Finn, "Kanye West Joins Forces with Scooter Braun—Why Working with Justin Bieber's Manager Actually Makes Perfect Sense for Him," *E! News*, March 31, 2016, https://www.eonline.com/news/752715/kanye-west-joins-forces-with-scooter-braun-why-working-with-justin-bieber-s-manager-actually-makes-perfect-sense-for-him.

178 **"say to all":** "Taylor Swift Fires Back at Kanye West in Acceptance Speech," *Hollywood Reporter*, February 15, 2016, https://www.hollywoodreporter.com/news/music-news/grammys-2016-taylor-swift-acceptance-speech-album-year-kanye-west-famous-866096.

178 **recorded phone call:** Grace Gavilanes and Sophie Dodd, "A Complete Timeline of Taylor Swift and Kanye West's Feud," *People*, December 8, 2023, https://people.com/music/kanye-west-famous-inside-his-and-taylor-swifts-relationship-history.

178 **"career death":** Gavilanes and Dodd, "A Complete Timeline."

178 **"incessant, manipulative bullying":** Gavilanes and Dodd, "A Complete Timeline."

178 **"revenge porn":** Gavilanes and Dodd, "A Complete Timeline."

178 **"Why don't you just die":** Mark Savage, "Scooter Braun's Family 'Received Death Threats' Following Taylor Swift Feud," *BBC News*, November 22, 2019, https://www.bbc.com/news/entertainment-arts-50503713.

178 **to the Disney family:** Ingham, "Reliving the Taylor Swift Catalog."

178 **"Taylor's Version" soundalikes:** Constance Grady, "Why Taylor Swift Is Rerecording All Her Old Songs," *Vox*, August 10, 2023, https://www.vox.com/culture/22278732/taylor-swift-re-recording-1989-speak-now-enchanted-mine-master-rights-scooter-braun.

178 **Each rerecorded album:** Dorian Lynskey, "It's the Age of Swiftonomics—but Will Taylor Swift's Phenomenal Success Trickle Down?," *Guardian*, June 1, 2024, https://www.theguardian.com/music/article/2024/jun/01/its-the-age-of-swift

onomics-but-will-taylor-swifts-phenomenal-success-trickle-down.

178 **canonical version:** "Next time you listen to any of Taylor Swift's first six albums, make sure to listen to 'Taylor's Version' to avoid supporting the men who took advantage of Swift's fame and talent." Adelyn Rabbitt, "Why 'Taylor's Version' Is Important," *Tower*, November 3, 2023, https://sbadamsthetower.com/10394/ae/why-taylors-version-is-important.

179 **Iovine's "greatest hits":** Allen Hughes, dir., *The Defiant Ones*, Alcon Entertainment, 2017.

179 **2014 *Variety* survey:** Susanne Ault, "Survey: YouTube Stars More Popular Than Mainstream Celebs Among U.S. Teens," *Variety*, August 5, 2014, https://variety.com/2014/digital/news/survey-youtube-stars-more-popular-than-mainstream-celebs-among-u-s-teens-1201275245.

180 **"intimate and authentic" connection:** Ault, "YouTube Stars More Popular."

180 **"Social media was practically":** Taylor Lorenz, *Extremely Online: The Untold Story of Fame, Influence, and Power on the Internet* (Simon & Schuster, 2023), 38–39.

180 **Bethany Mota's "haul videos":** Sean Hollister, "Meet Bethany Mota, the Teen Who Turned YouTube Shopping Sprees into a Fashion Career," *Verge*, January 20, 2014, https://www.theverge.com/culture/2014/1/20/5329356/bethany-mota-youtube-shopping-celebrity-turned-teen-fashion.

180 **accelerated this trend:** Emily Hund, *The Influencer Industry: The Quest for Authenticity on Social Media* (Princeton University Press, 2023), 28.

180 **raised this business model:** Zameena Mejia, "Kylie Jenner Reportedly Makes $1 Million per Paid Instagram Post—Here's How Much Other Top Influencers Get," *CNBC*, July 31, 2018, https://www.cnbc.com/2018/07/31/kylie-jenner-makes-1-million-per-paid-instagram-post-hopper-hq-says.html.

180 **$26.5 million in 2018:** Amy Chozick, "Keeping Up with the Kardashian Cash Flow," *New York Times*, March 30, 2019, https://www.nytimes.com/2019/03/30/style/kardashians-interview.html.

180 **getting cosmetic surgery:** Chase Peterson-Withorn, "Inside Kylie Jenner's Web of Lies—and Why She's No Longer a Billionaire," *Forbes*, June 1, 2020, https://www.forbes.com/sites/chasewithorn

/2020/05/29/inside-kylie-jennerss-web-of -lies-and-why-shes-no-longer-a-billionaire.

181 **"lip kits":** Natalie Robehmed, "At 21, Kylie Jenner Becomes the Youngest Self-Made Billionaire Ever," *Forbes*, March 5, 2019, https://www.forbes.com/sites/natalie robehmed/2019/03/05/at-21-kylie-jenner -becomes-the-youngest-self-made -billionaire-ever.

181 **"youngest-ever self-made billionaire":** Robehmed, "At 21, Kylie Jenner Becomes."

181 ***Forbes* retracted the title:** Peterson-Withorn, "Inside Kylie Jenner's Web."

181 **scouts, and support teams:** Lorenz, *Extremely Online*, 212.

181 **"hype houses":** Lorenz, *Extremely Online*, 178.

181 **boutique Paul Smith:** Lorenz, *Extremely Online*, 212.

181 **"Absent a notable skill":** Amanda Mull, "It's All So . . . Premiocre," *Atlantic*, April 2020, https://www.theatlantic.com/maga zine/archive/2020/04/its-all-so-premiocre /606775.

181 **Rich Kids of Instagram:** Robert Wabash, "The Very Best of the Rich Kids of Insta-gram Tumblr," Ranker, October 19, 2023, https://www.ranker.com/list/the-very -best-of-the-rich-kids-of-instagram -tumblr/robert-wabash.

181 ***Rich Kids of Beverly Hills*:** Zara Wong, "Rich Kids of Instagram Tumblr Inspires a Television Show," *Vogue Australia*, August 9, 2013, https://www.vogue.com.au/culture /features/rich-kids-of-instagram -tumblr-inspires-a-television-show/news -story/5d261475127e2dc3e6a32d0693d bba64.

182 **Bot farms in Indonesia:** Emma Grey El-lis, "Fighting Instagram's $1.3 Billion Problem—Fake Followers," *Wired*, Sep-tember 10, 2019, https://www.wired.com /story/instagram-fake-followers; "3 Best Sites to Buy Chinese Instagram Followers (from China)," Semiocast, January 28, 2025, https://semiocast.com/best-sites-to -buy-chinese-instagram-followers.

182 **"Instagram rapture":** Allison P. Davis, "The Instagram Rapture Threw Us into Existential Crisis," *Cut*, December 18, 2014, https://www.thecut.com/2014/12 /insta-rapture-caused-an-existential -crisis.html.

182 **in one day:** Davis, "Instagram Rapture Threw Us."

182 **Private Jet Studio:** See "Салон самолета Gulfstream 650 (фотостудия)," Private Jet Studio, 2017, https://pjstudio.ru/airplane.

182 **The "pioneering drill sound":** Jaimie Hodgson, "The Secret History of Drill," *Vice*, July 25, 2023, https://www.vice.com /en/article/secret-history-drill-music.

182 **Ed Sheeran sixty:** Frances Perraudin, "How Tattoos Went from Subculture to Pop Culture," *Guardian*, October 26, 2018, https://www.theguardian.com/fash ion/2018/oct/26/how-tattoos-went-from -subculture-to-pop-culture.

182 **implanted a diamond:** Danielle Cohen, "Exactly How Do You Embed a 10-Carat Diamond in Your Forehead, Anyway?," *GQ*, February 4, 2021, https://www.gq .com/story/how-to-embed-a-diamond-in -your-forehead.

183 **"keys to success":** Hua Hsu, "The Goofy Charm of DJ Khaled's 'The Keys,'" *New Yorker*, December 15, 2016, https://www .newyorker.com/books/page-turner/the -goofy-charm-of-dj-khaleds-the-keys.

183 **"connection that feels":** Josh Duboff, "It's the Golden Age of Celebrity Snap-chat," *Vanity Fair*, March 9, 2016, https:// www.vanityfair.com/hollywood/2016/03 /snapchat-celebrities-kylie-jenner-dj -khaled.

183 **"parasocial gap":** Montell, *Age of Magi-cal Overthinking*, 18.

183 **just fifty videos:** Lorenz, *Extremely Online*, 242.

183 **Trade Commission decreed:** Lorenz, *Extremely Online*, 242.

183 **#sponsored hashtags:** Lorenz, *Extremely Online*, 224.

184 **Burnout became rampant:** Lorenz, *Extremely Online*, 352.

184 **Phan disappeared:** Kathleen Hou, "Mi-chelle Phan Was YouTube's Biggest Beauty Star. Then She Vanished." *Cut*, September 26, 2019, https://www.thecut.com/2019/09 /michelle-phan-youtube-beauty-star-on -why-she-left.html.

184 **partnership with Disney:** "Disney Drops YouTuber PewDiePie over Anti-Semitism Claims," *BBC News*, February 14, 2017, https://www.bbc.com/news/business -38965377.

184 **PewDiePie was no longer:** "Disney Drops YouTuber."

184 **"fake acid attack":** "Arya Mosallah: Prankster Apologises for 'Acid Attack' Style Video," *BBC News*, February 5, 2018, https://www.bbc.com/news/blogs-trend ing-42948610.

184 **Aokigahara "suicide forest":** Tarleton Gillespie, "The Logan Paul YouTube Con-troversy and What We Should Expect

from Internet Platforms," *Vox*, January 16, 2018, https://www.vox.com/the-big-idea /2018/1/12/16881046/logan-paul-you tube-controversy-internet-companies.

184 **pedophilic comments:** "YouTube Cuts Off Shane Dawson's Ad Money," *BBC News*, July 1, 2020, https://www.bbc.com /news/entertainment-arts-53248775.

184 **by a rape scandal:** Florence O'Connor and Zoe Haylock, "A Timeline of the David Dobrik Allegations and Controversies," *Vulture*, January 10, 2025, https:// www.vulture.com/article/david-dobrik -allegations-controversies-timeline.html.

184 **"jail right now":** "Cancelled Youtuber List Tier List Community Rankings," Tiermaker, July 24, 2024, https://tiermaker.com /categories/youtube-and-streaming/can celled-youtuber-list-551131.

184 **XXXTentacion was murdered:** Nadine El-Bawab, "3 Men Found Guilty of Killing Rapper XXXTentacion," ABC News, March 20, 2023, https://abcnews.go.com/Enter tainment/3-men-found-guilty-killing -rapper-xxxtentacion/story?id=97767286.

184 **got an early release:** Caroline Busta, "The Internet Didn't Kill Counterculture—You Just Won't Find It on Instagram," *Document*, January 14, 2021, https://www.documentjournal.com/2021 /01/the-internet-didnt-kill-countercul ture-you-just-wont-find-it-on-instagram.

185 **Super Bowl commercials:** Brian Steinberg, "Bud Light Asks Super Bowl Viewers to Pick the Ad They Want to See," *Variety*, January 29, 2020, https://variety.com/2020 /tv/news/bud-light-super-bowl-commer cial-post-malone-1203485188.

185 **Grant Rindner observed:** Grant Rindner, "Comfort in the Discomforting: The History of SoundCloud Rap, the Face-Tatted, Hair-Dyed Vision That Showed Hiphop's Future," The Ringer, December 16, 2021, https://www.theringer.com/2021/12 /16/22838951/juice-wrld-soundcloud-rap -history-retrospective.

185 **allegations of bullying:** "Chrissy Teigen Says She's Depressed After Bullying Accusations," *BBC News*, July 15, 2021, https:// www.bbc.com/news/newsbeat-57846663.

185 **show fell through:** Kelly Connolly, "Josh Ostrovsky: Fat Jew's Comedy Central Pilot Dropped 'Several Months Ago,'" *Entertainment Weekly*, August 17, 2015, https:// ew.com/article/2015/08/17/josh-ostrovsky -fat-jew-comedy-central-deal-dropped.

185 **routinely stole jokes:** Alex Abad-Santos, "The Fat Jew's Instagram Plagiarism Scan-

dal, Explained," *Vox*, August 19, 2015, https://www.vox.com/2015/8/19/9178145 /fat-jew-plagiarism-instagram.

185 **"now deeply cognizant":** Lorenz, *Extremely Online*, 7.

185 **"There are no hooks":** Pharrell Williams, *Pharrell-isms*, ed. Larry Warsh (Princeton University Press, 2023), 83.

CHAPTER 13:
CAPITALIST SURREALISM

186 **Fleischmann yeast empire:** John Carreyrou, *Bad Blood: Secrets and Lies in a Silicon Valley Startup* (Vintage Books, 2018), 12.

186 **"I want to be a billionaire":** Carreyrou, *Bad Blood*, 11.

186 **gruff masculine timbre:** Danielle Cohen, "Elizabeth Holmes Has Changed Her Voice Again," *Cut*, May 8, 2023, https:// www.thecut.com/2023/05/elizabeth -holmes-voice-new-york-times-interview .html.

186 **valued at $9 billion:** Carreyrou, *Bad Blood*, 257.

186 **billionaire woman:** Katia Savchuk, "Youngest of the Richest Self-Made Women," *Forbes*, May 27, 2015, https:// www.forbes.com/pictures/gefl45eeee/eliz abeth-holmes.

186 **"golden age of fraud":** Harriet Agnew, "Jim Chanos: 'We Are in the Golden Age of Fraud,'" *Financial Times*, July 24, 2020, https://www.ft.com/content/ccb46309 -bba4-4fb7-b3fa-ecb17ea0e9cf.

187 **"the election of Donald Trump":** Jia Tolentino, *Trick Mirror: Reflections on Self-Delusion* (Fourth Estate, 2019), 162.

187 **former secretary of state:** Carreyrou, *Bad Blood*, 298–309.

187 **"one's internal thoughts":** Amanda Montell, *The Age of Magical Overthinking: Notes on Modern Irrationality* (Thorsons, 2024), 5.

187 **"This is what happens":** Abigail Stevenson, "Theranos CEO Fires Back at WSJ: I Was Shocked," CNBC, October 15, 2015, https://www.cnbc.com/2015/10/15/ther anos-ceo-fires-back-at-wsj-i-was-shocked .html.

188 **herself as Anna Delvey:** Jessica Pressler, "Maybe She Had So Much Money She Just Lost Track of It," *Cut*, May 28, 2018, https://www.thecut.com/article/how -anna-delvey-tricked-new-york.html.

188 **"show them the money":** Pressler, "Maybe She Had So Much."

188 **Sorokin signed a deal:** Chris Murphy, "Anna Sorokin, a.k.a. Anna Delvey, Is Getting a Docuseries," *Vanity Fair*, February 15, 2022, https://www.vanityfair.com /hollywood/2022/02/anna-sorokin-aka-anna-delvey-is-getting-a-docuseries.

189 **Holy Trinity moment:** Carmela Chirinos, "Inventing Anna Got It Right. Anna Delvey Did in Fact Know Billy McFarland and Martin Shkreli," *Fortune*, May 19, 2022, https://fortune.com/2022/05/19/in venting-anna-anna-delvey-billy-mcfar land-martin-shkreli-friends.

190 **Rockefeller University:** Landon Thomas Jr. "Jeffrey Epstein: International Moneyman of Mystery," *New York Magazine*, October 28, 2002, https://nymag.com/nym etro/news/people/n_7912.

190 **his private jet:** David Folkenflik, "A Dead Cat, a Lawyer's Call and a 5-Figure Donation: How Media Fell Short on Epstein," NPR, August 22, 2019, https://www.npr .org/2019/08/22/753390385/a-dead -cat-a-lawyers-call-and-a-5-figure-dona tion-how-media-fell-short-on-epstei.

190 **"It is even said":** Thomas, "Jeffrey Epstein."

190 **stormed their offices:** Folkenflik, "A Dead Cat."

190 **severed cat's head:** Folkenflik, "A Dead Cat."

190 **allegations about the abuse:** Folkenflik, "A Dead Cat."

190 **"on his cell phone":** Thomas, "Jeffrey Epstein."

190 **"He couldn't really":** Michael E. Hartmann, "In Distancing Himself from Epstein, Pinker Offers Insight into Relationship Between Some Givers and 'Smart Set,'" *Philanthropy Daily*, July 24, 2019, https:// philanthropydaily.com/in -distancing-himself-from-epstein-pinker -offers-insight-into-relationship-between -some-givers-and-smart-set.

190 **"If you actually really":** Andrew Rice, "The Jeffrey Epstein Mystery Roundtable," *Intelligencer*, December 16, 2021, https://nymag.com/intelligencer/2021/12 /jeffrey-epstein-unanswered-questions .html.

191 **lenient plea deal:** Michael Balsamo and Eric Tucker, "Justice Dept.: 'Poor Judgment' Used in Epstein Plea Deal," Associated Press, November 12, 2020, https:// apnews.com/article/jeffrey-epstein-flor ida-e2a4431f7319afd037023d9a586aa291.

191 **believe it was murder:** John Gage, "Majority Believe Epstein Was Murdered

'Because He Knew Too Much': Poll," *Washington Examiner*, January 9, 2020, https://www.washingtonexaminer.com /news/1717246/majority-believe-epstein -was-murdered-because-he-knew-too -much-poll.

191 **"storm of screw-ups":** Katie Benner, "Barr Says Epstein's Suicide Resulted from 'Perfect Storm of Screw-Ups,'" *New York Times*, November 22, 2019, https://www .nytimes.com/2019/11/22/nyregion/wil liam-barr-jeffrey-epstein-suicide-investi gation.html.

191 **"lifestyle is very different":** Emily Flitter and James B. Stewart, "Bill Gates Met with Jeffrey Epstein Many Times, Despite His Past," *New York Times*, October 12, 2019, https://www.nytimes.com/2019/10 /12/business/jeffrey-epstein-bill-gates .html.

191 **"referring only to the unique décor":** Flitter and Stewart, "Bill Gates Met."

192 **persistent allegations:** Yuri Kageyama, "Johnny & Associates Founder Kitagawa Sexually Assaulted Hundreds of Teens, Investigation Finds," Associated Press, August 29, 2023, https://apnews.com/arti cle/japan-johnnys-sexual-abuse-execu tive-resign-investigation-cd1b8c226ae 52ef4ff3c8e7d5d78bcc4.

192 **to print calendars:** Philip Brasor, "Media Watch: How Johnny's Exploits the Pin-up Factor to Keep Publishers in Line," *Philip Brasor* (blog), May 31, 2023, https://philip brasor.com/2023/05/31/media-watch -how-johnnys-exploits-the-pin-up-factor -to-keep-publishers-in-line.

192 **demanded compensation:** Frances Mao and Jean Mackenzie, "Johnny Kitagawa: Hundreds Seek Compensation over J-Pop Agency Founder's Abuse," *BBC News*, October 2, 2023, https://www.bbc.com/news /world-asia-66979993.

192 **like every US state:** "States," Homesick, https://homesick.com/collections/state -candles.

193 **"Magazines aren't democracies":** Dana Brown, *Dilettante: True Tales of Excess, Triumph, and Disaster* (Ballantine, 2022), 88.

193 **underwear subscriptions:** Amanda Tarlton, "15 Products Advertised on Podcasts That Are Actually Worth Buying," *USA Today*, January 30, 2020, https://www.usa today.com/story/tech/reviewedcom/2019 /10/07/15-products-advertised-podcasts -actually-worth-buying/3891429002.

193 **Nutritionists consistently questioned:** Scott C. Forbes, Jayna M. Holroyd-Leduc,

Marc J. Poulin, and David B. Hogan, "Effect of Nutrients, Dietary Supplements and Vitamins on Cognition: A Systematic Review and Meta-Analysis of Randomized Controlled Trials," *Canadian Geriatrics Journal* 18, no. 4 (2015): 231–45, https://doi.org/10.5770/cgj.18.189; Julia Belluz, "How Dietary Supplements Evade Regulation—with Dangerous Results," *Vox*, April 8, 2015, https://www.vox.com/2015/4/8/8366619/dietary-supplement-regulation.

193 **ballooned to $30 billion:** Kaitlyn Tiffany, "When Did Vitamins Get So Cool?," *Vox*, April 16, 2019, https://www.vox.com/the-goods/2019/4/16/18312030/vitamin-subscription-startups-careof-ritual-persona.

193 **proprietary "cognamine" blend:** Sasha de Beausset Aparicio, "BrainQuicken Review—Is It Effective?," Brain Reference, November 13, 2022, https://brainreference.com/brainquicken-review.

193 **sales of "nutraceuticals":** Ben Taub, "How the Biggest Fraud in German History Unravelled," *New Yorker*, February 27, 2023, https://www.newyorker.com/magazine/2023/03/06/how-the-biggest-fraud-in-german-history-unravelled.

194 **pundits propped up:** Richard Cooke, "Right Brain," *New Republic*, September 3, 2019, https://newrepublic.com/article/154629/right-brain-ben-shapiro-alex-jones-conservatives-love-affair-nootropics.

194 **involving gold bullion:** Jeremy B. Merrill and Hanna Kozlowska, "How Right-Wing News Powers the 'Gold IRA' Industry," *Washington Post*, July 25, 2023, https://www.washingtonpost.com/business/2023/07/25/gold-ira-conservative-media.

194 **famously bankrolled Infowars:** Anna Merlan, "Alex Jones Is Now Trying to Divert Money to His Father's Supplements Business," *Wired*, June 17, 2024, https://www.wired.com/story/alex-jones-bankruptcy-money-dr-jones-supplement-business/.

194 **Why Am I So Effing Tired?:** Nikhil Sonnad, "All the 'Wellness' Products Americans Love to Buy Are Sold on Both Infowars and Goop," *Quartz*, June 29, 2017, https://qz.com/1010684/all-the-wellness-products-american-love-to-buy-are-sold-on-both-infowars-and-goop.

194 **called Nerd Alert:** Kaitlyn Tiffany, "The All-Too-Understandable Urge to Buy a Better Brain," *Vox*, July 8, 2019, https://www.vox.com/the-goods/2019/7/8/18772467/nootropics-silicon-valley-brain-fitness-goop-smart-drugs.

194 **"personalized" vitamin packs:** Anthony Ha, "Subscription Vitamin Company Care/of Is Shutting Down," *TechCrunch*, June 15, 2024, https://techcrunch.com/2024/06/15/subscription-vitamin-company-care-of-is-shutting-down.

194 **"traceable" ingredients:** Emma Sandler, "Ritual Vitamins Wants 'Traceability' to Become the New 'Transparency,'" *Modern Retail*, September 13, 2022, https://www.modernretail.co/operations/ritual-vitamins-wants-traceability-to-become-the-new-transparency.

194 **strategy called "manifesting":** Rebecca Jennings, "Shut Up, I'm Manifesting!," *Vox*, October 23, 2020, https://www.vox.com/the-goods/21524975/manifesting-does-it-really-work-meme.

194 **"more affluent lifestyles":** Victoria Moore, "It's Become the Fastest-Selling Self-Help Book Ever, but Is the Secret Doing More Harm Than Good?," *Mail Online*, April 26, 2007, https://www.dailymail.co.uk/femail/article-450745/Its-fastest-selling-self-help-book-The-Secret-doing-harm-good.html.

195 **"compassionate guard":** Paris Hilton, *Paris: The Memoir* (Dey Street Books, 2023), 283.

195 **"anything you want":** Harland Highway Podcast, "Insane Clown Posses Violent J Speaks on Manifesting!," YouTube video, 0:46, November 26, 2023, https://youtu.be/nY9EPEJGdTc.

195 **devoted several episodes:** Peter Birkenhead, "Oprah's Ugly Secret," *Salon*, March 5, 2007, https://www.salon.com/2007/03/05/the_secret.

195 **Celebrity 100 list:** "Oprah 'Most Powerful Celebrity' in Annual Forbes List," *BBC News*, June 26, 2013, https://www.bbc.com/news/entertainment-arts-23068924.

195 **Oprah's "signature power":** Brian Lowry, "Experts Key to Winfrey Formula," *Variety*, December 18, 2010, https://variety.com/2010/tv/columns/experts-key-to-winfrey-formula-1118029220.

195 **"miracle elixirs, homeopathy":** Kurt Andersen, "Oprah Winfrey Helped Create Our American Fantasyland," *Slate*, January 10, 2018, https://slate.com/health-and-science/2018/01/oprah-winfrey-helped-create-our-irrational-pseudoscientific-american-fantasyland.html.

195 **James Frey's 2003 memoir:** David Carr, "How Oprahness Trumped Truthiness,"

New York Times, January 30, 2006, https://www.nytimes.com/2006/01/30/business/media/how-oprahness-trumped-truthiness.html.

195 **"mensch of the year":** Carr, "How Oprahness Trumped Truthiness."

195 **fabricated quotes:** Julia Rickert, "A Little Secret About the Secret," *Chicago Reader*, May 31, 2007, https://chicagoreader.com/news/a-little-secret-about-the-secret.

195 **danger of manifesting:** Fred Small, "Psst: 'The Secret' Isn't Total Bunk," *UU World*, November 19, 2007, https://www.uuworld.org/articles/unitarian-universalist-view-se.

196 **"is just one law":** "Letters to Oprah," March 26, 2007, *Oprah*, https://www.oprah.com/oprahshow/letters-to-oprah/all.

196 **"satanic cults, and more":** Andersen, "Oprah Winfrey Helped Create."

196 **back into popularity:** Jennings, "Shut Up, I'm Manifesting!"

196 **"the sentence (*sic*) I told you":** @kayley_2120, "HERES THE TUTORIAL EVERYONES ASKED FOR!!!🦋💗," TikTok, July 11, 2020, https://www.tiktok.com/@kayley_2120/video/6847964175956839686.

196 **took on the moniker *woo-woo*:** RationalWiki, "woo," last modified December 18, 2024, https://rationalwiki.org/wiki/Woo.

196 **found new relevance:** Hilary George-Parkin, "The Anxieties and Apps Fuelling the Astrology Boom," BBC, February 8, 2021, https://www.bbc.com/worklife/article/20210205-why-astrology-is-so-popular-now.

196 **"something that's happened":** Julie Beck, "The New Age of Astrology," *Atlantic*, January 16, 2018, https://www.theatlantic.com/health/archive/2018/01/the-new-age-of-astrology/550034.

197 **"High-functioning adults":** Montell, *Age of Magical Overthinking*, 179.

197 **"'I'm a Scorpio'":** Hanna Wickes, "Taylor Swift's Connection to Astrology: Every Time She's Referenced the Stars in Her Songs," Yahoo! Entertainment, April 12, 2024, https://www.yahoo.com/entertainment/taylor-swift-connection-astrology-every-141430923.html.

197 **"People tend to turn":** Beck, "New Age of Astrology."

197 **"symbols and shorthand":** Beck, "New Age of Astrology."

197 **Aliza Kelly, for example:** Christine Smallwood, "Astrology in the Age of Uncertainty," *New Yorker*, October 21, 2019, https://www.newyorker.com/magazine/2019/10/28/astrology-in-the-age-of-uncertainty.

197 **"new moon in Scorpio":** Smallwood, "Astrology in the Age of Uncertainty."

198 **"sun in Aquarius":** Smallwood, "Astrology in the Age of Uncertainty."

198 **$1,499 fee:** Katie Heaney, "The Most Serious Astrologer on TikTok," *Cut*, January 14, 2021, https://www.thecut.com/2021/01/maren-altman-viral-tiktok-astrologer.html.

198 **Apps like Co-Star:** Smallwood, "Astrology in the Age."

198 **Aetna, General Mills:** Michelle Goldberg, "The Long Marriage of Mindfulness and Money," *New Yorker*, April 18, 2015, https://www.newyorker.com/business/currency/the-long-marriage-of-mindfulness-and-money.

198 **"delicious look inward":** Tom Wolfe, *Mauve Gloves & Madmen, Clutter & Vine* (Farrar, Straus and Giroux, 1976), 164.

198 **"individualism and supernaturalism":** Andersen, "Oprah Winfrey Helped Create."

198 **"The book is proposing":** Michael Hobbes and Peter Shamshiri, hosts, *If Books Could Kill*, podcast, "The Secret," January 12, 2023, https://www.buzzsprout.com/2040953/episodes/12025809-the-secret.

199 **adhered to the "prosperity gospel":** Tara Isabella Burton, "The Prosperity Gospel, Explained: Why Joel Osteen Believes That Prayer Can Make You Rich," *Vox*, September 1, 2017, https://www.vox.com/identities/2017/9/1/15951874/prosperity-gospel-explained-why-joel-osteen-believes-prayer-can-make-you-rich-trump.

199 **faith with material success:** Burton, "Prosperity Gospel, Explained."

199 **"hundredfold" returns:** Burton, "Prosperity Gospel, Explained."

199 **"Rolls-Royces, private jets":** Michael Luo, "Preaching a Gospel of Wealth in a Glittery Market, New York," *New York Times*, January 15, 2006, https://www.nytimes.com/2006/01/15/nyregion/preaching-a-gospel-of-wealth-in-a-glittery-market-new-york.html.

199 **"face of Christianity":** Luo, "Preaching a Gospel."

199 **"focus on money":** Brianna Griff, "The Invention of Joel Osteen: How a Houston Boy Became the World's Pastor," *Chron*, October 9, 2022, https://www.chron.com

/culture/article/The-invention-of-Joel
-Osteen-How-a-Houston-boy-17494201
.php.

199 **airport gift shops:** Edward Wyatt, "Religious Broadcaster Gets Rich Contract for Next Book," *New York Times*, March 15, 2006, https://www.nytimes.com/2006/03/15/business/media/religious-broadcaster-gets-rich-contract-for-next-book.html.

199 **$12 million mansion:** Griff, "Invention of Joel Osteen."

199 **open his megachurch:** Laurel Wamsley, "After Pressure Mounts, Joel Osteen Says His Houston Megachurch Is Open to Evacuees," NPR, August 29, 2017, https://www.npr.org/sections/thetwo-way/2017/08/29/547035773/after-pressure-mounts-joel-osteen-says-his-houston-megachurch-is-open-to-evacuee.

200 **"alternative slates of electors":** Lisa Mascaro and Mary Clare Jalonick, "WATCH: Trump Advisers Tell Jan. 6 Committee They Knew Pence Had No Legal Standing to Challenge Electoral Votes," PBS News, June 16, 2022, https://www.pbs.org/newshour/politics/watch-trump-advisers-tell-jan-6-committee-they-knew-pence-had-no-legal-standing-to-challenge-electoral-votes.

200 **"@Mike_Pence comes through":** Jill Colvin, "What We Know About How Pence's Day Unfolded on Jan. 6," PBS News, June 16, 2022, https://www.pbs.org/newshour/politics/as-jan-6-hearings-what-we-know-about-how-pences-day-unfolded-on-jan-6.

200 **"We fight like hell":** Brian Naylor, "Read Trump's Jan. 6 Speech, a Key Part of Impeachment Trial," NPR, February 10, 2021, https://www.npr.org/2021/02/10/966396848/read-trumps-jan-6-speech-a-key-part-of-impeachment-trial.

200 **discovered pipe bombs:** Carrie Johnson, "Still on the Hunt, the FBI Shares New Details About Pipe Bombs Placed Ahead of Jan. 6," NPR, January 2, 2025, https://www.npr.org/2025/01/02/nx-s1-5244008/fbi-pipe-bomb-jan6-dnc-rnc.

200 **online-right symbols:** Mallory Simon and Sara Sidner, "Decoding the Extremist Symbols and Groups at the Capitol Hill Insurrection," CNN, January 11, 2021, https://edition.cnn.com/2021/01/09/us/capitol-hill-insurrection-extremist-flags-soh/index.html.

200 **"QAnon Shaman":** Jacques Billeaud, "Jan. 6 Rioter Known as 'QAnon Shaman' Sentenced to 41 Months," *PBS News*, November 17, 2021, https://www.pbs.org/newshour/nation/jan-6-rioter-known-as-qanon-shaman-sentenced-to-41-months.

200 **follower Ashli Babbitt:** Ellen Barry, Nicholas Bogel-Burroughs, and Dave Philipps, "Woman Killed in Capitol Embraced Trump and Qanon," *New York Times*, December 11, 2023, https://www.nytimes.com/2021/01/08/us/who-was-ashli-babbitt.html.

201 **"You're very special":** Travis Caldwell, "Trump's 'We Love You' to Capitol Rioters Is More of the Same," CNN, January 7, 2021, https://edition.cnn.com/2021/01/07/politics/trump-history-comments-trnd/index.html.

201 **"democracy would enter":** Li Zhou, "'Our Democracy Would Enter a Death Spiral': Mitch McConnell Urges Republicans to Back the Election Results," *Vox*, January 6, 2021, https://www.vox.com/2021/1/6/22217204/mitch-mcconnell-trump-election-results.

201 **"Let's just do it":** Chloe Gordon, "I Worked at Fyre Festival. It Was Always Going to Be a Disaster," *Cut*, April 28, 2017, https://www.thecut.com/2017/04/fyre-festival-exumas-bahamas-disaster.html.

PART FOUR:
2020–2025

CHAPTER 14:
THE OMNIVORE MONOCULTURE

205 **first pocket money:** ProducerGrind, "YoungKio Talks Making of 'Old Town Road,' Selling Beat for $30, Signing to CashMoneyAP + More," YouTube video, 59:08, September 19, 2019, https://youtu.be/w2dJ_kcfvN0.

205 **additional twenty:** "Lil Nas X Takes Gayle King Inside the Studio Where He Recorded 'Old Town Road,'" CBS News, September 30, 2019, https://www.cbsnews.com/news/lil-nas-x-inside-the-recording-studio-where-rapper-made-old-town-road.

205 **"Yeehaw Agenda":** Amanda Petrusich, "Lil Nas X Is the Sound of the Internet, Somehow," *New Yorker*, June 24, 2019, https://www.newyorker.com/culture/cultural-comment/lil-nas-x-is-the-sound-of-the-internet-somehow.

206 **Michael Pelchat posted:** Petrusich, "Lil Nas X Is the Sound."

206 **off the country charts:** Petrusich, "Lil Nas X Is the Sound."

206 **"'Old Town Road' incorporates":** Lauren Katz, "How 'Old Town Road' Revealed a Deep Divide Within Country Music," *Vox*, August 26, 2019, https://www.vox.com/2019/8/23/20826730/lil-nas-x-old-town-road-vma-podcast.

206 **a jaw-dropping 143 million streams:** Halle Kiefer, "Lil Nas X's 'Old Town Road' Breaks Streaming Record Set by Drake's 'In My Feelings,'" *Vulture*, April 15, 2019, https://www.vulture.com/2019/04/lil-nas-xs-old-town-road-breaks-drakes-streaming-record.html.

207 **"the two forms of pop music":** Nadine Smith, "How Hip-Hop Beats Took Over Country Music," *Fader*, September 28, 2023, https://www.thefader.com/2023/09/28/country-rap-jelly-roll-morgan-wallen-nashville-hip-hop.

207 **"Meant to Be":** Katz, "How 'Old Town Road' Revealed."

207 **country star Morgan Wallen:** Gil Kaufman, "Morgan Wallen and Lil Durk Drop Country Drill Ode to Untrustworthy Women 'Broadway Girls,'" *Billboard*, December 17, 2021, https://www.billboard.com/music/country/morgan-wallen-lil-durk-broadway-girls-1235012032.

207 **Shaboozey topped:** Spencer Kornhaber, "The Next Great American Mega-Genre," *Atlantic*, June 11, 2024, https://www.theatlantic.com/culture/archive/2024/06/hip-hop-country-billboard-charts-shaboozey/678652.

207 **"feels increasingly irrelevant":** Amanda Petrusich, "Genre Is Disappearing. What Comes Next?," *New Yorker*, March 8, 2021, https://www.newyorker.com/magazine/2021/03/15/genre-is-disappearing-what-comes-next.

207 **"a politically correct way":** Petrusich, "Genre Is Disappearing."

207 **dropped the term:** "Grammys Drop 'Urban' from Major Award Category," *BBC News*, June 10, 2020, https://www.bbc.com/news/entertainment-arts-52996675.

208 **more than $1 million:** Andre Paine, "IFPI: $1 Million to Break an Act," *Billboard*, March 9, 2010, https://www.billboard.com/music/music-news/ifpi-1-million-to-break-an-act-1210148.

208 **achieved eight *Billboard*:** Halle Kiefer, "Taylor Swift Has Some Tricks up Her Sleeve, Conjures Her Eighth Number One Album with *Evermore*," *Vulture*, December 20, 2020, https://www.vulture.com/2020/12/taylor-swifts-evermore-eighth-no-1-album-second-of-2020.html.

208 **over $2 billion:** Ben Sisario, "Taylor Swift's Eras Tour Grand Total: A Record $2 Billion," *New York Times*, December 9, 2024, https://www.nytimes.com/2024/12/09/arts/music/taylor-swift-eras-tour-ticket-sales.html.

208 **documentary of all time:** Steven J. Horowitz, "Taylor Swift's 'Eras Tour' Becomes Highest-Grossing Concert Film of All Time, Surpassing Michael Jackson," *Variety*, January 7, 2024, https://variety.com/2024/film/news/taylor-swifts-the-eras-tour-highest-grossing-theatrical-concert-film-1235863956.

208 **vinyl revival:** Dorian Lynskey, "It's the Age of Swiftonomics—but Will Taylor Swift's Phenomenal Success Trickle Down?," *Guardian*, June 1, 2024, https://www.theguardian.com/music/article/2024/jun/01/its-the-age-of-swiftonomics-but-will-taylor-swifts-phenomenal-success-trickle-down.

208 **"Commerce used to be":** Lynskey, "It's the Age of Swiftonomics."

208 **"the interminable length":** Sinéad O'Sullivan, "Why Normal Music Reviews No Longer Make Sense for Taylor Swift," *New Yorker*, April 30, 2024, https://www.newyorker.com/culture/cultural-comment/why-normal-music-reviews-no-longer-make-sense-for-taylor-swift.

208 **"creating standalone albums":** O'Sullivan, "Why Normal Music Reviews."

209 **314.5 million streams:** O'Sullivan, "Why Normal Music Reviews."

209 **hired a dedicated reporter:** Shannon Doyne, "A Newspaper Chain Hired a Dedicated Taylor Swift Reporter. Is It OK If He's a Swiftie?," *New York Times*, November 17, 2023, https://www.nytimes.com/2023/11/17/learning/a-newspaper-chain-hired-a-dedicated-taylor-swift-reporter-is-it-ok-if-hes-a-swiftie.html.

209 **"very, very good":** Mark Hemingway, "Taylor Swift's Popularity Is a Sign of Societal Decline," *Federalist*, September 5, 2023, https://thefederalist.com/2023/09/05/taylor-swifts-popularity-is-a-sign-of-societal-decline.

209 **"isn't entirely comfortable":** Cathy Horyn, "The Real Reason Taylor Swift Dresses Like That," *Cut*, April 18, 2024, https://www.thecut.com/article/taylor-swift-style.html.

209 **"Greatest Pop Star":** Andrew Unterberger, "Billboard's Greatest Pop Stars of

the 21st Century: No. 1—Beyoncé," *Billboard*, December 3, 2024, https://www.billboard.com/music/pop/beyonce-greatest-pop-stars-21st-century-1235842572.

209 **won thirty-five:** Recording Academy, "Beyoncé," Grammy Awards, https://www.grammy.com/artists/beyonce-knowles/12474.

209 **"So Deathly Afraid":** Cassie Da Costa, "Why Are People So Deathly Afraid of Criticizing Beyoncé?," *Daily Beast*, August 5, 2020, https://www.thedailybeast.com/why-are-people-so-deathly-afraid-of-criticizing-beyonce; see also "What If You Don't Like Beyonce's Album?," *Grantland*, December 20, 2013, https://grantland.com/hollywood-prospectus/what-if-you-dont-like-beyonces-album.

209 **expanded into consumer goods:** Frazier Tharpe, "The Business of Being Beyoncé Knowles-Carter," SirDavis, September 10, 2024, https://www.sirdavis.com/media/business-being-beyonce-knowles-carter.

209 **Tiffany & Co. advertising:** Vanessa Friedman, "The Mystery of That Basquiat Painting—and Its Tiffany Blue," *New York Times*, September 1, 2021, https://www.nytimes.com/2021/09/01/style/tiffany-basquiat-jay-z-beyonce.html.

210 **akin to a racial epithet:** Aaron Williams, "Jay-Z Compared Being Called a 'Capitalist' to Being Called a Slur and Fans Are Astounded," Uproxx, September 1, 2022, https://uproxx.com/music/jay-z-capitalist-slur-fan-reactions.

210 **Top 10 hits:** Andrew Unterberger, "Billboard's Greatest Pop Stars of the 21st Century: No. 4—Drake." *Billboard*, November 12, 2024, https://www.billboard.com/music/pop/drake-greatest-pop-stars-21st-century-1235824907.

210 **not conqueror:** Jason England, "50 Years Later, Is There Anything Left of Hip Hop?," *Defector*, August 28, 2023, https://defector.com/50-years-later-is-there-anything-left-of-hip-hop.

210 **"*Rich Dad Poor Dad*":** England, "50 Years Later."

210 **Ice Spice Munchkins Drink:** "Twice as Nice: Dunkin' Debuts New Commercial Starring Ice Spice, Created by Ben Affleck's Artists Equity," Dunkin', September 12, 2023, https://news.dunkindonuts.com/blog/dunkin-ben-affleck-ice-spice.

210 **rise in interpolations:** Charlie Harding, "Invasion of the Vibe-Snatchers: Pop Music Is Regurgitating Itself Faster Than

Ever," *Vulture*, September 15, 2022, https://www.vulture.com/article/pop-music-regurgitations-switched-on-pop.html.

210 **"I Ain't Worried":** Harding, "Invasion of the Vibe-Snatchers."

211 **their most celebrated albums:** Peter C. Baker, "No More Nostalgia Concerts, Please," *New York Times*, November 20, 2024, https://www.nytimes.com/2024/11/20/magazine/nostalgia-concerts.html.

211 **"onward acceleration":** Baker, "No More Nostalgia Concerts."

211 **"disconnecting from each other":** "Pharrell Williams: 'Faith Is About What You Feel,'" *i-D*, June 10, 2020, https://i-d.co/article/pharrell-williams-interview-i-d-magazine.

212 **"one of the worst films":** A. S. Hamrah, "Hollywood Crawls Out of the Trump Era," *Frieze*, February 23, 2021, https://www.frieze.com/article/a-s-hamrah-hillbilly-elegy-rebuilding-paradise-nomadland.

212 **"comfort food TV":** Emily St. James, "Why Ted Lasso Became the Hit That Put AppleTV+ on the Map," *Vox*, February 24, 2021, https://www.vox.com/culture/22290391/ted-lasso-explained-apple-tv-plus-jason-sudeikis.

212 **felt distinctly underwhelming:** Angela Watercutter, "2021 Was Bound to Be a Year of Pop Culture Disappointments," *Wired*, December 20, 2021, https://www.wired.com/story/2021-year-of-cultural-disappointments.

212 **new slang *mid*:** Stephen Marche, "Today's Teenagers Have Invented a Language That Captures the World Perfectly," *New York Times*, June 25, 2024, https://www.nytimes.com/2024/06/25/opinion/gen-z-slang-language.html.

212 **as "premium mediocre":** Amanda Mull, "It's All So . . . Premiocre," *Atlantic*, April 2020, https://www.theatlantic.com/magazine/archive/2020/04/its-all-so-premiocre/606775.

212 **"unconvinced that anyone":** Mull, "It's All So . . . Premiocre."

212 **thousand coffee brands:** James Hoffmann, "How Celebrity Coffee Brands Really Work," YouTube video, 20:58, August 2, 2024, https://youtu.be/yG8vp_UkCVg.

213 **dubbed "AirSpace":** Kyle Chayka, "Welcome to AirSpace," *Verge*, August 3, 2016, https://www.theverge.com/2016/8/3/12325104/airbnb-aesthetic-global-minimalism-startup-gentrification.

213 **phrase "Instagram face":** Jia Tolentino, "The Age of Instagram Face," *New Yorker,* December 12, 2019, https://www.newy orker.com/culture/decade-in-review/the -age-of-instagram-face.

213 **"an overly tan skin tone":** Tolentino, "Age of Instagram Face."

213 **The "patients zero":** Tolentino, "Age of Instagram Face."

213 **90 percent increase:** Kaitlin Clark, "Supply and Demand: How Surgeons Are Navigating the BBL Boom," American Society of Plastic Surgeons, December 22, 2022, https://www.plasticsurgery.org/news/arti cles/supply-and-demand-how-surgeons -are-navigating-the-bbl-boom.

213 **Brazilian butt lift:** Zoe Applegate and Helen Burchell, "Brazilian Butt-Lift Surgery: What Are the Risks and Why Is It So Popular?," *BBC News,* September 15, 2023, https://www.bbc.com/news/uk-eng land-norfolk-66798236.

213 **"more conventionally attractive":** Tolentino, "Age of Instagram Face."

213 **"thirty per cent of people":** Tolentino, "Age of Instagram Face."

214 **collaborated with 165 brands:** Natasha Degen, "The Marketing Hurricane of 'Wicked' Says a Lot About Our Culture," *New York Times,* December 14, 2024, https://www.nytimes.com/2024/12/14 /opinion/wicked-marketing-collaboration -culture.html.

214 **collaborations at 400:** Degen, "Marketing Hurricane."

214 **Casamigos tequila brand:** Michael J. de la Merced, "George Clooney's Tequila Company Sold for Up to $1 Billion," *New York Times,* June 21, 2017, https://www .nytimes.com/2017/06/21/business/george -clooney-tequila-casamigos-diageo.html.

214 **$610 million:** Desiree Murphy, "Ryan Reynolds Pens Hilarious Out of Office Message After Selling Aviation Gin Company for $610 Million," *Entertainment Tonight,* August 18, 2020, https://www .etonline.com/ryan-reynolds-pens-hilari ous-out-of-office-message-after-selling -aviation-gin-company-for-610.

214 **acquired in 2023:** Marisa Dellatto, "Ryan Reynolds' Mint Mobile Acquired by T-Mobile for $1.3 Billion," *Forbes,* March 15, 2023, https://www.forbes.com/sites /marisadellatto/2023/03/15/ryan-reyn olds-mint-mobile-acquired-by-t-mobile -for-13-billion.

214 **declared a billionaire:** Madeline Berg, "Fenty's Fortune: Rihanna Is Now Offi-

cially a Billionaire," *Forbes,* August 6, 2021, https://www.forbes.com/sites/mad dieberg/2021/08/04/fentys-fortune -rihanna-is-now-officially-a-billionaire.

214 **Japanese TV commercials:** Anthony Faiola, "American Stars Shine Again in Japan Ads," NBC News, January 14, 2007, https://www.nbcnews.com/id/wbna1 6618822.

215 **no longer just spokespeople:** Amy McCarthy, "Trudging Through the Tedious Swamp of Celebrity Brand Deals," Eater, May 7, 2024, https://www.eater.com/24150 484/celeb-brand-deals-how-do-they-work -interviews.

215 **bagging a $7.5 million film role:** Heather Schwedel, "The Sydney Sweeney Industrial Complex," *Slate,* December 15, 2024, https://slate.com/life/2024/12/sydney -sweeney-movie-endorsements-shoes.html.

215 **TikTok video of 2020:** Rebecca Jennings, "This Week in TikTok: And the Most Popular Video of the Year Is . . ." *Vox,* December 8, 2020, https://www.vox.com/the-goods /2020/12/8/22160034/tiktok-top-100 -bella-poarch.

216 **"absolute favorite thing":** Jesse David Fox, *Comedy Book: How Comedy Conquered Culture—and the Magic That Makes It Work* (Farrar, Straus and Giroux, 2023), 245.

216 **Chinese glycine factory:** Elaine Lee, "TikTok's Latest Obsession Is Donghua Jinlong, a Chinese Company Producing Glycine," *Straits Times,* April 13, 2024, https://www.straitstimes.com/asia/east -asia/tiktok-s-latest-obsession-is-donghua -jinlong-a-chinese-company-producing -glycine.

216 **"Harness Your Hopes":** Tom Skinner, "Pavement's 'Harness Your Hopes' Goes Viral on TikTok Again," *NME,* April 11, 2024, https://www.nme.com/news/music /pavements-harness-your-hopes-goes -viral-on-tiktok-again-3616479.

216 **"mishmash of stimuli":** Kieran Press-Reynolds, "This Is Corecore (We're Not Kidding)," *No Bells,* November 29, 2022, https://nobells.blog/corecore.

216 **They drank less, smoked less:** Ryan Burge (@RyanBurge), "Here's substance use by high school seniors in 1976," X (formerly Twitter), July 12, 2024, https://x.com /ryanburge/status/1811446674495074644.

216 **experienced teenage pregnancy:** Jenin Abu-Hashem and Sara Srygley, "Are the Kids Alright? How Gen Z Girls' Well-Being Compares with Their Mothers' and

Grandmothers' Teenage Years," Population Reference Bureau, December 14, 2023, https://www.prb.org/articles/are-the-kids-alright-how-gen-z-girls-well-being-compares-with-their-mothers-and-grandmothers-teenage-years.

216 **environmentally conscious:** Jacopo Paoletti, "Gen Z and Environmental Issues: How to Earn Young Consumers' Trust," *Forbes*, June 1, 2022, https://www.forbes.com/councils/forbescommunicationscouncil/2022/06/01/gen-z-and-environmental-issues-how-to-earn-young-consumers-trust.

216 **"full of corporate triumph":** Marche, "Today's Teenagers Have Invented."

216 **"OK boomer":** Anne Helen Petersen, *Can't Even: How Millennials Became the Burnout Generation* (Houghton Mifflin Harcourt, 2020), 2.

217 **crying-laughing-face emoji:** Helen Coffey, "How Millennials Became the Least Cool Generation," *Independent*, June 26, 2024, https://www.independent.co.uk/life-style/millennials-gen-z-uncool-boomers-socks-b2568557.html.

217 **had become "cringe":** Marche, "Today's Teenagers Have Invented."

217 **kitschy taste "cheugy":** Taylor Lorenz, "What Is 'Cheugy'? You Know It When You See It," *New York Times*, April 29, 2021, https://www.nytimes.com/2021/04/29/style/cheugy.html.

217 **"Millennial pause":** Kate Lindsay, "Are You Sure You're Not Guilty of the 'Millennial Pause'?," *Atlantic*, August 6, 2022, https://www.theatlantic.com/technology/archive/2022/08/tiktok-gen-z-millennial-pause-parody/671069.

217 **"Millennials, as a group":** Jean M. Twenge, "The Myth of the Broke Millennial," *Atlantic*, April 17, 2023, https://www.theatlantic.com/magazine/archive/2023/05/millennial-generation-financial-issues-income-homeowners/673485.

217 **households out-earned:** Twenge, "Myth of the Broke."

217 **massive wealth transfer:** Michael Savage, "Middle Class Millennials Set to Gain Most from 'Unprecedented' Wealth Transfer," *Guardian*, November 16, 2024, https://www.theguardian.com/inequality/2024/nov/16/middle-class-millennials-set-to-gain-most-from-unprecedented-wealth-transfer.

217 **7 percent of the workforce:** Emily Hund, "Why the Influencer Industry Needs Guardrails," *Harvard Business Review*, May 1, 2024, https://hbr.org/2024/05/why-the-influencer-industry-needs-guardrails.

217 **Gen Z set the bar at $587,800:** Ben Berkowitz, "What It Takes to Be 'Financially Successful' by Generation," *Axios*, November 22, 2024, https://www.axios.com/2024/11/22/boomers-gen-z-millennials-financial-success.

217 **over half of Gen Z respondents:** Jessica Dickler and Ana Teresa Solá, "'Recession Pop' Is In: Why So Many Listeners Are Returning to Music from Darker Economic Times," CNBC, July 21, 2024, https://www.cnbc.com/2024/07/21/recession-pop-explained-how-music-collides-with-economic-trends.html.

217 **built-in advantages:** Nate Jones, "How a Nepo Baby Is Born," *Vulture*, December 19, 2022, https://www.vulture.com/article/what-is-a-nepotism-baby.html.

218 **"vertical domain portfolios":** "Welcome to Rob Grant.net," Rob grant.net, http://robgrant.net/aboutus.html.

218 **his viral hit "Boyfren":** Beatrice Hazlehurst, "How Popstar LoveLeo Became the Internet's New BOYFREN," *i-D*, June 15, 2021, https://i-d.co/article/loveleo-leo-reilly-music-interview.

218 **"Stassie" Karanikolaou:** Mariah Espada, "How Internet Nepo-Friends Have Cultivated Their Own Online Stardom," *Time*, September 26, 2023, https://time.com/6316756/nepo-friend-influencers.

218 **"wealth comes close":** Thomas Piketty, *Capital in the Twenty-First Century*, trans. Arthur Goldhammer (Belknap Press, 2014), 22.

218 **pocket of lower Manhattan:** Ben Smith, "They Had a Fun Pandemic. You Can Read About It in Print," *New York Times*, March 7, 2021, https://www.nytimes.com/2021/03/07/business/media/the-drunken-canal-media-nyc.html.

218 **"understand Valerie Solanas":** Smith, "They Had a Fun Pandemic."

219 **number one creator:** Tuhin Das Mahapatra, "MrBeast Makes History, Becomes First YouTuber to Reach 300 Million Subscribers," *Hindustan Times*, July 10, 2024, https://www.hindustantimes.com/world-news/us-news/mrbeast-makes-history-becomes-first-youtuber-to-reach-300-million-subscribers-10172063 23424789.html.

219 **serving undercooked meat:** Mura Dominko, "This Popular New Burger Chain Is Being Called Out for Terrible,

Raw Food," Eat This, Not That! May 18, 2021, https://www.eatthis.com/news-mr-beast-criticized-for-terrible-raw-food.

219 **cheese sometimes molded:** Jennifer Zhan, "MrBeast Accused of Selling Moldy Meals to Kids," *Vulture*, October 25, 2024, https://www.vulture.com/article/mrbeast-lunchables-mold-controversy.html.

219 **"relatable, mass-appeal content":** Ryan Broderick, "Coolness Is Just Scarcity," Garbage Day, June 17, 2024, https://www.garbageday.email/p/coolness-just-scarcity.

219 **exclusivity and scarcity:** Broderick, "Coolness Is Just Scarcity."

219 **secured a record deal:** Jason Lipshutz, "TikTok Star Bella Poarch Signs with Warner Records, Shares Debut Single," *Billboard*, May 14, 2021, https://www.billboard.com/pro/bella-poarch-warner-records-label-deal-single-build-a-bitch.

219 **"cringe" appearance:** Arvan Mehta, "Addison Rae's Appearance on Jimmy Fallon Labelled 'Cringe' After Clip of Her Teaching Him TikTok Dances Goes Viral," SK Pop, March 28, 2021, https://www.sportskeeda.com/pop-culture/addison-rae-s-appearance-jimmy-fallon-labelled-cringe-clip-teaching-tiktok-dances-goes-viral.

220 **in Gen Z waters:** Chantal Fernandez, "Where Were All the TikTok Influencers at the Met Gala?," *Cut*, May 6, 2024, https://www.thecut.com/article/where-are-all-the-tiktok-influencers-at-the-met-gala.html.

220 **Wisdom Kaye attended:** Fernandez, "Where Were All the TikTok."

220 **internet-born creators:** Callie Holtermann, "From Teen Star to Entrepreneur," *New York Times*, November 10, 2024, https://www.nytimes.com/2024/11/10/style/emma-chamberlain-warby-parker.html; Taylor Lorenz, "Emma Chamberlain Is the Most Important YouTuber Today," *Atlantic*, July 3, 2019, https://www.theatlantic.com/technology/archive/2019/07/emma-chamberlain-and-rise-relatable-influencer/593230.

220 **"radically changed the idea":** Biz Sherbert, "Emma Chamberlain Doesn't Care About Being Famous," *Face*, September 14, 2024, https://theface.com/culture/emma-chamberlain-style-voice-of-a-generation-young-people-social-media-famous.

220 **demolished "traditional barriers":** Taylor Lorenz, *Extremely Online: The Untold Story of Fame, Influence, and Power on the Internet* (Simon & Schuster, 2023), 1.

221 **open Chamberlain Coffee:** Michelle Santiago Cortés, "Emma Chamberlain Talks Chamberlain Coffee's New Look & Products," Refinery 29, September 23, 2020, https://www.refinery29.com/en-us/2020/09/10042481/emma-chamberlain-coffee-merch-brand-interview.

221 **commodity business:** Hoffmann, "How Celebrity Coffee Brands Really Work."

221 **"own my masters":** Shaad D'Souza, "Charli XCX Knows You're Obsessed with Her," *Face*, February 19, 2024, https://theface.com/music/charli-xcx-interview-new-album-xcx6-vol-4-issue-18.

221 **"getting up onstage and waving":** Brock Colyar, "Creature from the Brat Lagoon," *Vulture*, October 11, 2024, https://www.vulture.com/article/charli-xcx-interview-brat-summer-fall-kamala-harris.html.

221 **"hedonistic, bra-less":** Zoe Williams, "Brat Summer: Is the Long Era of Clean Living Finally Over?," *Guardian*, July 16, 2024, https://www.theguardian.com/lifeandstyle/article/2024/jul/16/brat-summer-is-the-long-era-of-clean-living-finally-over.

221 **impending "vibe shift":** Allison P. Davis, "A Vibe Shift Is Coming," *Cut*, February 16, 2022, https://www.thecut.com/2022/02/a-vibe-shift-is-coming.html.

221 **"flash photography":** Davis, "A Vibe Shift Is Coming."

221 **musician the Dare:** Delia Cai, "According to the Cobrasnake, We Haven't Hit the Tip of the Indie-Sleaze Iceberg," Ssense, September 20, 2024, https://www.ssense.com/en-us/editorial/culture/cobrasnake-interview-mark-hunter-indie-sleaze.

222 **"I'm going to make a record":** Colyar, "Creature from the Brat Lagoon."

222 **"or a hamburger":** B. D. McClay, "My Crank Theory of Cultural Longevity," *Notebook* (Substack), December 9, 2023, https://notebook.substack.com/p/my-crank-theory-of-cultural-longevity.

222 **concocted loony conspiracies:** John Ganz, "The Race to the Swift," Unpopular Front, February 1, 2024, https://www.unpopularfront.news/p/the-race-to-the-swift.

222 **extreme parasocial relationships:** Habi Diallo, "Crazy Fans Are Making Chappell Roan Want to Quit Music," *Dazed*, July 19, 2024, https://www.dazeddigital.com

/music/article/63159/1/chappell-roan-drew-afaulo-podcast-fans-obsessive-parasocial.

222 **"Thank you, Beyoncé":** Dani Di Placido, "'TikTok's 'Thank You, Beyoncé' Meme, Explained," *Forbes*, October 8, 2024, https://www.forbes.com/sites/danidiplacido/2024/10/08/tiktoks-thank-you-beyonc-meme-explained.

222 **Drake sued Universal Music:** Sian Cain, "Drake Claims UMG and Spotify 'Artificially Inflated' Kendrick Lamar's Diss Track Not Like Us," *Guardian*, November 26, 2024, https://www.theguardian.com/music/2024/nov/26/drake-kendrick-lamar-umg-spotify-not-like-us-claims-ntwnfb.

222 **world's biggest pop star:** Isabelia Herrera, "In 2022, Bad Bunny Made Pop Stardom a Subversive Act," NPR, December 15, 2022, https://www.npr.org/2022/12/15/1134910331/how-bad-bunny-became-the-biggest-pop-star-2022.

223 **"Skeptics and xenophobes take note":** Herrera, "In 2022, Bad Bunny."

223 **arguably had the most influence:** Lexi Pandell, "How *RuPaul's Drag Race* Fueled Pop Culture's Dominant Slang Engine," *Wired*, March 22, 2018, https://www.wired.com/story/rupauls-drag-race-slang.

223 **"spiritually lobotomized":** Alex Quicho, "Everyone Is a Girl Online," *Wired*, September 11, 2023, https://www.wired.com/story/girls-online-culture.

CHAPTER 15:
TECHNO-NIHILISM

225 **AI tool Midjourney:** Chris Stokel-Walker, "We Spoke to the Guy Who Created the Viral AI Image of the Pope That Fooled the World," *Buzzfeed News*, March 27, 2023, https://www.buzzfeednews.com/article/chrisstokelwalker/pope-puffy-jacket-ai-midjourney-image-creator-interview.

225 **"real AI-generated hoax":** Ryan Broderick, "Pope in a Coat," *Garbage Day*, March 27, 2023, https://www.garbageday.email/p/pope-in-a-coat.

226 **poured into start-ups:** Cade Metz, Karen Weise, and Tripp Mickle, "A.I. Start-Ups Face a Rough Financial Reality Check," *New York Times*, April 29, 2024, https://www.nytimes.com/2024/04/29/technology/ai-startups-financial-reality.html.

226 **often "hallucinated" facts:** Kyle Wiggers, "Are AI Models Doomed to Always Hallucinate?," *TechCrunch*, September 4, 2023, https://techcrunch.com/2023/09/04/are-language-models-doomed-to-always-hallucinate.

226 **"When computer technology":** Jean Baudrillard, *Impossible Exchange* (Verso, 2001), 53.

226 **"A.I. could rapidly eat":** Yuval Harari, Tristan Harris, and Aza Raskin, "You Can Have the Blue Pill or the Red Pill, and We're Out of Blue Pills," *New York Times*, March 24, 2023, https://www.nytimes.com/2023/03/24/opinion/yuval-harari-ai-chatgpt.html.

227 **630 billion words:** Dana G. Smith, "A 630-Billion-Word Internet Analysis Shows 'People' Is Interpreted as 'Men,'" *Scientific American*, April 1, 2022, https://www.scientificamerican.com/article/a-630-billion-word-internet-analysis-shows-people-is-interpreted-as-men.

227 **14 billion visible YouTube videos:** Ryan McGrady, "What We Discovered on 'Deep YouTube,'" *Atlantic*, January 26, 2024, https://www.theatlantic.com/technology/archive/2024/01/how-many-videos-youtube-research/677250.

227 **uploading 100,000 songs:** Andy Price, "'More Music Is Being Released Today (in a Single Day) Than Was Released in the Calendar Year of 1989': How the Music Production Industry Has Taken Note of the Huge Number of Self-Releasing Artists," Music Radar, November 14, 2024, https://www.musicradar.com/music-industry/more-music-is-being-released-today-in-a-single-day-than-was-released-in-the-calendar-year-of-1989-how-the-music-production-industry-has-taken-note-of-the-huge-number-of-self-releasing-artists.

227 **"classist and ableist undertones":** Meghan Herbst, "NaNoWriMo Organizers Said It Was Classist and Ableist to Condemn AI. All Hell Broke Loose," *Wired*, September 4, 2024, https://www.wired.com/story/nanowrimo-organizers-classist-and-ableist-to-condemn-ai.

227 **"this entire side":** Pavel Bevlov, "Suno AI: The World Where Everyone Could Be a Musician," LinkedIn, April 15, 2024, https://www.linkedin.com/pulse/suno-ai-world-where-everyone-could-musician-pavel-belov-l96re.

228 **known as "slop":** Jason Koebler, "Where Facebook's AI Slop Comes From," *404*

Media, August 6, 2024, https://www
.404media.co/where-facebooks-ai-slop
-comes-from.

228 **"beautiful cabin crew"**: Ryan Broderick,
"The AI Flight Attendants of Facebook,"
Garbage Day, April 15, 2024, https://
www.garbageday.email/p/ai-flight
-attendants-facebook.

228 **"prompts that are written"**: Koebler,
"Where Facebook's AI Slop."

228 **platforms like X**: Erik Hoel, "A.I.-
Generated Garbage Is Polluting Our Culture," *New York Times*, March 29, 2024,
https://www.nytimes.com/2024/03/29
/opinion/ai-internet-x-youtube.html.

228 **AI-written "study guides"**: Hoel, "A.I.-
Generated Garbage"; my previous book
Status and Culture also directly experi-
enced this phenomenon.

228 **used AI tools**: Hoel, "A.I.-Generated Garbage."

228 **LinkedIn's long-form posts**: Kate Knibbs,
"Yes, That Viral LinkedIn Post You Read
Was Probably AI-Generated," *Wired*, November 26, 2024, https://www.wired.com
/story/linkedin-ai-generated-influencers.

228 **synthetic, AI-generated data**: Rahul
Rao, "AI-Generated Data Can Poison Future AI Models," *Scientific American*, July
28, 2023, https://www.scientificamerican
.com/article/ai-generated-data-can
-poison-future-ai-models.

229 **AI slop became fodder**: Jason Koebler,
"Hurricane Helene and the 'Fuck It' Era of
AI-Generated Slop," *404 Media*, October
8, 2024, https://www.404media.co/hurri
cane-helene-and-the-fuck-it-era-of-ai
-generated-slop.

229 **"where this photo"**: Koebler, "Hurricane
Helene and the 'Fuck It' Era."

229 **once synonymous with precision**: Charlie Warzel, "The Open Secret of Google
Search," *Atlantic*, June 20, 2022, https://
www.theatlantic.com/ideas/archive/2022
/06/google-search-algorithm-internet
/661325; Rachel Cunliffe, "The Internet
Is Unusable Now," *New Statesman*, June 7,
2023, https://www.newstatesman.com/the
staggers/2023/06/internet-is-unusable
-now-google-technology.

229 **"Is Japan owned by China?"**: "Is Japan
Owned by China?," Quora, https://www
.quora.com/Is-Japan-owned-by-China.

229 **Internet Archive**: Wes Davis, "The Internet Archive Is Under Attack, with a
Breach Revealing Info for 31 Million Accounts," *Verge*, October 9, 2024, https://
www.theverge.com/2024/10/9/24266419

/internet-archive-ddos-attack-pop-up
-message.

229 **vapid AI-generated clickbait videos**:
Freddie Deboer, "The Bitter End of 'Content,'" *Freddie Deboer* (Substack), February
20, 2023, https://freddiedeboer.substack
.com/p/the-bitter-end-of-content.

229 **reaching 275 million users**: Ivan Mehta,
"Threads Now Has 275M Monthly Active
Users," *TechCrunch*, November 3, 2024,
https://techcrunch.com/2024/11/03
/threads-now-has-275m-monthly-active
-users.

229 **"without ever having any"**: Katie No-
topolous (@KatieNotopoulos), Threads,
November 4, 2024, https://www.threads
.net/@katienotopoulos/post/DB84DT
7u-Wm.

230 **Techno Mechanicus**: Rania Aniftos,
"Grimes Opens Up About Custody Battle
with Elon Musk, Says She 'Didn't See
One of My Babies for 5 Months,'" *Billboard*, November 26, 2024, https://www
.billboard.com/music/music-news/grimes
-custody-battle-elon-musk-says-didnt-see
-baby-1235839921.

230 **"heaps of unfiltered posts"**: Charlie Warzel, "X Is a White-Supremacist Site," *Atlantic*, November 5, 2024, https://www
.theatlantic.com/technology/archive
/2024/11/x-white-supremacist-site/680
538.

230 **fell out of love**: Paul Roberts, "Once a
Must for Wealthy Seattle Liberals, Teslas
Feel an Elon Backlash," *Seattle Times*, December 1, 2024, https://www.seattletimes
.com/business/once-a-must-for-wealthy
-seattle-liberals-teslas-now-feel-an-elon
-backlash.

230 **"culture war on wheels"**: Joseph Bernstein, "A Culture War on Wheels," *New
York Times*, July 23, 2024, https://www
.nytimes.com/2024/07/22/style/elon
-musk-tesla-cybertruck.html.

230 **to Kekius Maximus**: "Elon Musk Changes
His Name on X to 'Kekius Maximus', Uses
Pic of 'Pepe the Frog,'" NDTV, December 31, 2024, https://www.ndtv.com/world
-news/elon-musk-changes-his-name-on-x
-to-kekius-maximus-uses-pic-of
-pepe-the-frog-7369514.

230 **anti-"woke" content**: Elon Musk (@Elon-
Musk), "YES!," X (formerly Twitter), December 13, 2024, https://x.com/ElonMusk
/status/1867652149012001262.

231 **"they grew up with"**: Kate Knibbs, "The
Internet Isn't Dead. It's Saturday Night
Live," *Wired*, December 23, 2023, https://

www.wired.com/story/the-internet-isnt-dying-its-saturday-night-live.

231 **"Knee Surgery Is Tomorrow":** Sakshi Rakshale, "What's Up with the Blue Grinch Saying 'That Feeling When Knee Surgery Is Tomorrow'? The Oddly Specific Meme Explained," Know Your Meme, November 4, 2024, https://knowyourmeme.com/editorials/guides/whats-up-with-the-blue-grinch-saying-that-feeling-when-knee-surgery-is-tomorrow-the-oddly-specific-meme-explained.

231 **"Just because you aren't":** Knibbs, "Internet Isn't Dead."

231 **"enshittification":** Cory Doctorow, "The 'Enshittification' of TikTok," *Wired*, January 23, 2023, https://www.wired.com/story/tiktok-platforms-cory-doctorow.

231 **"tends to be accessible":** Kyle Chayka, *Filterworld: How Algorithms Flattened Culture* (Doubleday, 2024), 5.

231 **pervasive "averageness":** Chayka, *Filterworld*, 9.

231 **"People tend to watch":** McGrady, "What We Discovered on 'Deep YouTube.'"

231 **"useless platform Kremlinology":** Doctorow, "The 'Enshittification' of TikTok."

231 **"Given my understanding":** Matthew Yglesias, "The Case Against Meta," *Slow Boring*, August 29, 2022, https://www.slowboring.com/p/the-case-against-meta.

232 **Silicon Valley dwindled:** Nico Grant, "What Is (or Was) 'Perks Culture'?," *New York Times*, December 16, 2024, https://www.nytimes.com/2024/12/13/technology/tech-perks-culture.html.

232 **"It sometimes seems":** Derek Thompson, "White-Collar Work Is Just Meetings Now," *Atlantic*, July 9, 2024, https://www.theatlantic.com/ideas/archive/2024/07/white-collar-meetings-more-frequent/678941.

232 **Cal Newport gained traction:** Jennifer Szalai, "The Very Busy Writer Telling Everyone to Slow Down," *New York Times*, March 6, 2024, https://www.nytimes.com/2024/03/06/books/review/slow-productivity-cal-newport.html.

232 **"lights just turned on":** Erin Griffith, "The End of Faking It in Silicon Valley," *New York Times*, April 15, 2023, https://www.nytimes.com/2023/04/15/business/silicon-valley-fraud.html.

232 **Frank's Charlie Javice:** Arwa Mahdawi, "30 Under 30-Year Sentences: Why So Many of Forbes' Young Heroes Face Jail," *Guardian*, April 7, 2023, https://www.the guardian.com/business/2023/apr/06/forbes-30-under-30-tech-finance-prison.

233 **"tall, long-haired, barefoot":** Matthew Zeitlin, "Why WeWork Went Wrong," *Guardian*, December 20, 2019, https://www.theguardian.com/business/2019/dec/20/why-wework-went-wrong.

233 **"dark forest" era:** Knibbs, "Internet Isn't Dead."

234 **Jeff Bezos bulked up:** Arwa Mahdawi, "Buff Billionaires Are Latest Sign That Bulk Is Now Beautiful for Male Body Image," *Guardian*, June 3, 2023, https://www.theguardian.com/commentisfree/2023/jun/03/buff-billionaires-jeff-bezos-mark-zuckerberg-body-image.

234 **doomsday-ready concrete bunker:** Mark O'Connell, "Why Silicon Valley Billionaires Are Prepping for the Apocalypse in New Zealand," *Guardian*, February 15, 2017, https://www.theguardian.com/news/2018/feb/15/why-silicon-valley-billionaires-are-prepping-for-the-apocalypse-in-new-zealand.

234 **ketamine to treat his depression:** Clare Duffy, "Elon Musk Details His Prescription Ketamine Use, Says Investors Should Want Him to 'Keep Taking It,'" CNN, March 18, 2024, https://edition.cnn.com/2024/03/18/tech/elon-musk-ketamine-use-don-lemon-interview/index.html.

234 **sold for $61.6 million:** "Here Are the 10 Most Expensive Works of Art Sold at Auction in 2021—and Why They Fetched the Prices They Did," Artnet, December 29, 2021, https://news.artnet.com/market/ten-expensive-lots-sold-auction-2021-2051948.

234 **astonishing $69.3 million:** Eileen Kinsella, "'This Is Going to Be a Billion-Dollar Piece Someday': The Buyer of the $69 Million Beeple NFT on Why It's the Greatest Artwork in a Generation," Artnet, March 12, 2021, https://news.artnet.com/market/the-buyer-of-the-69-million-beeple-nft-metapurse-1951561.

234 **"gender-swapped Captain Crunch":** Ben Davis, "I Looked Through All 5,000 Images in Beeple's $69 Million Magnum Opus. What I Found Isn't So Pretty," Artnet, March 17, 2021, https://news.artnet.com/art-world-archives/beeple-every-days-review-1951656.

234 **hadn't even looked:** Kinsella, "'This Is Going to Be.'"

234 **"billion-dollar piece":** Kinsella, "'This Is Going to Be.'"

235 **world's Bitcoins:** Nathaniel Popper, "How the Winklevoss Twins Found Vindication in a Bitcoin Fortune," *New York Times*, December 19, 2017, https://www.nytimes.com/2017/12/19/technology/bitcoin-winklevoss-twins.html.

235 **a single Bitcoin hit:** Julia Kollewe, "Bitcoin Surges Through $60,000 in Biggest Monthly Rally Since Late 2020—as It Happened," *Guardian*, February 28, 2024, https://www.theguardian.com/business/live/2024/feb/28/thames-water-lobbying-higher-bills-lower-fines-avoid-bailout-report-claims-somerset-gigafactory-bridgend-tata-us-gdp-business-live.

235 **turning the Winklevoss twins:** Giacomo Tognini, "Rihanna, the Winklevoss Twins, and More: Here Are the Most Notable New Billionaires of 2021," *Forbes*, April 21, 2022, https://www.forbes.com/sites/giacomotognini/2021/12/24/rihanna-the-winklevoss-twins-and-more-here-are-the-most-notable-new-billionaires-of-2021.

235 **"hard-hitting" band:** Mars Junction official site, accessed June 26, 2025, https://www.marsjunction.com.

235 **with a new outlet:** Zachary Small, *Token Supremacy: The Art of Finance, the Finance of Art, and the Great Crypto Crash of 2022* (Alfred A. Knopf, 2024), 21.

235 **"NFTs were about creating":** Small, *Token Supremacy*, 5.

236 **Investors balked:** Steve Rose, "'The Metaverse Will Be Our Slow Death!' Is Facebook Losing Its $100bn Gamble on Virtual Reality?," *Guardian*, December 7, 2022, https://www.theguardian.com/technology/2022/dec/07/metaverse-slow-death-facebook-losing-100bn-gamble-virtual-reality-mark-zuckerberg.

236 **"But seriously," Zuckerberg asserted:** Shirin Ghaffary, "Legs Are Finally Coming to Mark Zuckerberg's Metaverse," *Vox*, October 11, 2022, https://www.vox.com/recode/2022/10/11/23399439/metaverse-mark-zuckerberg-connect-avatar-legs-meta-microsoft-apple-vr-ar.

236 **labeled its momentum "dead":** Kyle Barr, "Apple Vision Pro U.S. Sales Are All but Dead, Market Analysts Say," Gizmodo, July 11, 2024, https://gizmodo.com/apple-vision-pro-u-s-sales-2000469302.

236 **"meatspace," or physical world:** Peter Coy, "'Meatspace'? Technology Does Funny Things to Language," *New York Times*, April 1, 2022, https://www.nytimes.com/2022/04/01/opinion/language-technology-economics.html.

236 **"Business Art":** Natasha Degen, *Merchants of Style: Art and Fashion After Warhol* (Reaktion Books, 2023), 29.

237 **"has no brief against":** Arthur Danto, *After the End of Art: Contemporary Art and the Pale of History* (Princeton University Press, 1997), 3.

237 **"mediocrity squared":** Jean Baudrillard, *The Conspiracy of Art* (Semiotext(e), 2005), 27.

237 **"mysterious collectors":** Calvin Tomkins, "A Fool for Art," *New Yorker*, November 4, 2007, https://www.newyorker.com/magazine/2007/11/12/a-fool-for-art.

237 **paid $143.5 million:** Tomkins, "A Fool for Art."

237 **"critiques against consumer culture":** Degen, *Merchants of Style*, 164.

237 **"Luxury brands neutralize":** Degen, *Merchants of Style*, 164.

237 **"ambition to explore":** Dean Kissick, "The Painted Protest," *Harper's*, December 2024, https://harpers.org/archive/2024/12/the-painted-protest-dean-kissick-contemporary-art.

237 **traditional European capitals:** Maxwell Rabb, "How Miami Became an Art World Capital," Artsy, November 30, 2023, https://www.artsy.net/article/artsy-editorial-miami-art-capital.

237 **prices to crash:** Zachary Small and Julia Halperin, "Young Artists Rode a $712 Million Boom. Then Came the Bust," *New York Times*, August 18, 2024, https://www.nytimes.com/2024/08/18/arts/design/young-artists-auctions-collectors.html.

237 **"NFTs as a symbol":** Small, *Token Supremacy*, 12.

238 **"When you say":** Kyle Chayka, "How Beeple Crashed the Art World," *New Yorker*, March 22, 2021, https://www.newyorker.com/tech/annals-of-technology/how-beeple-crashed-the-art-world.

238 **"aesthetic complexity":** Rebecca Alter, "Paris Hilton and Jimmy Fallon Go Ape for Printouts of NFTs," *Vulture*, January 25, 2022, https://www.vulture.com/2022/01/paris-hilton-jimmy-fallon-bored-ape-yacht-club-nft.html.

238 **"just trying to expand":** KK Ottesen, "The Digital Artist Known as Beeple: 'I'm Just Trying to Expand People's Idea of What Art Is,'" *Washington Post*, March 22,

2022, https://www.washingtonpost.com
/magazine/2022/03/22/digital-artist
-known-beeple-im-just-trying-expand
-peoples-idea-what-art-is.

238 **Zoë Roth of Disaster Girl:** Marie Fazio,
"The World Knows Her as 'Disaster Girl.'
She Just Made $500,000 off the Meme,"
New York Times, April 29, 2021, https://
www.nytimes.com/2021/04/29/arts/disas
ter-girl-meme-nft.html.

238 **"Doge" meme:** Kalhan Rosenblatt,
"Iconic 'Doge' Meme NFT Breaks Record,
Selling for $4 Million," NBC News, June
11, 2021, https://www.nbcnews.com/pop
-culture/pop-culture-news/iconic-doge
-meme-nft-breaks-records-selling
-roughly-4-million-n1270161.

238 **"don't want to be broke":** Hiji Nam,
"Price of Entry," *Artforum*, April 28, 2023,
https://www.artforum.com/columns
/price-of-entry-252684.

238 **"The way I describe it":** Kevin Roose, "I
Joined a Penguin NFT Club Because Ap-
parently That's What We Do Now," *New
York Times*, June 23, 2023, https://www
.nytimes.com/2021/08/12/technology
/penguin-nft-club.html.

239 **with Madonna's agent:** Zeke Faux,
*Number Go Up: Inside Crypto's Wild Rise
and Staggering Fall* (Currency, 2023), 154;
Small, *Token Supremacy*, 100.

239 **Curry paid $180,000:** Ambrose Leung,
"Steph Curry Just Bought a Bored Ape
Yacht Club NFT for $180,000 USD Worth
of ETH," Hypebeast, August 30, 2021,
https://hypebeast.com/2021/8/stephen
-curry-bored-ape-yacht-club-nft-55
-ethereum-purchase.

239 **Bieber owned one:** Andrew Hayward,
"Justin Bieber Paid $1.3 Million for a
Bored Ape NFT. It's Now Worth $69K,"
Yahoo! Finance, November 17, 2022,
https://finance.yahoo.com/news/justin
-bieber-paid-1-3-195705336.html.

239 **BAYC-themed products:** Hannah Miller,
"Bored Ape Yacht Club NFTs: Where Are
They Now?," *Bloomberg*, February 29,
2024, https://www.bloomberg.com/news
/newsletters/2024-02-29/what-happened
-to-yuga-labs-bored-ape-yacht-club
-nfts.

239 **showcased their apes:** Faux, *Number Go
Up*, 141.

239 **"friendly neighborhood bartender":**
Sarah Emerson, "Someone Stole Seth
Green's Bored Ape, Which Was Supposed
to Star in His New Show," *BuzzFeed News*,
May 24, 2022, https://www.buzzfeed
news.com/article/sarahemerson/seth
-green-bored-ape-stolen-tv-show.

239 **in a phishing attack:** Zoe Guy, "Seth
Green Gets Scammed out of His Show's
Main Character," *Vulture*, May 24, 2022,
https://www.vulture.com/2022/05/seth
-green-stolen-nft-tv-show.html.

239 **precisely why NFTs failed:** W. David
Marx, "Are NFTs Status Symbols?," Dirt,
September 8, 2021, https://dirt.fyi/article
/2021/09/are-nfts-status-symbols.

239 **"I'm here in a Brioni":** Faux, *Number Go
Up*, 130.

239 **plummeted over 90 percent:** Shaurya
Malwa, "Bored Ape NFT Prices Tank to
August 2022 Levels, Down 90% from
Peak," CoinDesk, April 16, 2024, https://
www.coindesk.com/web3/2024/04/16
/bored-ape-nft-prices-tank-to-august
-2022-levels-down-90-from-peak; Jessica
Sier, "Bored Ape Owners Sent Broke After
NFT Price Collapse," *Australian Financial
Review*, July 10, 2023, https://www.afr
.com/technology/bored-ape-owners-sent
-broke-after-nft-price-collapse-20230706
-p5dm7c.

239 **Kingship never launched:** Marc Schneider, "Bored Ape Supergroup KINGSHIP
Now Has a Habitat in Roblox," *Billboard*,
November 30, 2023, https://www.billboard
.com/business/tech/bored-ape-group
-kingship-roblox-level-environment
-1235518319.

240 **"stand less chance":** Tyler Cowen, "Recession Can Change a Way of Life," *New
York Times*, January 31, 2009, https://
www.nytimes.com/2009/02/01/business
/01view.html.

240 **turned her powers:** Hilary George-
Parkin, "The Anxieties and Apps Fuelling
the Astrology Boom," BBC, February 8,
2021, https://www.bbc.com/worklife/arti
cle/20210205-why-astrology-is-so
-popular-now.

240 **$830 to $19,783:** Nellie Bowles, "Everyone
Is Getting Hilariously Rich and You're
Not," *New York Times*, January 13, 2018,
https://www.nytimes.com/2018/01/13
/style/bitcoin-millionaires.html; David Z.
Morris, "Bitcoin Hits a New Record High,
but Stops Short of $20,000," *Fortune*, De-
cember 17, 2017, https://web.archive.org
/web/20181114132600/http://fortune
.com/2017/12/17/bitcoin-record-high
-short-of-20000

240 **then crossed $100,000:** Rafael Nam, "Bit-
coin Hits $100,000 for the First Time.
3 Things to Know About an Incredible

Ride," NPR, December 4, 2024, https://www.npr.org/2024/12/04/nx-s1-5202832/bitcoin-rally-100-000-crypto-trump.

240 **Ethereum went to market**: "Ethereum's Price History," GlobalData, accessed June 26, 2025, https://www.globaldata.com/data-insights/financial-services/ethereums-price-history.

240 **"all going to make it"**: LiterallyAustin, "WAGMI / NGMI," Know Your Meme, June 17, 2021, https://knowyourmeme.com/memes/wagmi-ngmi.

240 **"value masculinity highly"**: Katherine Hamilton, "Young Men Are Making Risky Bets on Crypto and Politics—and Raking It In Right Now," *Wall Street Journal*, December 7, 2024, https://www.wsj.com/finance/investing/young-men-investing-bitcoin-stocks-sports-betting-1d44cf8c.

240 **"Invest heavily in crypto"**: Faux, *Number Go Up*, 140.

240 **was a "degen"**: Small, *Token Supremacy*, 68–69.

241 **80 percent of ICOs**: Faux, *Number Go Up*, 51.

241 **"Bitcoin maxi now"**: *Money Electric: The Bitcoin Mystery*, directed by Cullen Hoback (HBO Documentary Films, 2024).

241 **$10-billion-plus industry**: German Lopez, "The Rise of Sports Betting," *New York Times*, April 5, 2024, https://www.nytimes.com/2024/04/05/briefing/the-rise-of-sports-betting.html.

241 **retooled its programs**: Jason Quick, "'I Literally Can't Stop.' The Descent of a Modern Sports Fan," *New York Times*, October 14, 2024, https://www.nytimes.com/athletic/5777632/2024/10/14/sports-betting-addiction-problem-fans.

242 **"So many smart people"**: Faux, *Number Go Up*, 237.

CHAPTER 16:
A NEW LUXURY

243 **Shanghai screening**: John Pasden, "The Martian in China: Two Observations," *Sinosplice*, December 1, 2015, https://www.sinosplice.com/life/archives/2015/12/01/the-martian-in-china-two-observations.

243 **like in 2012**: Peter Ford, "Why 2012 Movie Is a Hit in China," *Christian Science Monitor*, November 23, 2009, https://www.csmonitor.com/World/Global-News/2009/1123/why-2012-movie-is-a-hit-in-china.

243 ***Transformers: Age of Extinction***: Ben Child, "Transformers: Age of Extinction Becomes Highest-Grossing Film of All Time in China," *Guardian*, July 8, 2014, https://www.theguardian.com/film/2014/jul/08/transformers-age-extinction-highest-grossing-china.

243 **gutted factory jobs**: Peter Dizikes, "Q&A: David Autor on the Long Afterlife of the 'China Shock,'" *MIT News*, December 6, 2021, https://news.mit.edu/2021/david-autor-china-shock-persists-1206.

243 **was just $959**: "GDP per Capita (Current US$)—China," World Bank Group, accessed January 28, 2025, https://data.worldbank.org/indicator/NY.GDP.PCAP.CD?locations=CN.

243 **pool of millionaires**: Ali Hassan, "12 Countries Millionaires Are Moving To," Yahoo! Finance, September 17, 2024, https://finance.yahoo.com/news/12-countries-millionaires-moving-074936042.html; Charmaine Jacob, "Mumbai Overtakes Beijing to Become Asia's Billionaire Capital for the First Time," CNBC, March 27, 2024, https://www.cnbc.com/2024/03/27/mumbai-overtakes-beijing-to-become-asias-billionaire-capital-for-first-time.html.

243 **473 in 2024**: "World's Billionaires List," *Forbes*, 2024, https://www.forbes.com/billionaires.

244 **domestic freedoms tightened**: Elizabeth C. Economy, "The Great Firewall of China: Xi Jinping's Internet Shutdown," *Guardian*, June 29, 2018, https://www.theguardian.com/news/2018/jun/29/the-great-firewall-of-china-xi-jinpings-internet-shutdown.

244 **Umbrella Movement**: Zen Soo and Huizhong Wu, "How Democracy Was Dismantled in Hong Kong in 2021," Associated Press, December 29, 2021, https://apnews.com/article/china-hong-kong-beijing-democracy-national-security-9e3c405923c24b6889c1bcf171f6def4.

244 **Ai Weiwei was arrested**: Ian Williams, "'This Is a Massacre of Thoughts': The Exiled Chinese Artist Ai Weiwei on His Cancellation," *Spectator*, December 16, 2023, https://www.spectator.co.uk/article/this-is-a-massacre-of-thoughts-the-exiled-chinese-artist-ai-weiwei-on-his-cancellation.

244 **visas for journalists**: Marc Tracy, Edward Wong, and Lara Jakes, "China Announces That It Will Expel American Journalists," *New York Times*, November 16, 2021, https://www.nytimes.com/2020/03/17/business/media/china-expels-american-journalists.html.

244 **censorship of Pooh-related memes:** Vanessa Romo, "Why a Horror Film Starring Winnie the Pooh Has Run into Trouble in Hong Kong," NPR, March 23, 2023, https://www.npr.org/2023/03/23/1165504942/winnie-the-pooh-xi-jinping-china-film.

244 **Hollywood also agreed:** Deeper into Movies, and Erich Schwartzel, "9 Movies That Reveal the Weird Relationship Between China and Hollywood," *Vice*, March 25, 2022, https://www.vice.com/en/article/is-china-involved-in-hollywood.

245 *tang ping* **("lying flat"):** Ivana Davidovic, "'Lying Flat': Why Some Chinese Are Putting Work Second," *BBC News*, February 16, 2022, https://www.bbc.com/news/business-60353916.

245 **remain surprisingly sparse:** Sean Keeley, "How '3 Body Problem' Gets Lost in Translation," *Dispatch*, April 13, 2024, https://thedispatch.com/article/how-3-body-problem-gets-lost-in-translation.

245 **"balanced twentysomethings":** Keeley, "How '3 Body Problem' Gets Lost."

245 **taken off the air:** Andreas Illmer, "Yanxi Palace: Why China Turned Against Its Most Popular Show," *BBC News*, February 7, 2019, https://www.bbc.com/news/world-asia-china-47084374.

246 **in the global spotlight:** Amy Hawkins, "Chinese Rival App Xiaohongshu Is Overwhelmed by 'TikTok Refugees' in US," *Guardian*, January 18, 2025, https://www.theguardian.com/technology/2025/jan/18/chinese-rival-app-xiaohongshu-is-overwhelmed-by-tiktok-refugees-in-us.

246 **new designs daily:** Astha Rajvanshi, "Shein Is the World's Most Popular Fashion Brand—at a Huge Cost to Us All," *Time*, January 17, 2023, https://time.com/6247732/shein-climate-change-labor-fashion.

246 **exploiting laborers:** Rajvanshi, "Shein Is the World's."

246 **plagiarizing designs:** Ellie Violet Bramley, "'Details I Made, They Made'—Designers Hit Back at Shein's Imitation Game," *Guardian*, September 2, 2023, https://www.theguardian.com/business/2023/sep/02/details-i-made-they-made-designers-hit-back-at-sheins-imitation-game.

246 **Uyghur Forced Labor Prevention Act:** Hope O'Dell, "The Cost of Shein and Temu's Low Prices," Chicago Council on Global Affairs, October 19, 2023, https://globalaffairs.org/bluemarble/how-shein-and-temu-get-around-us-labor-laws-ban-products-made-forced-labor.

246 **Western influencers:** Vanessa Romo, "Shein Invited Influencers on an All-Expenses-Paid Trip. Here's Why People Are Livid," NPR, June 30, 2023, https://www.npr.org/2023/06/30/1184974003/shein-influencers-china-factory-trip-backlash.

246 **"The gaslighting is CRAZY!":** Jordyn Holman and Sapna Maheshwari, "Shein Flew Influencers to China to Help Its Image. A Backlash Ensued," *New York Times*, June 29, 2023, https://www.nytimes.com/2023/06/29/business/shein-influencers-backlash.html.

246 **author Haruki Murakami:** Stephen Teo, *Wong Kar-Wai: Auteur of Time* (Bloomsbury, 2005), 50–51.

247 **"most important person":** Jake Woolf, "The 25 Most Powerful People in Streetwear," *Complex*, January 23, 2013, https://www.complex.com/style/a/jake-woolf/the-25-most-powerful-people-in-streetwear.

248 **to Chinese factories:** This is one of the major themes of Dana Thomas, *Deluxe: How Luxury Lost Its Luster* (Penguin Books, 2008).

248 **hired a Japanese consultant:** Kyojiro Hata, *Louis Vuitton Japan: The Building of Luxury* (Assouline, 2004).

248 **Louis Vuitton's sales:** Suzy Menkes, "Capitalizing on the Power of Asia," *New York Times*, October 9, 1993, https://www.nytimes.com/1993/10/09/IHT-capitalizing-on-the-power-of-asia.html.

248 **global luxury sales:** Bruno Lannes and Weiwei Xing, "2023 China Luxury Goods Market: A Year of Recovery and Transition," Bain & Company, March 8, 2024, https://www.bain.com/insights/2023-china-luxury-goods-market.

248 **40 percent by 2030:** Shilpa Dhamija, "Chinese Consumers Set to Lead Personal Luxury Goods Market by 2030, According to Bain & Co.," *Jing Daily*, November 16, 2023, https://jingdaily.com/posts/china-personal-luxury-goods-market-2030-bain.

248 **generation in China:** Gracia Ventus, "Mao's Disappointment—a Look into China's Materialism," Rosenrot, March 11, 2018, https://the-rosenrot.com/chinese-materialism.

248 **"super rich are trading":** Ventus, "Mao's Disappointment."

249 **"brand for secretaries":** Megan Willett-Wei, "Louis Vuitton Is Now a 'Brand for

Secretaries' in China," *Business Insider*, February 27, 2015, https://www.business insider.com/louis-vuitton-losing-sales-in -china-2015-2.

249 **don't possess them:** Alex Imas and Kristof Madarasz, "Superiority Seeking and the Preference for Exclusion," *Review of Economic Studies*, August 7, 2023, https:// www.restud.com/superiority -seeking-and-the-preference-for-exclusion.

249 **more exclusive lines:** Rachel Tashjian, "The Rich Don't Dress like You Think They Do," *Washington Post*, May 7, 2023, https://www.washingtonpost.com/life style/2023/05/07/quiet-luxury-succession.

249 **"biggest fashion movement":** Sowmya Krishnamurthy, *Fashion Killa: How Hip-Hop Revolutionized High Fashion* (Gallery Books, 2023), 181.

249 **"single-minded vision":** Robert Sullivan, "Charting the Rise of Supreme, from Cult Skate Shop to Fashion Superpower," *Vogue*, August 10, 2017, https://www.vogue.com /article/history-of-supreme-skate -clothing-brand.

249 **the hybrid logo:** Alison Millington, "The Instagram-Famous Son of a Dubai Billionaire Wrapped a £200,000 Ferrari in Louis Vuitton Print—but Is 3 Years Too Young to Drive It," *Business Insider*, August 9, 2017, https://www.businessinsider .com/money-kicks-rashed-saif-belhasa -wraps-ferrari-in-louis-vuitton-print -2017-8.

249 **Harlem's Dapper Dan:** David Marchese, "Dapper Dan on Creating Style, Logomania and Working with Gucci," *New York Times Magazine*, July 1, 2019, https://www .nytimes.com/interactive/2019/07/01/mag azine/dapper-dan-hip-hop-style.html.

250 **met Abloh in 2009:** Vanessa Friedman and Elizabeth Paton, "Louis Vuitton Names Virgil Abloh as Its New Men's Wear Designer," *New York Times*, March 26, 2018, https://www.nytimes.com/2018/03/26 /business/louis-vuitton-virgil-abloh .html.

250 **"muse has always been":** Friedman and Paton, "Louis Vuitton Names Virgil Abloh."

250 **"pain and jealousy":** Brad Callas, "Kanye Says He Felt 'Pain and Jealousy' After Virgil Abloh Was Appointed to Louis Vuitton Position," *Complex*, October 7, 2022, https://www.complex.com/style/a/brad -callas/kanye-west-felt-pain-jealousy -louis-vuitton-deal-line-fell-through.

250 **offered him the role:** Callas, "Kanye Says He Felt."

250 **Hailey Baldwin's wedding dress:** Krishnamurthy, *Fashion Killa*, 179.

250 **"being at Louis Vuitton":** Nicole Phelps, "Virgil Abloh Shares Pics of His LV2 Collaboration with Nigo and Clarifies That 'Streetwear Is Dead' Comment," *Vogue*, March 9, 2020, https://www.vogue.com /slideshow/louis-vuitton-lv2-virgil-abloh -nigo-collaboration.

250 **modest $2.8 million:** "Hong Kong's I.T. Buys 90% of BAPE," *Complex*, February 1, 2011, https://www.complex.com/style/a /complex/hong-kongs-i-t-buys-90-of -bape.

250 **"my generation's Chanel":** Krishnamurthy, *Fashion Killa*, 175.

251 **"just as important":** Krishnamurthy, *Fashion Killa*, 175.

251 **50 percent of its shares:** Elizabeth Segran, "Cult Streetwear Brand Supreme Is Now a Unicorn," *Fast Company*, October 11, 2017, https://www.fastcompany.com /40480149/supreme-is-now-a-unicorn -500-million-carlyle-group-deal.

251 **Supreme for $2.1 billion:** "VF Corporation Completes Acquisition of Supreme," VF Corporation, December 28, 2020, https:// www.vfc.com/investors/news-events -presentations/press-releases/detail/1741/vf -corporation-completes-acquisition-of -supreme.

251 **Palace partnered with Polo:** Cam Wolf, "Ralph Lauren Is Collaborating with Skate Brand Palace," *GQ*, October 29, 2018, https://www.gq.com/story/ralph-lau ren-palace-collab.

251 **"McDonald's is an incredible brand":** Kyle MacNeill, "At McDonald's, a Growing Appetite for Fashion," *New York Times*, November 15, 2023, https://www.nytimes .com/2023/11/15/style/mcdonalds-crocs -moschino-vetements.html.

251 **"sneakers and T-shirts":** Vanessa Friedman, "Streetwear Is Dead," *New York Times*, February 10, 2022, https://www .nytimes.com/2022/02/10/style /streetwear-virgil-abloh-balenciaga.html.

251 **Dior Book Tote:** Amy Francombe, "Why Consumers Are Questioning Luxury's Markups," *Vogue Business*, July 23, 2024, https://www.voguebusiness.com/story /consumers/why-consumers-are-question ing-luxurys-markups.

252 **released a controversial video:** Maureen O'Connor, "The Trials of Diet Prada." *Vanity Fair*, September 16, 2021, https:// www.vanityfair.com/style/2021/09/diet -prada-roasting-the-runway.

252 **"Instead of dictating everything"**: Tiffany Ap, "China's Fashion Heavyweights React to Dolce & Gabbana Debacle," *WWD*, November 21, 2018, https://wwd.com/feature/chinas-fashion-heavyweights-react-to-dolce-gabbana-debacle-1202911319.

252 **criticism over a garment**: Ligaya Mishan, "What Does Cultural Appropriation Really Mean?," *New York Times Magazine*, September 30, 2022, https://www.nytimes.com/2022/09/30/t-magazine/cultural-appropriation.html.

252 **artist Sun Yitian**: Denni Hu, "Meet Sun Yitian, Artist Behind Louis Vuitton's Latest China Collaboration," *WWD*, April 18, 2024, https://wwd.com/eye/people/sun-yitian-artist-louis-vuittons-china-collaboration-1236318156.

252 **"whose creative universes"**: Elizabeth Paton and Guy Trebay, "Pharrell Williams Is Louis Vuitton's Next Men's Designer," *New York Times*, February 14, 2023, https://www.nytimes.com/2023/02/14/style/pharrell-williams-louis-vuitton-mens-creative-director.html.

253 **brown derby hat**: Krishnamurthy, *Fashion Killa*, 17.

253 **billion online views**: Natasha Degen, "'Barbie,' 'Saltburn,' Louis Vuitton: When Culture Becomes a TikTok Craze," *New York Times*, January 23, 2024, https://www.nytimes.com/2024/01/23/opinion/social-media-tiktok-marketing.html.

253 **a true "millionaire" version**: Joyce Li, "Pharrell's $1 Million USD Louis Vuitton Speedy Bag Revealed to Be Available in Four Additional Colorways," Hypebeast, November 7, 2023, https://hypebeast.com/2023/11/pharrells-one-million-usd-louis-vuitton-millionaire-speedy-bag-four-more-colorways-revealed.

253 **show in Hong Kong**: Joyce Li, "UPDATE: Louis Vuitton Reveals Location of Men's Pre-Fall 2024 Show in Hong Kong," Hypebeast, November 20, 2023, https://hypebeast.com/2023/10/pharrell-williams-louis-vuitton-mens-pre-fall-2024-collection-first-time-hong-kong-announcement.

253 **Pharrell's three-day tour**: Denni Hu, "Pharrell Williams' China Tour Ignites Fan Fervor, Drives VIP Sales," *WWD*, December 5, 2023, https://wwd.com/eye/scoops/pharrell-williams-china-trip-1236006638; Wenzhuo Wu, "Unveiling the Allure: China's Affection for Pharrell Williams," *Jing Daily*, December 14, 2023, https://jingdaily.com/posts/china-affection-pharrell-williams.

253 **saw its shares fall**: "Kering Revisits 2020 Lows, as Expected. Now What?," EWM Interactive, January 16, 2024, https://ewminteractive.com/kering-revisits-2020-lows-expected-now-what.

253 **"turned itself into"**: Bloomberg, "The End of Luxury? Gucci Slowdown Sends Alarms: 'Turned Itself into a Streetwear Brand but Later . . .'" *Hindustan Times*, March 25, 2024, https://www.hindustantimes.com/business/the-end-of-luxury-gucci-slowdown-sends-alarms-turned-itself-into-a-streetwear-brand-but-later-101711339131309.html.

253 **"I would definitely say"**: Friedman, "Streetwear Is Dead."

253 **"became almost like"**: Tom Barker, "Streetwear Has Lost Its Popularity. Is That a Good Thing?," Highsnobiety, November 27, 2024, https://www.highsnobiety.com/p/streetwear-popularity-2024.

253 **conglomerate EssilorLuxottica**: "Essilor-Luxottica to Acquire Supreme from VF Corporation," VF Corporation, July 17, 2024, https://www.vfc.com/news/press-release/1839/essilorluxottica-to-acquire-supreme-from-vf-corporation.

253 **"stealth wealth"**: Kristopher Fraser, "Quiet Luxury Explained: A Trend or a Fashion Subculture That's Gone Popular?," *WWD*, May 3, 2023, https://wwd.com/feature/quiet-luxury-trend-fashion-explained-1235630126.

254 **"the imperialist phase of his glow-up"**: Jacob Gallagher, "Mark Zuckerberg Tries His Hand at Fashion," *New York Times*, October 8, 2024, https://www.nytimes.com/2024/10/04/style/mark-zuckerberg-fashion-shirt.html.

254 **designer Mike Amiri**: Gallagher, "Mark Zuckerberg Tries."

254 **a "limited drop"**: Gallagher, "Mark Zuckerberg Tries."

254 **"a world without Caesars"**: Amanda Silberling, "Bluesky Made More Money Selling T-shirts Mocking Zuckerberg Than Custom Domains," TechCrunch, March 19, 2025, https://techcrunch.com/2025/03/19/bluesky-made-more-money-selling-t-shirts-mocking-zuckerberg-than-custom-domains.

254 **who sued Hermès**: Jacob Bernstein, "They Failed in Their Quests to Buy Birkin Bags. So They Sued," *New York Times*, March 21, 2024, https://www.ny

times.com/2024/03/21/style/birkin-bag
-hermes-lawsuit.html.

254 **"Luxury labels bulk up"**: Mimosa Spencer, "Luxury Labels Bulk Up on Lower-Priced Goods to Appeal to Middle-Class Shoppers," Reuters, December 19, 2024, https://www.reuters.com/business/retail-consumer/luxury-labels-bulk-up-lower-priced-goods-appeal-middle-class-shoppers-2024-12-20.

255 **"As costs climb"**: Katharine K. Zarrella, "Obscene Prices, Declining Quality: Luxury Is in a Death Spiral," *New York Times*, December 19, 2024, https://www.nytimes.com/2024/12/19/opinion/vuitton-chanel-lvmh-hermes.html.

255 **famed idea of simulation**: Jean Baudrillard, *Simulations* (Semiotext(e), 1983).

255 **that's "cottagecore"**: Mireille Silcoff, "Teen Subcultures Are Fading. Pity the Poor Kids," *New York Times*, February 22, 2024, https://www.nytimes.com/2024/02/21/magazine/aesthetics-tiktok-teens.html.

255 **"wear Nirvana shirts"**: Sarah Stankorb, "No Apologies," *Slate*, October 6, 2023, https://slate.com/human-interest/2023/10/nirvana-shirts-tiktok-trend-style-preppy-teens.html.

255 **"favorite clothing brand"**: Stankorb, "No Apologies."

CHAPTER 17:
BOYS GONE WILD

256 **made his first fortune**: Hadley Meares, "The Garbutt House in Silver Lake: Concrete Mansion That Capitalism Built," PBS SoCal, December 20, 2013, https://www.pbssocal.org/history-society/the-garbutt-house-in-silver-lake-concrete-mansion-that-capitalism-built.

256 **concrete mansion**: Bianca Barragan, "The 10 Weirdest Things About Dov Charney's All-Concrete Garbutt House in Silver Lake," Curbed Los Angeles, December 23, 2013, https://la.curbed.com/2013/12/23/10161108/the-10-craziest-things-about-dov-charneys-allconcrete-garbutt-house.

256 **sculpture of a middle finger**: Zach Behrens, "Found in LA: Dov Charney Gives LA the Finger," LAist, April 9, 2008, https://web.archive.org/web/20141227183645/http://laist.com/2008/04/09/found_in_la_dov.php.

256 **sell the mansion**: "Court Could Boot Dov Charney, Milo Yiannopoulos from Silver

Lake Mansion," *Real Deal*, October 23, 2023, https://therealdeal.com/la/2023/10/23/judge-could-boot-dov-charney-from-silver-lake-home.

256 **Leslie Jones "barely literate"**: Ameena Navab, "Who Is Milo Yiannopoulos, Kanye West's New Right Hand Man? Taking on Donald Trump for US President in 2024, Ye Is Reportedly in Cahoots with the Former Breitbart Writer and Banned Twitter Troll," *South China Morning Post*, November 25, 2022, https://www.scmp.com/magazines/style/celebrity/article/3200934/who-milo-yiannopoulos-kanye-wests-new-right-hand-man-taking-donald-trump-us-president-2024-ye.

256 **"gay conversion therapy"**: Kevin Dolak, "The Milo Yiannopoulos Makeover: The Alt-Right's Fallen Poster Boy Is Back for Trump 2.0," *Hollywood Reporter*, November 14, 2024, https://www.hollywoodreporter.com/news/politics-news/milo-yiannopoulos-career-new-ventures-1236059885.

256 **founder of a talent**: Dolak, "Milo Yiannopoulos Makeover."

257 **used space lasers**: Jonathan Chait, "Marjorie Taylor Greene Blamed Wildfires on Secret Jewish Space Laser," *Intelligencer*, January 28, 2021, https://nymag.com/intelligencer/article/marjorie-taylor-greene-qanon-wildfires-space-laser-rothschild-execute.html.

257 **"and fixing problems"**: Shweta Kukreti, "Kanye West's Ex-Chief Staff Makes Shocking Claims About Rapper's 'Self-Destruction', $850K Titanium Teeth," *Hindustan Times*, August 7, 2024, https://www.hindustantimes.com/entertainment/music/kanye-wests-ex-chief-staff-makes-shocking-claims-about-rappers-self-destruction-850k-titanium-teeth-101723028834757.html.

257 **Ye and Donald Trump**: Marc Caputo, "The Inside Story of Trump's Explosive Dinner with Ye and Nick Fuentes," NBC News, November 29, 2022, https://www.nbcnews.com/politics/donald-trump/story-trumps-explosive-dinner-ye-nick-fuentes-rcna59010; Gerard Baker, "Dinner at Hate for Donald Trump, Nick Fuentes and Kanye West," *Wall Street Journal*, November 28, 2022, https://www.wsj.com/articles/dinner-at-hate-for-donald-trump-at-mar-a-lago-kanye-west-nick-fuentes-anti-semitism-fascism-boundaries-2024-rapper-conspiracies-11669646030.

257 **denier Nick Fuentes:** Megan Twohey, "Kanye and Adidas: Money, Misconduct and the Price of Appeasement," *New York Times*, October 27, 2023, https://www.nytimes.com/2023/10/27/business/kanye-west-adidas-yeezy.html.

257 **"I wanted to show Trump":** Caputo, "The Inside Story of Trump's Explosive Dinner."

257 **"got along great":** Caputo, "The Inside Story of Trump's Explosive Dinner."

257 **over Ye's plans:** Tatiana Tenreyro, "Milo Yiannopoulos Resigns as Yeezy Chief of Staff amid Ye Porn Plans," *Hollywood Reporter*, May 16, 2024, https://www.hollywoodreporter.com/news/general-news/milo-yiannopoulos-resigns-kanye-ye-west-brand-yeezy-1235901411.

257 **"attitude on everything":** Amelia Butterly, "TL;DR Kanye West in Paper Magazine—Shortened for Your Convenience," *BBC News*, April 21, 2015, https://www.bbc.com/news/newsbeat-32399702.

258 **"There is no point":** Graeme Wood, "How Bronze Age Pervert Charmed the Far Right," *Atlantic*, August 3, 2023, https://www.theatlantic.com/magazine/archive/2023/09/bronze-age-pervert-costin-alamariu/674762.

258 **"shocking or controversial behavior":** Katherine Dee, "Adam Lanza Fan Art," *Tablet*, September 26, 2024, https://www.tabletmag.com/feature/adam-lanza-fan-art.

258 **$35 million in income:** Sopan Deb, "Louis C.K. Turns Up at a Comedy Club, but This Time It's No Secret," *New York Times*, October 30, 2018, https://www.nytimes.com/2018/10/30/arts/louis-ck-comedy-cellar.html.

258 **he made a surprise return:** Melena Ryzik, "Louis C.K. Performs First Stand-up Set at Club Since Admitting to #MeToo Cases," *New York Times*, August 27, 2018, https://www.nytimes.com/2018/08/27/arts/television/louis-ck-performs-comedy.html.

258 **"You can make a career":** Jesse David Fox, *Comedy Book: How Comedy Conquered Culture—and the Magic That Makes It Work* (Farrar, Straus and Giroux, 2023), 212.

259 **eighth album *Hitler*:** Twohey, "Kanye and Adidas."

259 **cozied up to prosperity:** Fernando Alfonso III and Amir Vera, "Kanye West Performs a Gospel Remix of Destiny's Child's 'Say My Name' at Joel Osteen's Megachurch," CNN, November 18, 2019, https://edition.cnn.com/2019/11/16/us/kanye-west-lakewood-church-ticket-scalping-trnd/index.html.

259 **wearing a "White Lives Matter" shirt:** Spencer Kornhaber, "Kanye's Creepy Comeback," *Atlantic*, March 18, 2024, https://www.theatlantic.com/culture/archive/2024/03/kanye-west-ty-dolla-sign-carnival-review/677789.

259 **merch from Burzum:** Kim Kelly, "Ye x Burzum Is Already the Worst Collab of 2024," *Vulture*, January 22, 2024, https://www.vulture.com/2024/01/kanye-burzum-photo-jpegmafia.html.

259 **allowed to perform:** Helen Davidson, "Kanye West Performs in China After Rare Approval by Country's Censors," *Guardian*, September 16, 2024, https://www.theguardian.com/music/2024/sep/16/kanye-west-performs-in-china-after-rare-approval-by-countrys-censors.

259 **"paranoiac selfishness":** Chris Richards, "The Pain of Giving Up on Ye," *Washington Post*, December 26, 2024, https://www.washingtonpost.com/entertainment/music/2024/12/26/kanye-west-ye-legacy-decline.

259 **Kyle Rittenhouse's acquittal:** Maya Yang, "Conservative Event Gives Rittenhouse a Standing Ovation a Month After Acquittal," *Guardian*, December 21, 2021, https://www.theguardian.com/us-news/2021/dec/21/kyle-rittenhouse-turning-point-usa-standing-ovation.

260 **"You're a hero to millions":** Yang, "Conservative Event Gives Rittenhouse."

260 **"magical amulet":** Raven Smith, "On Russell Brand's Troubling Rebrand," *Vogue*, October 16, 2024, https://www.vogue.com/article/russell-brand-troubling-rebrand.

260 **he faced charges:** Noor Nanji, "Russell Brand Charged with Rape and Sexual Assault," *BBC News*, April 4, 2025, https://www.bbc.com/news/articles/c0457d02e9go.

260 **"amorphous, fractious constellation":** Peter C. Baker, "Hunting the Manosphere," *New York Times*, June 13, 2017, https://www.nytimes.com/2017/06/13/magazine/hunting-the-manosphere.html.

260 **"no way you can":** Oana Marocico and Ben Milne, "'Tate Raped and Strangled Us'—Women Talk to BBC," *BBC News*, September 8, 2024, https://www.bbc.com/news/articles/cwyje823er4o.

261 **"Stand up straight"**: John Crace, "12 Rules for Life: An Antidote to Chaos by Jordan B Peterson—Digested Read," *Guardian*, January 28, 2018, https://www.theguard ian.com/books/2018/jan/28/12-rules-for -life-an-antidote-to-chaos-by-jordan -b-peterson-digested-read.

261 **"overwhelming sense"**: Emer O'Toole, "My Beef with Jordan Peterson's All-Cow Diet," *Guardian*, September 19, 2018, https://www.theguardian.com/comment isfree/2018/sep/19/my-beef-with-jordan -petersons-all-cow-diet.

261 **induced eight-day coma**: Aileen Donnelly, "Why Was Jordan Peterson Placed in a Medically Induced Coma? What We Know About Benzodiazepines and Treatment," *National Post*, February 11, 2020, https://nationalpost.com/health/jordan -peterson-benzodiazepines.

261 **introduced young men to Jungian mysticism**: Vincent Clarke, "Jordan Peterson: Shepherd of the Easily Freudened," *American Affairs*, May 17, 2018, https://ameri canaffairsjournal.org/2018/05/jordan-pe terson-shepherd-of-the-easily-freudened.

261 **better known as Bronze**: Wood, "How Bronze Age Pervert Charmed"; Rosie Gray, "How Bronze Age Pervert Built an Online Following and Injected Anti-Democracy, Pro-Men Ideas into the GOP," *Politico*, July 16, 2023, https://www.politico.com /news/magazine/2023/07/16/bronze-age -pervert-masculinity-00105427.

261 **"The only right government"**: Gray, "How Bronze Age Pervert Built."

261 **"In the spiritual war"**: Michael Anton, "Are the Kids Al(t) Right?," *Claremont Review of Books*, summer 2019, https://claremontrev iewofbooks.com/are-the-kids-altright.

261 **"gnarly virus"**: Wood, "How Bronze Age Pervert Charmed."

262 **"autonomous, high-tech nation"**: Joseph Bernstein, "Who Would Give This Guy Millions to Build His Own Utopia?," *New York Times*, December 12, 2023, https://www.nytimes.com/2023/12/12 /style/praxis-city-dryden-brown.html.

262 **"Fifteen years ago"**: Caroline Haskins, "Fashy Posturing and Rich-Kid Juvenilia? That's Praxis (Magazine)," *Hell Gate*, April 9, 2024, https://hellgatenyc.com/praxis -magazine-party-review-east-village.

262 **"halo-shaped wearables"**: Haskins, "Fashy Posturing and Rich-Kid Juvenilia?"

262 **the "trad wife"**: Sophie Elmhirst, "The Rise and Fall of the Trad Wife," *New Yorker*, March 29, 2024, https://www .newyorker.com/culture/persons-of-inter est/the-rise-and-fall-of-the-trad-wife.

263 **"live this lifestyle"**: Carter Sherman, "Sundresses and Rugged Self-Sufficiency: 'Tradwives' Tout a Conservative American Past . . . That Didn't Exist," *Guardian*, July 24, 2024, https://www.theguardian.com /lifeandstyle/ng-interactive/2024/jul/24 /tradwives-tiktok-women-gender-roles.

263 **"traditionally-minded wife"**: Mike Hammer, "Inside Kanye West's 'Twisted' Rules for Wife Bianca Censori: 'She Seems Dead Behind the Eyes,'" *InTouch Weekly*, August 29, 2024, https://www.intouchweekly.com /posts/inside-kanye-wests-twisted-rules -for-bianca-censori-exclusive.

263 **"Try That in a Small Town"**: Claretta Bellamy, "The Grim History of the Courthouse in Jason Aldean's New Music Video," NBC News, July 20, 2023, https:// www.nbcnews.com/news/nbcblk/jason -aldean-courthouse-black-teen-lynched -try-that-small-town-rcna95080.

263 **any historical allusion**: Rania Aniftos, "Jason Aldean Says He 'Probably' Wouldn't Have Filmed at the 'Try That in a Small Town' Courthouse If He Knew the History," *Billboard*, November 1, 2023, https://www.billboard.com/music/coun try/jason-aldean-reflects-try-that-in-a -small-town-courthouse-filming-location -1235461426.

263 **"Rich Men North of Richmond"**: Alexis Harton and Frédérick Guillaume Dufour, "How This Summer's Hit 'Rich Men North of Richmond' Was Appropriated by Both the Right and Left," *Conversation*, August 31, 2023, https://theconversation .com/how-this-summers-hit-rich-men -north-of-richmond-was-appropriated-by -both-the-right-and-left-212514.

264 **pairings with one another**: Dee, "Adam Lanza Fan Art."

264 ***Industrial Society and Its Future***: Caroline Busta, "The Internet Didn't Kill Counterculture—You Just Won't Find It on Instagram," *Document*, January 14, 2021, https://www.documentjournal.com/2021 /01/the-internet-didnt-kill-counterculture -you-just-wont-find-it-on-instagram.

264 **Luigi Mangione**: Aaron Katersky, Peter Charalambous, and Josh Margolin, "UnitedHealthcare CEO Shooting Suspect Inspired by Unabomber: NYPD Analysis," ABC News, December 10, 2024, https:// abcnews.go.com/US/unitedhealthcare -ceo-shooting-suspect-inspired-unabomber -nypd-analysis/story?id=116653076.

264 **delivered an instant classic:** Tim & Dee TV, "Hawk Tuah Girl Original Video," YouTube video, 13:57, June 23, 2024, https://youtu.be/C7tydu_erZo.

264 **4.7 million searches:** Olivia Craighead, "What's the Deal with 'Hawk Tuah' Girl?," *Cut*, September 3, 2024, https://www.the cut.com/article/hawk-tuah-girl-viral -tiktok-video-explained.html.

264 **costume collaboration:** Cassie Morris, "'Hawk Tuah' for Halloween: How Hailey Welch Is Turning Her Viral Catchphrase into a Blossoming Business," Yahoo! Entertainment, October 8, 2024, https:// www.yahoo.com/entertainment/hawk -tuah-for-halloween-how-haliey-welch-is -turning-her-viral-catchphrase-into-a -blossoming-business-185153297.html.

264 **old "granddaddy":** Chloe Stewart and Erin Rose Humphrey, "Hawk Tuah Girl Hailey Welch Jokes 'Old Grandaddy' Donald Trump Is 'Nice Man' but 'Ain't Getting a Hawk from Me,'" *Mirror US*, July 11, 2024, https://www.themirror.com/enter tainment/celebrity-news/breaking-hawk -tuah-donald-trump-586403.

264 **"left in the news cycle":** Luke Winkie, "Please, Make It Stop," *Slate*, July 12, 2024, https://slate.com/life/2024/07/hawk -tuah-girl-meaning-video-what-is-haliey -welch.html.

264 **agency the Penthouse:** Etan Vlessing, "'Hawk Tuah Girl' Hailey Welch Finds Representation," *Hollywood Reporter*, July 2, 2024, https://www.hollywoodreporter .com/business/business-news/hawk-tuah -girl-hailey-welch-1235937553.

264 **"Gen Z Dolly Parton":** Winkie, "Please, Make It Stop."

265 **judged a bikini contest:** Rudi Kinsella, Tom McGhie, and Erin Rose Humphrey, "Hawk Tuah Girl Joins in Bikini Contest as She Rakes in Whopping $30K for Appearances in NYC," MSN, July 10, 2024, https:// www.msn.com/en-us/tv/celebrity/hawk -tuah-girl-joins-in-bikini-contest-as-she -rakes-in-whopping-30k-for-appearances -in-nyc/ar-BB1pGWqI.

265 **Korea Blockchain Week:** Nimmi Mathai, "Hawk Tuah Girl Haliey Welch Attends Forbes Korea Blockchain Week for Viral Catchphrase, Internet Reacts as KBW Labels Her the 'Biggest Meme in History,'" LatestLY, September 4, 2024, https://www .latestly.com/socially/social-viral /hawk-tuah-girl-haliey-welch-attends -forbes-korea-blockchain-week-for-viral -catchphrase-internet-reacts-as-kbw -labels-her-the-biggest-meme-in-history -6239450.html.

265 **popular in the country:** "Hawk Tuah Girl's 'Talk Tuah' Podcast Hits Spotify's Top 3 in US, Behind Joe Rogan and Tucker Carlson," *Express Tribune*, September 29, 2024, https://tribune.com.pk /story/2499484/hawk-tuah-girls-talk-tuah -podcast-hits-spotifys-top-3-in-us-behind -joe-rogan-and-tucker-carlson.

265 **meme coin called Hawk:** Jason P. Frank, "Hawk Tuah, Insider Trade on That Thang," *Vulture*, December 20, 2024, https://www.vulture.com/article/hawk -tuah-memecoin-crypto-scam.html.

265 **disappeared for weeks:** Mashable, "Haliey Welch Releases First Statement After Going MIA Following 'Hawk Tuah' Crypto Crash," Yahoo! Tech, December 20, 2024, https://www.yahoo.com/tech /haliey-welch-releases-first-statement -160808862.html.

265 **"barstool conservative" corners:** Matthew Walther, "Rise of the Barstool Conservatives," *Week*, February 1, 2021, https://theweek.com/articles/964006/rise -barstool-conservatives.

265 **dubbed the "Zynternet":** Max Read, "Hawk Tuah and the Zynternet," *Read Max* (Substack), June 28, 2024, https:// maxread.substack.com/p/hawk-tuah-and -the-zynternet.

265 **"'edgy,' trollish, hedonistic":** Max Read, "A Guide to the Streamer Dipshits Trump Keeps Appearing With," *Read Max* (Substack), August 22, 2024, https://maxread .substack.com/p/a-guide-to-the-streamer -dipshits.

265 **full of "stinky guys":** Ryan Broderick, "The Internet's Stinkiest Guys," Garbage Day, September 23, 2024, https://www .garbageday.email/p/the-internet-s -stinkiest-guys.

265 **"flattening of digital media":** Ryan Broderick, "Hypebeasts Without the Hype," Garbage Day, June 26, 2024, https://www .garbageday.email/p/hypebeasts-without -hype.

265 **king of the Zynternet:** Devin Gordon, "Why Is Joe Rogan So Popular?," *Atlantic*, August 19, 2019, https://www.theatlantic .com/entertainment/archive/2019/08/my -joe-rogan-experience/594802.

265 **"male Oprah":** Helen Lewis, "How Joe Rogan Remade Austin," *Atlantic*, September 11, 2024, https://www.theatlantic.com /magazine/archive/2024/10/joe-rogan -austin-comedy-club/679568.

266 **"appearance of open inquiry"**: John Ganz, "Party Under Country: Dissecting the Democratic Malaise," *Nation*, November 15, 2024, https://www.thenation.com /article/politics/party-under-country -dissecting-the-democratic-malaise.

266 **"The main feature"**: Ganz, "Party Under Country."

266 **no college degree required**: Sirin Kale, "'It's Bullshit': Inside the Weird, Get-Rich-Quick World of Dropshipping," *Wired*, May 1, 2020, https://www.wired.com/story /dropshipping-instagram-ads.

266 **"Whenever I found"**: Alison Coleman, "The Teenage Entrepreneur Learning to 'Go Big' and Heading for a $250,000 Turnover," *Forbes*, May 6, 2018, https:// www.forbes.com/sites/alisoncoleman /2018/05/06/the-teenage-entrepreneur -learning-to-go-big-and-heading-for -a-250000-turnover.

266 **junior capitalist wunderkind**: "Disrupt Sits Down with Well Known Entrepreneur Aaron Grant," *Disrupt*, https://disruptmag azine.com/disrupt-sits-down-with-well -known-entrepreneur-aaron-grant.

267 **movement of "freedom fighters"**: Kale, "'It's Bullshit.'"

267 **first major sponsor**: Matt Flegenheimer, "Joe Rogan Is Too Big to Cancel," *New York Times*, February 17, 2022, https:// www.nytimes.com/2021/07/01/business /joe-rogan.html.

267 **film actress Asa Akira**: Anya Kamenetz, "David Choe's Fans Want to Follow Him to a World Beyond Conformity," *New Yorker*, May 25, 2023, https://www.new yorker.com/culture/culture-desk/david -choes-fans-want-to-follow-him-to-a -world-beyond-conformity.

267 **a.k.a. Adam22**: Broderick, "Hypebeasts Without the Hype."

267 **"People are just trying"**: Broderick, "Hypebeasts Without the Hype."

267 **declared Hawk Tuah Girl**: Alex Abad-Santos, "Hawk Tuah Girl, Explained by Straight Dudes," *Vox*, June 28, 2024, https://www.vox.com/internet-culture /357813/hawk-tuah-girl-meme-tiktok-explained.

268 **"the Costco Guys"**: Kyndall Cunningham, "It's Probably Time You Learned About the Costco Guys," *Vox*, November 19, 2024, https://www.vox.com/culture /386361/costco-guys-rizzler-tiktok-aj-big -justice-jimmy-fallon.

268 **"'real' or 'authentic' fans"**: Max Read, "What Does Jeff Bezos' Non-Endorsement Mean?," *Read Max* (Substack), November 1, 2024, https://maxread.substack.com/p /what-does-jeff-bezos-non-endorsement.

268 **Fallon was clearly annoyed**: Abby Zinman, "People Are Calling Out Jimmy Fallon for Appearing Super Annoyed at His Guests in a Recent Interview, and I Need to Know What You Think," *BuzzFeed*, October 31, 2024, https://www.buzzfeed.com /abbyzinman/jimmy-fallon-new-awkward -interview-tiktokers.

268 **"new Drip King?"**: Tim Marcin, "Livvy Rizzed Up Baby Gronk, the New Drip King Meme Explained," Mashable, June 8, 2023, https://mashable.com/article/baby -gronk-rizz-livvy-drip-king-meme-joke -explained.

268 **sixty million households**: Will Leitch, "Jake Paul vs. Mike Tyson Is the Absurd Spectacle We Deserve," *New York Times*, November 18, 2024, https://www.nytimes .com/2024/11/18/opinion/jake-paul-mike -tyson-fight.html.

268 **"inspires a lot of vitriol"**: Kelsey Weekman, "Fans Attending Mike Tyson–Jake Paul Fight Wanted a Spectacle. What They Got Was Resentment," Yahoo! Entertainment, November 16, 2024, https:// www.yahoo.com/entertainment/fans -attending-mike-tyson-jake-paul-fight -wanted-a-spectacle-what-they-got-was -resentment-215714075.html.

269 **"It's one thing to watch"**: Leitch, "Jake Paul vs. Mike Tyson."

269 **"Who would have guessed"**: Nick Gillespie (@NickGillespie), X (formerly Twitter), August 23, 2024, https://x.com /nickgillespie/status/182699261827 1650255.

269 **"Kamala IS brat"**: Charli (@Charli_XCX), "Kamala IS brat," X, July 21, 2024, https:// x.com/charli_xcx/status/18151823840 66707861.

270 **"Trump sat with all"**: Brian Barrett, "The Manosphere Won," *Wired*, November 6, 2024, https://www.wired.com/story/donald -trump-manosphere-won.

270 **more than $270 million**: Julia Ingram and Steve Reilly, "Elon Musk Spends $277 Million to Back Trump and Republican Candidates," CBS News, December 6, 2024, https://www.cbsnews.com/news/elon -musk-277-million-trump-republican -candidates-donations.

270 **sage-like "American Vulcan"**: Jeremy Stern, "American Vulcan," *Tablet*, https:// www.tabletmag.com/feature/american -vulcan-palmer-luckey-anduril.

270 **"cultural anxiety":** Olivier Roy, *The Crisis of Culture*, trans. Cynthia Schoch and Trista Selous (Oxford University Press, 2023), 37.

270 **"not cool or subversive":** "How Donald Trump Transformed Mass Culture," *Politico*, December 29, 2024, https://www.politico.com/news/2024/12/29/culture-wars-trump-woke-democrats-00195424.

270 **all donated to Trump's:** "Donald Trump Inauguration Day: From Apple to Amazon, Full List of Top US Companies That Have Donated for Swearing-In Ceremony," *Economic Times*, January 12, 2025, https://economictimes.indiatimes.com/news/international/global-trends/donald-trump-inauguration-day-apple-amazon-meta-google-microsoft-openai-boeing-uber-toyota-adobe-ford-full-list-of-top-us-companies-that-have-donated-for-swearing-in-ceremony/articleshow/117205135.cms.

271 **$40 million licensing fee:** Margaret Sullivan, "Melania's $40m Amazon Deal: Another Sign Bezos Is Capitulating to Donald Trump," *Guardian*, January 10, 2025, https://www.theguardian.com/commentisfree/2025/jan/10/melania-trump-amazon-documentary.

271 **market cap of $14.5 billion:** Tom Wilson and Michelle Conlin, "Exclusive: Trump's Meme Coin Made Nearly $100 Million in Trading Fees, as Small Traders Lost Money," Reuters, February 3, 2025, https://www.reuters.com/markets/currencies/trumps-meme-coin-made-nearly-100-million-trading-fees-small-traders-lost-money-2025-02-03.

271 **the manosphere's Andrew Tate:** Moira Donegan, "Andrew Tate Is Back in the US—And a Model of Trump's Worldview," *Guardian*, March 8, 2025, https://www.theguardian.com/commentisfree/2025/mar/08/andrew-tate-donald-trump.

271 **called "groyperification":** John Ganz, "Groyperfication," *Unpopular Front*, January 31, 2025, https://www.unpopularfront.news/p/groyperfication.

271 **"I'm a Nazi":** Michael Saponara, "'After Further Reflection,' Ye Declares: 'I'm Not a Nazi,'" *Billboard*, February 19, 2025, https://www.billboard.com/music/rb-hip-hop/kanye-west-says-not-nazi-1235905742.

271 **shot on an iPhone:** Michael Schneider, "How Kanye West Landed a Super Bowl Ad—Then Used It to Sell Swastika Shirts after It Aired," *Variety*, February 10, 2025, https://variety.com/2025/tv/news/how-kanye-west-super-bowl-ad-swastika-shirts-1236302946.

271 **with a black swastika:** Jonathan Wolfe, "Ye's Website Selling T-Shirts with Swastikas Is Taken Down," *New York Times*, February 11, 2025, https://www.nytimes.com/2025/02/11/arts/music/kanye-west-yeezy-website-swastika-shirts.html.

CONCLUSION: RESTORING CULTURAL INVENTION

272 **A 2024 study using:** Kara Manke, "Facial Recognition Technology Confirms Hollywood Is Getting More Diverse," Phys.org, November 4, 2024, https://phys.org/news/2024-11-facial-recognition-technology-hollywood-diverse.html.

273 **art without autonomy:** Natasha Degen, *Merchants of Style: Art and Fashion After Warhol* (Reaktion Books, 2023), 185.

273 **"If (Theodor) Adorno":** Alex Ross, "The Naysayers," *New Yorker*, September 8, 2014, https://www.newyorker.com/magazine/2014/09/15/naysayers.

273 **"deculturation of cultures":** Olivier Roy, *The Crisis of Culture*, trans. Cynthia Schoch and Trista Selous (Oxford University Press, 2023), 32.

273 **"codes of communication":** Roy, *Crisis of Culture*, 32.

273 **"it would be healthier":** Jason Farago, "Why Culture Has Come to a Standstill," *New York Times*, October 10, 2023, https://www.nytimes.com/2023/10/10/magazine/stale-culture.html.

273 **"There's a new culture":** Katherine Dee, "No, Culture Is Not Stuck," Wisdom of Crowds, October 4, 2024, https://wisdomofcrowds.live/p/no-culture-is-not-stuck.

274 **"conservatives in the arts":** Spencer Klavan, "A Matter of Taste," *American Mind*, June 18, 2024, https://americanmind.org/features/a-matter-of-taste.

276 **rewards and punishments:** Edna Ullmann-Margalit, *The Emergence of Norms* (Oxford University Press, 1977).

277 **like it was sports:** Adorno made this critique about pop culture long before poptimism; see Theodor Adorno, *The Culture Industry* (Routledge Classics, 1991), 89–90.

277 **bored with repetition:** Mark Fisher, *Capitalist Realism: Is There No Alternative?* (Zero Books, 2022), 76.

277 **"The media class's refusal":** Fisher, *Capitalist Realism*, 75.

278 "**products that are complex**": Fisher, *Capitalist Realism*, 75.

278 "**interested in being seen**": Caroline Busta, "The Internet Didn't Kill Counter-culture—You Just Won't Find It on Instagram," *Document*, January 14, 2021, https:// www.documentjournal.com /2021/01/the-internet-didnt-kill-counter culture-you-just-wont-find-it-on-insta gram.

279 "**these avant-gardes**": Jerry Saltz, "Glenn O'Brien and the Avant-Garde That Lost," *Vulture*, April 25, 2017, https://www .vulture.com/2017/04/glenn-obrien-and -the-avant-garde-that-lost.html.

280 **not audience analytics**: This was also true for the golden age of consumer maga-zines, see Dana Brown, *Dilettante: True Tales of Excess, Triumph, and Disaster* (Ballantine, 2022), 218.

INDEX

100 YEARS of PUBLISHING

Harold K. Guinzburg and George S. Oppenheimer founded Viking in 1925 with the intention of publishing books "with some claim to permanent importance rather than ephemeral popular interest." After merging with B. W. Huebsch, a small publisher with a distinguished catalog, Viking enjoyed almost fifty years of literary and commercial success before merging with Penguin Books in 1975.

Now an imprint of Penguin Random House, Viking specializes in bringing extraordinary works of fiction and nonfiction to a vast readership. In 2025, we celebrate one hundred years of excellence in publishing. Our centennial colophon features the original logo for Viking, created by the renowned American illustrator Rockwell Kent: a Viking ship that evokes enterprise, adventure, and exploration, ideas that inspired the imprint's name at its founding and continue to inspire us.

For more information on Viking's history, authors, and books, please visit penguin.com/viking.